CAFÉ BOULUD

THE CONDÉ NAST PUBLICATIONS
"GREAT TASTES OF OUR TIMES"

THURSDAY MAY 4, 2000

CHEF DANIEL BOULUD

Best wishes !

Daniel Boulud
04/00

CAFÉ BOULUD 20 EAST 76TH STREET NEW YORK, NY 10021 212 772 2600

Also by Daniel Boulud
Cooking with Daniel Boulud

Also by Dorie Greenspan
Desserts by Pierre Hermé
Baking with Julia
Pancakes from Morning to Midnight
Waffles from Morning to Midnight
Sweet Times

Daniel Boulud's

Café Boulud Cookbook

FRENCH-AMERICAN RECIPES FOR THE HOME COOK

Daniel Boulud and Dorie Greenspan

FOREWORD BY MARTHA STEWART

Color photographs by Gentl & Hyers

SCRIBNER

SCRIBNER
1230 Avenue of the Americas
New York, NY 10020

SCRIBNER and design are trademarks of Macmillan Library Reference USA, Inc.,
used under license by Simon & Schuster, the publisher of this work.

DESIGNED BY BRITTA STEINBRECHT

Set in News Gothic and Sabon

Manufactured in the United States of America

1   3   5   7   9   10   8   6   4   2

Library of Congress Cataloging-in-Publication Data
Boulud, Daniel.
[Café Boulud cookbook]
Daniel Boulud's Café Boulud cookbook : French-American recipes for
the home cook / Daniel Boulud and Dorie Greenspan.
p.   cm.
1. Cookery, French. 2. Café Boulud. I. Greenspan, Dorie.
II. Title.   III. Title: Café Boulud cookbook.
TX719.B724 1999
641. 5944—dc21   99-26665
CIP

ISBN 0-684-86343-X

The photograph on page 107, "Summer lunch *al fresco,* Café Boulud, 1999,"
was taken by Billy Jim; the photographs on page 185, "Daniel Boulud *en voyage,*"
and page 263, "Daniel Boulud at the farm," were taken by Martin Schreiber.

To Francine, who was the soul of the old Café Boulud

and

To Alix, who is the young spirit of the new Café Boulud
—Daniel Boulud

To Michael and Joshua, as always
—Dorie Greenspan

And in memory of
Andrew Bolsterli

Contents

Introduction

FOR ALMOST ONE HUNDRED YEARS, the locals of St.-Pierre-de-Chandieu, my small hometown outside Lyon, met daily at the roadside Café Boulud, the petit café and not-quite restaurant that my great-grandparents, grandparents, and later my parents took pride in tending on their family farm. It was the rendezvous point for generations of townsfolk. It was the place people went to begin and finish a day, to toast births and marriages and to mourn losses. It was where love affairs started and, of course, where some ended. It was warm, welcoming, and a vital part of village life. And, it was a memory I always carried with me.

From the time I was an apprentice, a fourteen-year-old living away from home, I dreamed of creating a restaurant that would capture the warmth and conviviality of my family's café. Thirty years later, I opened my own Café Boulud in New York City, the city that is today as much my home as St.-Pierre-de-Chandieu was when I was a child.

Café Boulud opened at the perfect moment in my life, at the time when I could truly say, "I am a French-American chef." The opening of Café Boulud, my thirtieth anniversary in the kitchen, and the midpoint in my French-American career share a date. Since I have now cooked in America for as long as I cooked in France, it was the ideal moment to pay tribute to the cuisine I grew up with, the kitchens I trained in, and the foods I've come to know and love in America, all of which Café Boulud and the *Café Boulud Cookbook* celebrate.

Just as I do at the Café, I have arranged the recipes in this book according to the four muses that have inspired my cooking: La Tradition, the classic, full-bodied foods of France; La Saison, the bounty of the market; Le Voyage, the foods of lands near and far; and Le Potager, vegetarian dishes that extol the goodness of the garden.

At Café Boulud, the menu is presented in four columns—La Tradition, La Saison, Le Voyage, and Le Potager—and we encourage people to move from column to column according to their cravings. I urge you to do the same: Please, choose recipes from each of the sections. There are no rules—you can plan an all-Tradition meal, or skip around, choosing, for example, a starter from Le Voyage, a main course from La Saison, and a dessert from any of the sections.

Similarly, I hope you'll feel free to pick and choose components within a recipe. I've presented the recipes just as I would serve them to you if you were my guest at Café Boulud. So, for instance, the recipe for Peppered Arctic Char includes the parsnip mousseline that we serve under the fish and the soft shallots, cooked in red wine and port, that we serve over it. I've given you the recipe for the complete dish so that you can understand the spirit of my cooking, the way I create a dish and the way it would be presented at the Café. At home, you may not want to make the dish in its entirety, or you may want to serve your favorite mashed potatoes with the peppered char. By all means, do it! I want you to have fun with these recipes, to use them often, to make them your own.

Following the sections dedicated to La Tradition, La Saison, Le Voyage, and Le Potager, you'll find a short chapter of basic preparations—pastry crusts and creams as well as simple stocks and condiments—that we use often in the kitchen; a glossary of terms, techniques, and ingredients that you can turn to if you have a question about how we do certain things at the Café; a short batterie de cuisine, including pots, pans, and a few gadgets that make cooking more efficient—and more pleasurable; and, finally, a source guide, a list of trusted suppliers who will send you the same ingredients I use at Café Boulud.

To create this collection, I have chosen the recipes that hold the dearest memories for me, the ones most tied to my culinary life in France and America, and the ones most enjoyed at Café Boulud. All of the recipes have been tested so that they will work as well in your kitchen as they do in mine, and all are offered to you with the hope that when you share this food with your family and friends, it will bring you as much satisfaction, indeed, as much joy, as it has brought me over the years.

Daniel Boulud, New York, 1999

Foreword
by Martha Stewart

WHEN I FIRST RECEIVED THE GALLEYS—the unillustrated, text-only version—of Daniel Boulud's new cookbook, I set it aside, waiting for the exact right moment of leisure to open it, read it, and enjoy it. Yesterday, I read the entire book cover to cover, and I now cannot wait to open it again, first to those pages where I've turned down the corners, marking those recipes that I want to try immediately, then systematically to all the other recipes, because I'd like to try them also.

It is with great pleasure that I write this foreword to Daniel's wonderful book. His musings, his rememberings, his reminiscences, his craft, his science, and his art are fully in evidence on each and every page. I was reminded as I read the first of four sections—La Tradition—of my own family's heritage and of all the wonderful tastes and treasures that emanated from my grandmothers' and mother's kitchens. I wonder if my mother's chrusciki tastes anything like Daniel's mother's Bugnes de Lyon. And I've always wanted an excellent recipe for Far Breton. Having eaten Daniel's Short Ribs Braised in Red Wine, I cannot wait to emulate the same, using his mouthwatering recipe.

The next section of the book is titled La Saison and contains recipes particularly designed to make use of seasonal ingredients. For Daniel Boulud, ingredients are 70 percent of a recipe's success—technique a mere 30 percent. I await with pleasure the opportunity to try the Jerusalem Artichoke Soup and the Beet and Tongue Salad. This chapter, more than the others, made me want to run out to the farmers' markets in search of the finest and rarest, and reading through the clear and concise and well-written recipes, I felt no sense of intimidation—only the desire to look for, find, and use fresh morels, pomegranates, fromage blanc, and quinces.

In the section Le Voyage, Chef Boulud takes us on a gastronomic exploration to countries real and imagined. Here flavors are mixed, herbs and spices sprinkled, and cultural and regional boundaries exceeded. We are tempted with a tuna vitello; a basquaise of cod, clams, and chorizo; an Oxtail Rioja; and a rice pudding called Arroz con Leche that appears simple to make.

Le Potager takes us outdoors to the vegetable garden. Ever respectful to the earth and its bounty, Daniel shows us how he enlivens vegetables, cooking them in odd combinations carefully, taking care always to make them flavorful and impeccably important. Having grown up on borscht—a hearty version made with beef shin and sour cream—I look forward to trying this version luxe, topped with a dollop of caviar. The Lemon-Lime Risotto with Asparagus must be made when the first stalks of asparagus pop out of the ground in the spring. And because I have a penchant for yellow tomatoes, home grown of course, the recipe for Candied Yellow Tomatoes is beguiling.

And at the very end of this very full and very wonderful and personal compilation is the last small section—Base Recipes, including the foundation combinations that enable us, as Daniel Boulud disciples, to easily create dishes that are very like his own. I am now off to my kitchen to make the Pâte Sublime, to be filled with Lemon Pastry Cream. Or should I make the Almond Cream today instead?

Café Boulud, St.-Pierre-de-Chandieu, circa 1900

la tradition the traditional dishes of French cooking

I think of this chapter as a culinary scrapbook of my life in France. Here are the dishes of my childhood, the soups, like golden, caramelized Onion Soup or Lobster and Duck Garbure, that are hearty enough to serve as supper; the dishes, like Short Ribs Braised in Red Wine, or Duck Civet, that simmer slowly and gently; and the sweets, such as custardy Far Breton studded with fruit or simple sugar-topped Bugnes de Lyon, that are at once rustic and satisfying. Here too is a sampling of the marvelous dishes I learned when I worked with some of France's great chefs, and the foods my colleagues and mentors made in their restaurants throughout the country. From hanger steaks topped with shallots to haricots verts wrapped in strips of bacon, these are dishes that revive my memories of the myriad deep, rich, satisfying flavors of classic French cooking.

Soups, Starters, Small Dishes, Lunches, and Anytime Food

Onion Soup with Braised Beef Shank

My hometown is just twenty miles from Lyon, France, the onion soup capital of the world. In Lyon, there were—and still are—small eateries (restaurant is too fancy a name for these places) known as *bouchons,* where workingmen would come for a simple meal with equally simple wine. A bowl of good (and it was invariably good) onion soup and a glass of Beaujolais was the quintessential bouchon combination and, indeed, it's a great combination no matter where you enjoy it. In France and in America, I've made onion soup with everything from water as the base to black truffles as the crust, and I can attest to the fact that this soup is so inherently satisfying that you can do nothing or everything to it and it will always taste wonderful.

The recipe that follows makes my favorite onion soup these days. Like every onion soup recipe, its success depends on plenty of onions and on cooking them very, very slowly until they are soft, sweet, and caramel-colored. The pot is deglazed with white wine (the soup needs that touch of acidity) and then—here's where my version is a little different and a lot heartier than most—I simmer the onions with pieces of roasted beef shank, which enrich the broth profoundly and turn it into a full meal.

Onion soup is most traditionally served au gratin, with a crouton of melted cheese forming a crust over the bowl. (If you want to serve it this way, see the note at the end of the recipe.) Usually I skip the cheese and, instead, scoop out the marrow from the beef shanks, spoon it onto a hunk of crusty sourdough bread, sprinkle it with fleur de sel (or lightly crushed coarse sea salt), and serve it alongside the soup. Whether the soup is gratinéed or served with marrow, you can still finish off the bowl the way diners at a Lyonnaise bouchon would by doing what's called *chabrot*. When there's just a little soup left in your bowl and only a lick of wine left in your glass, pour the wine into the soup, swirl it around, and then drink the soup right from the bowl. It may not be very polite, but it's very traditional.

MAKES 6 STARTER OR 4 MAIN-COURSE SERVINGS

1 tablespoon vegetable oil

1 beef shank—ask the butcher to remove the
    marrow bone and cut it into 6 pieces (each
    about 1½ to 2 inches long), to trim off the fat
    and nerves from the shank, and to cut the
    meat into 1-inch cubes

Salt and freshly ground white pepper

3 tablespoons unsalted butter

2 cloves garlic, peeled, split, germ removed,
    and finely chopped

2 pounds yellow or Spanish onions, peeled,
    trimmed, quartered, and finely sliced

2 teaspoons all-purpose flour

1 cup dry white wine

Herb sachet (2 sprigs Italian parsley,
    2 sprigs thyme, 8 black peppercorns,
    and 1 bay leaf, tied in cheesecloth)

2 quarts unsalted Beef or Chicken Stock (page
    347 or 346), store-bought low-sodium beef
    or chicken broth, or water

4 to 6 (1 per serving) thick slices sourdough
    country bread

Fleur de sel or lightly crushed coarse
    sea salt

1. WARM THE OIL in a large nonstick sauté pan or skillet over high heat. When it is hot, season the cubes of beef all over with salt and pepper and toss them into the pan. Cook, turning as needed, until the cubes are well browned on all sides. Transfer the meat to a plate and set aside until needed.

2. MELT THE BUTTER in a Dutch oven or large casserole over medium heat. Put the garlic and sliced onions into the pot, season with salt and pepper, and cook, stirring regularly, until the onions are very well colored—they should be a deep caramel color—about 30 to 40 minutes (depending on your onions, you might need even more time to color them seriously—be patient). Dust the onions with the flour and cook, still stirring, for about 5 minutes, to toast the flour, rid it of its raw taste, and incorporate it into the onions. Add the white wine and cook, stirring, until the wine evaporates almost completely.

3. TOSS THE SEARED BEEF CUBES into the pot along with the herb sachet and stock or water. Bring the soup to the boil, then lower the heat and simmer for 40 to 60 minutes, or until the beef is very tender. Make certain to skim the soup often as it cooks.

4. WHILE THE SOUP IS SIMMERING, prepare the marrow bones. Put the pieces of marrow bone into another pot and add enough cold water to cover them by about 2 inches. Bring the water to the boil, lower the heat so that it simmers gently, and cook the bones for 20 to 30 minutes. Remove from the heat and set the pot of bones aside, leaving the bones in the water. (If you're making the soup ahead or plan to chill it, don't simmer the marrow bones until about 30 to 40 minutes before serving time.)

5. WHEN THE BEEF CUBES ARE TENDER, remove the sachet. Taste the soup and add more salt and pepper if needed. *(If you're not serving the soup immediately, set it aside to cool, then cover and chill it; the soup can be kept in the refrigerator overnight. Once the soup is cold, spoon off and discard any fat on the surface. Reheat before serving.)*

6. AT SERVING TIME, toast the slices of bread—you can do this under the broiler.

to serve: Drain the marrow bones and place them on a platter. Ladle the steaming-hot soup into warm soup bowls and serve the marrow bones and croutons on the side. With everything on the table, everyone can help themselves to a bone, scooping out the marrow (with a marrow or espresso spoon), spreading it over a piece of toast, and finishing the crouton with a sprinkling of fleur de sel or lightly crushed coarse sea salt.

note: If you'd like to serve the soup au gratin, omit the marrow bones. Pour the soup into a large ovenproof serving bowl or into individual ovenproof bowls. Cover the toasted slices of bread with grated Gruyère or Swiss cheese, float the bread in the soup, and run the soup under the broiler until the cheese melts. Serve immediately.

to drink: A red Saint-Joseph or Cornas from France's Rhône Valley

Potage Parisien with Sorrel Cream

There is little simpler or more warming than this leek and potato soup, a slightly more refined version of the homey Parmentier Soup. The recipe gets its name from the potatoes; they are cut "Parisian-style" into cubes about ¼ inch on a side. (If the soup were Parmentier, the cubes would be twice as large.) To give the soup piquancy, I finish each bowl with a spoonful of sorrel cream, a blend of fresh sorrel purée and whipped cream. If the season for sorrel is over when you've got a craving for this soup, you can create almost the same effect with romaine or Bibb lettuce. Just to be on the sour side, give the lettuce cream a splash of fresh lemon juice.

MAKES 4 SERVINGS

1 tablespoon unsalted butter

3 medium leeks, white and light green parts only, split lengthwise, cut into thin slices, washed, and dried

6 cups unsalted Chicken or Vegetable Stock (page 346 or 348) or store-bought low-sodium chicken or vegetable broth

3 medium Yukon Gold potatoes, peeled and cut into ¼-inch dice

Salt and freshly ground white pepper

3 ounces sorrel leaves, stemmed, washed, and dried, or an equal amount of romaine or Bibb lettuce leaves, washed and dried

⅓ cup heavy cream, whipped to firm peaks

4 lemon wedges (if you are using romaine or Bibb)

1. **MELT THE BUTTER** in a stockpot over low heat. Add the leeks and cook, stirring, until they are tender but not colored, 8 to 10 minutes. Pour in the stock, increase the heat, and bring just to the boil. Add the potatoes, season with salt and pepper, lower the heat, and cook at a slow simmer for 8 to 10 minutes, or until the potatoes are cooked through. Taste the soup and add salt and pepper as needed. *(The soup can be made up to a day ahead and kept covered in the refrigerator; reheat before serving.)*

2. **PUT THE SORREL** or lettuce in the container of a blender and whir until you've got a smooth purée. (If the purée seems stiff, add a tablespoon of the whipped cream to get things moving.) Delicately fold the purée into the whipped cream and season with salt and pepper.

to serve: Ladle the hot soup into warm bowls and top each with a spoonful of sorrel or lettuce cream, which will quickly melt into the soup. Serve immediately. If you've made lettuce cream, offer lemon wedges and encourage your guests to give the cream a squirt of juice as soon as the soup is served.

to drink: A mineraly Savennières from the Loire

Lobster and Duck Garbure

In the France of my childhood, the classic farmhouse garbure was a thick, coarse cabbage and bacon stew with root vegetables, duck confit, and pork, the cuts of meat depending on the stores in the larder. It was cooked in an iron pot hung in the chimney and then reheated for the next day's meal—and the one after that and after that (as many times as possible until, finally, it was thick enough to hold a spoon upright). This was my inspiration, but after years of cooking in America, I've found that my garbure has become a reflection of the place in which it was cooked and the people for whom it was cooked. In looking to lighten the garbure and give it a flash of luxe, I ended up creating a soup for urban sophisticates. This New York garbure retains the lustiness of the original—certainly it has cabbage, bacon, root vegetables, and even white beans—but it's cooked quickly and its major ingredients are Maine lobster, strips of duck confit, and salty duck breast prosciutto. While you can't get fancier with a garbure, you also can't get closer to its roots—taste it and see if it doesn't call to mind the warmth of a slow-simmered stew and the coziness of a farmhouse meal.

I finish the soup with a few strips of duck prosciutto or prosciutto di Parma, the Italian air-dried ham. You can omit the prosciutto, but I like the additional flavor and complex saltiness a cured meat brings to the soup.

MAKES 6 STARTER OR 4 MAIN-COURSE SERVINGS

Salt

Two 1½-pound live lobsters, rinsed under cold water

2 ounces slab bacon, cut into ½-inch dice

3 tablespoons unsalted butter

2 medium carrots, peeled, trimmed, and cut into ½-inch dice

2 medium turnips, peeled, trimmed, and cut into ½-inch dice

1 large onion, peeled, trimmed, and cut into ½-inch dice

1 medium leek, white and light green parts only, split lengthwise, cut into ½-inch dice, washed, and dried

1 stalk celery, peeled, trimmed, and cut into ½-inch dice

8 cups unsalted Chicken Stock (page 346) or store-bought low-sodium chicken broth

2 legs duck confit (see Source Guide, page 385), meat removed from the bones and cut into small cubes

Herb sachet (1 bay leaf, a few black peppercorns, 1 sprig thyme, and 1 sprig Italian parsley, tied in cheesecloth)

Freshly ground white pepper

½ small head savoy cabbage, trimmed, quartered, cored, and cut into ½-inch-wide slices

1 medium potato, peeled and cut into ½-inch dice

1 cup cooked white beans (see Glossary, page 366), or 1 cup canned white beans (if they're not too soft), rinsed and drained
½ cup (loosely packed) Italian parsley leaves

¼ pound duck breast prosciutto (see Source Guide, page 385), fat removed and meat cut into thin strips, or 6 slices prosciutto di Parma, for serving (optional)

1. **BRING 1½ GALLONS** of water and 1 tablespoon salt to the boil in a deep pot. Add the lobsters and cook for just 5 minutes, then remove them and let them cool at room temperature for 15 minutes. Using a nutcracker, break the claws and remove the claw and knuckle meat. Work the tail meat out of the body—you should be able to pull it out of the shell in one piece with a fork—then put the tail, claw, and knuckle meat on a plate and cover with paper towels and plastic wrap; chill until needed. Crack the heads and middle sections. Toss away any small shells from the tails, knuckles, and claws (they'll be too small to find and scoop out of the finished garbure). Rinse or wipe off any soft parts in the remaining shells, cover the shells with plastic wrap, and refrigerate them until needed.

2. **PUT THE BACON** in a Dutch oven or large casserole and cook over medium heat until it renders its fat and colors lightly. Add 2 tablespoons of the butter along with the carrots, turnips, onion, leek, and celery. Cook, stirring, for 5 to 8 minutes, or until the vegetables soften but don't color. Add the chicken stock, the reserved lobster shells, the duck confit, and herb sachet and bring to a boil. Season the broth with a touch of salt and pepper, then toss in the cabbage and potato, lower the heat to a simmer, and cook for 20 minutes. Add the beans and parsley and cook for 5 minutes more.

3. **JUST BEFORE SERVING,** cut each lobster tail crosswise into 6 slices, or medallions, and add them to the pot along with the remaining lobster meat. Reheat for 2 minutes—don't cook the lobster any longer, or you'll risk it getting rubbery. Remove the pot from the heat and stir in the remaining 1 tablespoon butter. Using a slotted spoon, scoop out and discard the lobster shells and herb sachet. Taste the soup and add more salt and pepper if needed.

to serve: Ladle the garbure into warm soup bowls, top with the strips of prosciutto, if you're using it, and hurry to the table—you want everyone to have the pleasure of that first warming whiff while the soup is steaming hot.

to drink: A white Hermitage from the Rhône Valley

Billi-Bi Cressonnière

Given France's centuries-long culinary history, Billi-Bi, a creamy mussel soup, is an arriviste. Some say it was created in Paris in 1925 at Ciro's restaurant, perhaps for the American industrialist William B. (Billy B.) Leeds. Others claim it was first made by the chef of Maxim's in Paris. And still others think it was served for the first time aboard the *Normandie* at a farewell party for an American named Billy, and that the name of the dish derives from "Billy, bye-bye."

I have sampled Billi-Bi many times in France, but my fondest memory of it is attached to America. Soon after I came to New York, I was taken to the legendary Lutèce restaurant for my birthday and there, André Soltner made me a Billi-Bi that comes to mind every time I make the dish myself. Like the classic, my Billi-Bi extracts the essence of the mussels' best flavor for the broth, which is based on aromatic vegetables, crème fraîche, and white wine. But I've added chicken stock to the broth and used a lighter hand with the cream. The taste is crisp, clean, and appropriately briny—just like the classic. Recently, I decided to play with the soup a bit more. I wanted to add something peppery, and that's when I hit on making a Billi-Bi Cressonnière, a mussel soup with watercress. So that the watercress doesn't lose its color or its verve, I drop it into the soup at the last moment, just before everything is puréed. Then, when I'm ready to serve the soup, which can be offered hot or cold, I garnish it with mussels and a cloud of whipped cream—the cream adds just the right amount of richness.

MAKES 6 SERVINGS

2 tablespoons unsalted butter, plus a little extra for reheating the mussels

3 medium shallots, peeled, trimmed, thinly sliced, rinsed, and dried

2 pounds mussels, scrubbed

1½ cups dry white wine

Freshly ground white pepper

1 medium onion, peeled, trimmed, and thinly sliced

1 medium leek, white and light green parts only, thinly sliced, washed, and dried

1 stalk celery, peeled, trimmed, and thinly sliced

4 cups unsalted Chicken Stock (page 346) or store-bought low-sodium chicken broth

Bouquet garni (1 bay leaf, 1 sprig Italian parsley, and 1 sprig thyme, wrapped in a leek green and tied)

1 medium potato, peeled and cut into ½-inch dice

½ cup crème fraîche

3 bunches watercress, tough stems discarded, washed, and roughly chopped

Salt

½ cup heavy cream

Pinch of curry powder

Finely chopped chives

1. MELT 1 TABLESPOON of the butter in a Dutch oven or large casserole over medium heat. Add the shallots and cook, stirring, just until they turn translucent, about 5 minutes. Add the mussels and turn the heat to high. Pour in the white wine, season with a little pepper, put the lid on the pot, and cook just until the mussels open, 3 to 4 minutes. While the mussels are cooking, give the pot a few shakes to move the mussels around or stir the mussels a couple of times with a slotted spoon to help them cook evenly. When all the mussels have popped, turn them into a large cheesecloth-lined sieve set over a bowl to catch the flavorful cooking broth; reserve the mussels and the broth separately.

2. AS SOON AS THE MUSSELS are cool enough to handle, remove the meat from the shells and pull off and discard any black fibers attached to the mussels. Set the mussels aside, covered; discard the shells and any shallots in the sieve. (If you are going to serve the soup chilled, or keep the soup until the next day, refrigerate the mussels, well covered.)

3. RINSE OUT THE POT, drop in the remaining 1 tablespoon butter, and melt it over medium heat. Add the onion, leek, and celery and cook, stirring, until the vegetables are tender but not colored, 7 to 10 minutes. Pour in the reserved mussel broth and the chicken stock. Add the bouquet garni and potato and bring to the boil. Lower the heat and simmer for 20 minutes, at which point the potatoes should be well cooked through. Stir in the crème fraîche and watercress and remove the pot from the heat.

4. LET THE WATERCRESS SOFTEN in the soup off the heat for 3 minutes, then carefully transfer the soup to the container of a blender. (Depending on the size of your blender, you may have to do this in batches.) Whir the soup until it is puréed, then push it through a fine-mesh sieve; add salt and pepper as needed. *(The soup can be cooled to room temperature and then chilled for a day. It can be served cold or reheated. If you reheat it, do so gently—boiling will weaken the beautiful green color of the watercress.)*

5. JUST BEFORE SERVING, whip the heavy cream until it holds firm peaks, then season it with salt and pepper and the curry powder. Reheat the mussels by warming them gently in a small pan with a bit of butter.

to serve: Ladle the soup into warm bowls and top each serving with some of the mussels, a dollop of the whipped cream, and a sprinkling of chopped chives. Alternatively, the soup can be cooled and served chilled, garnished in the same way.

to drink: A very crisp Sancerre Blanc

Chilled Bouillabaisse Velouté

If you want the garlicky, saffron-scented seafood flavors of bouillabaisse and the taste of Provence that comes from combining some of that sunny region's most typical vegetables, then this soup will become a summer specialty at your house. Cold and velvety—indeed, *velouté* means velvety—this bouillabaisse retains its character even after it's been chilled because I thicken and smooth it with chickpeas, a regular in the South-of-France diet. Chickpeas' mild but distinctive flavor is perfect with fennel, tomatoes, saffron, and shrimp, the chief players in this surprisingly quick-to-make soup.

MAKES 4 SERVINGS

the bouillabaisse broth:

5 cups water

¼ cup extra-virgin olive oil

1 large onion, peeled, trimmed, and thinly sliced

2 stalks celery, peeled, trimmed, and thinly sliced

1 medium leek, white and light green parts only, split lengthwise, thinly sliced, washed, and dried

1 small head garlic, cut crosswise in half

¼ medium fennel bulb, trimmed and thinly sliced

Salt and freshly ground white pepper

1½ tablespoons tomato paste

4 medium tomatoes, quartered

1 pound medium to large shrimp in the shell

1 teaspoon saffron threads

1 sprig thyme

1 bay leaf

½ teaspoon fennel seeds

½ teaspoon coriander seeds

½ teaspoon red pepper flakes

⅔ cup cooked chickpeas (see Glossary, page 366), or ⅔ cup canned chickpeas, rinsed and drained

1. **PUT THE WATER** up to boil and keep it at a simmer.

2. **POUR THE OLIVE OIL** into a large stockpot or casserole set over medium heat. When the oil is hot, add the onion, celery, leek, garlic, and fennel, season with salt and pepper, and cook, stirring regularly, for 8 to 10 minutes, or until the vegetables soften but do not color. Add the tomato paste and fresh tomatoes and continue to cook and stir for 4 minutes more. Toss in the shrimp, herbs, and spices and cook, stirring, for 2 minutes, or until the shrimp turn pink. Add the simmering water and cook for 2 minutes more, then, with a slotted spoon or skimmer, remove the shrimp. Set the shrimp aside for about 10 minutes, so that they'll be cool enough for you to remove their shells.

3. **SHELL AND DEVEIN** the shrimp, reserving the shells, and refrigerate, covered, until needed. Toss the shells back into the pot and let simmer with the soup for another 30 to 40 minutes, regularly skim-

ming off the foam and any solids that rise to the surface. When the soup has only 5 minutes left to cook, add the chickpeas. Bring the soup back to the boil, then pull the pot from the heat.

4. POUR THE SOUP into a blender and purée until smooth (you may have to do this in batches). Push the soup through a fine-mesh strainer, so that it is smooth and creamy enough to live up to its name, velouté—it should be just thick enough to coat a spoon. If it is too thick, stir in a little water. Check the seasoning, add salt and pepper, if needed, and then cover and chill.

the vegetables:

3 tablespoons extra-virgin olive oil

1 small onion, peeled, trimmed, and cut into
¼-inch dice

½ red bell pepper, cored, seeded, deveined,
and cut into ¼-inch dice

½ yellow bell pepper, cored, seeded, deveined,
and cut into ¼-inch dice

1 small zucchini, scrubbed, trimmed, and cut
into ¼-inch dice

1 small purple or white eggplant, trimmed and
cut into ¼-inch dice

2 cloves garlic, peeled and crushed

Pinch of red pepper flakes

Salt and freshly ground white pepper

1 tablespoon finely chopped chives

3 leaves purple or green basil, coarsely
chopped

⅓ cup cooked chickpeas, or ⅓ cup canned
chickpeas, rinsed and drained

12 Niçoise olives, pitted and quartered

1. WARM 1 TABLESPOON of the olive oil in a large sauté pan or skillet over medium heat. When the oil is hot, add the onion and peppers and cook, stirring, until the vegetables start to soften but not color, about 3 minutes. Pour in the remaining 2 tablespoons olive oil and add the zucchini, eggplant, garlic, red pepper flakes, and salt and pepper to taste. Cook and stir for 6 to 8 minutes more, until the vegetables are tender. Turn the vegetables into a serving bowl to cool to room temperature.

2. WHEN THE VEGETABLES are cool, remove and discard the garlic. Stir in the chives, half the basil, and the chickpeas. *(At this point, you can cover and chill the vegetables a few hours, until needed.)*

to serve: Put the vegetables in a serving bowl, scatter over the shrimp, and sprinkle over the olives and the remaining basil. Pour the soup into a tureen and, at the table, ladle the soup into individual bowls, then top each with a spoonful of the shrimp and vegetables.

to drink: A Saint-Aubin with some oak

Artichokes and Mushrooms à la Grecque

When you see "à la grecque" on a menu, you can be sure that whatever is being served is pickled. Most often it's mushrooms à la grecque, and the dish is served alone as a starter or part of the French equivalent of an antipasto platter—*hors d'oeuvres variés*. An à la grecque preparation is always slow-cooked in olive oil and often includes, as this dish does, aromatic vegetables, such as carrots, celery, peppers, and licoricey fennel, and plenty of sharp flavors. For sharpness, I've chosen dry white wine, three kinds of vinegar, and lots of lemon juice. It's a well-balanced pickling blend and it's right with this mix, which features artichokes and pearl onions as well as mushrooms. You can make this dish successfully using only button mushrooms, but it's better with a variety. It's also better—and very convenient—to prepare anything à la grecque at least a day ahead, if not three or four, making this an excellent party dish.

MAKES 6 TO 8 SERVINGS

½ cup freshly squeezed lemon juice (from 3 to 4 lemons)

12 baby artichoke hearts, trimmed (see Glossary, page 362) and halved

8 Jerusalem artichokes, peeled and cut into ½-inch dice

3 cups plus 2 tablespoons extra-virgin olive oil

3 ounces slab bacon, cut into 3 pieces

Herb sachet (4 sprigs cilantro, 2 sprigs tarragon, 1 tablespoon crushed coriander seeds, 1 tablespoon fennel seeds, and 1½ teaspoons crushed white peppercorns, tied in cheesecloth)

12 pearl onions, peeled and trimmed

1 red bell pepper, cored, seeded, deveined, and cut into ¼-inch-thick strips

1 yellow bell pepper, cored, seeded, deveined, and cut into ¼-inch-thick strips

1 small fennel bulb, trimmed and cut into ½-inch-thick strips

1 carrot, peeled, trimmed, and cut on the bias into ¼-inch-thick slices

1 stalk celery, peeled, trimmed, and cut on the bias into ½-inch-thick slices

Salt and freshly ground white pepper

1 cup dry white wine

½ cup sherry vinegar

½ cup white wine vinegar

¼ cup balsamic vinegar

16 button mushrooms, stemmed and cleaned (or 48 if you are using only button mushrooms)

8 large shiitake mushrooms, stemmed, cleaned, and quartered

8 large chanterelle mushrooms, trimmed, cleaned, and quartered

1 cup trumpet mushrooms (choose whichever are in season), trimmed, cleaned, and dried

1. STIR 1 TABLESPOON of the lemon juice into a bowl filled with a quart of cold water and keep both the baby artichokes and Jerusalem artichokes in the acidulated water until needed.

2. PUT 2 TABLESPOONS of the olive oil and the bacon in a large sauté pan or skillet set over medium heat. Cook the bacon until it renders its fat, then add the herb sachet and all of the vegetables except the mushrooms. Season with salt and pepper and cook the vegetables gently, stirring them often, until they begin to soften without taking on any color, 10 to 15 minutes. Add all the other ingredients—the liquid should almost cover the vegetables. Cut a circle of parchment paper to fit inside the pan (see Glossary, page 369), press the paper lightly against the ingredients, and cook at a simmer (this shouldn't boil) for about 25 minutes more, until the Jerusalem artichokes and pearl onions are tender. (They are the test—if they're tender, everything else will be perfectly cooked too.)

3. REMOVE AND DISCARD the bacon chunks and the sachet, then pour the vegetables and their pickling liquid into a nonreactive container. Cover, cool, and chill overnight. *(Tightly covered in the refrigerator, the vegetables will keep for 3 to 4 days.)*

to serve: You can present the artichokes and mushrooms family-style, serving them in an earthenware bowl or arranged on a platter, or you can spoon them into small soup bowls along with their pickling liquid and vegetables. In either case, make sure there's bread on the table—you won't want to miss a bit of the vinegary sauce.

to drink: A sparkling wine such as a Crémant d'Alsace or a sparkling Vouvray

Cervelle de Canut

I don't know why this Lyonnaise cheese spread—it has to have been the inspiration for Boursin cheese—is called "the brains of the silk weaver"; its name has never made sense to me. It's a mixture of chopped herbs, shallots, a drop of vinegar, and a little olive oil beaten with soft fresh cheese. I use fromage blanc, but you can substitute ricotta—just make sure to drain it for a couple of hours before using it. In Lyon, it is served in a bowl and accompanied by toast and small warm boiled potatoes, and it's delicious that way. But I also like to use it as a salad dressing on bitter greens, such as frisée, as I do here; arugula; or, when I see them in the market, dandelion greens. The salad is wonderful paired with air-cured beef, such as bresaola or *viande des grisons*.

MAKES 6 SERVINGS

the cervelle de canut:

1½ cups fromage blanc (see Glossary, page 367) or fresh whole-milk ricotta

1 tablespoon finely chopped chives

1 tablespoon finely chopped Italian parsley leaves

1 teaspoon finely chopped tarragon leaves

1½ teaspoons finely chopped shallots, rinsed and dried

1 teaspoon finely chopped garlic

2 tablespoons extra-virgin olive oil

1½ teaspoons red wine vinegar

Salt and freshly ground white pepper

1. **IF YOU ARE USING** fromage blanc, whisk together the cheese, herbs, shallots, garlic, olive oil, and vinegar in a bowl and season with salt and pepper. If you are using ricotta cheese, you'll have to drain it: Put the ricotta in a cheesecloth-lined sieve set over a bowl. Draw up the ends of the cheesecloth and squeeze the cloth to extract some of the liquid from the ricotta. Put the ricotta, still wrapped in cheesecloth, back in the sieve, put the sieve and bowl in the refrigerator, and allow the ricotta to drain for 2 hours. When you are ready to make the cervelle de canut, put the ricotta in the work bowl of a food processor and process until the cheese is smooth, about 30 seconds. Add the remaining ingredients to the processor and pulse just to blend, taking care not to process the mixture too much.

2. **NO MATTER WHICH** cheese you use, the cervelle de canut should be chilled, covered, until needed. *(It can be made several hours ahead and kept covered in the refrigerator.)* If the mixture seems a little thick for your taste, you can thin it with a touch of milk.

the frisée:

3 heads frisée, white and light yellow parts
only, trimmed, washed, and dried (or 1
pound other bitter greens, trimmed, washed,
and dried)

2 tablespoons extra-virgin olive oil
2 teaspoons red wine vinegar
Salt and freshly ground white pepper

TOSS THE FRISÉE together with the oil, vinegar, and salt and pepper to taste. The frisée will be very lightly dressed, which is just right—the fromage blanc will finish the dressing.

to serve: Place a mound of frisée on each plate and top with a scoop of the cervelle de canut.

to drink: A fruity, fresh red wine from the Beaujolais region, a Saint-Amour or a Chiroubles

Boston Mackerel au Vin Blanc

Anyone who's ever eaten in a French bistro must surely have eaten mackerel pickled in white wine. It is so much the quintessential bistro starter that one bite can be enough to evoke the image of red-checkered tablecloths and wine in carafes. However, this typically French dish may actually have derived from Scandinavian pickled herring—it's similar—and may also have served the same purpose: to preserve an inexpensive fish.

What makes mackerel good for this dish is also what can make it problematic—its richness. Mackerel is rich in nutritious oils, which means it spoils quickly. Buy the mackerel from a reliable fishmonger, pickle it at its peak, and then sit back—it will keep deliciously for two days.

You can serve mackerel au vin blanc with nothing more than buttered bread, but I like it with a potato and leek salad dressed with crème fraîche. That little bit of creaminess rounds out the dish. And, when I want to give this humble dish a touch of class, I mix a little more crème fraîche with some caviar and drizzle it around the plate. It's hardly in keeping with the dish's bistro upbringing, but it is awfully good.

MAKES 6 SERVINGS

the mackerel:

1¼ pounds Boston mackerel fillets, skin on, small pinbones removed and each fillet cut on the bias into 6 pieces

4 shallots, peeled, trimmed, thinly sliced, and rinsed

2 small carrots, peeled, trimmed, and thinly sliced

2 small stalks celery, peeled, trimmed, and thinly sliced

1½ lemons, the whole lemon cut into 12 wedges, the half cut into 6

2 bay leaves

2 sprigs thyme

18 black peppercorns

18 coriander seeds

3 whole cloves

1½ tablespoons salt

3 cups dry white wine

½ cup white wine vinegar

1. **PUT THE MACKEREL** in a single layer in a large heatproof rectangular pan—a 7- by 11-inch Pyrex baking dish would work here—and keep the pan close at hand.

2. **PUT ALL THE REMAINING INGREDIENTS** in a medium saucepan over medium heat, bring to the boil, lower the heat so that the liquid simmers, and cook for 20 minutes.

3. POUR THE WINE MIXTURE over the mackerel and immediately cover the pan with plastic wrap. Allow the mackerel and its marinade to cool to room temperature, then chill it overnight in the refrigerator. *(The mackerel can be pickled up to 2 days ahead and kept covered in the refrigerator until needed.)*

the potatoes:

1½ pounds Yukon Gold potatoes, peeled and
  cut into ½-inch dice
2 small leeks, white parts only, split lengthwise, cut into ½-inch-thick slices, washed,
  and dried
¾ cup crème fraîche

1 tablespoon sherry vinegar
2 tablespoons finely chopped chives
Salt and freshly ground white pepper
Optional: 4 ounces sevruga or osetra caviar,
  plus an additional 3 tablespoons crème
  fraîche, for serving

1. BRING A MEDIUM SAUCEPAN of salted water to the boil, add the potatoes, and boil for 10 minutes before tossing in the leeks. Cook for 5 minutes more, or until the potatoes are tender enough to be pierced easily with the tip of a knife. Drain the potatoes and leeks and cool them under cold running water. Drain again and pat the vegetables dry between paper towels; reserve.

2. IN A MEDIUM BOWL, mix together the crème fraîche, vinegar, and chives and season well with salt and pepper. Add the potatoes and leeks and stir gently to combine; keep covered in the refrigerator until serving time. *(The potato salad can be prepared up to 2 hours ahead and kept tightly covered in the refrigerator.)*

to serve: The mackerel is meant to be served cool, so just lift it out of its marinade and arrange it over the seasoned potatoes and leeks on a serving platter. Top the mackerel with some of the carrots, celery, and shallots from the marinade and moisten with a few spoonfuls of the liquid. If you're serving the caviar, gently mix it with the additional crème fraîche and drizzle it around the fish.

to drink: A full wine with good acidity, such as a white Coteaux du Languedoc

Salt Cod Brandade With or Without Truffles

Brandade is one of those dishes in the French repertoire that plays humble against haute. The salt cod, brandade's brawn, is the humble part; the cream and the not-so-uncommonly used truffles are the obviously haute element. Salt cod, without which centuries of fishermen and explorers would never have survived, is at the heart of brandade. Inedible until it has been soaked for at least twenty-four hours and then gently poached, salt cod becomes irresistible once it is beaten into tender shreds and mixed with garlic and cream. The truffle is really the ultimate touch, but it's a traditional one: Capped with truffles, brandade has long been a mainstay of the customary Christmas Eve supper served in the South of France. The best way to serve brandade—with or without truffles—is the easiest: Panfry pieces of bread in olive oil, rub each piece of toast with a cut clove of garlic, and then lay on the brandade.

The most effective game plan for this dish is to have the cream, oil, potatoes, and cod all ready to be mixed together while they're hot. To do this, you need to have a few things going at the same time—it's not hard, you just need to do a little planning. Give the instructions a read-through before embarking on the recipe.

MAKES 4 SERVINGS

1¾ pounds salt cod (see Glossary, page 371)
½ cup extra-virgin olive oil
1 head garlic, cut crosswise in half
1 cup heavy cream
1 quart whole milk
1 pound Yukon Gold potatoes, peeled and cut
   into 1-inch chunks

Herb sachet (4 sprigs thyme, 2 bay leaves, and
   ½ teaspoon black peppercorns, tied in
   cheesecloth)
Freshly ground white pepper

1. **THE DAY BEFORE** you make the brandade, trim the salt cod, cutting away all the dry parts around the belly and tail. Once trimmed, you should have about 1½ pounds of perfectly white cod fillet. Cut the fillet into 2- to 3-inch chunks, put the pieces in a Dutch oven or stockpot, and cover with cold water. Keep the fish submerged in cold water and refrigerated for 24 hours, changing the water three to four times during this period.

2. **THE NEXT DAY,** put the olive oil and one half of the garlic in a small saucepan, turn the heat to the lowest possible setting, and cook for 20 minutes, to infuse the oil with the garlic. While the oil is infusing, pour the cream into another small saucepan, add the remaining garlic, and cook over the lowest possible heat for 15 to 20 minutes, or until the cream has reduced slightly and it, too, is thoroughly infused with the garlic's flavor.

3. ONCE THE OIL and cream have been set over heat, start working on the potatoes and cod. Pour the milk and 4 cups water into a Dutch oven or casserole, toss in the potatoes and herb sachet, and bring to the boil. Lower the heat and simmer for 10 to 12 minutes, or until the potatoes are almost tender enough to be pierced easily with a knife. Add the drained cod to the pot and continue to cook at a simmer for another 10 to 12 minutes, or until the potatoes are tender and the cod flakes easily.

4. LIFT OUT AND discard the herb sachet. Drain the potatoes and cod. Remove the garlic from the oil and cream. Turn the potatoes and cod into the bowl of a mixer fitted with the paddle attachment and, working on low speed, add three quarters of the hot oil in a fine stream, followed by three quarters of the hot cream. Take care not overprocess the brandade—you want the mixture to be well crushed but still coarse and even a bit lumpy. It should mound and hold its shape on a spoon, like mashed potatoes. Add the remaining oil and cream, if you think the brandade needs them, and season with pepper. If the brandade is still warm, you can serve it as soon as the bread is toasted; if it's not warm enough, warm it gently—stirring regularly—in a double boiler while you toast the bread.

the bread:

Extra-virgin olive oil
Slices of sourdough baguette
1 clove garlic, peeled and split

WARM A LITTLE olive oil in a large sauté pan or skillet over medium heat. When it's hot, slip in the slices of baguette and toast the bread until it's golden on both sides. Remove the bread from the pan and immediately rub the cut clove of garlic over one side of each slice.

to serve:

1 black truffle (optional)

SPOON THE BRANDADE into a warm bowl and, if you're using black truffle, shave it generously over the top. Serve with slices of the pan-toasted baguette.

to drink: A white Bandol, a light, thirst-quenching wine from Provence

Crayfish Salad with French Cocktail Sauce

You might think of this as my take on the American shrimp cocktail—it's a salad of lettuce, grapefruit, avocado, and tomato, topped with crayfish and finished with a sauce that will probably remind you of Thousand Island or Russian dressing—but most of the dish is based on foods and flavors from my youth. I first made the cocktail sauce when I was an apprentice at a restaurant in Lyon. I learned to love crayfish when I was an eighteen-year-old assistant cook at Georges Blanc— my kitchen mates and I would eat them by the bushelful at the local bars and truck-stop cafés, the only places we could afford—but the salad's tart Florida grapefruit and buttery avocado are flavors I've learned to appreciate since I came to America. Surprisingly, the cocktail sauce's typically American ingredients—ketchup and Worcestershire sauce—are original to the recipe, as is the very French touch of tossing in a drop of Cognac, to cut the ketchup's sweetness.

A note on crayfish: They're good in spring and summer, best bought from a reliable supplier and, ideally, purchased live. If you can't find them live, opt for freshly cooked and peeled ones and skip the boiling step in the recipe. And, yes, you can replace the crayfish with shrimp.

MAKES 4 SERVINGS

the salad:

1 pink grapefruit

2 ripe avocados

½ lemon

1 head Boston lettuce, washed, dried, and cut
   into thin strips

4 plum tomatoes, peeled, seeded, and finely
   chopped

12 leaves tarragon, finely sliced

1. **PEEL THE GRAPEFRUIT,** reserving the rind for cooking the crayfish. Using a small knife, slice away the bitter white pith and with it the thinnest possible layer of fruit. Cutting against the membranes, release each section of grapefruit intact; remove any seeds. Set the sections aside for the moment and, working over a bowl, squeeze as much juice from the membranes as you can, to use in the cocktail sauce; discard the membranes.

2. **HALVE, PIT, AND PEEL** the avocados, then rub the exposed fruit with the cut lemon to keep it from darkening. Slice each avocado half into 3 wedges and give the wedges a squirt of lemon juice.

3. **ARRANGE THE LETTUCE** in an even layer in the bottom of a large shallow bowl. Mound the tomatoes in the center of the bowl and surround them with alternating slices of grapefruit and avocado. Sprinkle the tarragon over the tomatoes. Cover the salad and keep it refrigerated until serving time. (*The salad can be made a couple of hours ahead of time and kept tightly covered and chilled.*)

the crayfish:

The reserved grapefruit rind (from above)
½ bunch tarragon, leaves and stems
¼ cup salt
1 teaspoon cracked peppercorns

Pinch of cayenne pepper
3 pounds crayfish, preferably live, rinsed under cold running water, or 1 pound peeled cooked crayfish

1. IF THE CRAYFISH are cooked and peeled, move on to the cocktail sauce. If they're live, bring 1 gallon of water to a boil in a stockpot. Add all the ingredients, return to the boil, and simmer, uncovered, for 2 minutes. Remove the pot from the heat and cool the crayfish in the water for 10 minutes. Drain and discard the cooking liquid.

2. TO PEEL CRAYFISH, twist off and discard the head. Peel off the upper three sections of shell, then, holding the meat in one hand and the tip of the tail in the other, squeeze the tail while pulling the meat out of the shell. The vein in the center of the crayfish should come off with the shell. If it doesn't, remove it by hand, then use your finger to rub off any yellow coral that clings to the meat. Set the crayfish aside.

the cocktail sauce:

The reserved grapefruit juice (from above)
1 large egg yolk
1 tablespoon Dijon mustard
Salt and freshly ground white pepper
Small pinch of cayenne pepper
¼ cup vegetable oil, preferably grapeseed or safflower oil

2½ tablespoons ketchup
1 teaspoon white wine vinegar
1 teaspoon Worcestershire sauce
½ teaspoon Cognac or Armagnac
2 tablespoons sliced blanched almonds, toasted, for serving

1. BOIL THE GRAPEFRUIT JUICE until it is reduced to 2 teaspoons; cool.

2. WHISK THE YOLK, mustard, salt and pepper to taste, and cayenne together in a medium bowl. Whisking constantly, add the oil in a slow stream. When the mixture is emulsified, like mayonnaise, whisk in all the other ingredients, including the cooled grapefruit juice. Taste and adjust the seasonings if necessary. *(The sauce can be kept in a tightly covered container in the refrigerator for 2 to 3 days.)*

to serve: Arrange the crayfish on the tomatoes, sprinkle with almonds, and serve the sauce on the side.

to drink: A light, dry Alsatian Gewürztraminer or, perhaps, a Muscat Sec

Frisée and Chicken Liver Salad

This warm salad, at once bitter and sweet, mild and sharp, soft and crunchy, is one of my favorites. Each element—the curly frisée, the rounds of Yukon Gold potatoes, the quickly sautéed chicken livers, and the shallot confit—has its own vinegar-based dressing, everything is seasoned separately with salt and freshly ground pepper, and the potatoes are given a shower of sage, thyme, and chives. But it's the simple poached eggs that unify the salad and smooth the vinegar's sharp edges. Compose the salads and, as you're about to bring them in from the kitchen, break each egg yolk and let it flow around the plate, creating a second sauce for each of the salad's players. It's a small part of the dish, but it's the part that sets everything else in balance.

For a deluxe version of this salad, toss in a few slices of sautéed porcini mushrooms. And for a lighter version, replace the chicken livers with chunks of moist chicken breast.

MAKES 4 SERVINGS

the shallot confit:

3 medium shallots, peeled, trimmed, finely
    chopped, and rinsed
1 cup dry white wine

¼ cup sherry vinegar
1 tablespoon balsamic vinegar
Salt and freshly ground white pepper

PUT THE SHALLOTS and white wine in a small saucepan and boil over medium heat until the wine evaporates. Add the vinegars and cook, stirring occasionally and watching the pan closely, until they evaporate. The shallots, now pale red, will be soft and jammy. Season with salt and pepper, and set aside until needed. *(This can be made up to 2 days ahead and kept covered in the refrigerator.)*

the potatoes:

3 small Yukon Gold potatoes, peeled and each
    cut into four ½-inch-thick rounds (discard
    the ends)
1 sprig sage
1 sprig thyme

Salt
1 tablespoon sherry vinegar
1½ tablespoons extra-virgin olive oil
Freshly ground white pepper

PUT THE POTATOES, sage, and thyme in a medium saucepan, cover with water, season with salt, and bring to the boil. Lower the heat and simmer until the potatoes are tender enough to be pierced easily with the point of a knife, about 8 to 10 minutes. Drain and pat the potatoes dry. Keep the potatoes warm or at room temperature. Right before you are ready to serve, toss them gently with the vinegar and oil and season with salt and pepper.

the poached eggs:

1 teaspoon white vinegar
4 large eggs

HEAT A FEW INCHES of water in a large sauté pan or skillet until the water is just under the boil; add the vinegar. Break each egg into a teacup and carefully slide the eggs, one by one, into the pan. Keeping the water at no more than a simmer, cook the eggs for 3 to 4 minutes, just until the whites set but the yolks are still soft. Carefully lift the eggs out of the water with a wide slotted spatula. If you are not going to use the eggs immediately, let them cool *(you can keep them for an hour or so in the refrigerator)*. Then, 10 to 15 minutes before you need them, slip them into a bowl of very hot water. When you are ready to serve, lift the eggs out of the water with the slotted spatula and pass the bottom of the spatula over a kitchen towel to dry the eggs.

the frisée and livers:

1 large head frisée, white and yellow parts only, trimmed, washed, dried, and cut into 1-inch-long sections
1 tablespoon finely chopped chives
3 tablespoons extra-virgin olive oil

4 whole chicken livers, cleaned, trimmed, and cut into 1-inch pieces
Salt and freshly ground white pepper
1 tablespoon sherry vinegar

1. **TOSS THE FRISÉE** and chives in a bowl and set aside.
2. **WARM 1 TABLESPOON** of the olive oil in a medium nonstick sauté pan or skillet set over medium-high heat. Season the chicken livers with salt and pepper and add them to the pan. Cook, stirring, until the livers are cooked through, about 3 minutes on a side. Reduce the heat, add the shallot confit, and stir well, then add the remaining 2 tablespoons olive oil and the vinegar and toss to combine. Remove the pan from the heat and pour the livers, shallots, and all their pan juices over the frisée. Mix the salad well and season with more salt and pepper, if needed.

to serve: Arrange 3 rounds of potatoes on one side of each warm dinner plate and slide a poached egg on top of the potatoes. Arrange a mound of the frisée and chicken liver salad in the center of the plate. Just before serving, break each egg yolk and allow it to run over the plate. If there's any extra vinaigrette or shallots in the bottom of the salad bowl, drizzle them around the plates.

to drink: A red Rully without much oak

Game Bird and Foie Gras Pâté

My father, like the other fathers and farmers around him in our part of France, was a hunter, and my mother, like her neighbors, always had a recipe at the ready for whatever the day's take might be. Game bird pâté was a staple during hunting season—it was the dish that made the best use of the birds that weren't young or tender enough to roast. What was second nature and given by Mother Nature to my parents is a bit more complicated and costly for us, who must purchase the partridges, squab, and pheasant at specialty stores or by mail order, but the result is unfailingly worth the expense and time. Few things are as welcoming as a crock filled with highly seasoned, coarsely ground pâté, its natural jelly coating the top. Put a jar of cornichons on the table along with mustard and a basket of brown bread, plant a sturdy knife in the center of the pâté so that everyone can dig in, put your elbows on the table, and count yourself among the lucky.

Keep in mind that the game birds have to marinate for twenty-four hours and that, once cooked, the terrine needs at least twelve hours in the refrigerator. But all this advance preparation pays off in the end—not only is the terrine a triumph, it will keep for a week in your refrigerator.

MAKES 12 TO 14 SERVINGS

2 partridges or 4 quail (see Source Guide, page 385)

2 squab (see Source Guide)

1 pheasant (see Source Guide)

2¼ pounds fatty pork jowl or other boneless fatty cut of pork, cut into small chunks

6 ounces fresh duck foie gras, cleaned and cut into 6 pieces

6 ounces chicken livers, cleaned and cut into 6 pieces

¼ cup dry white wine

2 tablespoons Cognac

2 juniper berries, finely chopped

1 sprig thyme, leaves only, finely chopped

2 tablespoons vegetable oil

½ cup finely chopped white mushrooms

¼ cup finely chopped shallots

1 teaspoon finely chopped garlic

1½ tablespoons salt

1 teaspoon freshly ground white pepper

1. **REMOVE AND DISCARD** the skin, bones, tendons, and nerves from the partridges or quail, squab, and pheasant (or ask the butcher to do this). Cut the meat into chunks and put them, the pork jowl, foie gras, and chicken livers in a pan that is just large enough to hold them snugly. Mix the wine, Cognac, juniper berries, and thyme together, add them to the pan, and turn the meat until all the pieces are coated evenly with the liquid and herbs. Cover the pan with plastic wrap and refrigerate for 24 hours.

2. **WHEN THE PIECES OF MEAT** have marinated for 24 hours, drain the meat and discard the marinade. Push the meats through the large-hole blade of a grinder—you want this to be a coarsely ground and very rustic pâté—into a bowl. Cover the bowl and chill until needed.

3. WARM THE VEGETABLE oil in a small sauté pan or skillet over medium heat. Add the mushrooms, shallots, and garlic and cook, stirring, until they are cooked through but not colored, about 8 minutes. Turn the ingredients out onto a plate and allow them to cool for about 10 minutes.

4. WORKING GENTLY WITH your hands, mix the mushroom mixture into the ground meats along with the salt and pepper.

5. CENTER A RACK in the oven and preheat the oven to 300°F. Line a roasting or baking pan with two layers of aluminum foil and keep nearby.

6. CHOOSE A TERRINE—I use a porcelain terrine that's 10 inches long by 3½ inches wide at the top, 3½ inches deep, and 9 inches long and 2½ inches wide at the bottom, but you can use any similar-size terrine. Cut two pieces of parchment paper to fit inside the top of the terrine. Fill the terrine with the ground meat—you'll have more than you can fit into the terrine and that's just fine: Mound the pâté mixture over the top of the terrine. Cover the top of the terrine with one piece of parchment paper and press the paper against the meat, then press the second sheet over the first. Place the terrine in the lined baking pan.

7. BAKE THE PÂTÉ until it reaches 150°F as measured on an instant-read thermometer, about 1¾ hours. (Make sure to measure the temperature of the pâté at the center of the terrine.) At this point, the meat will be very moist and quite pink—it will continue to cook as it cools. Remove the terrine from the oven and allow it to cool, still in its baking pan, for 2 hours.

8. WHEN THE PÂTÉ is cool, it should be weighted. If your pâté comes above the rim of the terrine, just place a small baking sheet over the top of the terrine and weight the sheet down by evenly placing a few cans or, better yet, a few bags of pie weights on it. If your pâté has fallen below the rim of the terrine, you'll need to do a little arts-and-crafts work. Cut a piece of Styrofoam or heavy cardboard to fit just inside the top of the terrine and wrap the Styrofoam or cardboard in parchment paper. Lay it on top of the terrine and then weight it down with cans or bags of pie weights. Transfer the terrine and its weighting system to the refrigerator and chill for at least 12 hours before serving. *(The terrine can be kept covered in the refrigerator for up to 1 week.)*

to serve: This pâté is meant to be served in the most rustic way: Plunge a knife into the center of the pâté and bring the terrine to the table. Everyone should help themselves to a wedge of pâté, a hunk of hearty bread, and a few vinegar-spiked cornichons.

to drink: A Cahors, from the Southwest of France

Crusty Marrow and Porcini Fricassee

This is a voluptuous, elegant dish served in a rustic, homey way. Essentially a richly flavored fricassee of thick, meaty porcini mushrooms cooked with diced vegetables and thin strips of smoky bacon, it is moistened and enlivened with red wine, then topped with an herbed bread crumb crust. Where other recipes might have the bread crumbs dotted with butter so that they will brown under the broiler, this crust is dotted with small cubes of beef marrow. Of course, the marrow helps brown the crust, but it brings so much more to the dish. It contributes its sensuous texture, its extravagantly deep flavor, and its compatibility with porcini and wine. I make the fricassee in a round baking dish, top it with the crust, run it under the broiler, and then spoon generous portions over a salad dressed with mustardy vinaigrette. If dandelion greens are in the market when you make this fricassee, grab them for the salad; if not, choose frisée. For a change, you might want to serve the fricassee over steak—it's supremely good over a hanger steak (page 68).

A note on the marrow: In order to get the full flavor of the marrow, you need to soak it overnight, so plan ahead. Once it's soaked, you've got nothing to do but drop it into boiling water for half a minute. After that, you're on your way to a very special recipe.

MAKES 4 SERVINGS

the marrow:

6 ounces beef marrow (removed from about
    2 pounds marrow bones)
2 teaspoons salt

ONE DAY AHEAD, put the marrow in a bowl with about a quart of cold water (you want to be sure that the water covers the marrow generously). Add the salt, cover the bowl, and soak overnight in the refrigerator, changing the water several times during this period if you can.

the fricassee:

Salt
The soaked marrow (from above)
1 ounce slab bacon, cut into short, thin strips
½ pound porcini or other wild mushrooms,
    trimmed, cleaned, and cut into
    ⅛-inch dice

1 small carrot, peeled, trimmed, and
    cut into ⅛-inch dice
1 stalk celery, peeled, trimmed, and cut into
    ⅛-inch dice
1 small onion, peeled, trimmed, and
    cut into ⅛-inch dice

4 cloves garlic, peeled, split, germ removed, and finely chopped

1 teaspoon finely chopped rosemary leaves

Pinch of finely chopped thyme leaves

1 cup dry red wine

Freshly ground white pepper

¼ cup fresh bread crumbs, preferably from sourdough bread

1 teaspoon finely chopped tarragon leaves

1 teaspoon finely chopped Italian parsley leaves

Dandelion or other salad, dressed with Mustard Vinaigrette (page 351), or Hanger Steak (page 68), for serving

1. **BRING A QUART OF WATER** and 1 teaspoon salt to the boil in a medium saucepan. Remove the marrow from its soaking liquid and cut it into ½-inch cubes. Drop the cubes into the boiling water and count 30 to 45 seconds before lifting the marrow out of the water with a slotted spoon. Put the marrow on a plate and set it aside for the moment.

2. **WARM A LARGE SAUTÉ PAN** or skillet over medium heat, then toss in the bacon. Cook and stir just until the bacon starts to render its fat, about 2 minutes. Leaving the bacon in the pan, discard the fat. Stir in the porcini, carrot, celery, onion, garlic, rosemary, and thyme, cover the pan, and cook, stirring occasionally, until the vegetables soften slightly, about 5 minutes. Pour in the red wine and let it boil down until only ¼ cup remains. At this point, you should have a juicy, well-blended mixture. Taste, season as needed with salt and pepper, and remove the pan from the heat.

3. **POSITION THE RACK** so that it is as far from the broiler as possible and turn on the broiler.

4. **SPOON THE FRICASSEE** into an 8- to 10-inch round baking dish. Gently toss the bread crumbs with the marrow, tarragon, and parsley and season with salt and pepper. Sprinkle the crumb mixture evenly over the fricassee and run the dish under the broiler until the crumbs are crusty and lightly browned.

to serve: The fricassee should be eaten immediately. Either spoon it over the dressed salad or serve it on top of hanger steaks.

to drink: An earthy Gevrey-Chambertin

Main Courses

Lobster à la Nage

Lobster à la Nage, lobster in a soupy herbal sauce that's briny and flavored with white wine, is one of the fabled dishes of the French kitchen. And, naturally, it's one I'd made myself many times. But making the dish is not the same as eating it, and I'd never had the opportunity to enjoy it as a guest in someone else's restaurant until I went to Fredy Girardet in Crissier, Switzerland. Girardet, one of the twentieth century's greatest European chefs, was closing his Michelin-three-star restaurant and I was there for a final dinner. He served Lobster à la Nage and since then the dish has been—and I'm sure always will be—tied in my memory to that extraordinary evening. Lobster à la Nage epitomizes simplicity—the simplicity that comes from using the best ingredients, treating them carefully, and allowing their flavors to shine brightly. Girardet's dish followed tradition and gave lobster the star turn; the nage was sparkling and crisp but very much the supporting player. My dish is traditional as well, except that lately I've been using a dry Riesling rather than the more usual Chardonnay in the nage. I like the acidity, fruit, and complexity I get from a Riesling. If you don't have a Riesling, try this with a dry Sauvignon Blanc.

the lobsters:

1 tablespoon coarse sea salt
Four 1-pound live lobsters, rinsed under cold
water

1. PUT 1 1/2 GALLONS of water and the salt in a deep stockpot and bring to the boil, then plunge the lobsters into the pot. Cook the lobsters for just 4 minutes; remove them from the pot and set aside to cool. Reserve 2 cups of the cooking water to make the fumet.

2. WHEN THE LOBSTERS are cool enough for you to handle, use a nutcracker to break the claws, then remove the claw and knuckle meat, working gently so that you don't damage the meat. Next, using shears, split the lobster tails in half down the back. You're going to leave the tail meat in the shell—the shell will protect the meat from overcooking—but you need to pull out the vein that runs through the tail. Cover and chill the tail, claw, and knuckle meat until needed; to keep the meat moist, cover it with damp paper towels and then wrap it in plastic wrap. As for the rest of the lobsters, the carcasses will be used to flavor the fumet. Crack the heads and the middle sections and remove and discard everything that's soft inside these shells. Then, using a pair of poultry shears, cut the shells into small pieces. Put the pieces in a pot and pound them with the end of a French-style rolling pin (or put them on a wooden board, cover them with parchment, and pound them with the bottom of a pan). Do the best you can to crush the carcasses. The smaller the pieces of shell, the more surfaces there will be to give their flavor to the fumet.

the fumet:

1 tablespoon unsalted butter
1 tablespoon extra-virgin olive oil
The crushed lobster carcasses (from above)
1 small carrot, peeled, trimmed, and quartered
1/2 onion, peeled, trimmed, and quartered
  (save the other half for the nage)
1/2 stalk celery, peeled, trimmed, and split
  lengthwise

1 strip lemon zest (pith removed)
1 teaspoon fennel seeds
1 teaspoon coriander seeds
1 bay leaf
1 whole clove
1/2 teaspoon black peppercorns
2 cups reserved lobster cooking water
  (from above)

1. WORKING IN THE rinsed-out stockpot you cooked the lobsters in or in a Dutch oven, warm the butter and olive oil over medium heat. Toss the crushed carcasses into the pot and cook them, stirring, for about 5 minutes. Add the carrot, onion, celery, lemon zest, and spices and cook and stir for 5 minutes more, taking care not to color the vegetables. Pour in the reserved lobster cooking water and bring the fumet to the boil, then lower the heat and simmer for 20 minutes.

2. POUR THE FUMET through a cheesecloth-lined chinois or other fine-mesh strainer; discard the solids and reserve 1 cup of the fumet for the nage.

the nage:

2½ tablespoons unsalted butter

½ onion, peeled, trimmed, and finely sliced

1 carrot, peeled, trimmed, and finely sliced

1 stalk celery, peeled, trimmed, and finely sliced

1 petal fennel (1 peel-away layer of fennel), finely sliced

Salt and freshly ground white pepper

1 cup dry white wine, preferably a Riesling

1 cup reserved lobster fumet (from above)

2 tablespoons finely chopped chives

2 tablespoons finely chopped chervil leaves

4 lemon wedges, for serving

1. MELT 1 TABLESPOON of the butter in a large sauté pan or skillet over medium heat. Add the onion, carrot, celery, and fennel and cook for 3 to 5 minutes, keeping the vegetables uncolored; they should be slightly undercooked. Season with salt and pepper, pour in the wine, stir, and cook at a steady simmer until the wine has reduced by half and the vegetables are almost cooked through. Add the reserved fumet, adjust the heat so that the liquid simmers slowly, and cook, regularly skimming off the foam and impurities that rise to the surface, for about 5 minutes, until the vegetables are just tender.

2. PUT ALL THE PIECES of lobster (still keeping the tails in their shells) into the pan and heat gently—don't boil—until the meat is warmed through, about 2 minutes. Pull the pan from the heat and swirl in the remaining 1½ tablespoons butter in a few additions. The butter shouldn't melt, but instead blend with the nage to form a satiny emulsion. Add the chives and chervil.

to serve: Divide the lobster pieces among four warm shallow soup plates, making sure that each plate has 2 pieces of tail meat and 2 claws. Spoon over the nage—both liquid and vegetables—and serve with lemon wedges in case guests want a drop of juice over their lobsters.

to drink: A very dry Alsatian Riesling

Scallops on Crushed Potatoes, Sauce Charcutière

Anytime you see "charcuterie" or "charcutièr(e)" on a menu, you're going to find something with pork. *Charcuterie* usually refers to the sausages, bacon, pâtés, and terrines that the charcutier makes from pork. Here, I use a sauce charcutière that would normally be served with pork, but I allow plump, naturally sweet American sea scallops and potatoes, another naturally sweet ingredient, to stand in for the pork and to stand up to the robust sauce. The sauce is vinegary— it has to be—sparked with tiny strands of also vinegary cornichons, and finished with a few strips of julienned ham, in part to keep its connection to the original, but mainly to provide another salty element that can play against the sweet scallops. Just a word on the potatoes—don't go overboard: They're meant to be crushed, not mashed, and certainly not puréed; keep their texture coarse.

MAKES 4 SERVINGS

the potatoes:

Coarse sea salt or kosher salt

2 pounds Idaho potatoes, scrubbed

10 tablespoons (1 stick plus 2 tablespoons)
   unsalted butter, at room temperature

2 shallots, peeled, trimmed, finely chopped,
   rinsed, and dried

½ bunch Italian parsley, leaves only,
   roughly chopped

Salt and freshly ground white pepper

1. PREHEAT THE OVEN to 400°F.

2. SPREAD AN EVEN ¼-inch-thick layer of coarse sea or kosher salt in the bottom of an ovenproof sauté pan, skillet, or baking pan large enough to hold the potatoes (an 8-inch pan should be fine). Arrange the potatoes in the pan, slide the pan into the oven, and roast for 45 minutes to an hour, or until the potatoes can easily be pierced with a thin knife. Remove the potatoes from the pan and let them cool for about 5 minutes.

3. SPLIT THE POTATOES in half and, using a spoon, scoop the flesh into a heatproof bowl. Still using the spoon, crush the potatoes with the butter, shallots, and parsley. Don't be overzealous—these are meant to be coarsely crushed and pleasantly lumpy. Season with salt and pepper, cover the bowl with plastic wrap, and set the bowl over a pan containing a few inches of simmering water—the water shouldn't touch the bowl. Keep the potatoes warm over very low heat while you cook the scallops.

the scallops:

1 tablespoon extra-virgin olive oil
12 or 16 large sea scallops (about
    1½ pounds), preferably live jumbo
    scallops from Maine (see Source
    Guide, page 385)
Salt and freshly ground white pepper
Flour for dredging
2 tablespoons unsalted butter

1 small red onion, peeled, trimmed, and thinly
    sliced
1 tablespoon red wine vinegar
¼ cup dry white wine
1 ounce boiled ham, cut into matchstick-sized
    pieces
2 cornichons (bottled French gherkins), cut into
    matchstick-sized pieces

1. **WARM THE OLIVE OIL** in a large sauté pan or skillet over medium-high heat. While it's heating, season the scallops with salt and pepper and dredge them in flour, shaking off the excess. Slip the scallops into the hot oil and cook on one side for 3 minutes. Add 1 tablespoon of the butter, lower the heat, flip the scallops over, and cook for 3 minutes more, or until just cooked through. Transfer the scallops to a warm plate and set aside while you finish the sauce. Do not wipe out the pan—you want to keep the cooking fats.

2. **RETURN THE PAN** to medium heat and add the onion. Season with salt and pepper and cook for a few minutes, just until translucent. Pour in the vinegar and, stirring and scraping the bottom of the pan, let it cook away. Add the white wine and cook until only half of it remains, then return the scallops, along with any juices that may have accumulated on the plate, to the pan. Cook just until the scallops are warmed through. Toss in the ham and cornichons—the ingredients that give the sauce its name—and pull the pan from the heat. Swirl the remaining 1 tablespoon butter into the sauce.

to serve: Spoon the potatoes into the center of a warm serving platter and arrange the scallops on top. Pour over the sauce charcutière and serve immediately.

to drink: A Montlouis Sec from France's Loire Valley

Sea Bass en Croûte

If one dish can be said to epitomize haute cuisine of the 1950s, it would have to be the legendary Fernand Point's whole sea bass inside layers of puff pastry, the pastry decorated to resemble the sea bass itself and baked to a burnished gold. For a chef to prepare a dish like this, and for a waiter to carry it through the dining room and present it to a guest, was a form of high drama. I remember that drama vividly from my time with Paul Bocuse, who learned the dish directly from Point (1897 to 1955) when he cooked at Point's famous restaurant, La Pyramide, in Vienne, France. This recipe, inspired by the original, is still dramatic, but it's more in keeping with the way we eat today. Rather than using a large whole fish, I use two fillets, stuff them with a blend of tiny cubed vegetables, and bake them, as the original was baked, between sheets of puff pastry. This is a serious gastronomic treat, a sophisticated dish, and a fish for a special occasion. But it should also be fun. Let yourself go when it comes time to decorate the puff pastry. Cut it out in a fanciful fish shape, give the fish fins, make sure it has scales, and don't forget to add eyes and a mouth. And serve the dish with a little pomp and a lot of circumstance—it deserves it.

This recipe makes enough for two main-course servings—perfect for dinner tête-à-tête—but it can easily be doubled.

MAKES 2 SERVINGS

¼ cup extra-virgin olive oil

2 small to medium carrots, peeled, trimmed, and cut into ⅛-inch dice

3 stalks celery, peeled, trimmed, and cut into ⅛-inch dice

1 small yellow squash, scrubbed, trimmed, and cut into ⅛-inch dice

1 small zucchini, scrubbed, trimmed, and cut into ⅛-inch dice

1 medium red onion, peeled, trimmed, and cut into ⅛-inch dice

¼ small celery root, peeled and cut into ⅛-inch dice

1 teaspoon finely chopped thyme leaves

Salt and freshly ground white pepper

1¾ pounds all-butter puff pastry (see Glossary, page 371)

One 1½-pound sea bass, cleaned, skinned, and filleted, or two 6-ounce skinless sea bass fillets

2 egg yolks, beaten with 1 teaspoon cold water, for egg wash

1. WARM THE OLIVE OIL in a large sauté pan or skillet over medium-low heat. When it's hot, add the vegetables and chopped thyme, season with salt and pepper, and cook, covered, for 15 to 20 minutes, or until the vegetables are truly tender. They're not going to really cook again once they're in the crust, so taste them now and make certain they're ready-to-eat soft. Taste for seasoning too and add more salt or pepper if needed. Set the vegetables aside to cool.

2. CENTER A RACK in the oven and preheat the oven to 450°F.

3. CUT THE PUFF PASTRY in two, making one piece slightly larger than the other (keep the larger piece in the refrigerator while you're working on the smaller one). Working on a lightly floured surface, roll the smaller piece of dough into a rectangle that's about ⅛ inch thick and 3 to 4 inches larger all around than the fish fillets. Brush any excess flour off the dough and lift the dough onto a parchment-lined baking sheet. Cover the pastry with a piece of plastic wrap and put it in the refrigerator for the moment while you roll out the second piece of dough. This piece of dough, which will be the top piece, should also be rolled to a thickness of ⅛ inch, but it should be 6 inches larger all around than the fish fillets. Brush off any excess flour and lift this piece of dough onto a parchment-lined baking sheet; cover the pastry with plastic and chill it while you stuff the fish.

4. REMOVE THE BAKING SHEET with the first piece of rolled-out pastry from the refrigerator. Season both sides of the fish fillets with salt and pepper and place one of the fillets, skinned side down, in the center of the dough. Top the fillet with an even layer of the cooled vegetables and lay the other fillet skinned side up on the vegetables. With a pastry brush, brush an inch-wide border of the egg wash around the stuffed fish. Carefully drape the second piece of puff pastry over the fish. (The easiest way to do this is to roll the dough up around your rolling pin and then unroll it over the fish.) With the back of a knife, very gently press against the fish to seal the pastry layers, then use the knife to trim away the excess dough. Be creative here: Trim the dough so that it is shaped like a fish, complete with a top fin and a decorative tail; in trimming, make sure to leave at least a 1-inch border of dough all around the fillets—of course, you'll need to leave more if you're designing a seaworthy fish. (Save the scraps—you'll want them to decorate the fish.) Use your fingers or the back of a fork to press down on the border around the fish, again to make certain that the layers are sealed. With a paring knife, cut out a small inverted V of dough from the border every inch or so—this will help the dough to puff more evenly; cutting into the dough helps seal it as well.

5. BRUSH THE ENTIRE SURFACE of the dough with a coat of the egg wash, taking care not to let it drip over the edges of the dough—any drips will glue the pastry down and keep it from puffing evenly. Now, you're free to decorate the fish any way you wish. You can use the tip of a paring knife to draw scales across the body of the fish—just don't cut all the way through the pastry. Use the dough scraps to fashion an eye for the fish and, if you'd like, a smiling mouth—glue these in place with egg wash and then give them another coat of wash so they'll shine. Try to work as quickly as you can. If, when you've finished, the dough seems soft, put the fish in the refrigerator for about 20 minutes, and then add 5 minutes or so to its baking time. *(The fish can be prepared to this point up to 2 hours ahead and kept covered with plastic wrap in the refrigerator until you are ready to bake it.)*

6. **BAKE THE FISH** for 7 minutes, lower the oven temperature to 375°F, and bake for 15 minutes more, or until the pastry is beautifully puffed and richly browned. While the fish is cooking, make the sauce.

the sauce:

2 teaspoons extra-virgin olive oil

1 shallot, peeled, trimmed, finely chopped, rinsed, and dried

1 cup heavy cream

1 medium tomato, peeled, seeded, and cut into tiny dice

1 tablespoon finely chopped chives

Salt and freshly ground white pepper

WARM THE OLIVE OIL in a small saucepan and toss in the shallot. Cook, stirring, until the shallot is softened but not colored, about 3 minutes. Pour in the heavy cream and bring to the boil, then lower the heat to medium and cook until the cream is reduced by one quarter, about 4 to 5 minutes. Stir in the tomato and chives and pull the pan from the heat. Season the sauce with salt and pepper as needed and serve while still hot.

to serve: Don't even consider cutting the fish in the kitchen. Present your creation on a large platter and cut it crosswise into slices at the table. Serve the sauce spooned around—not over—the fish.

to drink: A rich, floral white wine with good acidity such as a Châteauneuf-du-Pape or a Saint-Péray

Salmon and Sorrel Troisgros

The celebrated Troisgros brothers created thousands of dishes for their Michelin-three-star restaurant in Roanne, France, but this dish, Salmon and Sorrel Sauce, became a touchstone in French culture. It, more than any dish created by any other chef, marked the passage from the classic cooking of Escoffier to *la nouvelle cuisine*. Today, with food so spare and light, it might be hard to imagine the excitement—and discord—this dish provoked. The components of the dish were not the newsmakers—they'd been used singly and in combination for years by chefs in France. It was the way in which the salmon was cooked and the manner in which the plate was arranged that rocked the culinary establishment. In the old order of things, the salmon would have been poached and placed on a warm plate, and the sauce would have been spooned over it. In the Troisgros's instant classic, the salmon was flash-cooked in a pan, a radically new way to cook fish, and it was the sauce that was put on the plate—the salmon topped it. It may not sound like much now, but then, it changed the way food was experienced.

If the dish did nothing but start a revolution, it would be interesting enough, but it is, in fact, a pleasure to eat. The salmon, cut into thin slices (you can cut the salmon at home with a long thin very sharp knife or ask the fishmonger to do this for you), is seared on the outside so that the inside—what little of it there is—is pink, velvety, and only just warm; the cream sauce is rich, smooth, and sorely sour. Saumon à l'Oseille is still on the Troisgrois menu and still, as the *Michelin Guide* would say, worth a journey.

This dish is a replica of the original Troisgros recipe; or, at least, it comes as close as a French dish made in America with American ingredients can come. While many of the ingredients in this country are very comparable to those found in France, cream is the exception, so my sauce may taste just a little different from the Troisgros sauce.

MAKES 4 SERVINGS

the sauce:

1 teaspoon unsalted butter

2 medium white mushrooms, trimmed but stems left on, cleaned, and finely chopped

1 large shallot, peeled, trimmed, finely chopped, rinsed, and dried

1 cup dry white wine

Salt and freshly ground white pepper

1 cup heavy cream

2 ounces sorrel, stemmed, washed, dried, and cut into very thin strands

1. **MELT THE BUTTER** in a small saucepan over medium heat, then add the mushrooms, shallot, and white wine and season with salt and pepper. Bring the wine to a boil and cook, keeping a close eye on the pan, until the wine has completely evaporated. Pour in the heavy cream, lower the heat—it should

be at its lowest possible setting—and let cook very slowly for about 15 minutes, until the cream is just thick enough to barely coat a metal spoon. Strain the cream into another small saucepan. *(You can make the sauce to this point up to 2 hours ahead and keep it covered at room temperature.)*

2. **WHEN YOU ARE READY** to sear the fish, add the sorrel to the cream and put the saucepan over medium heat. Bring the cream just to the boil and then pull the pan from the heat; taste and season with salt and pepper if needed.

the salmon:

2 center-cut salmon fillets, each about 1¼
   inches thick, 6 inches long, and 4 to 5
   inches wide (size is more important than
   weight here, but each fillet will probably be
   about ¾ pound)
Salt and freshly ground white pepper

1. **USING A LONG KNIFE** with a very sharp thin blade, slice each salmon fillet into 2 scallops by cutting across the top of the salmon—you're cutting horizontally in order to have 4 slices that are each about 6 inches long, 4 to 5 inches wide, and about ⅓ inch thick. The sliced salmon will look like the fish version of veal scallopini—and, because you cut the salmon across, not downward, you'll have a scrap of flesh and skin left over. Season the fillets on one side with salt and pepper.

2. **COAT THE BOTTOM** of four warm dinner plates with sorrel sauce and keep them warm while you cook the fish.

3. **HEAT A LARGE NONSTICK**—it must be nonstick—sauté pan or skillet (or 2 smaller pans) over medium-high heat. When the pan is hot, slip in the fillets. Cook for no more than 2 minutes (seriously)—you want the salmon to be only half-cooked (the edges will be cooked and the center will be raw, but warm)—then flip the fish over for 10 seconds before serving.

to serve: Quickly lift the salmon out of the pan and place one fillet in the center of each sauce-napped plate. Serve immediately—there's no time to lose—before the salmon cools.

to drink: The classic accompaniment to this nouvelle classic dish is a Pouilly-Fuissé

Skate with Brown Butter and Capers

I doubt that there's a chef in France who didn't make this dish as an apprentice. I know I certainly did. It was a perennial on menus from bistro to haute, but it was a dish almost entirely unknown in America until the mid-1980s, when the late French chef Gilbert LeCoze introduced it at his New York restaurant, Le Bernardin. Pre-LeCoze, fishmongers were just about giving skate wings away; now they are a specialty—and one worth getting to know. The edible part of the fish is the wing, and its sweet white meat, arranged on the wing like tufts on a cushion, is soft and mild, the perfect foil for brown butter—which has a light hazelnut flavor—and zesty vinegar-soaked capers. If you'd like, you can make this dish *amandine* by slipping a few toasted sliced almonds into the butter at the last minute. With or without almonds, the skate should be served with boiled potatoes.

MAKES 4 SERVINGS

the potatoes:

1 teaspoon salt

1 tablespoon freshly squeezed lemon juice

2 pounds small Yukon Gold potatoes, peeled
   and cut into 1-inch chunks

PUT 4 CUPS WATER, the salt, lemon juice, and potatoes in a large saucepan and bring to the boil. Lower the heat and simmer until the potatoes are tender, 10 to 15 minutes. You can start cooking the skate while the potatoes are simmering. (*If the potatoes are cooked before the skate is ready, turn off the heat and let the potatoes rest in the water—they can stay for about 10 minutes.*) Just before serving, drain the potatoes well.

the skate:

2 tablespoons coarse sea salt

1 teaspoon crushed white peppercorns

1 tablespoon red wine vinegar, plus extra for
   drizzling

Four 7-ounce boneless, skinless trimmed pieces
   skate fillet

9 tablespoons (1 stick plus 1 tablespoon)
   unsalted butter

¼ cup chopped Italian parsley leaves

¼ cup drained capers, plus 2 tablespoons of
   the vinegar the capers are packed in

1. COMBINE 2 CUPS WATER, the coarse salt, peppercorns, and wine vinegar in a fish poacher or a roasting pan and bring to the boil. Lower the heat to a simmer, fold each skate fillet in half for easier handling, and slip the fillets into the pan. Poach the fish gently for 8 to 10 minutes. Lift the fish out of the water using either the poacher's perforated tray or a large skimmer. Drain the fish well, then transfer it to a warm plate. Keep the fish warm (you can put it in a 200°F oven) while you prepare the brown butter.

2. COOK THE BUTTER in a small pan over medium heat just until it turns a light caramely brown. Add the parsley, capers, and their vinegar and cook only long enough to warm the capers, about 1 minute.

to serve: Lift the fillets onto a large warm serving platter, surround with the potatoes, and pour the warm butter, capers, and parsley over the fish and potatoes. Drizzle a little red wine vinegar sparingly over the fish. Serve immediately.

to drink: A Juraçon Sec or, if you want to break the bank, an older Hermitage Blanc

Chicken Grand-mère Francine

Chicken grand-mère, a savory fricassee, is a classic in French cuisine in general, but it was a classic in my family too. It was a specialty and a favorite of my Grandmother Francine, the grandmother who cooked at the original Café Boulud outside Lyon, and at no time was it better than at mushroom harvest time. Mushrooms are a typical chicken grand-mère ingredient, but there was nothing typical about the dish when my grandmother would add *rose des prés,* pink field mushrooms, newly dug potatoes, and new garlic. Fortunately, this dish always seems to be both satisfying and soothing whether you're making it plain, with cultivated cremini or oyster mushrooms and creamer potatoes, or fancy, dressing it up with exotic mushrooms and any of the small fingerling or banana potatoes that many greenmarkets now offer.

MAKES 4 SERVINGS

2 tablespoons extra-virgin olive oil

One 3-pound chicken, cut into 8 pieces (see
    Glossary, page 365)

Salt and freshly ground white pepper

2 tablespoons unsalted butter

12 cipollini onions, peeled and trimmed

4 shallots, peeled and trimmed

2 heads garlic, cloves separated but not peeled

3 sprigs thyme

4 small Yukon Gold potatoes, peeled and cut
    into 1½-inch chunks

2 small celery roots, peeled and cut into
    1½-inch chunks

2 ounces slab bacon, cut into short, thin strips

12 small cremini or oyster mushrooms,
    trimmed and cleaned

2 cups unsalted Chicken Stock (page 346) or
    store-bought low-sodium chicken broth

1. **CENTER A RACK** in the oven and preheat the oven to 375°F.

2. **WORKING OVER MEDIUM-HIGH HEAT,** warm the olive oil in a large ovenproof sauté pan or skillet—choose one with high sides and a cover. Season the chicken pieces all over with salt and pepper, slip them into the pan, and cook until they are well browned on all sides, about 10 to 15 minutes. Take your time—you want a nice, deep color and you also want to partially cook the chicken at this point. When the chicken is deeply golden, transfer it to a platter and keep it in a warm place while you work on the vegetables.

3. **POUR OFF ALL BUT 2 TABLESPOONS** of the cooking fat from the pan. Lower the heat to medium, add the butter, onions, shallots, garlic, and thyme, and cook and stir just until the vegetables start to take on a little color, about 3 minutes. Add the potatoes, celery root, and bacon and cook for 1 to 2 minutes, just to start rendering the bacon fat. Cover the pan and cook for another 10 minutes, stirring every 2 minutes.

4. ADD THE MUSHROOMS, season with salt and pepper, and return the chicken to the pan. Add the chicken stock, bring to the boil, and slide the pan into the oven. Bake, uncovered, for 20 to 25 minutes, or until the chicken is cooked through. Spoon everything onto a warm serving platter or into an attractive casserole.

to serve: Bring the chicken to the table, with plenty of pieces of crusty baguette to sop up the sauce and spread with the soft, sweet, caramely garlic that is easily squeezed out of its skin.

to drink: A rustic Bandol Rouge

Cornish Hens à la Diable

The ingredients—and hence the flavors—of this dish seem so all-American that even I, who grew up with it, have to remind myself that this is a preparation deeply rooted in the French repertoire. Translated, the name means deviled Cornish hens, but I don't want you to think of deviled eggs or crab. In the French kitchen, anything cooked *à la diable* is coated with mustard, dredged in bread crumbs, and grilled. To get the best texture and taste, I sear the butterflied hens on the stovetop, cook them through in the oven on a bed of potatoes, onions, and garlic—the potatoes absorb the hens' cooking juices and make a wonderful accompaniment—and then run them under the broiler for a last-minute crisping. I serve the hens with the sauce diable on the side. Don't laugh when you see the ingredients in the sauce—they're hardly what you'd expect from a French chef, but they're just what you're going to want with this piquant dish.

MAKES 2 SERVINGS

the sauce:

2 tablespoons Dijon mustard

1 tablespoon ketchup

1 tablespoon A-1 steak sauce

1 teaspoon Worcestershire sauce

3 drops Tabasco sauce

WHISK THE INGREDIENTS TOGETHER. Keep the sauce covered in the refrigerator until needed. *(The sauce can be made up to 3 days ahead and kept covered in the refrigerator.)*

the hens:

1 teaspoon dry mustard

½ teaspoon water

6 tablespoons Dijon mustard

Two 1- to 1¼-pound Cornish hens

Salt and freshly ground white pepper

5 tablespoons extra-virgin olive oil

1 cup panko (see Glossary, page 369) or bread crumbs

1 medium onion, peeled, trimmed, and cut into ¼-inch dice

1 clove garlic, peeled, split, germ removed, and finely chopped

1 sprig thyme

2 medium Yukon Gold potatoes, peeled, halved, and cut into ½-inch-thick slices

2 tablespoons finely chopped Italian parsley leaves

2 tablespoons unsalted butter, melted

1. **PREHEAT THE OVEN** to 400°F.

2. **DISSOLVE THE DRY MUSTARD** in the water and then mix it into the Dijon mustard; reserve.

3. **WORKING ON ONE HEN** at a time, cut down either side of the backbone with shears and remove the backbone (or ask the butcher to do this for you). Lay the hens out flat, skin side up, on a work surface and, using your hands, press down on the breastbone of each hen to flatten it. Don't be afraid to use some force—you want to break the breastbone and butterfly the bird. Season the Cornish hens on both sides with salt and pepper.

4. **WARM 2 TABLESPOONS** of the oil in a large sauté pan or skillet over medium heat. When the oil is hot, add the hens and cook for 4 to 5 minutes on each side, so that the birds take on color. (Because of their size, it may be easier to cook each bird separately or to use two pans, in which case you'll need to use a little more oil.) Remove the birds from the pan, brush their skin sides with the reserved mustard mixture, and top with the panko or bread crumbs, patting the crumbs onto the mustard mixture, then shaking off the excess; set aside.

5. **WIPE OUT THE PAN,** return it to medium heat, and add the remaining 3 tablespoons oil. Add the onion, garlic, thyme, and potatoes, season with salt and pepper, and cook, stirring, for about 8 minutes. Stir in the chopped parsley.

6. **SPREAD THE POTATO MIXTURE** over the bottom of a small roasting pan or a large ovenproof sauté pan or skillet and arrange the Cornish hens skin side up over the potatoes. Pour over the melted butter and put the birds in the oven to roast for 25 to 30 minutes, or until they are cooked through—pierce a thigh, and the juices should run clear. Remove the pan from the oven and turn on the broiler. Wrap the ends of the hens' legs with foil and run the birds under the broiler for 3 to 5 minutes, or until the mustardy crumbs are brown and crisp.

to serve: For each serving, arrange a cushion of potatoes on a warm plate and top with a Cornish hen. Serve the sauce diable on the side.

to drink: A good dark beer, perhaps a Fischer d'Alsace

Duck Civet

A duck civet, a slowly braised red wine ragout, is a hearty dish that can be prepared without fuss over a day or two. The pieces of duck must marinate overnight, time enough for them to absorb the acidity and fruit of the wine, the sweetness of the shallots and root vegetables, and the essence of the juniper berries. Afterward, they must be pan-roasted to a deeply golden color and then, reunited with the marinade, slipped into the oven to braise until tender. The final touch is a simple one: a shower of lightly browned bacon strips and freshly chopped chives. Because you can—in fact, must—do everything in advance, this civet makes a wonderful dinner-party dish. Just add friends.

A note on the duck: At Café Boulud, we use Muscovy ducks, which are slightly leaner and meatier than Long Island, or Pekin, ducks. Whether you use Muscovy or Pekin ducks is not crucial—either will produce an outstanding civet. And either should be cut into eight pieces, a job you can do at home or leave to the butcher.

MAKES 6 SERVINGS

to marinate:

Two 3½-pound ducks, Muscovy or Long Island (Pekin)

Salt and freshly ground white pepper

12 shallots or cipollini onions, peeled, trimmed, thinly sliced, and rinsed

10 cloves garlic, peeled

5 medium carrots, peeled, trimmed, and thinly sliced

5 stalks celery, peeled, trimmed, and cut into 1-inch-thick slices

20 black peppercorns, crushed

8 sprigs thyme

2 bay leaves

8 juniper berries

Two 1-inch-wide strips orange zest (pith removed)

3 bottles dry red wine

Freshly squeezed juice of 1 orange

1. **CUT EACH OF THE DUCKS** into 8 pieces. The easiest way is to first remove the legs and then split each leg in half. With the legs out of the way, detach the backbone all the way to the neck (you can do this with poultry shears) and chop both the backbones and neck into 2 to 3 pieces; reserve. Split each pair of breasts down the center and then split each breast crosswise in half.

2. **TO MARINATE THE DUCKS,** pull off and discard as much of the fat as you can. Season the meat and the bones all over with salt and pepper and toss them into a deep pot or pan—a small stockpot or a Dutch oven would be good. Scatter the vegetables, herbs, and zest over the duck and pour over the red wine and orange juice. Cover the pan and marinate the duck overnight in the refrigerator. If you have a chance, turn the duck and bones in the marinade once or twice.

to roast:

2 tablespoons unsalted butter
1 tablespoon vegetable oil
2 tablespoons all-purpose flour

1 tablespoon tomato paste
Salt and freshly ground white pepper

1. CENTER A RACK in the oven and preheat the oven to 350°F.

2. LIFT THE DUCK MEAT and bones out of the pot and dry the pieces between layers of paper towels. Try to get them as dry as you can so they'll roast to a nice dark color.

3. BRING THE MARINADE, along with its vegetables and spices, to a simmer. Keep the marinade over low heat while you brown the duck.

4. WARM THE BUTTER AND OIL over medium heat in the largest ovenproof sauté pan, skillet or Dutch oven you have. (Choose one with a lid.) Slip the meat and bones into the pan and brown them very well on all sides. If your pan isn't large enough to accommodate everything in one uncrowded layer, work in batches or use two pans (adding more oil and butter as needed). When the pieces are browned, add the flour and cook, stirring, to brown the flour. Stir in the tomato paste, pour in the warm marinade, including the vegetables and spices, and give everything a good stir. Bring to the boil and season with salt and pepper.

5. CUT A PARCHMENT PAPER CIRCLE (see Glossary, page 369) to fit inside the pan, press it gently against the ingredients, then cover the pan with its lid. Slide the pan into the oven and braise for 2 hours, skimming the fat that rises to the surface and giving the pot a gentle stir every 30 minutes. When the duck is ready, pull the pan from the oven, taste the sauce and add more salt and pepper if needed. *(This can be made a day ahead, cooled, covered, and refrigerated. One hour before serving, reheat in a 300°F oven.)*

to finish:

2 ounces thick-sliced bacon, cut into ¼-inch-wide strips

2 tablespoons finely chopped chives or Italian parsley leaves

TOSS THE BACON into a small sauté pan or skillet set over medium heat. Cook, stirring, until the bacon renders its fat and browns lightly, 8 to 10 minutes; drain on paper towels.

to serve: You can serve the civet directly from its pan or transfer it to a serving casserole. Spoon the bacon into the casserole and sprinkle the chives or parsley over the duck.

to drink: A highly alcoholic Châteauneuf-du-Pape

Spiced Fresh Pork Belly

Traditional French cooking, the cooking I grew up with, is like the traditional cooking of so many countries, including America—a cuisine based on thrift. As much as possible of any animal is used, little is discarded, and no part is ever thrown away if the tiniest bit of flavor can still be extracted from it. Certainly this is the case with the pig, whose entire flesh, from the meat on the feet to that on the snout, is savored.

It's always true that the poorest parts of the pig need the greatest amount of attention—but they're always worth it. Here it's the belly that gets TLC. First I rub it with a mix of toasted spices, salt, and sugar and leave it to cure in the refrigerator for two days, then I simmer it with vegetables and herbs before slipping it into a pot of lentils to finish cooking. At the end of a few hours, the pork is robustly flavored and spoon-tender.

With the exception of smoked bacon, which is made from the same cut I use here, most Americans are unfamiliar with fresh pork belly and are surprised to find it on the Café Boulud menu. Yet, this dish has become a personal classic—if I took pork belly off the menu, there'd be cries of protest.

MAKES 6 SERVINGS

the spice cure:

3 whole star anise

2 cinnamon sticks

4 teaspoons black peppercorns

2 teaspoons coriander seeds

1 teaspoon fennel seeds

½ teaspoon whole cloves

½ cup coarse sea salt

2 tablespoons sugar

1 teaspoon finely chopped garlic

One 3-pound square piece boneless fresh
    pork belly (a slab about 10 inches
    on a side)

1. PUT THE STAR ANISE, cinnamon sticks, peppercorns, coriander, fennel seeds, and cloves in a heavy-bottomed skillet and place the skillet over medium heat. Toast the spices, shaking the pan frequently, for 3 to 5 minutes. The spices won't color, but they will give off a wonderful aroma. Coarsely crush the spices in a spice grinder or mortar and pestle, or bash them with the bottom of a clean very heavy pot. Stir the spices together with the salt, sugar, and garlic.

2. WITH A SMALL SHARP KNIFE, score the skin of the pork belly in a crosshatch pattern of 1-inch squares or diamonds, making each cut only about ⅛ inch deep. Rub the spice mixture on both sides of the pork, covering the entire surface evenly, and put the pork in a nonreactive pan—a Pyrex baking pan or a small roasting pan would be good. Cover the dish with plastic wrap and refrigerate for 48 hours.

to cook:

2 celery stalks, peeled, trimmed, and cut in
    half
1 large carrot, peeled, trimmed, and cut in half
1 large onion, peeled, trimmed, and
    halved
Bouquet garni (4 sprigs thyme, 2 bay leaves,
    1 sprig rosemary, and 1 bunch Italian pars-
    ley, stems only—reserve the leaves to finish
    the dish—tied together with kitchen twine)

Salt and freshly ground white pepper
2 whole cloves
1 whole star anise
½ cinnamon stick
½ teaspoon coriander seeds
¼ teaspoon fennel seeds
2 cloves garlic, peeled

1. **REMOVE THE PORK BELLY** from the refrigerator and, using the back of a knife, gently scrape the seasoning off the meat; discard the scraped-off spices, then rinse the pork briefly under cold running water to remove any spices that remain. Put the belly in a deep stockpot along with the celery, carrot, and onion, pour in enough cold water to cover the meat and vegetables by 3 to 4 inches, and bring to the boil.

2. **ADD THE BOUQUET GARNI** to the pot. Reduce the heat so that the water is at a steady simmer and simmer gently for 3 hours, diligently skimming off the fat that rises to the surface. At this point, the pork will be fork-tender. Pull the pot from the heat and set it aside. *(You can make the pork to this point up to 2 days ahead. Cool the pork, then refrigerate it in its cooking liquid, covered with plastic wrap or foil.)* While the pork is cooking or resting, soak the lentils.

to finish:

1 cup dark green lentils (lentilles de Puy),
    picked over and rinsed
1 tablespoon extra-virgin olive oil
1 tablespoon unsalted butter
2 small carrots, peeled, trimmed, and cut into
    ½-inch dice
1 stalk celery, peeled, trimmed, and cut into
    ½-inch dice
½ small turnip, peeled, trimmed, and cut into
    ½-inch dice

½ small onion, peeled, trimmed, and cut into
    ½-inch dice
1 clove garlic, peeled
5 cups unsalted Chicken Stock (page 346) or
    store-bought low-sodium chicken broth
Salt and freshly ground white pepper
The reserved parsley leaves (from above),
    finely chopped

1. **PUT THE LENTILS** in a large bowl and add enough cold water to cover them by a couple of inches. Allow the lentils to soak at room temperature for 2 hours, then drain and rinse.

2. **DRAIN THE PORK BELLY** and discard the liquid, vegetables, and spices. Cut the belly into 6 equal pieces. You can cut the belly into long strips or rectangles—the shape isn't important. If you own an electric knife, this is a good time to use it, since the pork belly is very tender and the electric knife will not shred the meat. Set the pork aside for the moment.

3. **WARM THE OLIVE OIL** and butter in a large saucepan or a Dutch oven over medium heat and, when hot, add the carrots, celery, turnip, onion, and garlic. Cook, stirring, until the vegetables are softened, about 5 minutes. Add the lentils and stock, season with salt and pepper, and bring to a boil. Lower the heat to a simmer, slip the pieces of pork into the pan, and cook until the lentils are tender, 40 to 50 minutes.

to serve: Spoon some lentils and a piece of pork belly into each of six warm shallow soup plates. Sprinkle each serving with finely chopped parsley and serve immediately.

to drink: An aromatic Volnay from the Côte de Beaune

Short Ribs Braised in Red Wine

Short ribs are enjoying their moment in the spotlight these days. Once a homey dish served with mashed potatoes, short ribs—still homey—are now starring on restaurant menus all over America. I'm delighted, because I've always been a fan of their rich meat, appreciated their near-limitless capacity to accept the essential flavors of everything they are cooked with, and loved the almost spoon-food texture they take on after being gently braised in the oven.

I'm an old-fashioned guy when it comes to short ribs. I like them cooked, as they are here, the way they were cooked when I was a kid in France. I give the ribs a traditional base of aromatics— garlic, shallots, carrots, celery, and leeks—toss in fresh herbs, and braise them slowly in a mixture of stock and red wine. The success of this dish depends on browning the meat well at the start and tending the meat during its braising time—to get the best flavor from the sauce, you need to be diligent about skimming off the fat that rises to the surface. This is a good dish to plan a party around because it takes nicely to being made ahead: Do the cooking one day, reheat the dish the next.

At Café Boulud, we serve the braised short ribs with a Celery Duo (page 78), a double dish of braised quarters of stalk celery and puréed celery root and potato, but mashed potatoes, parsnip mousseline (page 142), creamy polenta, or rice would also be right with the ribs.

MAKES 8 SERVINGS

3 bottles dry red wine

2 tablespoons vegetable oil

8 short ribs, trimmed of excess fat

Salt

1 teaspoon black peppercorns, crushed

Flour for dredging

10 cloves garlic, peeled

8 large shallots, peeled, trimmed, split, rinsed, and dried

2 medium carrots, peeled, trimmed, and cut into 1-inch lengths

2 stalks celery, peeled, trimmed, and cut into 1-inch lengths

1 medium leek, white and light green parts only, coarsely chopped, washed, and dried

6 sprigs Italian parsley

2 sprigs thyme

2 bay leaves

2 tablespoons tomato paste

3 quarts unsalted Beef Stock (page 347) or store-bought low-sodium beef broth

Freshly ground white pepper

1. **POUR THE WINE** into a large saucepan set over medium heat. When the wine is hot, carefully set it aflame. Let the flames die out, then increase the heat so that the wine boils; allow it to boil until it cooks down by half. Remove from the heat.

2. CENTER A RACK in the oven and preheat the oven to 350°F.

3. WARM THE OIL in a Dutch oven or large casserole over medium-high heat. Season the ribs all over with salt and the crushed pepper. Dust half the ribs with about 1 tablespoon flour and then, when the oil is hot, slip the ribs into the pot and sear for 4 to 5 minutes on a side, until well browned. Transfer the browned ribs to a plate, dust the remaining ribs with flour, and sear in the same manner. Remove all but 1 tablespoon of fat from the pot, lower the heat under the pot to medium, and toss in the vegetables and herbs. Brown the vegetables lightly, 5 to 7 minutes, then stir in the tomato paste and cook for 1 minute to blend.

4. ADD THE REDUCED WINE, browned ribs, and stock to the pot. Bring to the boil, cover the pot tightly, and slide it into the oven to braise for 2½ hours, or until the ribs are tender enough to be easily pierced with a fork. Every 30 minutes or so, lift the lid and skim and discard whatever fat may have bubbled up to the surface. *(Not only can you make this a day in advance, it's best to make the recipe up to this point, cool and chill the ribs and stock in the pan overnight, and, the next day, scrape off the fat. Rewarm before continuing.)*

5. CAREFULLY (the tender meat falls apart easily) transfer the meat to a heated serving platter with a lip and keep warm. Boil the pan liquid until it thickens and reduces to approximately 1 quart. Season with salt and pepper and pass through a fine-mesh strainer; discard the solids. *(The ribs and sauce can be combined and kept covered in the refrigerator for 2 to 3 days. Reheat gently, basting frequently, on top of the stove or in a 350°F oven.)*

to serve: Pour the sauce over the meat. If you've made the Celery Duo, serve it on the same platter—the celery root purée can go under the ribs, the braised celery over them.

to drink: A young, brawny Médoc, such as a Pauillac or a Saint-Julien

Lamb-Haricots

A quintessential French supper casserole, this combination of white beans and lamb is lusty enough to stand alone. Everything in the casserole is transformed during its time in the oven. The beans, characterless at the start, finish with remarkable flavor, having absorbed the juices from large pieces of celery, fennel, onion, and carrot, moistened with white wine and stock, and accented with garlic, tomatoes, and herbs. Nestled within the casserole is a lamb shoulder that also yields its flavor to the mix and, in the process, is transformed as well. After hours in the oven, the shoulder emerges tender enough to be cut with a spoon. Soak the beans the night before and you'll have nothing to do to ready supper but brown the meat and vegetables, tuck them snugly into the casserole, and braise the dish in the oven. It doesn't even need stirring.

MAKES 6 SERVINGS

the beans:

1 pound assorted dried beans, such as
    Great Northern, flageolet, cranberry, and
    cannellini, picked over and rinsed

PUT THE BEANS in a large pot and cover them with about three times their volume of cold water; allow the beans to soak overnight in the refrigerator. Alternatively, you can hasten the process by bringing the water and beans to a boil, boiling for 2 minutes, and then letting the beans soak in the hot water for an hour. No matter which method you've used, drain and rinse the beans before proceeding.

the lamb:

3 tablespoons extra-virgin olive oil
One 3-pound boneless lamb shoulder, tied into
    a roast or cut into 6 pieces
Salt and freshly ground white pepper
6 cloves garlic, peeled, split, and germ removed
2 stalks celery, peeled, trimmed, and cut into
    1-inch lengths
1 onion, peeled, trimmed, and cut into
    1-inch chunks
1 carrot, peeled, trimmed, and cut into
    1-inch lengths
1 fennel bulb, trimmed and cut lengthwise
    into quarters

1 tablespoon tomato paste
5 large tomatoes, peeled, seeded, and finely
    chopped
2 cups dry white wine
Herb sachet (10 sprigs Italian parsley, 6 sprigs
    thyme, 2 sprigs rosemary, 2 bay leaves,
    1 branch fennel—reserved from the fennel
    bulb—and 1 teaspoon black peppercorns,
    tied in cheesecloth)
8 cups unsalted Chicken Stock (page 346),
    store-bought low-sodium chicken broth,
    or water

1. **CENTER A RACK** in the oven and preheat the oven to 325°F.

2. **WARM THE OIL** in a large sauté pan or skillet over medium heat. While it is heating, season the lamb all over with salt and pepper. Slip the lamb into the pan and brown it very well on all sides. When the lamb is deeply colored, transfer it to a Dutch oven or large casserole and set aside. Pour off all but 2 to 3 tablespoons of the fat in the sauté pan. Add the garlic, celery, onion, carrot, and fennel, season with salt and pepper, and cook, stirring, until the vegetables are translucent but not colored, about 10 minutes. Add the tomato paste and tomatoes and cook, stirring, until the tomatoes soften. Add the wine and simmer for about 5 minutes, to burn off the alcohol and reduce the liquid by half. Transfer everything from the pan to the Dutch oven and stir in the beans, herb sachet, and stock or water.

3. **PUT THE POT** over medium heat and bring the liquid to a simmer. Cut a parchment paper circle to fit inside the pot (see Glossary, page 369) and cover the pot with the parchment paper lid and its own lid. Slide the pot into the oven to braise undisturbed for about 2½ hours, or until the meat is so tender it can be cut with a spoon. (If the casserole seems dry, you can stir in up to 1 cup of water as it's braising. You want to keep the casserole moist and saucy.) Discard the herb sachet and taste the beans; add more salt or pepper if needed.

to serve: Serve this from the casserole, giving everyone a generous portion of beans topped with a piece of the tender lamb.

to drink: A Provençal rosé, such as a Tavel, or a crisp, dry white, like a Palette

Onion Soup with Braised Beef Shank (page 14) and marrow on crusty sourdough bread

la tradition

Top left: Ratatouille Méridionale (page 76)

Top right: Artichokes and Mushrooms
à la Grecque (page 24)

Bottom: Socca Stuffed
with Peppery Greens (page 80)

la tradition
Cervelle de Canut with Frisée (page 26)

la tradition
Sea Bass en Croûte (page 45)

la tradition
Chicken Grand-mère Francine (page 52)

la tradition
Cornish Hens à la Diable (page 54)

la tradition
Short Ribs Braised in Red Wine (page 61) with Celery Duo (page 78)

la tradition
Chocolate Mousse Trio (page 93)

Mustard-Crusted Calf's Liver

If you've never cooked calf's liver in a whole piece, as I do here, nor given it the three-step treatment it gets in this recipe, I think you'll be truly surprised by what you end up with—liver so rich, silky, and luxurious in texture it will make you think of foie gras. Liver's texture is its best quality; its flavor always needs a pick-me-up, and it receives several in this preparation. After the liver is seared to create a protective coating and roasted to cook it through to pink perfection, I give it a pungent crust of Dijon mustard. (Make sure to choose a mustard that's strong enough to make your eyes water—it will lose some of its zip as it cooks.) Then, the dish gets additional punch with vinegar-glazed sweet-and-sour onions and finally, just when the balance of the flavors might go awry, I even things out by putting a touch of cream in the sauce—it smooths, soothes, and completes the dish. I almost always serve Mustard-Crusted Liver on a bed of sautéed spinach because I like the way the spinach cuts the richness of the liver and adds its own mellow sweetness to play against the assertively flavored onions.

You can only be successful with the liver if you buy the right cut. You need one large, thick block of liver in order to sear it well and give it a good crust. (Don't try this with the thin slices of calf's liver found in the supermarket—they'll overcook before they're properly seared.) Since you will need to order the liver from your butcher, this is a dish to think about in advance.

MAKES 4 SERVINGS

the onions:

3 large red onions, peeled

1 tablespoon extra-virgin olive oil

3 tablespoons sherry vinegar

2 tablespoons aged balsamic vinegar

1 large leaf sage, finely chopped

Salt and freshly ground white pepper

1. CENTER A RACK in the oven and preheat the oven to 400°F.

2. TRIM WHATEVER ROOTS are attached to the onions, but don't cut through the root ends—they're what will keep the onions together during cooking—then cut each onion into 6 wedges from top to root. Working over medium heat, warm the olive oil in a large ovenproof sauté pan or skillet. Add the onions and cook, turning, until the onions are lightly but evenly colored, about 10 minutes. Reduce the heat to low and cook for 3 minutes more. Add the sherry and balsamic vinegars and the sage, season with salt and pepper, and slide the pan into the oven.

3. BRAISE THE ONIONS for 20 to 30 minutes, carefully turning them twice during this time so that they cook evenly. The liquid in the pan will reduce and the onions will glaze lightly. *(The onions can be made 30 to 60 minutes ahead of the liver and set aside at room temperature. Reheat for a few minutes in a hot oven before serving.)*

the sauce:

1½ teaspoons unsalted butter

1 shallot, peeled, trimmed, finely chopped, rinsed, and dried

2 tablespoons sherry vinegar

⅓ cup heavy cream

1 tablespoon Dijon mustard

Salt and freshly ground white pepper

MELT THE BUTTER in a small saucepan over medium heat. Add the shallot and cook, stirring, until the shallot is translucent but not colored, about 3 minutes. Pour in the vinegar and allow it to cook away before adding the heavy cream. Boil the cream for 2 minutes, then stir in the mustard. Taste and season the sauce with salt and pepper. Pass the sauce through a fine-mesh strainer into a pitcher or sauceboat. Set the sauce aside in a warm place, or reheat gently before serving. *(The sauce can be made a few hours ahead and reheated over low heat or in a double boiler just before serving.)*

the liver:

7 leaves sage

1¾ pounds calf's liver, in one piece and preferably of an even thickness, skin removed

Salt and freshly ground white pepper

Milk

Flour for dredging

2 tablespoons extra-virgin olive oil

1 tablespoon unsalted butter

3 cloves garlic, peeled and crushed

1 tablespoon Dijon mustard

1½ teaspoons finely grated Parmesan cheese

1½ teaspoons bread crumbs

1 tablespoon unsalted butter, melted

Simply Sautéed Spinach (page 74), for serving (optional)

1. CENTER A RACK in the oven and preheat the oven to 400°F.

2. CUT 3 OF THE SAGE LEAVES into quarters. Using a small pointed paring knife, cut a small slit in the liver and, using the point of the knife, immediately push a piece of the cut sage into it. (You need to work quickly because the slit will close quickly.) Continue to cut and fill slits until you've got all 12 pieces of sage tucked evenly into the top, bottom, and sides of the liver. Season the liver with salt and pepper, roll it in the milk, and dredge it in the flour, tapping off the excess.

3. WARM THE OLIVE OIL in a large ovenproof sauté pan or skillet over medium heat. Slip the liver into the pan and brown it evenly on all sides, cooking it for about 12 minutes. After about 5 minutes of cooking, add the 1 tablespoon butter, the remaining whole sage leaves, and the garlic. When the liver is browned, place the pan in the oven and roast for 6 minutes, turning the liver over halfway during the roasting time.

4. REMOVE THE LIVER from the oven and set the oven to broil. Coat the top of the liver evenly with the mustard, then toss together the Parmesan and bread crumbs and gently pat them onto the mustard. Drizzle the melted butter over the coating, place the pan about 6 inches from the heat, and broil until the crust is lightly browned, about 3 minutes. Transfer the liver to a cutting board.

to serve: Using an electric knife or a thin sharp knife, cut the liver crosswise on the bias into eight ½-inch-thick slices. The inside of the liver will be very pink, very moist, and not at all as firm as the outside. If you're serving the liver with the spinach, spoon the spinach into the center of a warm oval serving platter, surround with the onions, and top with the thick, juicy slices of liver; pass the sauce at the table.

to drink: A Saint-Émilion, a red wine with sweet fruit and good acidity

Hanger Steak with Shallots

Like lamb neck (page 70), hanger steak was, until recently, a cut of meat too humble to enter a restaurant dining room. In fact, it was even too poor a cut to sell. In France, and later, here too, it earned the name "the butcher's steak," because it was the piece the butcher took home for himself and his family. It is a very chewy cut of meat—not tough, just chewy. And, because it's so very chewy, it's also incredibly flavorful. I think the steak wasn't too lowly for the butcher to sell, it just tasted too good—he knew what he was doing when he kept it for himself. Sometime in the mid-1980s, a few butchers in America started cutting hanger steaks and a few French chefs started serving them. They were instant favorites among Americans and a delight to stateside French diners who already knew them. Now the steak is found on menus—and in butcher shops—all over America and France.

To my way of thinking, the traditional way of serving hanger steak is the best. The steaks are quickly pan-roasted—they're best served medium-rare (although in France they're often served *"bleu,"* so rare that they're almost blue and only just warm in the center)—and sauced with shallots that have been cooked to a compote's consistency with red wine and vinegar and then tossed with butter and herbs. Whether you sauce the steaks or not (sometimes small bistros in France will serve the steaks with just a spoonful of butter and some sea salt or a pot of strong mustard), I hope you'll serve them with the greatest and most classic accompaniment: Pommes Frites, French-fried potatoes (page 85).

MAKES 6 SERVINGS

1 tablespoon vegetable oil
Six 7-ounce hanger steaks
Salt and freshly ground white pepper
2 tablespoons unsalted butter
8 medium shallots, peeled, trimmed, thinly
   sliced, rinsed, and dried

2 tablespoons red wine vinegar
½ cup dry red wine
2 tablespoons finely chopped Italian
   parsley leaves

1. HEAT A LARGE heavy-bottomed sauté pan or skillet over high heat, then add the oil. When the oil is hot, season the steaks with salt and pepper, slip them into the pan, and brown evenly, turning as needed, until they're done the way you like them—6 minutes total will give you a medium-rare steak (remember, the steaks will continuing cooking while they rest); cook the steaks a minute longer for medium and 2 to 3 minutes longer for well-done. Transfer the steaks to a heated serving dish and set them aside in a warm place while you make the shallots.

2. PLACE THE PAN you used to cook the steaks over medium heat and add 1 tablespoon of the butter and the shallots. Season with salt and pepper and cook, stirring, for 3 to 5 minutes, until the shallots are softened but not colored. Add the vinegar and cook until it evaporates, then add the wine. Bring the wine to the boil and allow it to cook down until it is reduced by half. Pull the pan from the heat and swirl in the remaining 1 tablespoon butter, then stir in the chopped parsley.

to serve: Cut each steak on the bias into thin slices and, for each serving, fan the slices out on a warm dinner plate. Drizzle the warm shallot sauce over the meat and serve immediately.

to drink: A lightly chilled Beaujolais-Villages

Braised Stuffed Lamb Neck

When I was a cook in France, the lamb's neck wasn't considered haute enough fare for paying guests, so the restaurant's butcher would set it aside for staff meals—and there wasn't a time when the staff wasn't happy to see it on the table: It's the tastiest cut from the lamb. It's also a chewy, muscular cut, which was why the chefs didn't think it was right for guests. For years, I held to what I had learned in France and kept the neck out of the dining room, until I decided to serve an *épigramme* of lamb, a *plat de résistance* in which each part of the lamb is cooked differently and all the parts are presented at the table on one large platter. You can imagine my surprise when guests raved about the neck—now my problem is getting enough of them. When I served the *épigramme* of lamb, I treated the neck just as I do here, stuffing it with a flavorful ground pork mixture, tying it up like a roast, and braising it very slowly with herbs, garlic, and white wine, adding, toward the end, carrots and spring onions.

In all likelihood, you'll have to special-order the lamb neck from your butcher—even we have to place a special order—so plan ahead. And, when you give the butcher your order, give him a smile, too, and ask if he'll butterfly the neck for you. If he won't, don't give up: The job is easily done at home, even if you're a first timer. (If you end up with a piece that's uneven or that's got a little hole here or there, just trim and patch.) Finally, if you can't get a lamb neck, you don't have to forego this dish—it will work just fine with a lamb shoulder. Butterfly the shoulder just as you would the neck and then keep going.

MAKES 4 SERVINGS

the stuffing:

2 tablespoons extra-virgin olive oil

1 medium onion, peeled, trimmed, and finely diced

3 large white mushrooms, trimmed, cleaned, and coarsely chopped

Salt and freshly ground white pepper

1 clove garlic, peeled, split, germ removed, and finely chopped

1 teaspoon finely chopped thyme leaves

1 slice stale or oven-dried white bread, crust removed and cut into ¼-inch dice

1 tablespoon finely chopped Italian parsley leaves

2 tablespoons finely chopped basil leaves

½ pound ground pork

1. **WARM THE OLIVE OIL** in a medium sauté pan or skillet over medium heat. Add the onion and cook, stirring, just until it is translucent but not colored, about 5 minutes. Toss in the mushrooms, season with salt and pepper, and sauté until the mushrooms release their moisture, reabsorb it, and turn

tender. Add the garlic and thyme and continue to cook and stir for 2 minutes more. Finally, add the bread cubes and parsley and give them a few turns in the pan. Pull the pan from the heat, turn the stuffing into a large bowl, and let it cool.

2. WHEN THE STUFFING is cool, knead in the basil and ground pork, and season with more salt and pepper. (If you are unsure of the seasoning, sauté a tablespoonful of the stuffing, taste it, and make whatever adjustments you need.) Set the stuffing aside in a cool place while you ready the lamb. *(The stuffing can be made 1 day ahead and kept covered in the refrigerator.)*

the lamb:

1 whole lamb neck, about 10 to 12 inches long, split open lengthwise, bone removed, and meat deveined and butterflied so that it lies flat and is ½ inch thick, or 1 lamb shoulder, about 4 to 5 pounds, boned and butterflied

Salt and freshly ground white pepper

2 tablespoons extra-virgin olive oil

4 tablespoons unsalted butter

5 cloves garlic, peeled, split, germ removed, and thinly sliced

1 teaspoon finely chopped thyme leaves

12 medium carrots, peeled, trimmed, and cut diagonally into ½-inch-thick slices

6 medium white onions, peeled, trimmed, and cut in half from root to top

1 fennel bulb, trimmed and cut into 6 wedges

1 bottle dry white wine

1. CENTER A RACK in the oven and preheat the oven to 375°F.

2. OPEN THE BUTTERFLIED LAMB and place it flat on a work surface. Season it inside and out with salt and pepper and turn it so that the inside is face up. Spoon the stuffing down the length of the neck in a compact log, then roll up the meat tightly around the stuffing, shaping it into a roast. Tie the lamb at 1-inch intervals with kitchen twine so that the stuffing is secure and the neck—now looking very much like a rolled roast—will cook evenly.

3. SET A ROASTING PAN over medium-high heat and add the olive oil. When the oil is hot, slip the lamb into the pan and sear it on all sides, browning the meat evenly for about 6 minutes on a side. Halfway through the browning, when two of the sides have been seared, add 2 tablespoons of the butter and, as the meat continues to brown, baste it with the combined pan fats.

4. WHEN THE LAMB is beautifully browned on all sides, slide the pan into the oven and roast the lamb for 15 minutes, basting regularly. Give the lamb a quarter-turn and roast for 15 minutes more. Remove the pan from the oven and carefully pour off the fats that have accumulated. Toss the garlic and thyme into the pan along with the remaining 2 tablespoons butter, the carrots, onions, and fennel. Season the vegetables with salt and pepper and stir them around in the pan until they are well combined. Return the pan to the oven and continue to roast for 20 minutes more, turning and basting the meat and stirring the vegetables twice during this time.

5. POUR IN THE WINE and check on the vegetables—if they're browning too quickly, turn the heat down to 350°F. Braise the meat for an additional 1½ hours, turning and basting the meat and stirring the vegetables every 15 minutes. Remove the pan from the oven and discard the garlic.

6. TRANSFER THE LAMB to a cutting board and snip off the twine. Cut the roast into 8 slices and arrange them on a warm serving platter. Top with the vegetables and set the platter aside in a warm place. Pour the juices from the roasting pan into a saucepan and bring to a boil. Allow the sauce to cook at the boil until it is reduced to 1 cup.

to serve: Pour the pan juices over the lamb and vegetables and serve immediately.

to drink: A rich red, such as a Coteaux du Languedoc, preferably a Faugères

Side Dishes

Braised Carrots with Thyme and Garlic

Oven-braising carrots in chicken stock with fresh thyme and slivers of garlic is the best way to ensure carrots that are tender, sweet, and flavorful enough to accompany hearty dishes.

MAKES 6 SERVINGS

2 tablespoons unsalted butter

1½ pounds carrots, peeled, trimmed, and cut on the bias into ¼-inch-thick slices

2 cloves garlic, peeled and finely sliced

2 sprigs thyme

Salt and freshly white ground pepper

1 cup unsalted Chicken Stock (page 346) or store-bought low-sodium chicken broth

1. **CENTER A RACK** in the oven and preheat the oven to 375°F.

2. **WORKING OVER MEDIUM HEAT,** melt the butter in a large ovenproof sauté pan or skillet (one that you can serve from would be nice here). Add the carrots, garlic, and thyme, season with salt and pepper, and cook, stirring regularly, for 10 minutes, or until the vegetables soften a little but don't color.

3. **IF YOU'D LIKE,** you can arrange the carrots in decorative overlapping rows now—it's not necessary, just attractive. Add the chicken stock and bring to a boil. Cover the pan with a circle of parchment paper (see Glossary, page 369), pressing the paper against the carrots, and then cover the pan with its lid. Braise in the oven for 20 minutes, then remove the cover and the paper and cook for 15 to 20 minutes more, or until the carrots are very tender when pierced with a knife.

to serve: The carrots are best served directly from their braising pan—and immediately. Just remember to discard the sprigs of thyme before serving.

Simply Sautéed Spinach

Reach for this recipe any time you want quickly, simply prepared spinach to serve alongside—or under—roasted or grilled meats or fish. This is the spinach I serve with Mustard-Crusted Calf's Liver (page 65).

MAKES 4 SERVINGS

1½ teaspoons unsalted butter

1½ pounds spinach, stemmed, tough center veins removed, well washed, and dried

2 cloves garlic, peeled and crushed

Salt and freshly ground white pepper

MELT THE BUTTER in a large sauté pan or skillet over high heat. Add the spinach, garlic, and salt and pepper to taste and toss until the spinach is tender but still bright green, about 5 minutes. Discard the garlic and drain off any liquid remaining in the pan. Serve immediately.

Green Bean Bundles

These little packets of bacon-wrapped green beans are as practical as they are dressy (delicious goes without saying). Because the beans are cooked ahead of time and then neatly wrapped in strips of bacon, all you have to do at dinnertime is give the bundles a gentle sauté to cook the bacon, warm the beans, and encourage the thin haricots verts to take on a touch of the bacon's smokiness. At Café Boulud, we serve these beans with roasted meats.

MAKES 4 SERVINGS

6 ounces haricots verts or wax beans, tipped

2 slices bacon

2 tablespoons extra-virgin olive oil

Freshly ground white pepper

1. **BRING A MEDIUM SAUCEPAN** of salted water to the boil, plunge the beans into the water, and cook just until they are tender, 3 to 5 minutes. Drain the beans in a colander and immediately run them under very cold water to cool and set their color. When the beans are cool, dry them well between layers of paper towels.

2. **CUT EACH PIECE OF BACON** crosswise in half and place the pieces between sheets of plastic wrap. Using a meat tenderizer or the bottom of a pot, pound the bacon gently to flatten and thin it (the way you would veal scallopini). Cut each of the pieces of bacon crosswise in half again.

3. **DIVIDE THE BEANS** into 8 packets. Working with one packet and one piece of bacon at a time, lay the bacon out flat on a work surface, place a bundle of beans close to one end of the bacon, and roll up the bacon tightly around the beans. When the bacon is wrapped tightly, you usually won't need to secure the bundle with a toothpick. But if the bundles look a little shaky, run a toothpick through each piece of bacon to hold it fast.

4. **WARM THE OLIVE OIL** in a large sauté pan or skillet over medium-low heat. When the oil is hot, slip the bundles into the pan. Cook the packets slowly, just until the bacon is crisp, without allowing the beans to color.

to serve: Carefully lift the bundles out of the pan and serve immediately, placing 2 bundles on each dinner plate or piling up a pyramid of the bundles on a platter to serve family-style.

Ratatouille Méridionale

The Méridional is the southern region of France famous, among other reasons, for its ratatouille. This ratatouille is classic in that it contains tomatoes, peppers, zucchini, onions, and eggplant, but unusual in that it is cooked gently in the oven, not on the stovetop, and only until the vegetables are tender but neither mushy nor melded with one another. This rendition has its own personality because each of the vegetables is allowed to keep its individual taste and texture. I usually serve ratatouille at room temperature, but if you prefer it warm, you can reheat it. Whether it's warm or not, I like to add a splash of lemon juice and a handful of basil leaves right before serving—they bring a hint of garden freshness back to the cooked vegetables.

MAKES 4 TO 6 SERVINGS

3 tablespoons extra-virgin olive oil

2 cloves garlic, peeled, split, and germ removed

1 onion, peeled, trimmed, and cut into 1-inch chunks

2 red bell peppers, cored, seeded, deveined, and cut into 1-inch chunks

2 yellow bell peppers, cored, seeded, deveined, and cut into 1-inch chunks

Salt and freshly ground white pepper

1 small eggplant (about ¼ pound), trimmed and cut into 1-inch chunks

1 zucchini, scrubbed, trimmed, and cut into 1-inch chunks

1 yellow squash, scrubbed, trimmed, and cut into 1-inch chunks

2 tablespoons tomato paste

3 large tomatoes, peeled, seeded, and cut into 1-inch chunks

½ teaspoon finely chopped thyme leaves

2 bay leaves

½ teaspoon thinly sliced basil leaves

½ teaspoon freshly squeezed lemon juice

1. CENTER A RACK in the oven and preheat the oven to 300°F.

2. IN ORDER FOR THE VEGETABLES to retain their distinctive flavors, you will need either to cook them in batches or to cook them in two separate sauté pans or skillets. Warm 1 tablespoon of the olive oil in a large sauté pan over medium heat. When the oil is hot, add 1 clove of garlic, the onion, and the chunks of red and yellow pepper. Season with salt and pepper and cook, stirring, until the vegetables soften a bit but don't take on color, about 5 minutes. Either remove the vegetables and wipe out the pan or, while the peppers are cooking, take another sauté pan or skillet, and warm the remaining 2 tablespoons oil over medium heat. Add the second clove of garlic, the eggplant, zucchini, and squash and cook and stir for 8 to 10 minutes, this time allowing the vegetables to color a bit.

3. COMBINE THE SAUTÉED VEGETABLES in one large ovenproof sauté pan or skillet or a baking dish and stir in the tomato paste, tomatoes, thyme, and bay leaves. Cover the pan with a circle of parchment paper (see Glossary, page 369), pressing the paper against the vegetables. Put the pan in the oven and bake for 45 to 50 minutes, stirring the ratatouille every 15 minutes or so. The ratatouille is done when the vegetables are meltingly tender but still retain their shape. Remove the bay leaves and garlic. *(The ratatouille can be made up to 3 days ahead and kept covered in the refrigerator. Before serving, bring it to room temperature or warm it gently in a slow oven.)*

to serve: The ratatouille can be served now, while it's hot, or when it reaches room temperature. Just before serving, stir in the basil leaves and the squirt of lemon juice.

Celery Duo

This double dip of celery is served alongside braised short ribs (page 61) at Café Boulud, but it's a side dish that can play the field—it's equally good served with hanger steak (page 68) or peppered char (page 142). The duo comprises a purée of celery root, smoothed out with Yukon Gold potatoes, and a braise of celery in which heads of celery are quartered, then cooked until glossy in chicken stock with carrots and turnips. Each member of the duet sings its own tune, but together they hymn the variety and depth of flavors celery can offer.

MAKES 8 SERVINGS

the celery root:

1 quart whole milk

2 tablespoons coarse sea salt

2 pounds celery root, peeled and cut into
  8 pieces

1 pound Yukon Gold potatoes, peeled and
  cut in half

8 tablespoons (1 stick) unsalted butter, cut
  into 8 pieces, at room temperature

Salt and freshly ground white pepper

1. PUT THE MILK, 4 cups water, the coarse salt, celery root, and potatoes in a medium saucepan and bring to a boil over medium heat. Lower the heat and cook at a simmer until the vegetables can be easily pierced with the point of a knife, 20 to 25 minutes. Drain the vegetables and return them to the pan.

2. PUT THE PAN BACK over low heat and toss the vegetables in the pan just enough to cook off their excess moisture; transfer the vegetables to the work bowl of a food processor. Add the butter and process—taking care not to overwork the mixture—just until the purée is smooth and creamy. Season with salt and pepper. Keep the purée warm in the top of a double boiler over simmering water. *(The purée can be made up to 6 hours ahead. Cool it, cover it with plastic wrap, pressing the wrap against the purée, and refrigerate. When you're ready to serve, rewarm the purée in the top of a double boiler over simmering water.)*

the celery:

2 bunches celery
1 tablespoon extra-virgin olive oil
1 carrot, peeled, trimmed, and quartered
1 turnip, peeled, trimmed, and quartered

Salt and freshly ground white pepper
2½ cups unsalted Chicken Stock (page 346) or
store-bought low-sodium chicken broth

1. TRIM THE BOTTOM of each bunch of celery—but make certain the stalks remain together—then measure 4 to 5 inches up from the bottom and cut the celery top off at that point (you'll be using the bottom part). Remove and discard the 3 or 4 tough outer stalks. Run a vegetable peeler over the exterior of the outer celery stalks to remove the stringy part of the vegetable, then cut each bunch of celery lengthwise into quarters. Keep close at hand.

2. WARM THE OIL in a large sauté pan or skillet over medium heat. Add the carrot, turnip, and celery quarters, season with salt and pepper, and cook, without coloring the vegetables, for 3 minutes. Pour in the stock and bring to the boil. Adjust the heat so that the stock simmers steadily and cook the vegetables for about 25 minutes, or until they can be pierced easily with the point of a knife. When the vegetables are tender, the liquid should be just about gone, so that you should have tender vegetables lightly glazed with the stock. Remove and discard the carrots and turnips and serve the celery immediately. *(If it's more convenient, you can make the celery up to 6 hours ahead, chill it, and then rewarm it gently at serving time.)*

to serve: Serve the duo as a duo, choosing a large heated platter and spooning the purée onto one half, the glazed celery onto the other.

Socca Stuffed with Peppery Greens

Socca, a soft chickpea pancake, is as popular in Nice as pizza is in New York City. In fact, socca is so popular in Nice that you're as likely to be knocked down by a socca delivery man on his specially built socca-carrying bicycle as you are by a pizza man in Gotham. Along the French Riviera, and especially in the market at Nice, socca is made in huge round pans, baked in a pizza oven, and sold by the slice. The batter is similar to the one used to make crêpes, but for socca, you use chickpea flour, readily available in health food stores. While the Niçois in the marketplace eat their socca on the run—nursing their burnt fingers as they shop for the day's vegetables—at Café Boulud, I make it a little easier to enjoy this rustic treat. I prepare socca as I do crêpes, making them about eight inches across and then plumping them up with a highly seasoned filling of wilted arugula, watercress, and basil. At the Café, socca is often served with lamb, but it's equally good with roasted chicken or beef.

MAKES ABOUT 16 PANCAKES

the filling:

2 bunches chives

¼ cup extra-virgin olive oil

2 cloves garlic, peeled and crushed

4 bunches arugula, tough stems removed, washed, and dried

2 bunches watercress, tough stems removed, washed, and dried

Salt and freshly ground white pepper

2 bunches basil, leaves only, washed and dried

1. **BRING A SMALL POT** of salted water to the boil, toss in the chives, and boil for a minute. Drain the chives in a strainer and immediately run them under very cold water. When they are cool, pat them dry between layers of paper towels.

2. **PUT THE OLIVE OIL** and garlic in a large sauté pan or skillet over medium heat. As soon as you catch a healthy whiff of garlic, remove and discard the cloves. Add the arugula and watercress to the pan, season with salt and pepper, and cook, stirring, until the greens are wilted and have released their liquid, 2 to 3 minutes. Add the basil and cook for 30 seconds to wilt, then drain off all the liquid and transfer the greens to a plate to cool.

3. **WHEN THE GREENS** are cool, roughly chop them, as well as the chives, and season with salt and pepper. Cover and set the greens aside at room temperature while you make the socca. *(The filling can be made up to 2 hours ahead and kept covered in the refrigerator; bring it to room temperature before proceeding.)*

the socca:

2 cups chickpea flour

1 cup all-purpose flour

Salt and freshly ground white pepper

1 large egg

2½ cups tepid water

½ cup heavy cream

2 tablespoons extra-virgin olive oil, plus extra
   for the pan

1. SIFT THE CHICKPEA and all-purpose flours together into a large bowl; whisk in salt and pepper to taste. Use the tip of the whisk to push the flour to the sides and create a well in the center. Drop the egg into the well and gently whisk it into the flour as best you can—there isn't enough egg to go around, so stop when it runs out. Very slowly add the water and then the cream, whisking gently all the while. Right before you're ready to cook the pancakes, whisk in the oil. You should have a smooth batter that's the consistency of heavy cream. *(Without the oil, the socca batter can be made a few hours ahead and kept covered in the refrigerator; bring it to room temperature before adding the oil. If the batter is too thick, add tepid water by tablespoonfuls to get the consistency you need.)*

2. THE SOCCA COOK VERY WELL in an 8-inch crêpe or omelet pan—even better if the pan's non-stick. Warm the pan over medium heat until it's hot—the socca won't set quickly and evenly if the pan isn't hot enough—then drizzle in a tiny bit of olive oil. Pour in just enough batter to coat the bottom of the pan with a thin but even layer of batter—about 4 to 5 tablespoons. Cook the pancake until it bubbles on top and is set but not brown on the bottom. Flip it over and cook it for a minute or so on the other side. Slide the pancake out of the pan onto a plate and continue making pancakes with the remaining batter, laying them one on top of the other in stacks no more than 6 pancakes high. Set the socca aside, covered with a kitchen towel, until you're ready to serve. *(The pancakes can be kept at room temperature for an hour or two or covered tightly and refrigerated overnight. If the pancakes have been chilled, bring them to room temperature before filling and reheating.)*

to serve: Spread a thin layer of the filling over each pancake and fold the pancake in quarters. If you want, you can rewarm the pancakes in a 400°F oven for about 3 minutes.

Chickpea Fries

If the cuisine is French and chickpeas are the main ingredient, you're safe to bet that the dish is Niçois in inspiration, if not in origin. These fries, cut into rectangles like a child's wooden building blocks, rolled in semolina, and fried until their outside crusts are nicely crisped, are a great change of pace from fried potatoes—and just as irresistible. The base of the fries is a porridge made from chickpea flour; in fact, you can think of it as a chickpea polenta, since the cooking method is about the same. Plan ahead for these, because the porridge needs to be thoroughly cooled before it's fried. Two or three hours is enough to cool it down, but overnight is even better.

MAKES ABOUT 60 FRIES

1 quart whole milk
2 tablespoons extra-virgin olive oil
1 tablespoon unsalted butter
1 tablespoon fennel seeds, toasted
Salt and freshly ground white pepper

2¼ cups chickpea flour, sifted
Peanut oil for deep-frying
Semolina flour or finely ground cornmeal for
   dredging

1. LINE A 9- BY 12-INCH baking pan with parchment paper or plastic wrap and keep it close at hand, along with another sheet of parchment or plastic.

2. PUT THE MILK, olive oil, butter, and fennel seeds into a medium saucepan, season with salt and pepper, and bring to the boil. Lower the heat so that the milk simmers steadily and, stirring constantly with a wooden spoon, add the chickpea flour in a fine stream. When all the flour is incorporated, continue stirring for 10 minutes over low heat to thoroughly cook the flour. This is hard work—the mixture will get very thick—so if there's someone around, recruit him or her as your stirring partner. Pour the thickened chickpea mixture into the prepared baking pan and cover the pan with the second sheet of parchment or plastic, pressing against it lightly to smooth the top of the chickpea paste and create an airtight seal. Chill the chickpea paste in the refrigerator for 2 to 3 hours or, better still, overnight.

3. POUR 3 TO 4 INCHES of peanut oil into a deep pot or casserole and heat the oil to 350°F, as measured on a deep-fat thermometer.

4. PEEL THE TOP SHEET of parchment or plastic off the chickpea paste and cover a plate with an even layer of semolina or cornmeal. Using a long sharp knife, dipping it into hot water and drying it as necessary, cut 3-inch-long logs of the paste. (Ideally, the logs should be ½ inch by ½ inch by 3 inches, but perfection is not necessary—just don't cut them too thin.) Roll the logs in the semolina or cornmeal to coat them evenly and gently tap off any excess. Fry the logs in batches—you don't want to crowd the pot—until they're golden brown, 2 to 3 minutes. Carefully lift the fries out of the oil and onto a plate

lined with a double thickness of paper towels. Pat off any excess oil and sprinkle the fries with salt. Serve immediately or, if the fries have cooled while you were working on the later batches, reheat in a 300°F oven for 5 to 10 minutes.

to serve: Because of the log shape, these fries are fun stacked on a warm platter (or on each guest's dinner plate) like firewood near the hearth, tic-tac-toe fashion, as we do at Café Boulud.

Pommes "Boulangère"

Boulanger is the French word for a bread baker and it was the village bread baker's oven, often the only oven in town, in which these potatoes, lazily braised in fine chicken stock flavored with herbs and lots of thinly sliced onions, were once cooked. Prepared and served in an ovenproof skillet, the potatoes are started on the stovetop and slid into the oven to braise until all the liquid has been absorbed by the potatoes and they are so sublimely soft and savory they're tempting enough to make you forget there's a main course.

MAKES 6 SERVINGS

3 tablespoons unsalted butter

1 pound onions, peeled, trimmed, and thinly sliced

Salt and freshly ground white pepper

4 large Idaho potatoes, peeled and cut into ⅛-inch-thick slices

1 bay leaf

1 sprig thyme

3 cups unsalted Chicken Stock (page 346) or store-bought low-sodium chicken broth

1. **CENTER A RACK** in the oven and preheat the oven to 400°F.

2. **MELT THE BUTTER** in a large ovenproof sauté pan or skillet with high sides over medium heat. Add the onions, season with salt and pepper, and cook, stirring, until the onions are translucent but not colored, about 10 minutes. Add the potatoes, bay leaf, and thyme, stir to mix, and season with salt and pepper. Pour in the chicken stock and bring to a boil.

3. **CUT A PARCHMENT** paper circle to fit inside the pan (see Glossary, page 369) and press the parchment gently against the potatoes. Slide the pan into the oven. Braise the potatoes for 35 minutes, then remove the parchment and cook for 10 minutes more, or until the potatoes can be easily pierced with the point of a knife. Remove and discard the bay leaf.

to serve: Bring the skillet to the table and spoon out the potatoes, spooning some of the stock from the pan over each portion.

Pommes Frites

Pommes frites, or French-fried potatoes as we call them here, may be France's best-known export—France could be known for worse. Properly made, pommes frites can be as treasured a gastronomic icon as foie gras, duck confit, or perfectly roasted chicken. Unfortunately, pommes frites are often not properly made. Making frites that can live up to icon status is a three-step process: First the potatoes are soaked overnight in water to remove some of their starch; next they're blanched in oil to cook them through; and finally they're fried in very hot oil to color and crisp them. Forget the ketchup—all these need is sea salt. Pommes frites are the quintessential accompaniment to hanger steak (page 68)—the combo is abbreviated as "steak-frites" on French menus—but for lots of people the steak, as great as it is, is just the excuse for the frites, they're that good.

MAKES ABOUT 40 TO 50 FRITES

3 pounds Idaho potatoes, scrubbed
Peanut oil for deep-frying
Fine sea salt

1. **CUT THE UNPEELED POTATOES** into sticks that are ½ inch thick and 2½ to 3 inches long. Drop them into a bowl filled with enough cold water to cover and keep the potatoes in the refrigerator overnight.
2. **THE FOLLOWING DAY,** drain the potatoes and pat them dry between paper towels. Pour about 3 to 4 inches of oil into a deep pot and heat the oil to 300°F, as measured on a deep-fat thermometer. Working in batches, slip the potatoes into the oil, taking care not to crowd the pot—you should have twice as much oil as potatoes in the pot. Cook the potatoes for 10 to 12 minutes, during which time they should not take on much color. With a slotted spoon, remove the potatoes to a cooling rack set over a foil-lined pan and cook the remaining potatoes.
3. **RAISE THE HEAT** under the oil so that the temperature increases to 375°F. Slip the blanched potatoes into the oil, again working in batches, and cook until the fries are crisp and golden, about 3 to 5 minutes. Remove the potatoes from the oil and drain them on a baking sheet lined with several layers of paper towels.

to serve: You'll be lucky if you have any fries left to serve—these have a way of disappearing in the kitchen. Sprinkle whatever fries remain with sea salt and serve them immediately.

Desserts

Far Breton

The *far* is Brittany's answer to the Limoges region's clafoutis, a fairly firm custard baked like a cake and studded with fruit—here, Armagnac-soaked prunes, the most traditional filling. (Of course, you can be nontraditional—a far made with dried cherries is also excellent.) While many French home cooks will tackle elaborate savory dishes but then head for the local pâtisserie to purchase dessert, the far, with its quickly and easily mixed crêpe-like batter, is a sweet that's often made at home—and always with perfect results.

MAKES 8 SERVINGS

the prunes:

2 tablespoons sugar

1 cup (6 ounces) pitted prunes or 1 cup (about 5 ounces) dried cherries

2 tablespoons Armagnac

BRING 1 CUP OF WATER and the sugar to a boil in a small saucepan. Put the prunes or cherries in a heatproof bowl, pour over the Armagnac, and add the hot sugar syrup. Stir gently just to combine, then set the bowl aside until the liquid reaches room temperature. *(The prunes can be used now or covered with plastic wrap and refrigerated for up to 1 week.)*

the far:

3 large eggs, at room temperature

½ cup sugar

Pinch of salt

¾ cup plus 1 tablespoon all-purpose flour

2 cups whole milk, at room temperature

5 tablespoons unsalted butter, melted and
  cooled

1. WORKING WITH A WHISK (or a mixer fitted with the whisk attachment and set to medium-low), beat the eggs, sugar, and salt together in a medium bowl. Gently but thoroughly whisk in the flour, followed by the milk and then the melted butter. Cover the batter with plastic wrap and refrigerate for at least 1 hour or, preferably, overnight.

2. CENTER A RACK in the oven and preheat the oven to 425°F. Butter the inside of an 8- by 2-inch round cake pan. Fit the bottom with a circle of parchment paper, butter the paper, and then dust the bottom and sides of the pan with flour, tapping out the excess.

3. DRAIN THE PRUNES OR CHERRIES well and keep them close at hand. Remove the batter from the refrigerator and stir it gently just to bring it together again. Pour the batter into the pan and scatter over the fruit. Slide the pan into the oven and bake for 15 minutes. Turn the oven down to 350°F and bake for another 30 to 40 minutes, or until the top is browned and a knife inserted into the center of the far comes out clean. Transfer the far to a rack and let it cool to room temperature in its pan.

to serve: Run a blunt knife around the sides of the far, turn the far upside down onto a parchment-lined plate (a rack might cut into the delicate custard), remove the pan and the parchment paper, and then invert the far onto a decorative serving platter. The far is best eaten the day it is made, but it would be foolish to toss away leftovers—cover them well with plastic wrap and refrigerate them for up to 1 day.

to drink: A young, still-fruity Maury

Apple and Armagnac Croustade

The croustade, a covered tart, is a specialty of Gascony, in France's Southwest. Although it was once made of thin sheets of hand-pulled dough, not unlike strudel, and brushed with duck or goose fat, even the Gascons now use butter and phyllo, the dough used here. This croustade is constructed unlike any other type of tart in the French pastry chef's repertoire: It is built of layers of butter-brushed, sugar-dusted, and almond-sprinkled dough. Once filled and baked, the croustade is topped with two more layers of phyllo, each caramelized to a polished finish—it's gorgeous. While a croustade can take any number of fillings, buttery sautéed apples flamed with Armagnac, the brandy of Gascony, are not only traditional, they're delicious.

MAKES 6 SERVINGS

the apples:

3 tablespoons unsalted butter

1 moist, plump vanilla bean

6 Rome apples, peeled, cored, and each cut
    into 6 to 8 wedges

2 tablespoons sugar

⅓ cup Armagnac

MELT THE BUTTER in a large sauté pan or skillet over medium heat. Cut the vanilla bean lengthwise in half and, using the back of the knife, scrape the pulp out of the pod. When the butter is foamy, add the apples, the vanilla pulp and pod, and the sugar and cook, stirring constantly, until the apples are lightly caramelized, 7 to 10 minutes. Add the Armagnac and, standing away from the pan, set it aflame. When the flames subside, turn the apples over in the Armagnac; when the flames have died out and the Armagnac is reduced to a glaze, transfer the apples to a plate and cool to room temperature. *(Once cooled, the apples can be covered airtight and kept refrigerated for up to 12 hours.)*

the croustade:

8 sheets phyllo

6 tablespoons unsalted butter, melted and still
    warm

½ cup confectioner's sugar, sifted

⅓ cup sliced almonds

Crème fraîche, lightly sweetened, whipped
    cream, or vanilla ice cream (homemade, page
    341, or store-bought), for accompaniment

1. CENTER A RACK in the oven and preheat the oven to 350°F. Place a 10-inch tart ring or, in a pinch, a 10-inch springform pan minus the bottom on a nonstick baking sheet. Stack the phyllo on your work surface and cover it with a damp towel.

2. REMOVE THE TOP SHEET of phyllo (re-cover the remaining sheets), brush it with butter, and dust it with confectioner's sugar. Crumple the dough and press it into the ring—it should be fairly flat and shouldn't come up the sides of the ring. Sprinkle with about one fifth of the almonds. Repeat this procedure three more times, until you have four buttered, sugared, and almond-sprinkled sheets of phyllo in the ring. Spoon the apples into the center of the croustade, leaving a 1-inch border bare. Working as you did before, butter, sugar, and crumple a sheet of phyllo, fitting it into the ring to cover the apples. Sprinkle this layer with the remaining almonds and cover with another crumpled sheet of buttered and sugared phyllo.

3. SLIDE THE CROUSTADE into the oven and bake for about 10 minutes, watching the top of the tart carefully to make certain it doesn't brown too much. The top should be just lightly browned. Remove the croustade from the oven.

4. INCREASE THE OVEN TEMPERATURE to 400°F. Butter and sugar another sheet of phyllo, this time crumpling it very loosely so that when you place it on top of the croustade it creates a light, airy crown. Bake the tart for 7 minutes, or until lightly browned, before pulling the baking sheet from the oven.

5. BUTTER THE LAST SHEET of phyllo and, once again, crumple it to make a crown. Place it on top of the croustade and dust it heavily with the remaining confectioner's sugar. Return the tart to the oven and bake until the top layer caramelizes evenly, about 5 minutes. Check the progress of the sugar frequently, because it can go from brown to burnt in a flash. Pull the croustade from the oven as soon as the top is a golden caramel color and allow it to cool for 5 to 10 minutes.

to serve: Lift off the cake ring or remove the springform and, using two large wide metal spatulas, transfer the croustade to a serving plate. Serve the tart warm or at room temperature the day it is made, with crème fraîche, whipped cream, or vanilla ice cream.

to drink: To feel like a true Gascon musketeer, serve a shot of Armagnac alongside each slice of croustade

Souffléed Lemon Crêpes with Sauce Suzette

Crêpes may be among France's most famous desserts and Sauce Suzette, crêpes' most famous accompaniment. These crêpes, richly flavored with hazelnutty brown butter, Grand Marnier, and dark rum, are filled with an airy lemon mixture, baked until the filling is warm, puffed, and fragrant and served with my simplified rendition of the celebrated sauce, a citrusy sauce that's fortified with Grand Marnier and smoothed with a swirl of butter. According to legend, the sauce was created at the end of the nineteenth century by Henri Charpentier, a young chef in Monte Carlo. In the midst of preparing crêpes for the Prince of Wales, Charpentier's pan of cordials—meant for the sauce—caught flame. Certain of ruin but uncertain of what to do next, the young chef plunged the crêpes into the boiling cordials and thereby made culinary history as well as a stunning dessert. My sauce features the flavors of Charpentier's Suzette minus the flames—it's less dramatic but no less luscious.

MAKES 10 TO 12 SERVINGS

the crêpes:

5 tablespoons unsalted butter

½ cup all-purpose flour

2 tablespoons sugar

Pinch of salt

2 large eggs

2 teaspoons dark rum

2 teaspoons Grand Marnier

Grated zest of ½ navel orange

½ cup whole milk, at room temperature

¼ cup heavy cream, at room temperature

1. **PLACE 4 TABLESPOONS** of the butter in a small saucepan and cook over medium heat, swirling the pan, until the butter melts and turns a deep golden brown. Remove the pan from the heat and spoon off the clear browned butter; discard the sediment. For this recipe, you'll need 2 tablespoons of the browned butter. Set the butter aside for a couple of minutes—you want to use it when it is just warm.

2. **USING A WHISK** (or a mixer fitted with the whisk attachment and set on low speed), mix the flour, sugar, salt, and eggs together in a large bowl just until they are combined. Whisk in the 2 tablespoons browned butter, followed by the rum, Grand Marnier, zest, milk, and cream, whisking just until each ingredient is incorporated. For convenience, you might want to pour the batter into a pitcher with a spout. Whether it's in a bowl or pitcher, cover the batter with plastic wrap and refrigerate for at least 1 hour, or, preferably, overnight.

3. **WHEN YOU'RE READY** to make the crêpes, set a plate or a small baking sheet close to the stove and line it with a piece of plastic wrap. Heat a nonstick 8-inch crêpe pan over medium-high heat. While the pan is warming, melt the remaining 1 tablespoon butter. Gently stir the crêpe batter just to bring it together again.

4. SWIRL A FEW DROPS of melted butter over the bottom of the hot crêpe pan, then lift the pan off the heat and pour in about 2 tablespoons of batter, tilting the pan and swirling the batter so that the batter covers the bottom of the pan in a very thin, even layer. Return the pan to the heat and cook the crêpe until it starts to bubble on top—the underside should be golden brown. Run a blunt knife or spatula around the edge of the crêpe, then lift the crêpe up and flip it over—this is best done quickly and nimbly with your fingers. Cook the second side for only about 20 seconds, or until it is just speckled with golden dots—this side will never be as brown as the other. Transfer the crêpe to the plastic-lined plate or baking sheet and continue making crêpes, dotting the pan with melted butter and gently stirring the batter between crêpes, until you've used all the batter—you should have about 10 to 12 crêpes. (As the crêpes are made, stack them on the plate.) When the crêpes are cool, you can use them immediately or cover them with plastic wrap and store them in the refrigerator until needed. *(The crêpes can be made a day ahead and kept well covered in the refrigerator.)*

the sauce:

4 to 6 navel oranges	**3 tablespoons sugar**
2 to 3 small lemons	**1½ tablespoons Grand Marnier**
½ teaspoon cornstarch	**1½ tablespoons unsalted butter**
1½ teaspoons cold water	

1. USING A ZESTER, remove the zest from 2 of the oranges and 2 of the lemons. (Alternatively, you can use a sharp paring knife or a vegetable peeler to remove the zest—just be careful to avoid any of the bitter white cottony pith that's just under the zest. If you're not using a zester, you'll need to cut the zest into very thin strips before proceeding.) Put the zests in a small saucepan, cover with 2 cups cold water, and bring to the boil. Drain and cool the zests under cold running water. Repeat this boiling-draining-cooling process two more times, then drain the zests well and set them aside, covered with plastic wrap, until needed.

2. WORKING WITH THE ORANGES and lemons separately so that you can measure them properly, squeeze the juice from the fruits and strain it. Reserve 3 cups orange juice and ½ cup lemon juice (it's possible that there will be a little juice left over).

3. POUR THE ORANGE and lemon juices into a saucepan, bring to the boil, and simmer the juices until they are reduced to 1¼ cups. While the juices are reducing, dissolve the cornstarch in the cold water and whisk until smooth. Whisk the cornstarch into the hot cooked-down juices; cook, whisking, for 1 minute more. Whisk in the sugar, Grand Marnier, and the reserved orange and lemon zests and cook at the boil for another 3 to 4 minutes, or until the sauce thickens just enough to coat the back of a spoon.

Pull the pan from the heat and whisk in the butter. Set the sauce aside in a warm place while you finish the crêpes. *(The sauce can be made a few hours ahead and kept covered in the refrigerator; carefully rewarm it over gentle heat at serving time. Alternatively, you can keep the sauce warm in the top of a double boiler if you prepare it right before you're ready to soufflé the crêpes.)*

the filling:

3 large eggs, separated	4 tablespoons granulated sugar
2 tablespoons plus 1 teaspoon freshly squeezed lemon juice	Grated zest of 1 small lemon
	Confectioner's sugar for dusting

1. **POSITION THE RACKS** to divide the oven into thirds and preheat the oven to 400°F. Butter two large baking sheets.

2. **IF NECESSARY,** remove the crêpes from the refrigerator. Fold each crêpe in half and then in half again, so that you have a four-layer-thick fan shape, and place the crêpes on the buttered baking sheets, leaving at least 1 inch between them.

3. **PUT THE EGG WHITES** in the bowl of a mixer fitted with the whisk attachment (or work with a hand mixer). Add 1 teaspoon of the lemon juice and, working on low-medium speed, beat the whites just until they are foamy. Increase the speed to medium-high and whip the whites, gradually adding 1 tablespoon of the sugar, until they hold firm, glossy peaks.

4. **WHILE YOU'RE WHIPPING** the whites, whisk the remaining 3 tablespoons sugar and the egg yolks together in a large bowl until the mixture is pale and thick; whisk in the remaining 2 tablespoons lemon juice and the zest.

5. **WHEN THE EGG WHITES** are in peaks, use a flexible rubber spatula to gently fold the whites into the yolk mixture. Using a spoon and working quickly and gingerly, lift the top layer of each crêpe and spoon in a generous amount of filling—you're only filling that top quarter of each crêpe, but you're filling it until it is big-bellied. Immediately slide the baking sheets into the oven and bake the crêpes for 5 to 6 minutes, or until the filling puffs and the crêpes seem firm to the touch. Dust the crêpes with confectioner's sugar.

to serve: Lift 1 crêpe onto each warm dinner plate, drizzle over some of the warm sauce, and serve immediately.

to drink: A Cognac-spiked Pineau des Charentes

Chocolate Mousse Trio

This dessert was on our debut menu at Café Boulud and quickly became a never-to-be-sent-on-sabbatical signature dish. Since chocolate mousse is one of the most beloved French desserts, it's easy to understand why a dessert that combines three kinds of chocolate mousse—bittersweet, milk, and white—would win loyal fans. At the Café, we serve the three mousses layered in large martini glasses. It's a beautiful presentation and one that makes it easy to slip your spoon down through all three layers and come up with a little of each flavor for each mouthful. Of course, you could layer this dessert in coupes, coffee cups, wineglasses, or even serve it family-style, in one big bowl—the flavors will always be sensational.

As you read through the recipe, you'll see that each mousse is nothing more than chocolate, cream, and milk; therefore, it's vital that you use the finest chocolates you can find. The taste of the chocolate won't change much when it is made into mousse, so choose chocolates you love. (I suggest you use imported chocolates for the white and milk chocolate mousses, because they usually have a higher percentage of cocoa solids than domestic brands.) And give some thought to the chocolate sauce: It's optional, but easy to make and fun to have on the side—ditto the tic-tac-toe decoration.

MAKES 6 SERVINGS.

the bittersweet mousse:

3 ounces extra-bittersweet chocolate, preferably   ½ cup heavy cream
   one that is at least 70% cocoa solids, finely   ¼ cup whole milk
   chopped

1. **SET OUT SIX** 8-ounce martini glasses, or as many wineglasses or bowls.
2. **MELT THE CHOCOLATE** in a microwave oven set to low power or in a bowl over (not touching) simmering water. As soon as the chocolate is melted, remove it from the heat. If the chocolate is not in a bowl that's large enough to hold all the mousse's ingredients, transfer it now.
3. **WHIP THE HEAVY CREAM** just until it holds soft peaks.
4. **BRING THE MILK** to the boil in a small saucepan, then whisk it into the chocolate. When the milk is incorporated, whisk in the whipped cream. Divide the mousse among the glasses or bowls, using a pastry bag or a spoon to transfer the mousse to the glasses. Smooth the top, if necessary. In either case, make sure to keep the sides of the glasses clean—you'll want to see the dividing lines between the different-colored mousses. Refrigerate the glasses while you prepare the milk chocolate mousse.

the milk chocolate mousse:

9 ounces milk chocolate, preferably imported,
  finely chopped

¾ cup plus 2 tablespoons heavy cream
½ cup whole milk

1. **JUST AS YOU DID** with the bittersweet chocolate, melt the milk chocolate—be especially careful, though, since milk chocolate melts faster than bittersweet.

2. **WHIP THE CREAM** until it holds soft peaks.

3. **BRING THE MILK** to the boil. Whisk the milk into the chocolate, then whisk in the whipped cream—you'll have a loose, pourable mousse. Ladle or pour the mousse into the glasses, again keeping the tops smooth and the sides of the glasses clean. Refrigerate until the milk chocolate mousse is firm before working on the white chocolate mousse

the white chocolate mousse:

6 ounces white chocolate, preferably imported,
  finely chopped

½ cup heavy cream
¼ cup whole milk

1. **JUST AS YOU DID** with the bittersweet and milk chocolate mousses, melt the white chocolate—be especially careful, since white chocolate melts quickly and can't take a lot of heat.

2. **WHIP THE CREAM** until it holds soft peaks.

3. **BRING THE MILK** to the boil. Whisk the milk into the chocolate, then whisk in the whipped cream—you'll have a loose, pourable mousse. Ladle or pour the mousse into the glasses, again keeping the tops smooth and the sides of the glasses clean. Refrigerate until the mousse is firm. *(The dessert can be made up to this point and kept covered in the refrigerator for a day.)* If the trio of mousses is well chilled, let the glasses sit at room temperature for an hour before serving.

the chocolate sauce (optional):

1 cup water
⅔ cup sugar
½ cup unsweetened cocoa powder, preferably
  Dutch-processed, sifted
½ cup heavy cream

BRING THE WATER and sugar to a boil in a saucepan. Whisk in the cocoa and bring the mixture back to the boil, then whisk in the cream. Bring the mixture back to the boil, lower the heat, and simmer, whisking almost constantly, until the sauce reduces a little and thickens. You should have about 1 cup of chocolate sauce. Set the sauce aside. Right before serving, you can reheat the sauce if necessary— it should be only just warm.

the decoration (optional):

6 ounces bittersweet chocolate, finely chopped

1. PUT A BAKING SHEET in the freezer and leave it there until it is very cold, about 1 hour. Fold a piece of parchment or waxed paper into a cornet, or small pastry cone (or use a small zip-seal plastic bag); keep it close at hand.

2. MELT THE CHOCOLATE in a microwave oven set to low power or in a bowl over (not touching) simmering water. Remove from the heat. Fill the piping cornet (or plastic bag) with the warm chocolate and snip away a tiny piece of the tip of the cornet (or of a bottom corner of the bag). Working on the back of the frozen baking sheet, make six tic-tac-toe or crosshatch patterns with the chocolate. Each crisscross should be slightly larger than the rims of the glasses holding the mousses.

3. DIP A COOKIE CUTTER that's slightly smaller in diameter than the tops of the glasses into hot water, dry it, and cut the crisscrosses to size; or do this with a small knife.

to serve: If you've made the crisscrosses, place one on top of each glass of mousse. Serve the chocolate sauce, if you're using it, on the side.

to drink: A demi-sec Champagne; even better, a demi-sec Champagne Rosé

Tarte Tropézienne

While Tarte Tropézienne is almost completely unknown in America—there are only two bakeries that I know of in New York City that make it regularly—it's the stuff of legends in France. When we were testing this recipe in Café Boulud's kitchen, we had to hide it from the staff until we'd taken notes on it, because I knew it would disappear in an instant—which is just what happened when I gave the all clear.

Originally made in St.-Tropez on the Riviera, as its name suggests, the Tarte Tropézienne is in no way, shape, or form a tart, but rather a sweet yeast cake, really a not-too-rich brioche, filled, traditionally, with kirsch-scented buttercream or pastry cream (I use pastry cream), and topped, also traditionally, with sugar. The cake and its components are simple and simply made, yet the combination of brioche and kirsch cream is splendid beyond all reason.

MAKES 8 SERVINGS

the cake:

1¾ cups all-purpose flour

2½ teaspoons sugar

¼ teaspoon salt

½ teaspoon (firmly packed) crumbled fresh yeast

4 large eggs, at room temperature

4 tablespoons unsalted butter, at room
   temperature

1. WORKING IN A MIXER fitted with the dough hook, mix together the flour, sugar, salt, and yeast just to combine. Set the mixer to low speed and add the eggs one by one, waiting until each egg is incorporated before adding the next. Increase the speed to medium-low and beat, scraping the sides and bottom of the bowl as needed, until the dough wraps around the hook and cleans the sides of the bowl, about 20 minutes—the dough will be smooth, shiny, and satiny and will make a pleasant slapping sound as it hits the sides of the bowl. Don't skimp on the mixing time—this beating and kneading is what will give you the fine crumb you want in the cake. When the dough is properly kneaded, start adding the butter bit by bit. As the butter goes into the bowl, the beautifully homogenous dough may fall apart: Don't be concerned—just keep beating for another 5 minutes or so, and it will come together again.

2. LIGHTLY COAT THE INSIDE of a large bowl with butter and turn the dough into the bowl. Working your way around the bowl, lift the dough gently from the bottom and let it fall with a slap against the bowl until you've shaped the dough into a ball with a smooth top. Cover the bowl with plastic wrap and set it in a warm place (about 75° to 80°F) until the dough doubles in volume, about 1 to 2 hours.

3. REPEAT THE LIFTING and slapping—this is the best way to punch down a brioche dough (it knocks the air out of the dough but doesn't disturb the structure you've developed in the dough by kneading it)—and again cover the dough with plastic wrap. Place the bowl in the refrigerator and let the dough rest for 4 hours, during which time it will rise again.

4. LINE A BAKING SHEET with parchment paper and keep it close at hand. Lightly flour a work sur-face and turn the chilled dough out onto it. Working quickly, roll the dough out into a 9-inch disk that's about ¼ inch high. Transfer the dough to the baking sheet, cover it loosely with a damp towel, and place the baking sheet in a warm place (about 75° to 80°F) to allow the dough to barely double in volume, another hour or so. (The amount of time will depend on the temperature of the room.)

the filling and topping:

¼ **cup plus 1 tablespoon sugar**
1¼ **cups heavy cream**

½ **recipe Vanilla Pastry Cream (page 357)**
2 **tablespoons imported kirsch**

1. CENTER A RACK in the oven and preheat the oven to 350°F.

2. REMOVE THE TOWEL from the dough. Stir together ¼ cup of the sugar and ¼ cup of the heavy cream in a small bowl and, with a pastry brush, brush half of this mixture evenly over the top of the dough. Sprinkle the remaining 1 tablespoon sugar over the dough and slide the baking sheet into the oven. Bake the cake for 10 to 12 minutes, then remove it from the oven and brush the top with the rest of the sugar-cream mixture. Return the cake to the oven and bake for another 10 to 12 minutes, or until the top is golden brown and a knife inserted into the side or bottom of the cake comes out clean. (Avoid plunging the knife into the top of the cake and marring its beauty.) Remove the cake from the oven and transfer it to a rack to cool to room temperature.

3. WHEN THE CAKE IS COOL, cut it horizontally in half, using a long serrated knife and a gentle saw-ing motion. Turn the pastry cream into a bowl and whisk it just to loosen it. Pour in the kirsch and whisk to combine. Whip the remaining 1 cup heavy cream until it holds firm peaks, then fold the whipped cream into the pastry cream. Spread the cream evenly over the bottom layer of the cake, then put it in the refrigerator for about 20 minutes, or until the cream is firm enough to hold its shape.

4. GENTLY PLACE THE TOP LAYER of cake over the filling and return the Tropézienne to the refrig-erator for another 20 minutes to set the filling. *(The cake can be covered and refrigerated for up to 6 hours.)*

to serve: Using a serrated knife and a gentle sawing motion, cut the Tarte Tropézienne into 8 slices—a somewhat delicate operation, since the filling is soft. (A pastry chef's trick is to lift off the top layer of cake and cut it, then return the pieces to the cake and cut through the filling and bottom layer.) Serve the cake lightly chilled.

to drink: A honey-ish Sauternes

Trao-Mad with Peach Compote

Trao-Mad are the tenderest, meltingest, butteriest cookies imaginable. They are the pride of the Brittany region of France and they are delightfully, deliciously, and definitely addictive. At Café Boulud, we serve them with a little bowl of peach compote in the summer and then change the compote as the seasons change, but Trao-Mad are also good with ice cream or sorbet, mousse, pots de crème, or solo—a plate of Trao-Mad and a cup of tea are always welcome.

Like all my compotes and marmalades, this recipe makes more than you'll probably need at one sitting, but it keeps well and is infinitely versatile—if you do nothing more than spread it on toast, you'll be glad you made a surplus.

MAKES ABOUT 32 COOKIES

the compote:

1½ **pounds very ripe peaches**
Juice of ½ **lemon**
¼ **cup honey**

¼ **cup water**
Small pinch of saffron threads

1. **BRING A LARGE POT** of water to the boil. Plunge the peaches into the boiling water and blanch for 30 seconds, then drain them in a colander and run them under very cold water. When the fruit is cool enough to handle, peel the peaches and cut them in half along their "seams"; remove the pits. Set one peach (2 halves) aside and cut the remaining peaches into 1-inch cubes.

2. **PUT THE CUT-UP PEACHES,** the lemon juice, honey, and water in a medium saucepan over medium-low heat. Cook, stirring from time to time, for 20 to 30 minutes, or until the peaches are so soft they fall apart when stirred. Add the saffron and cook, stirring frequently, for 10 minutes more.

3. **WHILE THE COMPOTE** is cooking, cut the reserved peach into ¼-inch cubes. Line a baking pan with a large piece of plastic wrap, leaving enough of an overhang to fold over itself.

4. **WHEN THE COMPOTE** is cooked, pull the pot from the heat and stir in the fresh peach cubes. Turn the compote out into the plastic-lined baking pan and spread it out in a thin layer. Cover with the excess plastic wrap or another piece of plastic wrap, pressing the plastic against the compote to create an airtight seal. Chill in the refrigerator. *(Packed airtight, the compote will keep for at least 1 week in the refrigerator.)*

the cookies:

2 sticks (8 ounces) unsalted butter, at room
    temperature
¾ cup plus 2 tablespoons confectioner's sugar,
    sifted
¼ teaspoon salt

2 large egg yolks
1⅓ cups all-purpose flour
⅓ cup almond flour (see Glossary, page 362)
    or finely ground blanched almonds

1. **WORKING IN A MIXER** fitted with the paddle attachment (or in a large bowl with a wooden spoon), beat the butter, sugar, and salt together until creamy and smooth. Add the egg yolks and stir to blend. Add the all-purpose flour as well as the almond flour and continue to mix until the dough is homogenous.

2. **DIVIDE THE DOUGH** in half and, using plastic wrap to help you, roll each half into a log that's ¾ to 1 inch in diameter. Seal the logs in plastic wrap and freeze for 1 hour.

3. **POSITION THE RACKS** to divide the oven into thirds and preheat the oven to 400°F. Line two baking sheets with parchment paper.

4. **UNWRAP THE LOGS** of dough and, with a sturdy, thin-bladed knife, slice the logs into rounds about ⅓ inch thick. Arrange the cookies on the baking sheets so that there is 1 inch of space between each cookie. Slide the baking sheets into the oven and bake the cookies for 8 to 10 minutes, or until they are a light golden brown. (If some of the cookies are browning faster than others, rotate the cookie sheets front to back and top to bottom at the halfway point.) Using a wide metal spatula, transfer the cookies to racks to cool to room temperature. *(The cookies can be kept in an airtight tin in a cool, dry place for up to 1 week or frozen for up to a month.)*

to serve: Spoon the compote into a small bowl and put the bowl on a large serving plate. Surround with the cookies and serve, keeping a small jam spoon close by so that guests who are not dippers can spoon as much compote as they want onto each cookie.

to drink: A sweet but still crisp Coteaux du Layon

Bugnes de Lyon

This is my mother's recipe for a well-known Lyonnaise dessert, *bugnes,* or fried dough. Hometown pride makes me wish I could claim that Lyon is the only place you can find bugnes, but they are popular throughout France, and in Switzerland, where they are called *merveilles,* or marvels. In the United States, they are beloved in New Orleans. At home, my mother flavored the egg-rich dough with grated orange zest and formed the pastries into fanciful knot shapes before frying them. If you'd like, you can just roll out the dough and cut it into circles, squares, strips, or diamonds, small or large—they all look good and taste great. Whatever the shape, you should serve these freshly made, hot and showered with confectioner's sugar.

MAKES 20 TO 25 BUGNES

1½ tablespoons unsalted butter, at room temperature

1 teaspoon sugar

Pinch of salt

1 large egg

Grated zest of ½ navel orange

Rounded ¼ teaspoon baking powder

1 cup plus 2 tablespoons all-purpose flour

3 tablespoons whole milk

Peanut oil for deep-frying

Confectioner's sugar for dusting

1. **USING A WOODEN SPOON** (as my mother would) or working in a mixer fitted with the paddle attachment, beat the butter, sugar, and salt together until creamy. Add the egg and beat well, then beat in the orange zest. Stir the baking powder into the flour and then stir the flour into the bowl alternately with the milk, incorporating the flour in three additions and the milk in two. Turn the dough out onto a counter—or just reach into the bowl—and knead the dough lightly to form it into a ball. Cover the dough with plastic wrap and chill it in the refrigerator for at least 1 hour, or, preferably, overnight.

2. **DUST A BAKING SHEET** with flour and keep it close at hand. To shape the bugnes as my mother does, roll the dough out on a lightly floured work surface into a rectangle that's ¼ to ⅛ inch thick— these shouldn't be too thin. Cut the dough into 2-inch-wide strips and, using a sharp knife or a pastry cutter, cut each strip on the diagonal at 2-inch intervals—you'll have created diamonds. Now, cut a 1½-inch-long slit down the center of each piece of dough—the slit should run down the length of the diamond. Take the top or bottom corner of the dough and lift it up and into the slit, then pull it out the other side—you will have created a twisted, handkerchief-like knot. Place the bugnes on the floured baking sheet, cover them with plastic wrap, and refrigerate for 1 hour.

3. POUR AT LEAST 4 INCHES of oil into a deep pot and heat it to 350°F, as measured on a deep-fat thermometer. Line a baking sheet with a double thickness of paper towels and keep the baking sheet and a slotted spoon close at hand.

4. DROP 5 OR 6 BUGNES into the oil—you don't want to crowd the pot—and fry for about 2 minutes, or until the underside of each bugne is golden. Turn the bugnes over and fry for another 2 minutes or so, just until the second side is also golden. Lift the bugnes out of the oil with a slotted spoon and place them on the towel-lined baking sheet to drain. Repeat with the remaining bugnes.

to serve: Sprinkle the pastries generously with confectioner's sugar and serve while they're still warm.

to drink: A verveine infusion or an espresso with Cointreau on the side

Apricot and Raspberry Dartois

When you see the word *dartois,* you can be sure of three things: You'll find a dessert made with puff pastry, it will be filled with fruit, and it will be shaped as a strip, with the top layer of pastry cut so that you can see the fruit within. In America, it's called a peek-a-boo strip, a cute nursery name for what is really a rather stylish, grown-up sweet. For this version, I use a mixture of apricots and raspberries, a combination I like for its honey sweetness and touch of tartness; when the season for apricots ends, you can make the tart by substituting an equal amount of drained best-quality canned apricots or a marmalade or compote. Try this with apple and quince (page 336) or kumquat (page 249) marmalade during the fall and winter, or peach compote (page 98) or berry marmalade (page 172) during the summer.

MAKES 8 SERVINGS

1 pound all-butter puff pastry (see Glossary, page 371)
2 cups water
½ cup sugar
Juice of 1 lemon
4 large or 6 medium apricots, halved and pitted

¾ cup Almond Cream (page 359), at room temperature
½ cup raspberries
1 egg, lightly beaten, for egg wash
Vanilla ice cream, homemade (page 341) or store-bought, for serving

1. IF THE PUFF PASTRY is in one piece, cut it in half. Working on a lightly floured surface, roll each half out into a rectangle that's ⅛ inch thick and at least 16 inches by 7 inches. Put each piece of pastry on a parchment-lined baking sheet, cover with plastic wrap, and refrigerate for 1 hour, to allow the pastry to rest.

2. STIR THE WATER, sugar, and lemon juice together in a medium saucepan and bring to the boil. Put the apricot halves in a heatproof bowl and when the sugar is dissolved and the syrup is boiling, pour it over the apricots. Set aside to cool to room temperature. *(You can make the apricots ahead and refrigerate them, in their syrup and covered with plastic wrap, for up to 3 days.)* When you're ready to use the apricots, drain them, discarding the syrup, and pat them dry between paper towels.

3. LINE A BAKING SHEET with parchment paper. Remove the puff pastry sheets from the refrigerator. Cut one sheet into a 16- by 7-inch rectangle and return it to the refrigerator for the moment. Cut the second sheet into a 15- by 6-inch rectangle and place it on the parchment-lined baking sheet. Spread the almond cream over the pastry on the baking sheet, leaving a 1-inch border uncovered by cream all around. Arrange the apricots on the almond cream, placing the apricot halves at a slight diagonal and forming two rows down the length of the pastry—leave a narrow space in the middle and fill it in with the raspberries. Set the pastry aside for the moment, or, if it seems a little soft—and it might—cover it loosely with a piece of plastic wrap and put it back in the refrigerator while you make the top layer.

4. REMOVE THE SECOND SHEET of puff pastry from the refrigerator and fold it lengthwise in half. Using a paring knife, starting 1½ inches from the top of the pastry cut slits starting at the fold and slanting downward—the slits should stop 1½ inches from the sides of the pastry and 1½ inches from the bottom of it too, and each slit should be separated from its neighbor by ½ inch. Remove the bottom pastry strip from the refrigerator (if necessary) and brush the bare border with water. Lift the top layer of pastry onto the bottom, unfold it, and press down lightly on the edges of the pastry to seal the top and bottom layers. If necessary, trim the edges of the pastry, then crimp the edges with a fork. Place the dartois in the freezer for at least 1 hour. *(The dartois can be made up to this point and stored, covered, in the freezer overnight.)*

5. CENTER A RACK in the oven and preheat the oven to 400°F.

6. BRUSH THE TOP of the pastry with the egg wash, taking care not to let any drip down the sides (it will glue the layers together), then slide the baking sheet into the oven and bake the dartois for 40 minutes, or until the pastry is beautifully puffed and evenly golden. Let the dartois cool on the baking sheet.

to serve: Slice the dartois into 8 pieces and serve it warm or at room temperature, topped with a scoop of vanilla ice cream.

to drink: To continue the apricot flavor, a Tokay Pinot-Gris Sélection de Grains Nobles

Sweet Swiss Chard Tourte

In the covered market in Monte Carlo—indeed, in markets all along the Riviera—double-crusted Swiss chard tarts are a specialty. Typically French and Italian—I can't think of an American tart that's similar—this tourte, a tart with a top crust, is flavored with honey and orange, tastes of the Côte d'Azur, and is dotted with raisins and pine nuts. It's more unusual in the telling than the tasting, since the main ingredient, Swiss chard, turns out to have a natural sweetness and a remarkable affinity for the cream and sugar in the filling.

MAKES 6 SERVINGS

the crust:

**1 recipe Pâte Sablée (page 353), shaped into
disks and chilled**

LINE A BAKING SHEET with parchment paper. Butter the inside of an 8- by ³/₄-inch tart ring; keep it close at hand. Working on a lightly floured surface, roll one of the disks of pâte sablée into an ¹/₈-inch-thick circle. Place the tart ring on one end of the parchment-lined baking sheet and fit the dough into the ring, smoothing it over the bottom and up the sides. Trim away the excess dough, leaving a slightly raised rim. Roll the second piece of pâte sablée out to a thickness of ¹/₈ inch and cut it into a 9-inch circle. Lift the circle onto the other end of the parchment-lined baking sheet and, using a small fluted or scalloped cookie cutter, cut a circle out of the center of the dough; cut 6 more vents around the center hole. Cover this circle of dough as well as the dough in the tart ring with plastic wrap and refrigerate until needed. *(The crust can be prepared several hours ahead and kept covered in the refrigerator.)*

the tart:

¹/₂ **cup plump golden raisins**

1¹/₂ **pounds Swiss chard, stems and tough center veins removed and washed**

1 tablespoon honey

¹/₂ **cup pine nuts**

2 large eggs, plus 1 egg, lightly beaten, for egg wash

1 tablespoon sugar

¹/₂ **cup heavy cream**

2 tablespoons whole milk

1 teaspoon finely grated orange zest

1. BRING 2 CUPS OF WATER to the boil in a small saucepan. Add the raisins, remove from the heat, and allow the raisins to plump in the hot water for 30 minutes. Drain and pat dry before using.

2. BRING A LARGE POT of lightly salted water to the boil. Plunge the Swiss chard into the boiling water and blanch for 5 minutes, or until the leaves are tender but still very green. Drain the chard in a colander and run it under very cold water. When the leaves are cool enough to handle, drain them well, then squeeze them between your hands to remove the excess moisture. Roughly chop the Swiss chard and set it aside for the moment.

3. MELT THE HONEY in a small pan over medium heat and toss in the pine nuts. Cook, stirring, until the pine nuts turn golden brown. Pull the pan from the heat and cool to room temperature, then break the nuts apart if the honey has caused them to form clumps.

4. CENTER A RACK in the oven and preheat the oven to 400°F.

5. IN A MEDIUM BOWL, whisk together the 2 eggs, the sugar, cream, milk, and orange zest. Stir in the cooled pine nuts, the Swiss chard, and raisins. Spoon the filling into the tart shell and brush the rim of the tart with a little egg wash—this will be the glue for the top crust. Lift the circle of dough onto the tart and pinch the top and bottom crusts together. Trim off any excess dough and brush the top of the tart with an even coating of egg wash.

6. SLIDE THE BAKING SHEET into the oven and bake the tart for about 50 minutes, or until the top is beautifully golden. Transfer the tart to a rack and cool.

to serve: The tart should be served at room temperature. Cut it into 6 wedges and, if you'd like, serve each wedge with a dollop of lightly whipped cream.

to drink: A very late harvest wine from the Loire, perhaps a Quarts de Chaume

Summer lunch *al fresco*, Café Boulud, 1999

la saison   the seasonal specialties of the market

After thirty years in the kitchen, the sight of fine ingredients and the promise of what can be coaxed from them continue to excite me. Each season, I am thrilled by the prospect of creating new dishes for the ingredients coming into the market. Here are some of my favorite recipes, designed to showcase each season's bounty. Whether it's a smooth soup of chestnuts, celery root, and apples that epitomizes fall; winter's roasted halibut served with creamy endive; a crackly crusted chicken surrounded with the first of spring's fresh vegetables; or a peach tart that celebrates summer, each recipe captures the essence—the aromas, flavors, and character—of the season. Choose a casual dish, such as sautéed chicken with glazed fall apples and quinces, an elegant roast of tuna presented on a bed of potatoes puréed with sharply flavored spring ramps, or a whimsical dessert of chocolate lollipops and citrus sabayon that can brighten dreary winter days, and you'll find reason to rejoice in the changes each season brings.

Soups, Starters, Small Dishes, Lunches, and Anytime Food

Chestnut, Celery Root, and Apple Soup

Much as I love them, I know that chestnuts are an odd ingredient. They have a distinctive, delicious flavor, but that flavor is exceedingly mild—mix them with something, and you've got to take care not to overpower them. In this cold-weather soup, chestnuts have found their boon companions—celery root and apple. Together, they boost the chestnuts' flavor, enhance their satiny texture, and give them pizzazz. Built on a base of onions, leeks, herbs, and chicken stock, this soup is earthy and inviting, satisfying, but not too rich or too filling—in other words, it's the perfect opener for Thanksgiving or Christmas dinner.

This soup is just right just as it is, but if you'd like to dress it up, try topping it with some shredded duck confit, or thin strips of prosciutto; or go all out and sprinkle it with sliced truffles or small cubes of sautéed foie gras.

MAKES 4 SERVINGS

2 tablespoons extra-virgin olive oil

1 medium onion, peeled, trimmed, and thinly sliced

1 medium leek, white part only, thinly sliced, washed, and dried

2 McIntosh apples, peeled, cored, and cut into ½-inch cubes

10 ounces celery root, peeled and cut into ½-inch cubes

1 bay leaf

1 sprig thyme

Pinch of freshly grated nutmeg

Salt and freshly ground white pepper

¾ pound peeled fresh chestnuts (from about 1¼ pounds chestnuts in the shell; see Glossary, page 365) or dry-packed bottled or vacuum-sealed peeled chestnuts

2 quarts unsalted Chicken Stock (page 346) or store-bought low-sodium chicken broth

½ cup heavy cream

1. **HEAT THE OIL** in a stockpot or large casserole over medium heat. Add the onion, leek, apples, celery root, bay leaf, thyme, nutmeg, and salt and pepper to taste and cook, stirring occasionally, for about 10 minutes, or until the onions and leeks are soft but not colored. Add the chestnuts and chicken stock and bring to the boil. Lower the heat to a simmer and cook, skimming the surface regularly, for 35 to 40 minutes, or until the chestnuts can be mashed easily with a fork. Add the heavy cream and simmer for 5 to 10 minutes more, then remove from the heat and discard the bay leaf and thyme.

2. **PURÉE THE SOUP** until smooth using a blender, hand-held immersion blender, or a food processor, and working in batches if necessary, then pass it through a fine-mesh strainer. You should have about 2 quarts of soup. If you have more, or if you think the soup is too thin—it should have the consistency of a velouté or light cream soup—simmer it over medium heat until slightly thickened. Taste and, if necessary, adjust the seasoning. *(The soup can be cooled completely and stored in a covered container in the refrigerator for 3 to 4 days or frozen for up to a month. Bring the soup to a boil before serving.)*

to serve: Reheat the soup, if necessary—it really needs to be hot—and ladle it into warm bowls.

to drink: A light, lively, low-alcohol German Kabinett Riesling from the Pfalz

Jerusalem Artichoke Soup with Sage Croutons

Jerusalem artichokes, those knobby, gnarly, crunchy little bulbs that resemble misshapen potatoes or hunks of ginger, are the unexpected base for this creamy soup. These small, leafless artichokes, with their water chestnut–like texture and fresh, clean taste, are the roots of sunflower plants, the reason you sometimes find them labeled "sunchokes" in the market. Their season—late summer into midwinter—is longer than that of their pointy-leafed cousins, the more common globe artichokes, but they are sometimes more difficult to find. If you can't find Jerusalems, this soup is a standout made only with hearts of globe artichokes, which are readily available in the spring.

To provide a little crunch and a complementary flavor, I serve this soup with crisp croutons, small cubes of bread quickly sautéed with garlic and fresh sage.

A note on the Jerusalem artichokes: There's no need to peel them for this recipe. Just give them a good scrub—their skins will add character to the soup.

MAKES 6 SERVINGS

The soup:

4 tablespoons unsalted butter

3 ounces pancetta or slab bacon, cut into 3 chunks

1 large onion, peeled, trimmed, and thinly sliced

1 medium fennel bulb, trimmed and thinly sliced

1 medium leek, white part only, thinly sliced, washed, and dried

1 celery stalk, peeled, trimmed, and thinly sliced

3 cloves garlic, peeled, split, and germ removed

Salt and freshly ground white pepper

Bouquet garni (2 sprigs sage, 2 sprigs thyme, and 1 bay leaf, wrapped in a leek green and tied)

2 pounds Jerusalem artichokes, scrubbed and cut into ¼-inch-thick slices, or 8 to 10 globe artichoke hearts (see Glossary, page 362), cut into ¼-inch-thick slices

2 quarts unsalted Chicken or Vegetable Stock (page 346 or 348), store-bought low-sodium chicken or vegetable broth, or water

1 small potato, peeled and diced

½ cup heavy cream

1. **MELT THE BUTTER** in a Dutch oven or large casserole over medium heat. Add the pancetta or bacon and cook, stirring occasionally, until it renders its fat, 3 to 5 minutes. Add the onion, fennel, leek, celery, and garlic and season with salt and pepper. Toss in the bouquet garni and cook, stirring from time to time, for 5 minutes. Add the artichokes and cook for 15 to 20 minutes more, stirring occasionally.

2. **POUR IN THE STOCK OR WATER,** add the potato and 1½ teaspoons salt, and bring the mixture to the boil. Lower the heat so that the soup simmers and cook, uncovered, for 30 to 35 minutes, skimming

the foam from the surface as needed. Spoon out the pieces of pancetta or bacon, cut them into small dice, and set them aside until serving time. Discard the bouquet garni.

3. USING A BLENDER, hand-held immersion blender, or a food processor, and working in batches, purée the soup until it is very smooth. Strain the soup through a fine-mesh sieve into a large saucepan and taste for salt and pepper, adding seasoning as needed. Add the cream to the soup and bring to the boil, then lower the heat and keep the soup warm while you make the croutons. *(The soup can be made ahead, cooled, poured into a container with a tight-fitting lid, and stored overnight in the refrigerator. Reheat over gentle heat before serving.)*

the croutons:

2 tablespoons extra-virgin olive oil

2 slices bread, preferably country bread, crusts removed and cut into ¼-inch dice (to make about 1 cup)

3 leaves sage, finely sliced

1 clove garlic, peeled and crushed

Salt and freshly ground white pepper

WARM THE OIL in a small sauté pan or skillet over medium heat. Add the bread, sage, and garlic, season with salt and pepper, and sauté until the bread is crisp and golden brown. Discard the garlic and drain the croutons on a double thickness of paper towels. Save the crisp sage leaves to garnish the soup.

to serve: Ladle the soup into warm bowls and top each serving with some of the reserved diced pancetta or bacon, a few croutons, and some strands of crisped sage.

to drink: A barrel-fermented Sauvignon Blanc from California's Russian River region

Chilled Spring Pea Soup

There are many reasons to celebrate the arrival of spring, and garden peas are one of them. At Café Boulud, we're delighted when the first batch of peas shows up so we can make this sublime chilled soup swirled with a few spoonfuls of rosemary-infused cream and topped with bits of crisp bacon. Because only ingredients that blend with and intensify the flavors of peas are used, the soup tastes even fresher, brighter, and more pea-like than just-picked peas. When I can, I like to prepare this soup with a variety of peas—I love it with sweet peas, sugar snaps, snow peas, and fava beans, which become an honorary member of the pea family here—but if you make it with only English sweet peas, you'll re-create the French classic Potage St.-Germain, a creamy pea soup named for the town outside Paris where peas used to be grown. (Now that St.-Germain has become a chic suburb, I think they've given up their pea patches.)

MAKES 6 SERVINGS

1 ounce slab bacon, cut in half, or 4 slices bacon

1 tablespoon extra-virgin olive oil

2 stalks celery, peeled, trimmed, and thinly sliced

1 small onion, peeled, trimmed, and thinly sliced

1 leek, white part only, thinly sliced, washed, and dried

Salt and freshly ground white pepper

5 cups unsalted Chicken Stock (page 346) or store-bought low-sodium chicken broth

1 sprig rosemary

6 cups fresh peas, preferably an assortment, such as 1½ pounds English sweet peas, shelled; ¾ pound fava beans, shelled; ¼ pound sugar snap peas, thinly sliced; and ¼ pound snow peas, thinly sliced

1 bunch Italian parsley, leaves only

1. **HEAT A MEDIUM CASSEROLE** over medium heat and toss in the bacon. Brown the bacon very well, then pour off all of the rendered fat. Add the olive oil to the pot and warm it, then add the celery, onion, leek, and a little pepper. Lower the heat and cook the vegetables, stirring, until they soften but don't color, about 15 minutes.

2. **POUR IN THE CHICKEN STOCK** and toss in the sprig of rosemary. Bring to the boil, lower the heat, and simmer the soup for 15 minutes. Spoon out and discard the bacon and rosemary. Pour the soup into the container of a blender and purée until smooth. (You may have to do this in batches.) Set the soup aside to cool.

3. **BRING A LARGE POT** of salted water to the boil. Toss the sugar snap and snow peas into the pot and cook for 3 minutes. Add the sweet peas and cook for another 3 minutes. Put the fava beans in a

colander and plunge the colander into the pot so that the beans can boil for 1 minute. Toss the parsley into the colander and cook everything a final minute. Remove the colander, leaving the fava beans and parsley in it, turn the other peas into a strainer, and run all of the ingredients under cold water to cool them down quickly and to set their colors; drain again. Pop the fava beans out of their skins by pressing each bean between your thumb and index finger. (You may have to pinch the skin of some of the favas open with your fingernail.) Dry the parsley leaves by squeezing them between your palms.

4. PUT THE PEAS, fava beans, parsley, and a little of the soup into the container of a blender and whir until the vegetables are smooth. (You might have to add more of the soup to keep things moving in the container.) Add the remainder of the soup, in batches, and whir until you have a smooth mixture. Push the soup through a fine-mesh strainer to make certain it is smooth and free of small pieces of pea skin, then taste it for salt and pepper. Pour the soup into a container and refrigerate until cold.

the cream:

1 cup heavy cream	**Salt and freshly ground white pepper**
1 sprig rosemary	**5 slices bacon**
1 clove garlic, peeled, split, and germ removed	

1. BRING THE CREAM, rosemary, and garlic to a boil in a small pot, reduce the heat, and simmer for 5 minutes, just until the cream thickens a little. Strain the cream, discarding the rosemary and garlic, season with salt and pepper, and chill.

2. WHILE THE CREAM IS COOLING, brown and lightly crisp the bacon in a pan over medium heat, then drain it well between several layers of paper towels. When the bacon is cool, chop it into small bits.

to serve: Ladle the soup into cold bowls and drizzle a bit of rosemary cream over each portion; top with a sprinkling of bacon.

to drink: An Austrian Grüner Veltliner—it even smells like spring peas

Beet and Tongue Salad

This spring salad is a study in contrasts. There are the contrasts in texture: The meat of the salad, quite literally, is the simmered calf's tongue, which emerges from its slow cooking silky, slightly but very pleasantly chewy, and perfectly suited to play opposite the tender boiled beet cubes. Then there are the flavor contrasts: The meat is mild, the beets pickle-y, the salad bitter, the vinaigrette aptly vinegary, and the dressing, a wonderful blend of horseradish and heavy cream, razor-sharp, ultra-fresh tasting, and a good go-along with each of the salad's other elements.

MAKES 4 TO 6 SERVINGS

the tongue:

¼ cup white vinegar

1 calf's tongue (1 to 1½ pounds)

1 stalk celery, peeled, trimmed, and cut into
1-inch-long pieces

1 carrot, peeled, trimmed, and cut into
1-inch chunks

1 leek, white and light green parts only, cut
into 1-inch-long pieces and washed

Bouquet garni (4 sprigs Italian parsley, 1 sprig
thyme, 2 bay leaves, and 1 tablespoon black
peppercorns, wrapped in a leek green and tied)

2 tablespoons salt

1. **PUT 2 QUARTS OF COLD WATER,** the vinegar, and calf's tongue in a stockpot or other large pot (choose a pot that holds about 6 quarts). Bring the water to the boil and then pull the pot from the heat. Drain the tongue; discard the vinegar water.

2. **RETURN THE TONGUE** to the pot, pour in 4 quarts water, add all the remaining ingredients, and bring to the boil. Adjust the heat so that the liquid simmers and cook for about 3½ hours, or until the tongue is tender enough to be pierced easily with a fork. Drain and discard everything but the tongue; set the tongue aside to cool.

3. **WHEN THE MEAT** is cool enough to handle, peel off and discard the white skin that covers the entire tongue. Cover the tongue and chill it in the refrigerator. When it is cold, cut the tongue on the bias into slices about ⅛ inch thick. Cover the slices and chill until needed.

the beets:

2 large beets, trimmed

5 black peppercorns

5 sprigs thyme

1 leek, white part only, washed

1. **PUT ALL THE INGREDIENTS** except the leek in a large pot, pour in about 2 quarts water, and bring to the boil. Adjust the heat so that the water simmers and cook until the beets can be pierced easily with the tip of a knife, about 1 hour. Drain the beets and set them aside to cool.

2. WHILE THE BEETS are cooling, put a small pot of salted water up to boil. When the water is boiling, toss the leek into the pot and cook until tender, about 10 minutes. Drain the leek, run it under cold water until it is cool, and then dry it well between several layers of paper towels.

3. AS SOON AS THE BEETS are cool enough to handle, peel them and cut them into ¼-inch dice. Cut the leek in half and then into ¼-inch pieces. Cover and set aside until needed. *(The beets and leek can be prepared a day ahead and kept covered—in separate containers—in the refrigerator.)*

the vinaigrette:

2½ tablespoons extra-virgin olive oil

1 tablespoon sherry vinegar

Salt and freshly ground white pepper

WHISK EVERYTHING together until well blended.

the dressing:

½ cup very cold heavy cream

1½ tablespoons grated horseradish

1 tablespoon sherry vinegar

Salt and freshly ground white pepper

WHISK THE CREAM together with the horseradish and vinegar, then season with salt and pepper.

to assemble:

3 heads frisée, white and light yellow parts only, trimmed, washed, and dried

2 tablespoons walnuts, toasted and coarsely chopped

6 chives, cut into 1-inch lengths

JUST BEFORE SERVING, toss the beets and leeks together and season them with half the vinaigrette. (It's best to wait until the last minute to mix beets into a salad, since they quickly turn everything else red.) Season the tongue with half the remaining vinaigrette and use the last of the vinaigrette to toss with the frisée.

to serve: Place some of the beets and leeks in the center of each dinner plate, and surround with slices of calf's tongue, arranging the slices in overlapping concentric circles. Top with a bouquet of frisée and sprinkle with the chopped walnuts. Drizzle the dressing around each plate and scatter over the chives.

to drink: An Oregon Pinot Gris

Sardine and Red Pepper Terrine

As beautiful as it is luscious, with colors as brilliant as its flavors are bold, this warm-weather terrine is bright and beguiling. I created it for fresh sardines, wanting to find a way to call attention to their meaty texture as well as their wonderful oiliness. Pairing them with vegetables that are more sweet than earthy turned out to be the ideal way to show off the entire ensemble. I chose to layer the roasted sardines with sweet peppers, petals of equally sweet, plump tomato, and thin slices of roasted herb-strewn eggplant, a vegetable that has its own full flavor but melds well with others. I used the eggplant as the wrapper, lining the terrine with thin slices and then building up the strata of vegetables and fish within this wrapper. When you bring the terrine to the table, its eggplant wrapper moist, glistening, but inscrutable, no one will suspect—but everyone will appreciate—the burst of summer color and the flavor held within.

MAKES 8 SERVINGS

for the terrine:

2 pounds fresh sardine fillets (from about
4 pounds whole sardines)
Salt and freshly ground white pepper
¾ cup extra-virgin olive oil
8 leaves sage
6 sprigs thyme
4 sprigs rosemary

4 garlic cloves, peeled and crushed
3 pounds eggplant, trimmed, peeled, and cut into ½-inch-thick slices
40 pieces Tomato Confit (page 350) or drained oil-packed sun-dried tomatoes
12 ounces piquillo peppers (see Glossary, page 370) or roasted red bell peppers

1. **CENTER A RACK** in the oven and preheat the oven to 350°F.

2. **LINE A BAKING SHEET** with parchment paper and arrange the sardines in a single layer on the pan. Season the fillets on both sides with salt and pepper and one quarter of the olive oil. Scatter half the sage, thyme, rosemary, and garlic over the fillets and slide the pan into the oven. Roast the sardines for 7 minutes, or until they're just cooked through. Remove the sardines from the baking pan, cool, and then chill in the refrigerator.

3. **RE-LINE THE BAKING SHEET** with clean parchment paper and arrange the eggplant on the sheet. Season the eggplant slices with salt and pepper as well as the remaining oil and herbs. Bake the eggplant for 20 to 25 minutes, or until tender. Cool and then transfer to the refrigerator to chill.

4. **LINE AN 8½-** by 4½- by 2½-inch loaf pan with plastic wrap, allowing it to extend over the sides. The terrine will be built with the eggplant, peppers, sardines, and tomatoes in layers, starting with the eggplant. To begin, cut the eggplant slices to fit the terrine and lay a layer of eggplant over the bottom

and up the sides of the terrine, allowing the slices to overlap a little and overhang the edges. Top with peppers, then sardines, then tomatoes. Repeat with the remaining ingredients, finishing by folding the overhanging eggplant over the top of the terrine and leveling the top with an additional layer of eggplant slices. Cover the top with the plastic wrap that's hanging over the sides and press another piece of plastic wrap against the top for good measure. Cut a piece of corrugated cardboard to fit inside the top of the terrine and press it down firmly against the plastic wrap. Place a weight, such as a 1-pound can, on top of the cardboard, put the terrine on a parchment-lined tray (to catch any drips that result from the weighting), and refrigerate for at least 12 hours, or overnight.

to serve: If you have an electric knife, now's the time to use it; if not, choose a long thin serrated knife and work with a sawing motion. Remove the weight, the cardboard, and the sheet of plastic wrap from the terrine, invert it onto a cutting board, and remove the pan and the last of the plastic wrap. Carefully cut the loaf into slices, each no less than 1 inch thick (thinner slices will fall apart). If you'd like, serve the terrine with a small green salad dressed with lemon juice and olive oil.

to drink: A Spanish white Rueda, rich, oaky, and, even though it's white, berryish

Asparagus and Lobster Salad

The lobster for this salad may come from Maine, the lemons from Florida, and the asparagus from California, but the inspiration for the dish is French through and through. It's a typically French practice to build a salad by layering one luxurious ingredient over another. Here, the luxury begins with a tic-tac-toe board of thick tender asparagus tips, continues with lobster—each portion includes a steamed lobster, slices of the moist tail meat paired with the plump meat from the claws—and finishes with rounds of hearts of palm and a bouquet of greens. As with all French salads, every element is seasoned separately so that the whole will be fragrant and flavorful. The first seasoning is a lemon juice vinaigrette; the second is a creamy curried yellow pepper vinaigrette that's light and vibrant. Once assembled—and for all its specialness, it's extremely easy to assemble—this spring-through-summer salad presents a happy marriage of two cultures and many flavors.

A note on the asparagus: If you can find white asparagus—it's available in early spring—this salad is wonderful made with a mix of white and green asparagus.

MAKES 2 SERVINGS

the lemon vinaigrette:
3 tablespoons extra-virgin olive oil
1 tablespoon freshly squeezed lemon juice
Salt and freshly ground white pepper

WHISK ALL OF THE INGREDIENTS together. Set the vinaigrette aside until needed.

the lobster and asparagus:
Two 1½-pound live lobsters, rinsed under cold water, or freshly steamed lobsters (the lobsters should be bought and steamed the day you serve the salad)

8 stalks jumbo asparagus, preferably 4 green and 4 white, peeled

1. IF YOU ARE STEAMING the lobsters, bring a few inches of salted water to the boil in a lobster pot or stockpot. Plunge the lobsters into the pot, cover, and steam them for 7 minutes. Drain. When the lobsters are cool enough to handle, remove the meat from the claws. Shell and devein the tails and cut each of the tails crosswise into 5 slices, or medallions; reserve. *(The lobster can be prepared a few hours ahead and kept refrigerated, covered with damp paper towels and plastic wrap.)*

2. BRING A MEDIUM SAUCEPAN of salted water to the boil. Trim the asparagus spears so that each is about 5 inches long. Plunge the asparagus into the boiling water and cook until the point of a knife can be inserted easily into the stalk, about 5 minutes. Drain the asparagus and immediately run under cold water to stop the cooking and set the color. When the asparagus is cool, dry it well between layers of paper towels.

to assemble:

1 heart of palm, thinly sliced (optional)
Salt and freshly ground white pepper
Small handful of baby greens

½ recipe Curried-Pepper Vinaigrette
** (page 272)**

SEASON THE LOBSTER, asparagus, the heart of palm, if you're using it, and the greens with salt and pepper and enough of the lemon vinaigrette to give them flavor and a nice gloss.

to serve: Arrange 4 asparagus spears to form a tic-tac-toe square in the center of each dinner plate. Place one slice of lobster tail meat on each side of the square and fill the center of each square with the remaining lobster meat. Arrange the greens as a mound over the claw meat and scatter over the slices of heart of palm, if you have them. Drizzle the curried-pepper vinaigrette around the asparagus and serve the remaining pepper vinaigrette on the side.

to drink: A rich New Zealand Sauvignon Blanc

Crab-Stuffed Zucchini Flowers

If you're like me, you feel a pang of loss the summer day when zucchini flowers are no longer in the market. Zucchini flowers are a treat any way you prepare them—their scarcity as well as their taste and texture make them so. But fill them with the fixings for a great crab cake—fresh lump crabmeat, cornichons and capers, chopped herbs, a shake or two of Tabasco, a squirt of lemon juice, and a dab of Dijon mustard—and the treat becomes a triumph. Once the flowers are plumped up with the crab-cake mix, they're dredged in bread crumbs, fried, and served with a pesto-mayonnaise dipping sauce. They're as right for a casual outdoor meal as they are for a dress-up dinner. Outdoors, they're great served from a big basket as finger food. Put the dipping sauce in a bowl nearby and have a stack of paper napkins at the ready to wipe fingers that haven't been licked perfectly clean. Indoors, it's nice to arrange the stuffed flowers on dinner plates along with a small salad simply dressed with lemon juice and good olive oil, a few slices of black olives, and a drizzle of the pesto mayonnaise.

A note on crab cakes: The mixture that's used to fill the zucchini flowers is so good that you'll want to prepare it on its own. To make crab cakes, just form the crab mixture into patties and chill the cakes, covered, for about 3 hours. When you're ready to cook them, dredge them in flour, dip them in beaten egg, dust them with bread crumbs, and sauté them until golden.

MAKES 4 SERVINGS

the dipping sauce:

½ **cup mayonnaise**

¼ **cup pesto (page 274)**

BLEND THE MAYONNAISE and pesto together, spoon it into a small serving bowl, cover, and refrigerate until needed. *(The sauce can be made up to 4 hours ahead and kept covered in the refrigerator.)*

the crab and zucchini flowers:

¾ **pound fresh jumbo lump crabmeat (see Source Guide, page 385), picked through to remove small pieces of shell and cartilage**

4½ **tablespoons mayonnaise**

1½ **teaspoons chopped cornichons (bottled French gherkins)**

1½ **teaspoons capers, rinsed, dried, and chopped**

¾ **teaspoon Dijon mustard**

¾ **teaspoon freshly squeezed lemon juice**

¾ **teaspoon finely chopped chives**

¾ **teaspoon finely chopped Italian parsley leaves**

¾ **teaspoon finely chopped basil leaves**

2 **drops Tabasco sauce**

Salt and freshly ground white pepper

8 zucchini flowers, pistils removed at the base
    and dirt gently brushed off (don't wash the
    flowers)
Flour for dredging

2 large eggs, lightly beaten
1 cup bread crumbs, preferably panko
    (see Glossary, page 369)
2 tablespoons extra-virgin olive oil

1. **GENTLY MIX TOGETHER** the crabmeat, mayonnaise, cornichons, capers, mustard, lemon juice, chopped herbs, and Tabasco and season with salt and pepper. Using a small spoon (or a pastry bag fitted with a plain tip), spoon enough of the crab mixture into each flower to plump it up, taking care to leave enough space at the top to close the flower. Carefully draw the flower's petals closed around the stuffing—get the top closed as best you can—and then dredge each packet in flour, tapping off the excess. Dip the flowers into the beaten eggs and then dust them with the bread crumbs.

2. **WARM THE OLIVE OIL** in a large nonstick sauté pan or skillet over medium-high heat. When the oil is hot, place the stuffed zucchini flowers in the pan. Brown the flowers on all sides, turning them ever so carefully with a thin spatula as needed. The flowers will probably need 3 to 5 minutes of cooking time. Transfer the flowers to a double layer of paper towels to drain for a few seconds before serving.

to serve: If you're serving these family-style, just pile the stuffed flowers on a small platter and offer the dipping sauce on the side. If you want to arrange individual plates, consider drizzling the flowers with the dipping sauce and serving them with a small pouf of salad dressed lightly with lemon juice and olive oil.

to drink: A bone-dry Canadian Riesling

Savory Lemon Pots de Crème with Caviar

It's astonishing how changing the texture of an ingredient changes the way it blends with other foods. I would rarely consider interfering with the clear, clean, sea-fresh flavor of caviar by splashing it with lemon juice, and yet, when the flavor of lemon—zest, juice, and fruit—is softened by eggs, mellowed by cream, and then gently baked into a custard, as it is here, the difference in the way it pairs with caviar is dramatic. In this recipe, the lemon's sparkle emphasizes the caviar's best and briniest characteristics, while the custard's soft, velvety texture sets up a contrast that makes the caviar's grains seem even fuller, firmer, and more fun than ever to pop against the roof of your mouth.

If the lemon custard looks familiar, that's because it's an almost sugarless version of the filling for my lemon tart (page 181). Years ago, I started using the filling—without much sugar—in a tart that I served sometimes with fresh asparagus (it was like having a hollandaise contained in a crust) and often with caviar. Then, as I was searching for something exceptional to make at Café Boulud for Christmas and New Year's, I had the idea to turn the filling into a pot de crème, and it became an immediate holiday-season favorite. I like to serve these winter treats with crunchy chive twists made with puff pastry, but they are sumptuous solo.

MAKES 6 SERVINGS

the chive twists (optional):

2 ounces all-butter puff pastry (see Glossary, page 371)

2 tablespoons finely chopped chives

Salt

1 egg, lightly beaten, for egg wash

1. LINE A BAKING SHEET with parchment paper and set it aside for the moment. Working on a lightly floured work surface, roll the puff pastry into a rectangle about ⅛ inch thick (thickness is more important than size here). Brush the pastry with water, sprinkle with chives, and season with salt. Fold the pastry in half (the chives will be on the inside) and roll the pastry into a thin rectangle again. Brush the pastry with the egg wash and, using a thin knife or a pastry cutter, cut it into strips that are about 4 inches long and ¼ inch wide. You should have approximately 40 strips. Twist the pastry strips into corkscrew shapes and lay them on the parchment-lined baking sheet, leaving about 1 inch of space between them. Press the ends of each twist down against the parchment (this will help the twists keep their shape during baking) and stow the baking sheet in the refrigerator or freezer while you preheat the oven. (*If you don't want to bake the twists—or all of the twists—now, freeze them until firm, then pack them airtight. The twists can stay frozen for up to 1 month. Don't defrost them before baking, just add a few extra minutes to the baking time.*)

2. CENTER A RACK in the oven and preheat the oven to 450°F.

3. SLIDE THE BAKING SHEET into the oven and bake the twists for 12 to 15 minutes, or until they are beautifully puffed and golden brown. Transfer the twists to a rack. They can be served warm or at room temperature. *(Once cooled, the twists can be kept in an airtight container for several hours. To reheat the twists, arrange them on a baking sheet and bake for a few minutes in a 400°F oven.)*

the custards:

1½ **medium lemons**	¼ **teaspoon salt**
2 **large eggs**	**Pinch of sugar**
2 **large egg yolks**	**Freshly ground white pepper**
1 **cup heavy cream**	3 **ounces sevruga or osetra caviar**

1. CENTER A RACK in the oven and preheat the oven to 300°F.

2. FINELY GRATE and reserve the zest of the lemons. Then, using a small sharp knife, slice away all of the white cottony pith beneath the zest, as well as the slimmest possible layer of fruit, so that the moist, juicy flesh of the lemons is exposed. Cut the lemons crosswise into ½-inch-thick slices and remove the seeds.

3. TOSS THE LEMON SLICES (hold on to the zest), eggs, yolks, cream, salt, and sugar into the container of a blender (first choice) or food processor and purée until smooth. Strain the mixture into a bowl, season with pepper, and stir in the zest. Skim off the layer of foam that will have formed on the top of the mixture.

4. ARRANGE SIX 4-OUNCE CUPS (you can use pot-de-crème, espresso, or custard cups or ramekins) in a small roasting pan, leaving an equal amount of space between the cups, then fill each cup to the halfway mark with the lemon custard. Using a small pitcher, fill the roasting pan with enough hot water to come halfway up the sides of the cups. Cover the pan with a double layer of plastic wrap (don't worry— it can stand the heat) and poke two holes in two opposite corners.

5. BAKE THE CUSTARDS for 20 to 25 minutes, or until the edges color ever so slightly and the custards are lightly set but still jiggle a little in the center when you (gently) shake them. Remove the pan from the oven and let the custards sit in the water bath for 10 minutes. Peel off the plastic wrap, lift the cups out of the water, and either serve the custards or, if it's more convenient, let them sit at room temperature for up to 10 minutes.

to serve: Top each pot de crème with a generous spoonful of caviar and serve with chive pastry twists, if you've made them.

to drink: A Champagne as celebratory as the dish

Morels and Pea Shoot Gnocchi

I created this spring dish for the *New York Times* and then held on to it when Café Boulud opened —it was too good to give up. The main ingredients are delicate pea shoot gnocchi, soft, small dumplings built on ricotta cheese (they seem to disappear in a little puff of flavor the instant you put them in your mouth), and woodsy morels, mushrooms I dote on. Morels are conical, bulbous, and honeycombed and have a spongy texture that makes them just right for any dish with broth. Here the broth is the element that ties all the flavors together. There's just enough of it to moisten the dish—it's not a soup, although it's fine enough to be one if you want to play around with this recipe—and it's used to poach first the morels, then each of the other ingredients. With the addition of each ingredient, the broth gets richer, deeper, and more complex. You can tinker with the selection of vegetables—I always do—but I like to keep the earthy flavors and crunch of carrots and radishes, and the sweetness of fresh peas.

MAKES 4 SERVINGS

the gnocchi:

5½ ounces pea shoots, leaves only

¾ cup whole-milk ricotta cheese, wrapped in a tea towel and squeezed dry

3 tablespoons extra-virgin olive oil, plus additional for drizzling

2 tablespoons plus 1 teaspoon all-purpose flour

Salt and freshly ground white pepper

1. **BRING A MEDIUM POT** of salted water to the boil. Plunge the pea shoots into the boiling water and cook until the leaves are tender but still green, about 2 to 3 minutes. Drain the leaves in a strainer and run them under cold water to set their color and cool them. Press the leaves between your hands to remove the excess water and pat them dry between paper towels.

2. **PUT THE LEAVES** in a small food processor or blender along with the ricotta and olive oil and process until smooth. Add the flour, season with salt and pepper, and pulse just to blend, then taste and add more salt and pepper if needed. Press the gnocchi mixture through a sieve into a bowl.

3. **BRING A QUART OF WATER** and 1½ teaspoons salt to a boil in a medium saucepan, then lower the heat so that the water just simmers gently. Set a bowl filled with ice cubes and water close to the stove. Using two teaspoons, make dumplings, each about 1 inch in diameter, by picking up some of the gnocchi mixture on one spoon and scraping it off into the gently simmering water with the other. Make and poach the gnocchi in three batches, cooking each batch for 4 to 5 minutes. With a slotted spoon, transfer the gnocchi from the simmering water to the ice-water bath.

4. WHEN THE GNOCCHI ARE COLD, use the slotted spoon to transfer them to a plate. Drizzle a little olive oil over the dumplings to keep them from sticking together, cover with plastic, and, if you're not finishing the dish now, refrigerate until needed. *(The gnocchi can be made ahead and refrigerated for up to 6 hours.)*

the broth:

1 tablespoon unsalted butter

4 scallions, white and light green parts only, cut on the bias into 1-inch pieces

1 large shallot, peeled, trimmed, finely diced, rinsed, and dried

1 sprig rosemary

2 long thin carrots, peeled, trimmed, and cut on the bias into very thin slices

2 cloves garlic, peeled and thinly sliced

1½ cups (approximately) unsalted Vegetable Stock (page 348), store-bought low-sodium vegetable broth, or water

1 pound morels, trimmed, washed, and dried

Salt and freshly ground white pepper

1½ pounds English sweet peas, shucked

1 ounce pea shoots, leaves only

1 tablespoon extra-virgin olive oil, or more to taste

4 small pink radishes, scrubbed, trimmed, and cut into very thin rounds

1 tablespoon finely chopped chives

1. MELT THE BUTTER in a medium sauté pan or skillet over medium heat. Toss in the scallions, shallot, and rosemary and cook, stirring, for 3 to 4 minutes, or until the vegetables are translucent but not colored. Add the carrots, garlic, and 1½ cups stock or water and cook for 3 minutes. Add the morels and salt and pepper to taste, cover the pan, and cook for another 5 minutes. Uncover the pan, add the peas, and cook for 4 to 5 minutes more.

2. CHECK THE LIQUID to make sure that it is at a very gentle simmer, then add the gnocchi, pea shoot leaves, and olive oil. Heat the gnocchi gently for 3 minutes, then add the radishes, taste the broth, and add more salt and pepper, stock or water, or olive oil, if needed. Remove the pan from the heat.

to serve: Lift the gnocchi and vegetables out of the pan with a slotted spoon and divide them evenly among four warm shallow soup plates. Pour an equal amount of broth over each serving, sprinkle with the chives, and serve immediately.

to drink: A California wine made from a blend of Roussanne and Marsanne grapes

Crab Salad with Green Apple Gelée

If the mention of crab salad makes you think of a rich, mayonnaisey mixture in which it's hard to tell the crab from the celery—clear your mind. Every element in this fresh, clean-tasting cool-weather salad conspires to make this starter sparkle. Constructed in layers and centered in a shallow soup plate, from the bottom up you've got sweet crabmeat gently tossed with lemon juice and oil; a light rémoulade sauce enlivened with pickles, capers, and herbs; a few slivers of celery, root and stalk, for crunch; and a topknot of seasoned frisée or escarole for a spot of bitterness. The combination is great, but it becomes perfect when you add a pool of apple gelée dotted with tiny diced green apples and small cubes of fresh lime. At Café Boulud, we use peeky-toe crab (an East Coast specialty available nationwide by mail order), but fresh Maine, Louisiana, or Maryland lump crabmeat makes a good salad too.

MAKES 4 SERVINGS

the gelée:

4 Granny Smith apples, cored and halved, ½ apple cut into tiny dice, the remainder coarsely chopped

Pinch of vitamin C powder (to help keep the apples' color; available in health food stores)

1 lime

1 sheet gelatin (see Glossary, page 367), or ½ teaspoon powdered gelatin, softened in 1 tablespoon cold water and then dissolved over heat

1. **PUT THE APPLE CHUNKS** in the container of a food processor and whir, scraping down the sides of the container as needed, until finely puréed. Add the vitamin C powder to the purée and blend to mix. Line a strainer with a double thickness of damp cheesecloth, set the strainer over a bowl, pour in the purée, and allow it to drip through the strainer. When it looks as though all the liquid has gone through the strainer, press against the solids to extract whatever liquid remains. Pour 1 cup of the juice into a small bowl and save the leftovers to thin the rémoulade if necessary. (If it's not necessary, drink the juice: It's great.)

2. **PEEL THE LIME,** then, using a small knife, slice away the bitter white pith and with it the thinnest possible layer of fruit. Cutting against the membranes, release each segment of lime. Remove any seeds, cut each segment into tiny dice, and set aside for the moment.

3. **IF YOU ARE USING** sheet gelatin, drop the gelatin into a bowl of cold water to soften. Warm ¼ cup of the strained apple juice in a small saucepan. Lift the sheet gelatin out of the cold water, then stir it into the warm apple juice. If you are using powdered gelatin, stir the dissolved gelatin into the warm juice. When the gelatin is incorporated, mix it into the remaining ¾ cup apple juice; stir in the diced apple and

lime. Chill until the gelatin sets and the gelée is syrupy. *(The gelée can be kept, covered in the refrigerator, for up to 2 hours.)*

the rémoulade:

1 stalk celery, peeled, trimmed, and cut into matchstick-sized pieces

½ small celery root, peeled and cut into matchstick-sized pieces

1 large egg yolk

2 teaspoons freshly squeezed lemon juice

1 teaspoon Dijon mustard

½ teaspoon sherry vinegar

Salt and freshly ground white pepper

½ cup vegetable oil

2 teaspoons chopped cornichons (bottled French gherkins)

2 teaspoons chopped capers

2 teaspoons chopped Italian parsley leaves

½ teaspoon chopped tarragon

½ small clove garlic, peeled, germ removed, and finely chopped

1. BRING A MEDIUM SAUCEPAN of salted water to the boil. Plunge the strips of celery stalk and celery root into the water and cook for about 1 minute, until tender. Drain the celery pieces in a strainer and run them under cold water to cool. When they're cool, drain and pat them dry between layers of paper towels; set aside.

2. WORKING IN A MIXING BOWL, make the rémoulade's mayonnaise base by whisking together the yolk, lemon juice, mustard, and vinegar; season with salt and pepper. Whisking constantly, drizzle in the vegetable oil—start by adding the oil in droplets and then, when the mixture starts to look thick and creamy, pour in the oil in a slow steady stream. Fold in the remaining ingredients, taste the rémoulade, and add more salt and pepper if needed. If you think the rémoulade is too thick, just stir in a splash of the reserved apple juice. *(The sauce can be made up to 1 day in advance and kept well covered in the refrigerator. Leftovers make a good salad dressing or dip for raw vegetables.)*

the crab and salad:

1 pound peeky-toe or other best-quality fresh crabmeat (see Source Guide, page 385), picked through to remove any small pieces of shell or cartilage

Freshly squeezed lemon juice

Extra-virgin olive oil

Salt and freshly ground white pepper

1 head frisée, white and light yellow parts only, washed and dried, or tender center escarole leaves, washed and dried

2 tablespoons walnuts, toasted and roughly chopped

TOSS THE CRABMEAT very gently (you don't want to crush or shred it) with a little lemon juice and olive oil and season to taste with salt and pepper. Do the same with the frisée or escarole.

to serve: If you want to serve the salad as we do at Café Boulud, for each serving, place a 2¾-inch ring mold in the center of a shallow soup plate. Spoon a quarter of the crabmeat into the mold and top with about a tablespoon of rémoulade. Arrange a few slivers of celery stalk and celery root over the rémoulade and then carefully remove the ring. Alternatively, you can just mound the ingredients in layers in the center of each soup plate. Either way, spoon some of the gelée, with the small pieces of apple and lime, around each little tower of crab. Finish with a bouquet of the greens, sprinkle with the toasted nuts, and serve immediately.

to drink: A dry, refreshing, low-alcohol Austrian Riesling

la saison
Chilled Spring Pea Soup (page 112)

la saison
Beet and Tongue Salad (page 114)

la saison
Asparagus and Lobster Salad (page 118)

la saison
  Cod with Blood Orange Sauce
  and Creamy Grits (page 134)

la saison
Pancetta-Wrapped Tuna with Potato-Ramp Purée (page 136)

la saison

Chestnut-Crusted Loin of Venison with Spiced Braised Rutabaga (page 157)

la saison
Rhubarb Napoleon with Orange Flower Cream (page 164)

la saison
Light Vanilla Cake with Quick Berry Marmalade (page 172)

Endive, Prosciutto, and Pecan Clafoutis

Most clafoutis are rustic and fruity, and they're often improvised. The classic clafoutis batter is a crêpe batter's first cousin, the filling is usually whatever is ripest in the orchard, and the whole is normally very inexpensive to make. But this winter version of clafoutis is savory, chic, and indulgent. It's an unusual blend of mild (the mix of eggs and cream) and bitter (the endive), salty (the strips of prosciutto), and earthy (the pecans). And, it's an unusual preparation—unlike all other clafoutis, this one is made with a little yeast, the key to its lightness. At the Café, I prepare one-to-a-person clafoutis and serve them with a small salad of raw endive, mushrooms, and greens. Here, I've given you the recipe to make a larger clafoutis that can be sliced into servings and offered along with the salad as a starter, a showstopping lunch, or a late-night supper.

MAKES 4 SERVINGS

2 large eggs, at room temperature

3 large egg whites, at room temperature

2 tablespoons plus 2 teaspoons sugar

½ cup heavy cream

1 teaspoon (firmly packed) crumbled fresh
   yeast

¾ cup plus 1 tablespoon all-purpose flour

2 tablespoons unsalted butter, melted and
   cooled, plus 1 tablespoon unsalted butter

Juice of 1 lemon

5 large Belgian endive, outer leaves removed

Salt and freshly ground white pepper

¼ cup pecans, toasted and coarsely chopped

1½ ounces prosciutto or Virginia ham, cut into
   very thin strips

1. **WHISK THE EGGS,** whites, and 1 tablespoon plus 1 teaspoon sugar together in a medium bowl, beating just until the sugar dissolves. Warm the heavy cream in a microwave oven or over low heat for just a few seconds—it should feel only slightly warm to the touch—remove from heat, and stir in the yeast, mixing until it is dissolved. Whisk the dissolved yeast into the egg mixture, then gently whisk in the flour and the 2 tablespoons melted butter. Cover the bowl with plastic wrap and refrigerate for an hour.

2. **BRING A LARGE POT** of lightly salted water to the boil. Add the lemon juice and endive, lower the heat to a simmer, cover the pot, and cook for 15 to 20 minutes, or until the endive is tender. Drain very well, and when the endive is cool, cut it into 1-inch-thick rounds, discarding the tough bottoms.

3. **MELT THE REMAINING** tablespoon butter in a large sauté pan or skillet over medium heat and add the endive. Sprinkle with the remaining 1 tablespoon plus 1 teaspoon sugar and cook the endive, turning it as needed, until lightly caramelized on all sides, about 5 minutes. (Don't worry if some of the pieces come apart—it's unavoidable.) Remove the endive from the pan and cool.

4. CENTER A RACK in the oven and preheat the oven to 300°F. Lightly butter or spray a 6-inch round cake pan, preferably one with 2-inch-high sides (you can use a disposable foil cake pan for this), and set it on a baking sheet.

5. REMOVE THE BATTER from the refrigerator and season with salt and pepper. Pour about ¼ cup batter over the bottom of the cake pan. Arrange the fullest pieces of endive around the edge of the pan; fill in the center of the pan with the rest of the endive. Pour in half of the remaining batter and scatter over the pecans and prosciutto or ham; top with the rest of the batter. Bake the clafoutis for about 40 minutes, or until a knife inserted in the center comes out clean. Transfer the clafoutis to a rack to cool.

the salad:

¼ cup extra-virgin olive oil	¼ pound mâche or other small sweet salad
2 tablespoons sherry vinegar	greens, washed and dried
1 shallot, peeled, trimmed, finely chopped,	6 white mushrooms, trimmed, cleaned, and cut
rinsed, and dried	into thin strips
Salt and freshly ground white pepper	1 Belgian endive, trimmed and cut into thin strips

WHISK TOGETHER the oil, vinegar, and shallot and season to taste with salt and pepper. Toss the greens, mushrooms, and endive together and dress with some of the vinaigrette.

to serve: Put a slice of clafoutis and some salad on each plate; drizzle the remaining vinaigrette around the clafoutis.

to drink: A northern Italian Gewürz from the Alto Adige

Main Courses

Lobster with Sweet Corn Polenta

I start making this dish in early summer and continue through the fall, and it just keeps getting better and better as the corn and lobsters get fuller and sweeter. The combination of corn and lobster is an American summer classic, and I took to it almost as soon as I came to this country. (Who wouldn't?) In this recipe, lobster gets a double dose of corn, dried and fresh. The dried corn is polenta, whose texture retains a pleasant grittiness even after it's fully cooked and as soft and creamy as mashed potatoes. (I use instant polenta because it's creamier than long-cooking cornmeal.) And the fresh corn on the cob plays a wake-up role—it's added to the polenta to bring back some of its original vitality. I use the cobs to flavor the milk the polenta is cooked in, and I stir the sweet, fresh pulp into the finished polenta. It's a wonderful way to recycle and rejuvenate flavors and a great cushion for the lightly sautéed lobster. At Café Boulud, we finish the dish with a few pieces of oven-dried prosciutto—they contribute a different kind of saltiness as well as a different texture.

the oven-dried prosciutto (optional):

4 thin slices prosciutto or cured ham

1. CENTER A RACK in the oven and preheat the oven to 250°F.

2. LINE A BAKING SHEET with parchment paper, lay out the slices of prosciutto or ham, and bake for 45 minutes to an hour, or until dried. Remove from the oven and set aside on the baking sheet until needed.

the lobster and polenta:

Two 2-pound live lobsters, rinsed under cold water

8 large ears corn, shucked

1 quart whole milk

2 cups water

5 cloves garlic, peeled and crushed

2 shallots, peeled, trimmed, thinly sliced, and rinsed

2 sprigs rosemary

Salt and freshly ground white pepper

3 tablespoons unsalted butter

1 cup instant polenta

1 tablespoon finely grated Parmesan cheese

6 scallions, trimmed and cut into 1½-inch lengths

1 tablespoon finely chopped chives

1. FILL A LOBSTER POT or very large stockpot three-quarters full with salted water, place it over high heat, cover, and bring the water to a boil. Plunge the lobsters into the pot and cook them at a boil for 7 minutes. Drain them and cool them under cold running water.

2. YOU'RE GOING TO NEED the lobster shells to flavor the polenta cooking liquid, so pull the heads from the bodies, wipe them clean, and use your fingers to scoop out and discard all the soft parts from inside. Cut the shells into small pieces (poultry shears work well here) and toss them back into the empty lobster pot. Crack the tail, claw, and knuckle shells and carefully pull out the meat. (You should be able to pull the tail meat out of its shell in one piece with a fork.) Again, clean and cut up the shells and toss them into the pot. As for the tail meat, remove the vein running down the back of each tail and cut the meat crosswise into 6 slices, or medallions. Set the medallions aside with the claw and knuckle meat, covered with damp paper towels and plastic wrap.

3. FOR THE CORN, you'll use the pulp in the polenta and the cobs in the cooking liquid. To get the pulp, run the point of a chef's knife down the center of each row of corn kernels. Working over a deep wide bowl, run the back of the knife firmly down the rows of kernels to release as much pulp and liquid as possible—you should end up with about 1½ cups. Set the soupy pulp aside and toss the cobs into the pot with the lobster shells.

4. ADD THE MILK, water, 3 of the garlic cloves, the shallots, and 1 sprig of the rosemary to the pot and bring to the boil. Adjust the heat so that the liquid simmers and cook for 10 minutes. Season well with salt and pepper, then pour the liquid through a strainer and discard the solids.

5. POUR 4 CUPS of the liquid into a large saucepan (keep the rest of the liquid aside; you may need it for finishing the polenta), add 2 tablespoons of the butter, and bring to the boil. Lower the heat and, whisking constantly, add the polenta in a thin steady stream. Cook the polenta at a gentle simmer, whisking occasionally, for 5 minutes, then add the reserved corn pulp and its liquid and cook until the polenta has the consistency of loose mashed potatoes, about 5 minutes. If the polenta seems too thick or dry, whisk in some of the reserved liquid, little by little, as needed. Stir in the Parmesan cheese and season with salt and pepper. *(If you need to hold the polenta, transfer it to the top of a double boiler, press a sheet of plastic wrap against the surface, and keep warm over simmering water.)*

6. WHILE THE POLENTA IS COOKING, melt the remaining 1 tablespoon butter in a large sauté pan or skillet over medium heat. Add the scallions along with the remaining 2 garlic cloves and sprig of rosemary, cover, and cook until softened, 3 to 5 minutes. Add the lobster meat, replace the cover, and cook just until the lobster is hot, about 1 minute. Discard the rosemary and garlic, toss in the chives, and season to taste with salt and pepper.

to serve: Spoon the polenta into a warm large serving bowl. Make an indentation in the center of the polenta and spoon in the lobster. If you're using the dried prosciutto or ham, drape it over the lobster. Serve immediately.

to drink: A fruity Australian Semillon with some oak

Cod with Blood Orange Sauce and Creamy Grits

When winter's days grow colder, darker, and shorter, I grow more and more grateful for oranges—their light, clean, refreshing taste and sparkling color bring cheer to cold-weather cooking. In part because of the oranges (blood oranges with their brilliant red color are my first choice, but you can use regular oranges), this winter dish has an edgy freshness and clarity that's more characteristic of spring and summer foods. The sauce is a sweet and bitter mixture of orange juice and sliced endive that's caramelized and then cooked down to concentrate the flavors. The fish is a plump fillet of moist, flaky cod, which is at its prime in winter waters. And the serve-along is a mound of old-fashioned, straight-from-America's-South grits, cooked slowly in rosemary-infused milk until they're as creamy as polenta, as comforting as mashed potatoes, and as ritzy as grits can get.

MAKES 4 SERVINGS

the sauce:

8 to 10 blood oranges (or 1 cup freshly squeezed regular orange juice and the grated zest of 1 orange)

4 tablespoons unsalted butter

3 tablespoons sugar

1 sprig rosemary

4 medium Belgian endive, cut lengthwise in half, cored, and cut crosswise into ¾-inch-thick pieces

Salt and freshly ground white pepper

1. **GRATE THE ZEST** from 1 of the blood oranges, then squeeze the juice from as many oranges as necessary to get 1 cup of juice; strain the juice.

2. **MELT THE BUTTER** with the sugar in a large sauté pan or skillet over medium-high heat. Add the grated orange zest and rosemary and cook until the butter-sugar mixture is almost caramelized. Add the endive to the pan, season with salt and pepper, and pour in the orange juice: The caramel may bubble, so stand away, and, if the juice is cold, the caramel may seize—just keep cooking and stirring and it will smooth out. Continue to cook and stir until the endive is meltingly tender and only about 2 to 3 tablespoons of liquid remain, 10 to 15 minutes. Set the pan aside.

the grits:

3 cups whole milk

⅔ cup water

2 sprigs rosemary

⅔ cup old-fashioned (*not* quick-cooking) grits

Salt and freshly ground white pepper

PUT THE MILK, water, rosemary, and grits in a medium saucepan and bring to the boil, stirring, over medium heat. Adjust the heat so that the grits barely simmer—just a bubble or two at a time is perfect—add a little salt and pepper, and cook, stirring frequently, until all the liquid is absorbed and the grits are tender and creamy, about 15 minutes. Taste for salt and pepper and, if you're not ready to serve, set the grits in a bowl over—not touching—simmering water for a few minutes, while you cook the fish and finish its sauce.

the fish:

3 tablespoons unsalted butter
Four 6-ounce cod fillets, skin on
Salt and freshly ground white pepper

1. MELT 2 TABLESPOONS of the butter in a large sauté pan or skillet over medium heat. Season the fish with salt and pepper and slip the fillets into the pan. Sear the fish on both sides, about 4 to 5 minutes on a side, until the flesh is opaque but still very moist.

2. WHILE THE FISH IS COOKING, reheat the endive and sauce by bringing the mixture to a boil over medium heat. As soon as the sauce boils, pull the pot from the heat and swirl in the remaining 1 tablespoon butter. The sauce is ready and should be served quickly.

to serve: For each serving, spoon a mound of grits into the center of a warm dinner plate, top with a cod fillet, and surround with some endive and blood orange sauce.

to drink: A Raixas Baixas, a clean, slightly herbaceous white wine from Spain

Pancetta-Wrapped Tuna with Potato-Ramp Purée

If you were ever the least bit skeptical about just how much like meat tuna is, this dish, created to showcase tuna's meatiness, should erase all doubts: At every step, I've treated the tuna just as I would a traditional roast. The tuna is cut as a roast would be cut, wrapped in pancetta, tied like a roast, and, indeed, seared, roasted, and served with go-with-a-roast vegetables—sautéed chanterelles and mashed potatoes sparked with a purée of spring ramps. The cut of the tuna is unusual—it's a loin of tuna—and, in all likelihood, you'll have to have a chat with your fishmonger about it. Tell him you'd like a piece from the center of the fish cut into a rectangular block about 6 inches long, 1½ inches high, and 1½ inches wide.

If you can't find ramps—they're wild spring onions that look like skinny scallions or baby leeks but have a strong, sharp onion taste—you can substitute an equal amount of scallion greens; just include a clove of garlic to give the scallions an edge.

MAKES 6 SERVINGS

the tuna:

8 to 10 ounces slab pancetta, thinly sliced, or
   an equal amount of sliced bacon

1¼ pounds tuna loin, cut like a roast, approximately 6 inches long, 1½ inches high, and 1½ inches wide

Salt and freshly ground white pepper

SPREAD A PIECE OF PLASTIC WRAP on the counter and lay out the slices of pancetta (or bacon) vertically, so that each slice overlaps its neighboring slice just a bit. Season the tuna very lightly with salt and pepper (remember, the pancetta or bacon is salty) and place it crosswise in the center of the pancetta. One by one, wrap each piece of pancetta around the tuna, pressing the pancetta gently against the tuna and keeping the rows even. Secure the pancetta by tying the tuna at 1-inch intervals with kitchen twine, just as you would a meat roast. Wrap the tuna in the plastic wrap and refrigerate it while you prepare the potatoes.

the potatoes and ramps:

1¾ pounds potatoes, preferably fingerlings, peeled and cut into ½-inch pieces

¾ cup whole milk

8 tablespoons (1 stick) unsalted butter, cut into 8 pieces

3 ounces ramps, trimmed and washed,
   or 3 ounces scallion greens (from about
   4 to 5 ounces scallions) plus 1 clove garlic,
   peeled, split, germ removed, and finely
   chopped

1 bunch Italian parsley, leaves only
4 tablespoons extra-virgin olive oil
Salt and freshly ground white pepper

1. **PUT THE POTATOES** in a large pot of salted cold water, bring to the boil, and cook until the potatoes are tender enough to be pierced with the point of a knife, about 15 minutes.

2. **WHILE THE POTATOES ARE COOKING,** bring the milk and butter to the boil in a small saucepan. When the mixture reaches the boil and the butter melts, turn off the heat; keep this warm until you're ready to purée the potatoes.

3. **WHEN THE POTATOES ARE COOKED** through, drain them, then return them to the pot. Set the pot over medium heat and, shaking the pot to keep the potatoes from sticking, cook just until the potatoes are dry, a matter of a minute or two. Pull the pot from the heat and spoon the potatoes into a food mill fitted with the fine blade or a potato ricer. Push the potatoes through the food mill or ricer into a large bowl. In a slow, steady stream, add the hot milk and butter, stirring the liquid into the potatoes with a wooden spoon. Press a piece of plastic wrap against the surface of the potatoes and set the bowl aside in a warm place, or keep the potatoes warm in a covered heatproof bowl set over a pan of simmering water.

4. **BRING A SMALL POT** of water to the boil. Toss the ramps or scallion greens into the pot and boil for 3 to 4 minutes, until tender. Scoop the ramps or scallions out of the pot with a slotted spoon (keep the boiling water over the heat) and run them under cold water to cool; dry them well. Toss the parsley into the boiling water and cook for 2 minutes before draining and running it under cold water. When the parsley is cool, dry it as well.

5. **WARM 1 TABLESPOON** of the olive oil in a medium sauté pan or skillet over medium heat. If you're using it, add the garlic and sauté until it is tender but not colored, about 2 minutes. Toss in the ramps or scallions and cook, stirring, for 3 minutes. Scrape the ingredients into the container of a small processor or a blender. Add the drained and dried parsley and the remaining 3 tablespoons olive oil and whir, scraping down the sides of the container as needed, until you have a smooth purée. Stir the purée into the potatoes, season with salt and pepper, cover again, and keep warm while you cook the tuna.

to finish:

3 tablespoons unsalted butter

6 ounces chanterelles, trimmed and cleaned
(halved or quartered if large)

1 tablespoon finely chopped shallots, rinsed
and dried

Salt and freshly ground white pepper

¼ cup sherry vinegar

¼ cup dry white wine

¼ cup unsalted Chicken Stock (page 346) or
store-bought low-sodium chicken broth

2 tablespoons finely chopped chives

1. CENTER A RACK in the oven and preheat the oven to 350°F.

2. MELT 1 TABLESPOON of the butter in a large ovenproof sauté pan or skillet over medium heat and, when it's hot, slip the tuna into the pan. Sear the tuna for about 2 minutes on each of its four sides, then slide the pan into the oven for 5 minutes. (After 5 minutes in the oven, the tuna will be rare—cooked on the outside and warm but not colored anywhere else. If this is too rare for you, increase the tuna's time in the oven by 1 to 2 minutes and you'll have medium tuna.) Lift the tuna out of the pan and onto a warm serving platter (don't discard the cooking fat).

3. POUR OFF HALF THE FAT that's in the pan, return the pan to the stovetop, turn the heat to medium-low, and toss in the chanterelles. Cover the pan and cook the mushrooms until they're almost tender but not colored, 3 to 5 minutes. Add the shallots, season with salt and pepper, and cook another minute or so to soften the shallots. Pour in the vinegar and allow it to reduce by three quarters. Add the white wine, bring it to a boil, and allow it cook away before adding the chicken stock. Cook until the stock is reduced by half, then pull the pan from the heat and swirl in the remaining 2 tablespoons butter, a small piece at a time. (The idea is to melt the butter slowly so that it forms an emulsion.) Sprinkle in the chives.

to serve: Cut the tuna into 12 slices (this is done most easily with an electric knife or a very sharp long thin-bladed knife). On each of six warm dinner plates, center a scoop of potatoes, lean two slices of tuna against the potatoes, and surround with the chanterelles and sauce.

to drink: A wine with big fruit, perhaps a Sonoma Coast Pinot Noir

Truite Farcie

This is my favorite way to serve whole trout—stuffed with summer's abundant Swiss chard and tomato, spiraled in lightly smoked bacon, roasted in the oven along with small white potatoes, and drizzled with a glaze made of red wine and port. There's nothing in the dish to overpower the trout's mild, sweet flavor and fine, flaky flesh, and everything to make it exciting. The fish and potatoes can be presented on a platter, but if I've cooked them in a large copper pan, I'll serve straight from that. There's something both homey and haute about bringing the fish to the table with their heads and tails peeking out of their bacon wrap, the potatoes glistening with sage butter and ruby glaze, and the copper pan gleaming.

MAKES 4 SERVINGS

the stuffing:

2 tablespoons extra-virgin olive oil

2 cloves garlic, peeled, split, and germ removed

1½ pounds Swiss chard, stems and tough center veins removed, washed, and well dried

Salt and freshly ground white pepper

3 ounces slab bacon, cut into short, thin strips, or sliced bacon, cut crosswise into thin strips

2 slices white bread, crusts removed and cut into ¼-inch dice

2 tablespoons pine nuts

8 pieces Tomato Confit (page 350) or drained oil-packed sun-dried tomatoes, patted dry and cut into ¼-inch dice

6 leaves sage, finely chopped

1. WARM THE OLIVE OIL with the garlic in a large sauté pan or skillet over medium-high heat. When you catch a whiff of the garlic, remove and discard it, then add the chard to the pan. Season the chard with salt and pepper and cook, stirring, until the chard is tender, 3 to 4 minutes. Drain the chard and, as soon as it's cool enough for you to handle, wrap it in a kitchen towel and twist the towel to wring out as much moisture as you can from the leaves. Chop the leaves and toss them into a mixing bowl.

2. PUT A MEDIUM SAUTÉ PAN or skillet on the stove, toss in the bacon strips, and turn the heat to medium. Cook the bacon just until it renders its fat and browns lightly, then lift it out of the pan with a slotted spoon and onto several layers of paper towels to drain. Keep the pan on the heat and add the diced bread and pine nuts. Cook, stirring, until both the bread and nuts are toasted a golden brown. Add the bacon, bread, and nuts to the bowl with the Swiss chard. Stir the diced tomatoes into the bowl along with the sage and season with salt (check—it may be salty enough because of the bacon) and pepper. *(The stuffing can be made a few hours ahead, cooled, and then covered and refrigerated. Bring it to room temperature before using.)*

the glaze:

½ **cup port**
¼ **cup dry red wine**
1 **leaf sage**

PUT ALL THE INGREDIENTS in a small saucepan and bring to the boil over medium heat. Cook until the port and wine are reduced almost to a glaze. Remove the pan from the heat, strain (discard the sage leaf), and set aside. *(The glaze can be made up to a day ahead and kept covered in the refrigerator.)* Warm the glaze gently before serving.

the potatoes:

20 **small fingerling potatoes (about**
   ¾ **pound), scrubbed**
1 **shallot, peeled, trimmed, split, and rinsed**

1 **sprig thyme**
1 **sprig rosemary**

PUT ALL THE INGREDIENTS into a large pot with 2 quarts of salted cold water, bring to the boil, and boil for about 10 minutes, or until the potatoes are almost cooked. Cool the potatoes under cold running water and, when they're cool enough for you to handle, peel them. Dry the potatoes and set them aside for a moment while you ready the trout.

the trout:

Four 6- to 8-ounce trout, cleaned, boned, and
   cut open for stuffing
Salt and freshly ground white pepper
4 slices bacon (optional)
1 tablespoon extra-virgin olive oil
   (if you're not using the bacon,

you'll need another tablespoon or
   two of oil)
2 leaves sage, finely chopped
2 tablespoons unsalted butter

1. **CENTER A RACK** in the oven and preheat the oven to 350°F.
2. **OPEN ONE TROUT** on a work surface, skin side down, and season the inside with salt and pepper. Fill the trout with a quarter of the stuffing and close the fish. Wrap it in a strip of bacon, if you're using it, by spiraling the bacon around the fish from its tail to its head. Secure the bacon around the trout with kitchen twine. If you don't want to use the bacon, just tie the trout with twine. Continue until all four trout are stuffed and wrapped.

3. CHOOSE AN OVENPROOF PAN that's large enough to hold the trout as well as the potatoes and set it over medium heat. (An oval fish pan or a 12-inch ovenproof sauté pan or skillet will work well.) Warm the olive oil in the pan, then slip in the fish and potatoes. Cook, turning as needed, until the trout are almost cooked through, 8 to 10 minutes. Slide the pan into the oven and continue to cook for 4 minutes more, or until the fish are cooked through. Pull the pan from the oven and carefully transfer the trout and potatoes to a warm platter. Toss the chopped sage into the pan along with the butter and swirl until the butter melts and melds with the sage and pan juices.

to serve: The fish can be served in their pan or on warm dinner plates. In either case, cut each trout crosswise into thirds and surround with the potatoes, drizzle some of the glaze over and around the potatoes, and finish with a drizzle of the sage-butter pan juices. Serve immediately.

to drink: A lighter, traditional Chianti Rufina

Peppered Char with Shallot Compote and Parsnip Mousseline

The inspiration for this dish was the classic steak au poivre, in which coarsely cracked black peppercorns coat both sides of a steak. Sautéed and sauced, steak au poivre is often accompanied by potatoes to mellow the pepper's heat and always served with a robust red wine, the better to appreciate both the steak and its spice. With this in mind, it might be hard to imagine that delicate Arctic char—a fish whose pink flesh is reminiscent of salmon but whose flavor is more like sea trout—would prove a fine substitute for he-man beef, but it works splendidly. Peppered (not quite as heavily as you would a steak), sautéed, and served with a mousseline, a smooth parsnip-potato purée that's just a bit sweet (the parsnips do that), and a spoonful of shallots, cooked in red wine and port until they're soft and, like the mousseline, a bit sweet, the dish is winning, not as assertive as the original steak au poivre, but just as deserving of a great red wine. When you're looking for a change, you can substitute tuna for the char—it will be even more steak-like.

MAKES 4 SERVINGS

the shallots:

½ **pound shallots, peeled, trimmed, very finely sliced, and rinsed**

2 **cups dry red wine**

1 **cup ruby port**

Salt and freshly ground white pepper

PUT THE SHALLOTS, wine, and port in a saucepan that can hold them comfortably and bring to a boil over medium heat. Adjust the heat so that the wine simmers gently and cook until almost all the liquid has evaporated and the shallots are soft and jammy, about 20 to 40 minutes. Season the compote with salt and pepper and set it aside. *(The compote can be made up to a week ahead and refrigerated, covered.)* Warm the compote over gentle heat or in a microwave oven when you're ready to serve.

the mousseline:

¾ **pound parsnips, peeled, trimmed, and cut into ¾-inch pieces**

½ **pound Yukon Gold potatoes, peeled and cut into 1-inch chunks**

2 **tablespoons unsalted butter**

1 **tablespoon heavy cream**

Salt and freshly ground white pepper

1. **PUT THE PARSNIPS** and potatoes in a large saucepan with enough salted cold water to cover them by 2 inches and bring to the boil; cook until the vegetables are very tender. Drain the vegetables and

toss them back into the pan. Put the pan over medium heat and cook the vegetables another 1 to 2 minutes, shaking the pan or stirring the vegetables, just to cook off the excess moisture.

2. PURÉE THE PARSNIPS and potatoes through the fine blade of a food mill, using a potato ricer, or in a food processor. (If you're using a food processor, don't overdo it. Too much processing, and the purée will be pasty.) Transfer to the top of a double boiler and, with a wooden spoon, beat in the butter and cream. Season with salt and pepper. Keep the mousseline warm over simmering water for the few minutes it will take you to sauté the fish.

the fish:

Four 6-ounce skinless Arctic char fillets	**1 tablespoon extra-virgin olive oil**
Salt	**1 tablespoon unsalted butter**
About 1 teaspoon coarsely cracked black pepper	

SEASON THE CHAR with salt and the cracked pepper. Be generous with the pepper and use your hands to press it gently against the fish—you want it to stick to the fish during cooking. Warm the oil and butter in a large sauté pan or skillet over medium-high heat and, when the butter is bubbling, slip the fillets into the pan. Cook for about 3 minutes on a side, or until the fish is firm to the touch and still moist and rosy on the inside. If you like your fish more well done, add another 1 to 1½ minutes on a side for fish that is cooked through to an even degree of doneness—just take care not to overcook the fish, because it will dry out. Remove the pan from the heat and serve the fish immediately.

to serve: Place an equal amount of parsnip mousseline on each of four warm dinner plates. Arrange the fillets on top of the mousseline and top each with a generous spoonful of the red shallot compote.

to drink: A rich, soft red wine with good fruit and some tannic structure, such as a Saint-Joseph from the Rhône Valley

Roasted Halibut with Tapioca Broth and Creamy Endive

The greatness of this dish rests in its contradictory characteristics. It is celestially light but still has texture; it has body without bulk; and it achieves winter heartiness without heft. The fish at the center of the dish is halibut, a tender white-fleshed flatfish with a fresh, clean saltwater taste. I roast it until its skin is crisp and its meat sweet and set it on a bed of creamy endive, the only rich element in this rich-tasting composition. It's the addition of a little tapioca to the broth that creates the illusion of richness. Blended with beef broth and thyme, the tapioca turns these ingredients into a sensuous, luminescent sauce. Spooned around the halibut, the tapioca shimmers on the plate like so many minute pearls, melts instantly on the tongue, and captures and carries the broth's flavor to the halibut and endive. This is an exquisite dish for a cold-weather dinner party—and it's simple to make, because each of the elements is quick-cooking and, with the exception of the fish, can be prepared before your guests ring your doorbell.

MAKES 4 SERVINGS

the broth:

1 cup unsalted Beef Stock (page 347) or
   store-bought low-sodium beef broth
3 sprigs thyme, preferably lemon thyme

1 tablespoon instant tapioca
Salt and freshly ground white pepper

1. **BRING THE STOCK** to a boil in a small saucepan. Pull the pan from the heat, toss in the thyme, cover, and let steep for 30 minutes.

2. **STRAIN THE BROTH,** discarding the thyme, return it to the saucepan, and bring it back to the boil. Add the tapioca, cover the pan, remove it from the heat, and let it sit for 15 to 20 minutes, or until the tapioca is translucent. Season the broth with salt and pepper and set it aside until needed.

the chanterelles:

1 tablespoon unsalted butter
1 shallot, peeled, trimmed, finely chopped,
   rinsed, and dried

¾ pound chanterelles, trimmed and cleaned
   (halved or quartered if large)
Salt and freshly ground white pepper

MELT THE BUTTER in a large sauté pan or skillet over medium heat, then add the shallot and cook, stirring, until it softens but doesn't color, about 3 minutes. Toss in the chanterelles, season with salt and pepper, and cook and stir until the mushrooms are tender, 3 to 4 minutes. Set the mushrooms aside.

the endive:

2 tablespoons unsalted butter

2 medium Belgian endive, cut lengthwise in
   half, cored, and cut into very thin strips

2 medium leeks, white and light green parts
   only, split lengthwise, cut into very thin
   strips (about 1½ inches by ⅛ inch),
   washed, and dried

1 clove garlic, peeled

1 sprig thyme

Salt and freshly ground white pepper

½ cup heavy cream

MELT THE BUTTER in a large sauté pan or skillet over medium-low heat. Toss in the endive, leeks, garlic, and thyme, season with salt and pepper, and cook, stirring, until the endive and leeks are so tender they almost fall apart when stirred, 8 to 10 minutes. Add the cream and continue to cook at a simmer until the cream thickens just enough to coat the back of a spoon. Spoon out and discard the garlic and thyme, and keep the endive warm. (The endive can be gently reheated at serving time if necessary.)

the halibut:

2 tablespoons extra-virgin olive oil

2 tablespoons unsalted butter

1 clove garlic, peeled

2 sprigs thyme, preferably lemon thyme

Four 6-ounce halibut fillets, skin on

1. WARM THE OLIVE OIL in a large sauté pan or skillet over high heat. When the oil is hot, add the butter, garlic, and thyme, stir, and then slip the fillets into the pan, skin side down. Cook the fillets until they are opaque but still very moist, 2 to 3 minutes on a side.

2. WHILE THE FISH is pan-roasting, rewarm the tapioca broth, chanterelles, and, if necessary, the endive.

to serve: Divide the creamy endive evenly among four warm dinner plates. Place the halibut fillets over the endive, top with the chanterelles, and surround with the tapioca broth.

to drink: A Pinot Blanc from Oregon

Warm Seafood-Artichoke Salad

Everything about this warm salad is captivating, from its succulent seafood—shrimp, scallop, and squid—to its colorful cache of vegetables—baby artichokes, thin green beans, juicy cherry tomatoes, and a handful of arugula tossed into the pan at the last moment to warm it and intensify its peppery flavor. It's a great combination, but it's the final flourish that makes this salad unforgettable—a double dose of lemon. While the salad is still over the heat, I stir in a generous amount of lemon zest confit (thin strips of still-tart but lightly candied zest) and then, off the heat, just before I'm ready to spoon the salad onto plates, I add freshly squeezed lemon juice for a spirited finish. If you prepare the confit ahead of time, the salad is especially quick to make—quick enough for a weeknight meal.

For a change, make this an all-shrimp salad. Simply omit the scallops and squid and use 16 large shrimp.

MAKES 2 MAIN-COURSE OR 4 STARTER SERVINGS

the lemon zest confit:

3 lemons
¼ cup sugar

1. USING A VEGETABLE PEELER or small sharp knife, remove the zest from the lemons, taking care not to include any of the bitter white cottony pith. Cut the zest into very thin strands. Squeeze the juice from the lemons—you'll need ¼ cup juice for the confit and, in a separate bowl, the juice of 1 lemon for the salad. Toss the zest into a small pot of cold water (you don't need more than about a cup of water) and bring to the boil, then drain in a strainer and run the zest under cold water to cool it down. Repeat this blanching and cooling process twice more to rid the zest of some of its bitterness.

2. BRING THE ¼ CUP JUICE, the sugar, and ¼ cup water to a boil in a small saucepan and add the blanched zest. Cook, stirring occasionally, until the syrup coats the zest, 5 to 8 minutes. Spoon out the zest and set it aside on a plate; save the syrup—it's great in tea. *(The confit can be made a day ahead, cooled, and kept covered at room temperature, or packed airtight and refrigerated for up to 3 days. If you're not using the confit immediately, it's better to keep the zest in its syrup.)*

the beans:

6 ounces thin green beans, tipped and cut on
the bias into 1½-inch lengths

BRING A POT OF SALTED WATER to the boil. Cook the beans in the boiling water until they are tender, about 8 minutes, then drain them in a strainer and run them under cold water to set their color and cool them down. When cool, drain them, pat dry between paper towels, and set aside.

the seafood:

⅓ cup extra-virgin olive oil

1 sprig rosemary

3 cloves garlic, peeled and crushed

4 baby artichokes, trimmed (see Glossary, page 362) and halved

6 scallions, white part only, cut on the bias into 1-inch lengths

16 cherry tomatoes

Salt and freshly ground white pepper

8 large shrimp, peeled and deveined

8 bay scallops

8 cleaned squid (remove the tentacles, cut each body in half, and then cut a 1½-inch-long slit in the center of each piece)

The reserved lemon juice (from above)

⅓ cup Italian parsley leaves

1 bunch arugula, tough stems removed, washed, dried, and cut into very thin strands

1. WARM THE OIL and rosemary sprig in a large sauté pan or skillet over medium heat. Add the garlic and artichokes and cook, stirring, until the artichokes are tender and lightly golden, about 10 minutes. Toss the scallions into the pan and cook and stir until they're slightly softened, another 3 minutes or so, then add the cherry tomatoes. When the tomatoes just start to pop, pull the pan from the heat. Lift the vegetables out of the pan with a slotted spoon—you want to keep the oil in the pan—and transfer them to a plate. Season the vegetables with salt and pepper.

2. RETURN THE PAN to the heat, put the garlic and rosemary back in the pan, and, when the oil is once again hot, toss in the shrimp. Cook the shrimp for 1½ minutes, turn them over, and add the scallops to the pan. Give the seafood a stir, then add the squid and cook for a minute or so more, just until the squid turn opaque. Add the lemon confit, return the vegetables to the pan, along with the green beans, and give them a quick turn, just to warm them. Stir the lemon juice into the pan and season the salad with salt and pepper, then stir in the parsley and arugula. Pull the pan from the heat.

to serve: Serve the salad from the pan or divide it among dinner plates.

to drink: A tart, crisp, well-chilled Sancerre Blanc

Spring Collection Chicken

This recipe is my rite of spring—I've been making it every year for more than fifteen years, ever since John Fairchild, publisher of *Women's Wear Daily,* and his good friend Bill Blass, the clothing designer, first asked me to make them a chicken dish with big flavor. Roasted in the oven with the best of spring's bounty—porcini, tiny fingerling potatoes, artichokes, a head of garlic, and bulbs of Texas spring onions—this chicken has the depth of flavor you'd expect from a stovetop fricassee. Although the dish is simple, it takes some babying: First, the chicken roasts alone in the pan, basted early and often; next the vegetables are added in batches; and then the chicken is misted with water during the last twenty minutes of roasting to keep the skin crisp and the meat and vegetables as moist as they'd be in a fricassee. Nothing that you've got to do is hard, you've just got to be there to do it.

I hope you won't skip the little watercress salad that accompanies this chicken. It provides a peppery contrast to the sweet roasted vegetables and—best of all—its dressing is made from the chicken's liver, a delicacy that's often discarded. Mixed with some of the garlic and a spoonful of the pan juices, it's a favorite of mine.

MAKES 4 SERVINGS

One 3½-pound chicken, neck and liver
   reserved
Salt and freshly ground white pepper
3 sprigs thyme
3 sprigs sage
2 tablespoons unsalted butter
3 tablespoons (approximately) extra-virgin olive
   oil
¾ pound small fingerling potatoes, scrubbed, or
   ¾ pound small Yukon Gold potatoes,
   scrubbed and quartered
1 head garlic, separated into cloves but not
   peeled

2 medium Texas or Vidalia spring bulb onions,
   bulbs and some green only, quartered
2 globe artichoke hearts (see Glossary, page
   362), quartered and tossed with 1 teaspoon
   freshly squeezed lemon juice (optional)
½ pound porcini or other spring mushrooms,
   trimmed and cleaned (halved or quartered if
   large)
2 bunches watercress, tough stems removed,
   washed, and dried
White wine vinegar (optional)

1. **CENTER A RACK** in the oven and preheat the oven to 425°F. Place a large roasting pan in the oven and let it heat for 5 minutes. Get the chicken ready for roasting while the pan is heating.
2. **USING POULTRY SHEARS** or a cleaver, clip off the chicken wings at the second joint. Set the clippings aside with the neck—these will serve as your "roasting rack." Season the chicken inside and out

with salt and pepper. Toss the liver, a sprig of thyme, and a sprig of sage into the cavity and truss the chicken with kitchen twine. Melt 1 tablespoon of the butter and brush it over the chicken.

3. WHEN THE PAN you put in the oven is hot, pour in 1 tablespoon of the oil, tilting the pan so that the oil coats the bottom evenly. Put the neck and wing pieces in the center of the roasting pan and rest the chicken on top of them. Slide the pan into the oven and roast the chicken for 20 minutes, brushing the chicken every 5 to 10 minutes with a little more olive oil.

4. ADD THE POTATOES, garlic, and the remaining 1 tablespoon butter, thyme, and sage sprigs to the roasting pan. Stir the ingredients around to coat them well with the fat in the pan and roast for 20 minutes more, this time brushing the chicken regularly with the fat in the pan and, just as regularly, stirring the vegetables to keep them coated with fat and cooking evenly. (If the vegetables seem to be browning too fast, you can turn the heat down to 400°F, or even 375°F.)

5. AFTER ABOUT 10 MINUTES (when the chicken has been in the oven a total of 30 minutes), begin preparing the rest of the vegetables by warming a large sauté pan or skillet over high heat. Pour 1 tablespoon olive oil into the pan and toss in the onions, artichoke quarters (if you're using them), and porcini. Season the vegetables with salt and pepper and cook, stirring, until they are very hot and lightly browned, 8 to 10 minutes. Transfer the vegetables from the sauté pan to the roasting pan, stirring well to incorporate them with the vegetables already in the pan.

6. CONTINUE TO ROAST the chicken for another 20 to 30 minutes (the total roasting time is 60 to 70 minutes). During this last roasting period, continue to stir the vegetables, but don't baste the chicken. Instead, fill a plant mister with water and mist the chicken and vegetables every 10 minutes. (This will keep the vegetables moist and develop a crackly skin on the chicken.)

7. WHEN THE CHICKEN is cooked through, pull the pan from the oven and set it in a warm place. Remove the chicken liver from the cavity and pick out 5 to 8 large cloves of garlic from the pan. Push the garlic out of its skin into a mixing bowl and add the liver and a spoonful of the pan juices. With a fork, lightly mash the garlic, liver, and juices to blend. Put the watercress into a serving bowl and toss with the mashed garlic and liver, adding more of the cooking fat, salt and pepper to taste, and a splash of vinegar, if desired.

to serve: Present and carve the chicken in its roasting pan or on a platter, accompanied by the roasted vegetables, including the remaining garlic, and the watercress salad.

to drink: A rich white Mâcon wine with some oak

Honey-Glazed Chicken with Quinces and Apples

For people who love quinces—and I'm one of them—everything about them is prized, from the trees' twisty branches laden with fragrant blossoms to their fruit, smooth, greenish yellow on the outside, and pale and unyielding within. A quince in hand gives little hint of the sensuous texture it reveals when cooked. And, unlike most other fruits, quinces are only eaten when cooked. Because the slightly tart quince takes so well to braising, sautéing, and roasting, it could be a cook's good friend in the kitchen—if it weren't such a fair-weather friend: Quinces are available in the fall—and that's it. But when they are in the market, I grab them for this chicken sauté.

In terms of preparation, this is a straightforward, quickly made dish (the whole thing's done in less than forty-five minutes), but, like the quince, it keeps its charms hidden until the end. It's only in the tasting that you realize what a dynamic combination the recipe's cider vinegar and honey make: They blend for the sauce, glaze the chicken, and give the dish an aigre-doux—tart-sweet— edge that echoes the essence of the quince.

MAKES 4 SERVINGS

½ cup plus 1 tablespoon cider vinegar

1 large quince, peeled, halved, cored, and cut into 1-inch chunks

2 tablespoons extra-virgin olive oil

One 3½-pound chicken, cut into 8 pieces (see Glossary, page 365)

Salt and freshly ground white pepper

6 ounces pearl onions, peeled and trimmed

Pinch of sugar

1 cinnamon stick

1 sprig rosemary

1 Granny Smith apple, peeled, cored, and cut into 1-inch chunks

1 tablespoon honey

¼ cup unsalted Chicken Stock (page 346), store-bought low-sodium chicken broth, or water

1. **BRING 2 QUARTS** of salted water to a boil in a medium pot. Add 1 tablespoon of the cider vinegar and the quince and boil gently for 10 minutes. Drain the quince well and set aside to cool; pat dry between paper towels, if necessary.

2. **CENTER A RACK** in the oven and preheat the oven to 375°F.

3. **HEAT THE OIL** in a large ovenproof sauté pan or skillet over high heat. Season the chicken with salt and pepper and add the pieces to the pan, skin side down. Brown the chicken for 5 to 7 minutes, then turn the pieces over and brown the other sides for 5 minutes. Transfer the chicken to a plate and reserve.

4. YOU NEED ABOUT 2 TABLESPOONS of oil for the next steps, so pour off any excess from the pan. Lower the heat to medium and add the onions, sugar, cinnamon, and rosemary to the pan. Season with salt and pepper and, turning often, brown the onions evenly, 8 to 10 minutes. Return the chicken to the pan along with the quince, apples, and honey. Turn to coat the ingredients with the honey, then cook for another 8 to 10 minutes to lightly caramelize everything. Add the remaining ½ cup cider vinegar, stirring and scraping up any bits that may have stuck to the bottom of the pan.

5. SLIDE THE PAN into the oven and roast the chicken for 10 minutes. Transfer the pan to the stovetop again, turn the heat to medium, and add the chicken stock or water, bringing it just to the boil. Stir to blend.

to serve: Discard the cinnamon and rosemary and spoon out the chicken, fruit, and sauce directly from the pan at the table.

to drink: A not-at-all-sweet New York State sparkling hard cider

Warm Chicken and Spinach Salad with Shallot Jus

This sophisticated spring salad is warm and cool, soft and crisp, mild and tart, and thoroughly French. It is a mix of sweet spinach and pan-roasted chicken breasts, tender-to-the-bite baby artichokes, and a remarkable dressing—a whisked-in-the-pan blend of the chicken's savory cooking juices, chopped shallots, sherry vinegar, fresh tarragon, and basil (two herbs that complement chicken beautifully). At Café Boulud, we serve smaller portions of this as a luncheon dish, but put a basket of country bread on the table, and this salad makes a perfect one-dish family supper.

MAKES 4 SERVINGS

the chicken:

⅔ cup plus 3 tablespoons extra-virgin
   olive oil
4 bone-in chicken breasts, skin removed and
   cut into small strips
Salt and freshly ground white pepper
6 baby artichokes, trimmed (see Glossary, page
   362) and quartered
1 clove garlic, peeled and crushed
1 sprig thyme

1 tablespoon water
2 medium shallots, peeled, trimmed, finely
   diced, rinsed, and dried
¼ cup sherry vinegar
2 tablespoons finely sliced basil leaves
1 tablespoon finely chopped tarragon leaves
4 plum tomatoes, peeled, seeded, and cut into
   thin strips

1. **CENTER A RACK** in the oven and preheat the oven to 400°F.

2. **WARM 2 TABLESPOONS** of the olive oil in a large ovenproof sauté pan or skillet over medium-high heat. Season the chicken with salt and pepper and, when the oil is hot, slip the breasts, skin side (or what would have been skin side) down, into the pan. Sear the chicken on one side until golden, 3 to 4 minutes, then turn it over and give the other side equal treatment. Turn the breasts again and slide the pan into the oven. Roast the chicken until it is cooked through, about 12 to 14 minutes.

3. **MEANWHILE, WARM 1 TABLESPOON** of the olive oil in a sauté pan or skillet over medium-high heat. Add the strips of chicken skin and cook until they start to color lightly. Add the artichokes, garlic, and thyme, season with salt and pepper, cover, and cook for 3 minutes. Lift the lid and stir in the water. Cover the pan and cook for another 3 to 4 minutes, until the artichokes are tender. Discard the garlic and thyme. Pull the pan from the heat and keep warm.

4. **WHEN THE CHICKEN IS COOKED**, transfer it to a cutting board and put the pan over medium heat. Add the shallots to the pan and cook, stirring, until they soften, about 2 minutes. Pour in the vinegar and stir it around, scraping up whatever little bits of meat may have stuck to the bottom of the pan.

Cook the vinegar down by about half, then whisk in the remaining ⅔ cup olive oil and the herbs—this is the dressing for your salad. Pull the pan from the heat, season as needed with salt and pepper, and stir in the tomatoes.

to finish:

8 cups (loosely packed) baby spinach, well
**   washed and dried**
Salt and freshly ground white pepper

PUT THE SPINACH in a large bowl and season with salt and pepper.

to serve: Slice the chicken breasts on the bias and put the chicken strips, along with the artichokes and pieces of chicken skin, in the bowl with the spinach. Toss the salad with the warm chicken pan juices and serve immediately.

to drink: A flowery Viognier from California

Crisp Potato Cakes with Chicken Livers and Herb Fromage Blanc

This full-meal-on-a-plate is composed around a potato cake that is undeniably—almost uncon-scionably—good. The cakes are made from baked Yukon Gold potatoes that are coarsely crushed with a fork, blended with plenty of sweet butter and chives, and then sautéed until they are crusty on the outside but still soft and moist within. If you love potatoes as much as I do, you may think that anything would be great with these potatoes—or that these potatoes need nothing else—but when you taste the potato cakes after a bit of the vinegary jus from the shallots and chicken liv-ers has seeped into them, or when you take a forkful holding every component of the dish, includ-ing the cool salad and the herb-flecked fromage blanc *(cervelle de canut)*, I think you'll agree that this is a cold-weather dish in which each part is sublime on its own, even more sublime in concert.

You may find the method I use for cooking the potatoes unusual—they are baked on a thick bed of salt—but it's the most effective method I know for drawing out the excess moisture from the potato flesh so that it's even more receptive to the addition of butter and seasonings. After the pota-toes are baked, cool the salt and pack it away—you can use it next time you want baked potatoes.

MAKES 6 SERVINGS

the herbed cheese:

1½ cups fromage blanc (see Glossary, page 367) or fresh whole-milk ricotta

1 tablespoon finely chopped chives

1 tablespoon finely chopped Italian parsley leaves

1 teaspoon finely chopped tarragon leaves

1½ teaspoons finely chopped shallots, rinsed and dried

1 teaspoon finely chopped garlic

2 tablespoons extra-virgin olive oil

1½ teaspoons red wine vinegar

Salt and freshly ground white pepper

1. IF YOU ARE USING fromage blanc, whisk together the cheese, herbs, shallots, garlic, olive oil, and vinegar in a bowl and season with salt and pepper. If you are using ricotta cheese, you'll have to drain it: Put the ricotta in a cheesecloth-lined sieve set over a bowl. Draw up the ends of the cheesecloth and squeeze the cloth to extract some of the liquid from the ricotta. Put the ricotta, still wrapped in cheese-cloth, back in the sieve, put the sieve and bowl in the refrigerator, and allow the ricotta to drain for 2 hours. When you are ready to make the herbed cheese, put the ricotta in the work bowl of a food proces-sor and process until the cheese is smooth, about 30 seconds. Add the remaining ingredients to the processor and pulse just to blend, taking care not to process the mixture too much.

2. NO MATTER WHICH CHEESE you use, the mixture should be chilled, covered, until needed. *(This can be made several hours ahead and kept covered in the refrigerator.)* If the mixture seems a little thick for your taste, you can thin it with a touch of milk.

the potato cakes:

Coarse sea salt or kosher salt

2 pounds Yukon Gold potatoes, washed and dried

7 tablespoons unsalted butter, at room
    temperature

Salt and freshly ground white pepper

1 teaspoon chopped chives

1. PREHEAT THE OVEN to 400°F. Spread an even layer, about ¼ inch thick, of coarse salt in the bottom of an ovenproof skillet or a baking pan large enough to hold the potatoes.

2. SPRINKLE THE POTATOES generously with coarse salt and arrange them in the pan. Slide the pan into the oven and roast for 70 minutes, or until the potatoes give easily when pierced with a knife. Remove the potatoes from the pan and let them cool for about 5 minutes.

3. WHILE THE POTATOES are cooling, arrange six doubled squares of foil (each about 6 to 8 inches on a side) on a baking sheet. Butter 6 ring molds, each 3 inches across and ¾ inch high, and place one on each square of foil. (If you don't have ring molds, you can use well-scrubbed tuna cans with both ends removed.)

3. TO GET THE BEST TEXTURE from the potatoes, you must work with them while they're hot. Peel the potatoes and place them in a bowl. Using a fork, crush the potatoes with 6 tablespoons of the butter. Season with salt and pepper and stir in the chopped chives. Spoon the potatoes into the molds, mounding them a little on the top.

4. PLACE A LARGE SAUTÉ PAN or skillet over medium heat and add the remaining 1 tablespoon butter. When the butter is melted and hot, turn the potato cakes into the pan, using the foil squares to lift the cakes to the pan and then to flip them over into the butter. Cook the cakes, still in their molds, on both sides just until golden, 3 to 5 minutes on a side. Return the cakes to the foil squares on the baking sheet and remove the ring molds. *(The potatoes can be made ahead to this point and left at room temperature for an hour or so; reheat in a 350°F oven for about 10 minutes.)*

the chicken livers:

1½ pounds chicken livers, trimmed and cut in
   half
Salt and freshly ground white pepper
5 tablespoons unsalted butter

½ cup finely chopped shallots, rinsed and dried
2 tablespoons sherry vinegar
2 tablespoons dry red wine

PAT THE CHICKEN LIVERS dry between paper towels and season them with salt and pepper. Melt 1 tablespoon of the butter in a large sauté pan or skillet over high heat. When the butter is hot, add the livers. Cook for about 2 minutes on one side, then turn the livers over, add the shallots, and cook for another 2 minutes. Add the vinegar and wine and boil for 1 minute. Lift the pan off the heat and lower the heat, then start adding the remaining 4 tablespoons butter to the pan a little at a time, swirling the pan as you work and moving it on and off the heat as needed, just until the butter is creamy. You don't want the heat to be so high that the butter melts completely, because then the sauce will separate. Pull the pan from the heat as soon as you've added all the butter.

to finish:

Salad greens
Salt and freshly ground white pepper

Extra-virgin olive oil
Sherry vinegar

SEASON THE SALAD GREENS with salt and pepper and dress with a little oil and vinegar.

to serve: For each serving, place a hot, crisp potato cake at the top of the plate, a spoonful of fromage blanc in the center, and some chicken livers at the bottom half of the plate. Drizzle the chicken livers with the pan sauce, put a small mound of salad on each plate, and serve immediately.

to drink: A light, fruity, easy-to-drink wine like a Saumur-Champigny

Chestnut-Crusted Loin of Venison

The days when a venison loin roast could be enjoyed only by those who hunted or knew hunters are gone. With premium-quality ranched and farmed venison available in neighborhood markets and through mail order, venison's virtues can now be explored by everyone. I count among venison's sterling qualities the fact that the meat is extremely lean, quick-cooking (a loin roasts in under fifteen minutes), full flavored, and easygoing—it pairs happily with nuts, spices, and herbs. And these are the qualities that are played to advantage in this dish, one of my favorites, in which I marinate the venison in an herb and spice mixture, roll it in blanched chestnuts—the "über nut" of autumn—brown it stovetop, and then roast it and serve it with a sweet-savory sauce based on vinegar, wine, and beef stock. At the Café, I serve the venison with spiced braised rutabaga, a novel way to prepare this underrated root vegetable.

A word on timing: The chestnuts for the crust need to dry overnight and the venison needs to marinate for at least four hours (overnight would be better), so plan ahead.

MAKES 6 SERVINGS

the crust:

¾ pound peeled fresh chestnuts (from about
    1¼ pounds in the shell; see Glossary, page
    365) or dry-packed bottled or vacuum-
    sealed peeled chestnuts

1. BREAK EACH CHESTNUT into a few pieces and spread the pieces out on a baking sheet. Allow the pieces to dry overnight in a warm place—inside an oven with a pilot light is perfect.

2. THE NEXT DAY, place the chestnuts in the work bowl of a food processor and pulse until they break into ¼-inch chunks. Sift the chestnuts, reserving the larger pieces that remain in the sieve, and discarding the powder or saving it for another use. Transfer these pieces to a plate and keep close at hand.

the marinade and venison:

1 teaspoon grated orange zest
½ cup freshly squeezed orange juice
2 tablespoons extra-virgin olive oil
1 teaspoon ground cinnamon
¼ teaspoon ground star anise
¼ teaspoon black peppercorns

Pinch of freshly grated nutmeg
2 cloves garlic, peeled and crushed
1 sprig thyme
Two 1½-pound venison loins, trimmed (see
    Source Guide, page 385)

MIX ALL THE MARINADE ingredients together in a shallow pan, then roll the venison around in the marinade to coat. Cover the pan tightly with plastic wrap and refrigerate for at least 4 hours, or, preferably overnight, turning the meat a few times during this period.

the rutabaga:

Zest from ½ orange (pith removed), cut into
very thin strands
2 tablespoons extra-virgin olive oil
1 large rutabaga, peeled and cut into
½-inch cubes
Large pinch of ground cinnamon
Small pinch of freshly grated nutmeg

Small pinch of ground star anise
1 clove garlic, peeled
1 sprig thyme
Salt and freshly ground pepper
1 cup unsalted Chicken Stock (page 346) or
store-bought low-sodium chicken broth

1. PUT THE ORANGE ZEST in a small pot of water and bring to the boil. Boil for 2 minutes; drain and set aside.

2. WARM THE OLIVE OIL in a large sauté pan or skillet over medium heat. Add the rutabaga, spices, garlic, thyme, and salt and pepper to taste and cook, stirring, for 5 minutes, without letting the rutabaga color. Add the chicken stock, bring to the boil, cover the pan, and lower the heat to keep the liquid at a simmer. Braise the rutabaga for 15 minutes, or until it can be pierced easily with the tip of a knife.

3. REMOVE THE COVER and cook the rutabaga, stirring and turning it gently, until it is glazed and the liquid in the pan has evaporated; discard the garlic and thyme. Just before serving, rewarm the rutabaga if necessary, stir in the orange zest. *(The rutabaga can be made several hours ahead, cooled, and kept covered in the refrigerator. Warm over gentle heat before serving; stir in the zest at serving time.)*

to cook the venison:

Salt and freshly ground white pepper
2 large eggs
1 large egg yolk

Flour for dredging
The dried chestnuts (from above)
¼ cup extra-virgin olive oil

1. CENTER A RACK in the oven and preheat the oven to 425°F.

2. REMOVE THE VENISON from the marinade and discard the marinade. Pat the meat dry with paper towels and season with salt and pepper. In a pan or dish large enough to accommodate the venison loins, beat together the eggs and yolk. Dust one side of each loin with flour, shake off the excess, and dip that side into the egg mixture and then into the chestnuts.

3. HEAT THE OLIVE OIL in a roasting pan over medium heat. When the oil is hot, add the venison, chestnut side down, and cook for about 2 minutes. Turn the loins over and place the roasting pan in the oven. Roast the venison for 10 to 12 minutes, until medium-rare. Pull the pan from the oven and transfer the loins to a warm platter. Set aside in a warm place while you make the sauce.

the sauce:

1 small shallot, peeled, trimmed, finely
   chopped, rinsed, and dried
2 teaspoons coarsely crushed black pepper
1 teaspoon grated orange zest
4 teaspoons balsamic vinegar
1 cup dry red wine

1 teaspoon sugar
1½ cups unsalted Beef Stock (page 347)
   or store-bought low-sodium beef broth
Salt and freshly ground white pepper
2 teaspoons unsalted butter

REMOVE AS MUCH FAT from the liquid in the roasting pan as possible and place the pan over medium heat. Add the shallot and cook, stirring, just until translucent. Add the pepper and orange zest, sauté for a minute more, and then deglaze the pan with the balsamic vinegar, cooking and stirring until the vinegar just about evaporates. Add the red wine and cook down again until the pan is almost dry. Add the sugar and beef stock and cook at a boil until the liquid is reduced by half. Taste and add salt and pepper as needed. Remove the pan from the heat, swirl, and strain the butter into the sauce.

to serve: Slice the loins into 12 to 16 slices and arrange them attractively on a platter. Moisten with the sauce and serve with the spiced rutabaga.

to drink: The oldest Rioja you can find

Braised Beef Brisket with Whole Turnips and Onions

It doesn't seem to make any difference to whom I mention this dish, the response is always the same: "My grandmother used to make that." No matter if grandma was from Romania, Russia, Rhode Island, or Roanne in Burgundy, braised brisket and glazed vegetables seems to have been her specialty and the memory of this dish brings a smile to every grandchild's face. I don't know whether or not this is the way your grandmother made brisket, but it's a way I like. I marinate the brisket for a day in a base of white wine and brown sugar, the start of a sweet-sour construction. Then, when I'm ready to cook the meat, I sear it on all sides, encouraging the sugar to caramelize and create a protective crust. When it's browned and burnished, I tuck the brisket into the oven to braise slowly and develop even deeper flavors. The final touch is a double shot of apple cider and cider vinegar, pungent ingredients that, because they are added at the last minute, retain their punch and enliven the entire dish. This is a brisket any grandmother would be proud to call her own.

MAKES 6 SERVINGS

One 2-pound first-cut beef brisket
¼ cup (packed) light brown sugar
1 cup dry white wine
5 cloves garlic, peeled and crushed
2 sprigs thyme
2 bay leaves, broken in half
Salt and freshly ground white pepper
2 tablespoons extra-virgin olive oil

5 cups unsalted Beef Stock (page 347) or store-bought low-sodium beef broth
18 small to medium turnips, peeled and trimmed
18 small Texas or Vidalia spring bulb onions, bulbs and some green only
½ cup apple cider
¼ cup cider vinegar

1. PLACE THE BRISKET in a shallow baking pan or refrigerator container that will hold it snugly. Mix together the brown sugar, wine, garlic, thyme, and bay leaves and pour this mixture over the beef. Cover the pan with plastic wrap and marinate in the refrigerator for 24 hours, turning the meat at least once during this period.

2. CENTER A RACK in the oven and preheat the oven to 325°F.

3. REMOVE THE BRISKET and scrape off the garlic and herbs—reserve these as well as the marinade. Pat the meat dry and season it all over with salt and pepper. Warm the olive oil in a small roasting pan (or use a Dutch oven) over medium-high heat. Slip the meat into the pan and brown it evenly, turning it carefully as needed, for 15 to 20 minutes, until all surfaces of the meat are caramel brown. Add the set-aside marinade, garlic, and herbs, bring the liquid to the boil, and then pour in the beef stock. When the stock comes to the boil, cover the pan (you can make a cover with foil if your roasting pan doesn't have one), slide the pan into the oven, and braise for 2 hours.

4. REMOVE THE COVER, add the turnips and onions, and continue to braise, uncovered, for 2 hours more, basting regularly—the vegetables will be fork-tender.

5. CAREFULLY TRANSFER THE BRISKET to a large heated serving platter, spoon the vegetables around the meat, cover loosely, and keep warm while you make the sauce. Skim the fat off the pan juices and put the roasting pan over medium heat. Add the cider and cider vinegar, bring to the boil, and cook until the sauce is reduced enough to coat the back of a spoon. Taste and season as needed with salt and pepper.

to serve: Strain the sauce over the meat and vegetables and serve immediately, cutting the meat on the bias into long thin slices.

to drink: A slightly sweet Primitivo from southern Italy

Lamb Chops with Lemon-Pignoli Crust

Here's a party dish that offers big flavors for little effort. The excitement is in the crust, a blend of spiced lemon, fresh herbs, and rich, buttery toasted pine nuts, pignoli. The lemon confit, more tart, salty, and spicy than the word *confit* would lead you to believe, can be cooked ahead, in which case you'll have just minutes of work to do before you roast the chops briefly, coat them with their crust, and run them under the broiler. This dish is ambrosial paired with oven-roasted vegetables (page 316), a casserole that reverberates with the flavors that make this lamb so seductive—lemon, basil, and garlic.

MAKES 4 SERVINGS

the confit:

1 tablespoon sugar
¾ teaspoon salt
Spice sachet (3 coriander seeds, 2 fennel seeds,
   1 clove, 1 point star anise, ½ bay leaf, and
   ¼ cinnamon stick, tied in cheesecloth)

1 small lemon, preferably a Meyer lemon

1. **POUR 3 CUPS** of water into a small saucepan, add the sugar, salt, and sachet, and bring to the boil. Make four lengthwise incisions in the lemon and add the whole lemon to the pan. Lower the heat and simmer for 1 hour, until the lemon is extremely soft.

2. **WHEN THE LEMON** is cool enough for you to handle, drain, dry it well, and slice away the peel, taking care not to include any of the fruit. Finely chop the peel and discard the fruit.

the crust:

2½ tablespoons pine nuts, toasted and cooled
¼ cup (loosely packed) Italian parsley leaves
Salt and freshly ground white pepper
¼ cup fresh bread crumbs
3 tablespoons cold unsalted butter, cut into
   ½-inch cubes

1 small clove garlic, peeled, split, germ
   removed, and coarsely chopped
The confit

PUT THE PINE NUTS, parsley, basil, and salt and pepper to taste in the work bowl of a food processor and pulse on and off until the nuts and herbs are finely chopped. One by one, pulsing after each addition, add the bread crumbs, butter, garlic, and confit. Continue to process until the mixture is smooth. Scrape the mixture out of the bowl onto a piece of plastic wrap, and use the plastic to help you shape the mixture into a short log about 1½ inches in diameter; chill until firm.

the lamb:

2 tablespoons extra-virgin olive oil
Eight 3-ounce lamb rib chops, cut
   1 inch thick, fat trimmed and bone
   cut to 2 inches
Salt and freshly ground white pepper

1. PREHEAT THE BROILER. Slice the chilled crust mixture into 8 rounds.

2. WARM THE OLIVE OIL in a large ovenproof sauté pan or skillet over high heat. Season the lamb on both sides with salt and pepper and slip the meat into the pan. Brown the meat on both sides, cooking it for a total of about 4 minutes if you like your lamb medium-rare, longer if you prefer lamb that is more well done.

3. COVER EACH CHOP with a piece of the crust mixture, then run the lamb under the broiler for about 2 minutes, or until the crust is golden brown.

to serve: Serve the lamb with its buttery crust on warm dinner plates along with a generous helping of the oven-roasted vegetable casserole, if you've made it.

to drink: A simple Dolcetto d'Alba, a light, fruity red wine

Desserts

Rhubarb Napoleon with Orange Flower Cream

Rhubarb appears in the market twice a year—once in late winter, usually in February and March, and once in late summer, in August and September—and when there's rhubarb in the market, there's rhubarb in various guises on my menu. I admire rhubarb for its versatility—bitter and stringy when raw, when poached, it softens, retains a judicious amount of its acidity, and allows itself to take on a measure of whatever flavors you offer it. For this dessert, which celebrates rhubarb's arrival in winter, the rhubarb is poached in a sweet grenadine syrup so that it turns bright red and becomes only just sweet enough to make an appearance as dessert. The poached fruit is spooned onto a cushion of whipped cream–lightened pastry cream, flavored with elusively fragrant orange flower water, and layered napoleon-like between spiced tuiles, French cookies of such flavor and delicacy that we often find ourselves short of them when it comes time to assemble dessert—it's impossible to keep snackers from nibbling their way through our tuile supply.

The word *tuile* means tile in French, and the classic French tuile is a thin round cookie that is removed from its baking sheet and instantly molded over a rolling pin or wine bottle so that it takes on the curved shape of French roof tiles. Not these. These tuiles are thinner than the norm (so thin you probably could read a newspaper through them), lightly spiced, and untuile-like in appearance—not only are they uncurved, they are rectangular.

MAKES 6 SERVINGS

the tuiles:

¾ cup confectioner's sugar, sifted

¼ cup plus 1 tablespoon all-purpose flour

¼ teaspoon ground cinnamon

Pinch of freshly grated nutmeg

Pinch of ground star anise

2 large egg whites

4 tablespoons unsalted butter, melted

1. WHISK THE DRY INGREDIENTS together in a medium bowl just to combine. Whisk in the egg whites, followed by the melted butter, whisking to create a smooth but not airy batter. Press a piece of plastic wrap against the batter's surface and refrigerate for at least 1 hour. *(The batter can be kept tightly covered in the refrigerator for up to 2 days.)*

2. CENTER A RACK in the oven and preheat the oven to 300°F.

3. WORKING ON A NONSTICK baking sheet with a small offset spatula, spread out a very thin layer of batter to make a rectangle that's about 5 inches long by 2 inches wide. Fill the baking sheet with tuiles and then, if you need more, work on another sheet. (You'll need 24 to 30 to make 6 napoleons, but it's best to make extra, since they're fragile and it's inevitable that a couple will break or that even more will be nibbled before dessert.) Bake the tuiles for 10 to 12 minutes, or until they turn a light golden brown. Because the tuiles are so thin and ovens so often uneven, some tuiles may finish baking before others. To avoid burning the fast-bakers, remove them from the baking sheet as soon as they're properly baked. Lift the tuiles off the baking sheet using a plastic dough scraper or a thin offset spatula and invert them onto a flat surface—marble is ideal, the back of a baking sheet fine too. If there are still tuiles on the baking sheet, return the sheet to the oven to finish the batch. Continue until you've made as many tuiles as you need. When the tuiles are cool—they cool quickly—store them in an airtight container with sheets of parchment or waxed paper between the layers. *(If it's not too humid, you can make the tuiles a day in advance and keep them in the airtight container at room temperature.)*

the rhubarb:

4 cups water
1 cup sugar

1 cup grenadine
1 pound rhubarb, trimmed and peeled

1. BRING THE WATER, sugar, and grenadine to the boil in a large pot. While the water is coming to the boil, cut each stalk of rhubarb lengthwise into 3 pieces, then cut each piece into 2-inch-long segments.

2. WHEN THE LIQUID is at the boil, toss in the rhubarb, bring the syrup back to the boil, lower the heat, and simmer for just 1 to 2 minutes more, until the rhubarb is barely tender. Pull the pot from the heat and allow the rhubarb to cool to room temperature in the syrup. *(The rhubarb can be made 1 day in advance and kept in its syrup covered in the refrigerator. Bring to room temperature before using.)*

the cream:

½ recipe Vanilla Pastry Cream (page 357)
1 teaspoon orange flower water
½ cup heavy cream, whipped to soft peaks

TURN THE PASTRY CREAM into a medium bowl and whisk it to bring it back to its original smoothness. Whisk in the orange flower water. Switch to a rubber spatula and fold in the lightly whipped cream.

to serve: For each portion, place one tuile in the center of a dessert plate. Spoon a dollop of the orange flower cream into the center of the tuile. Gently press some pieces of rhubarb into the cream and top with another tuile. Repeat this layering twice more so that, in total, you'll have three layers of cream and rhubarb and four tuiles. (If you want a taller tower, you can repeat the layering three times.) This napoleon won't have the precision of a puff pastry napoleon, and that's just fine. Serve immediately.

to drink: A sparkling wine with a drop of the rhubarb's grenadine poaching syrup stirred into it

Crunchy Apricot Tart

If you take as much pleasure in the sweet-pungent flavor of summer's ripe, aromatic apricots as I do, then you're bound to appreciate this tart. It is simple to the point of plain and it is its plainness that makes it so special. The tart's other elements—its almond crust, the couple of spoonfuls of almond cream spread across the crust, and the crackly royal icing half-moons that top it—are supporting players to the apricot compote; they're there to accentuate the compote's natural goodness. It just about goes without saying that for this tart to succeed, the apricots must be impeccable: If their aroma almost knocks you out, you know you've got the right fruit. If you can't find perfectly ripe apricots, take heart—this recipe is lovely made with ripe red plums.

The recipe for the compote produces more than you'll need for this tart, but extras will become a treat. For starters, think of spreading the compote over toast for breakfast, serving it with cookies at tea time, or using it as a topping for vanilla ice cream.

MAKES 8 SERVINGS

the crust:

**1 fully baked 8- by ¾-inch tart shell (in a tart
ring) made from Pâte Sublime (page 355),
cooled to room temperature**

LEAVE THE COOLED CRUST, with the tart ring still in place, on the parchment-lined baking sheet. *(You can make the crust up to 8 hours ahead and keep it in its ring at room temperature.)*

the compote:

½ moist, plump vanilla bean
**2 pounds ripe fragrant apricots (or ripe red
plums), halved and pitted**
¼ cup sugar

1. CUT THE VANILLA BEAN lengthwise in half and, using the back of the knife, scrape the pulp out of the pod. Put the pod and pulp along with the apricots and sugar in a saucepan over low heat and stir to combine. When the apricots begin to give up some of their juice, increase the heat to medium-low and cook, stirring often, for 30 to 35 minutes, or until the fruit is so soft that it falls apart. Pull the pan from the heat.

2. LINE A BAKING PAN or a plate with a sheet of plastic wrap and spread the apricot compote over the plastic in a thin layer. Top with another piece of plastic wrap, pressing the wrap against the apricot compote to create an airtight seal. Chill in the refrigerator; when the compote is cool, remove the vanilla bean. *(Packed airtight, the compote will keep about 1 week in the refrigerator.)*

the topping:

1 large egg white
1 cup plus 3 tablespoons confectioner's sugar,
   sifted

1. POSITION THE RACKS to divide the oven into thirds and preheat the oven to 250°F. Line two baking sheets with parchment paper and set them aside for the moment. Make a template so that you'll be able to shape the topping into half-moons of a consistent size. To create a template that's ⅛ inch thick— the thickness that's ideal—you'll need to make two templates from large plastic tops, the type that comes with yogurt or ice cream, and tape them together. Cut out a semicircle 2½ inches long and 1¼ inches wide from each top, leaving the rims intact, then tape the templates together.

2. BEAT THE EGG WHITE (either in a standing mixer fitted with the whisk attachment or with a handheld mixer) on low speed until it is broken up and foamy. Increase the speed to medium-high and whip to soft peaks. Gradually add the confectioner's sugar and continue to whip until the egg white holds very firm, marshmallowy peaks but is still glossy—this is the royal icing.

3. SECURE THE PARCHMENT paper onto the baking sheets by dabbing a drop of the icing in each corner. To make the half-moons, lay the template flat against the parchment and, using a small offset metal spatula, spread a thin layer of the royal icing over the template; lift the template off and, if necessary, wipe it clean before making the next half-moon. Make as many half-moons as you can with the icing, since, once baked, they'll be fragile and it's inevitable that you'll break a few.

4. SLIDE THE BAKING SHEETS into the oven and bake for 45 minutes to 1 hour, or until the half-moons are crisp, dry, and barely colored. Cool the half-moons—still on the parchment paper—to room temperature, then carefully peel away the paper. *(The half-moons can be stored for a day or two in an airtight container if kept in a cool, dry place. If you live in a humid climate, however, the half-moons will have to be used right away.)*

to assemble:

¼ **cup Almond Cream (page 359)**

1. **CENTER A RACK** in the oven and preheat the oven to 400°F.

2. **SPREAD THE ALMOND CREAM** evenly over the bottom of the baked tart shell (which should still be on its parchment-lined baking sheet). Slide the sheet into the oven to bake the almond cream for 3 to 5 minutes, until it puffs and browns lightly. Cool to room temperature.

3. **JUST BEFORE SERVING,** spoon the apricot compote into the tart shell, gently spreading it evenly over the almond cream. Starting at the outside edge of the tart, position the half-moons—each over-lapping half of its preceding neighbor—to form a circle on top of the compote. Repeat, forming a second circle in the center and completely covering the compote.

to serve: The easiest way to serve this tart is to present it to your guests and then bring it back to the kitchen to slice—the royal icing half-moons can be tricky. Lift up a few of the half-moons to make way for your knife, make a cut, replace the half-moons, and continue in this way until you've cut 8 wedges. Serve immediately.

to drink: A Barsac—its flavors match those in the tart

Pear and Quince Tart

This tart brings together two of fall's most fragrant fruits: pears and quinces. While quinces are treasured for their perfume and sought after for their gelling qualities—the word *marmalade* comes from the Portuguese word for quince—quinces are also just plain delicious, especially when poached, as they are here, with sugar and spice. Once their seemingly unyielding fruit is softened, quinces acquire an irresistibly soft and slidey consistency that plays perfectly with the poached pears and crunchy sweet almond crust. The crust, really an almond streusel that resembles a nut cookie, is very easy to make: It's a no-roller—you just pat it into the tart ring.

MAKES 8 SERVINGS

for the crust:

1 cup slivered or sliced blanched almonds
½ cup sugar
¾ cup all-purpose flour
8 tablespoons (1 stick) unsalted butter,
**   at room temperature**

1. PUT THE ALMONDS and 3 tablespoons of the sugar into the work bowl of a food processor fitted with the metal blade. Pulse and process until the almonds are as finely ground as possible. Take care not to overprocess the almonds and have them turn into almond butter—what you're after is almond powder, or flour. Turn the mixture into a bowl and whisk it together with the all-purpose flour.
2. PUT THE BUTTER and the remaining 5 tablespoons sugar in the bowl of a mixer fitted with the paddle attachment. (Alternatively, you can work in a bowl with a large rubber spatula.) Beat on medium speed until the mixture is light and fluffy, about 2 minutes. Set the mixer speed to low, add the flour mixture, and mix just until the dough looks as if it's ready to form a ball—don't overmix it. Remove the dough, press it gently into a disk, and wrap it in plastic wrap; chill for at least 1 hour. *(The dough can be kept refrigerated for up to 3 days.)*
3. LINE A BAKING SHEET with parchment paper and set a buttered 9- by ¾-inch tart ring on the sheet. (The tart can also be constructed in a 9½-inch fluted metal tart pan with a removable bottom.) Pinch off small pieces of the dough and pat the pieces evenly over the parchment paper bottom and up the sides of the ring. Chill the dough while you preheat the oven.
4. CENTER A RACK in the oven and preheat the oven to 350°F.
5. BAKE THE TART SHELL just until it is golden brown, 15 to 20 minutes. Transfer it to a rack to cool to room temperature.

the fruit:

½ **moist, plump vanilla bean**

1 cup sugar

3 tablespoons freshly squeezed lemon juice

1 cinnamon stick

1 whole star anise

3 ripe Comice pears

1 quince

1. CUT THE VANILLA BEAN lengthwise in half and, using the back of the knife, scrape the pulp out of the pod. Put the pulp and pod, sugar, lemon juice, and spices into a large pot with 1 quart water and bring to the boil. Lower the heat to keep the liquid at a simmer, peel the pears (you don't want to do this earlier—they'll darken), and add them to the pot. Cook the pears at a gentle simmer just until they can be pierced with the tip of a knife, 30 to 40 minutes. Remove the pot from the heat and allow the pears to cool in the poaching liquid.

2. WHEN THEY ARE COOL, remove the pears with a slotted spoon and set them aside, covered. Bring the liquid back to the boil while you peel, quarter, and core the quince. Reduce the heat so that the poaching liquid is at a simmer, add the quince, and cook until it too is soft, 50 to 60 minutes. Cool the quince in the liquid. (*The fruits can be used now or packed in their poaching syrup for storage; they'll keep for 3 days under refrigeration. Drain the fruit before using.*)

to finish:

½ **cup sugar**

TO ASSEMBLE THE TART, chop the cooled and drained quince so that it resembles a chunky applesauce. Spread the chopped quince evenly over the bottom of the tart shell. Carefully halve and core the pears and thinly slice them lengthwise. Arrange the pears in a decorative pattern over the quince—concentric circles of slightly overlapping slices are nice here. Sprinkle the sugar over the pears and caramelize the top with a propane torch, or run it under the broiler. If you're using the broiler method, cover the edges of the tart with aluminum foil to keep them from burning and keep a close watch on the tart's progress—once the sugar melts, the process goes very quickly.

to serve: Remove the tart ring (or take the tart out of its pan) and, if possible, serve immediately, cutting the tart into 8 wedges. (It's best as soon as it's made, and should be eaten the same day.) The tart, delicious unaccompanied, can be served with lightly whipped cream, sweetened or not.

to drink: A German ice wine

Light Vanilla Cakes with Quick Berry Marmalade

These little cakes, so delicious and so much in demand at Café Boulud, look as if they could be in a French pastry shop window. Actually, they were inspired by a cake I'd never eaten until I came to America—angel food cake. Of course, I couldn't resist tinkering with the recipe, adding some melted butter (almost turning the batter into a French-American creation, an egg-white génoise) and miniaturizing the cake—but the spirit remains the same: A soft, airy sponge cake with a melt-on-the-tongue evanescence, a warm vanilla flavor, and a welcoming personality—it takes to berry marmalade as happily as toast takes to butter.

The recipe for the summer-berry marmalade will make more than you'll need for the vanilla cakes, but it keeps well and is scrumptious stirred into yogurt or spread on toast. And when the season for berry marmalade is over, or you're in the mood for a variation, serve the cakes with some of the oranges from the Orange Salad (page 333), Vanilla Blueberries (page 340), any of my other marmalades, such as apple-quince (page 336) or kumquat (page 249), or even a puff of chicory cream (page 330).

MAKES 8 SERVINGS

the marmalade:

1¼ cups strawberries, hulled

1 cup raspberries

¼ cup blackberries, halved

¼ cup blueberries, halved

¼ cup sugar

½ teaspoon powdered pectin

Grated zest and juice of ¼ lime

½ moist, plump vanilla bean

1. DICE ¼ CUP of the strawberries. Cut ¼ cup of the raspberries in half. Gently mix these berries with the blackberries and blueberries, and set aside.

2. SLICE EACH OF THE REMAINING strawberries into 8 to 12 pieces, depending on their size, and toss the slices along with the remaining ¾ cup raspberries, the sugar, pectin, and lime zest and juice into a medium saucepan. Cut the vanilla bean lengthwise in half and, using the back of the knife, scrape the pulp out of the pod; toss the pulp and the pod into the pot. Gently stir, then set aside for 5 minutes.

3. PLACE THE SAUCEPAN over low heat and cook, stirring occasionally and always gently, just until the berries begin to render their juices, about 5 minutes. Increase the heat to medium and continue to cook and stir until the raspberries lose their shape and the strawberry slices are soft but still intact, about 8 minutes. Turn the marmalade into a bowl, press a piece of plastic wrap against the surface to create an airtight seal, and cool to room temperature.

4. WHEN THE MARMALADE IS COOL, remove and discard the vanilla bean and fold in the reserved fresh berries. (*The marmalade can be made up to 2 days in advance and kept in an airtight container in the refrigerator. Use it at room temperature or slightly chilled.*)

the cakes:

½ **cup all-purpose flour**

¼ **teaspoon baking powder**

5 large egg whites, at room temperature

Pulp scraped from ½ **moist, plump vanilla bean**
    (scraped as above; reserve the pod for
    another use, if desired)

½ **cup sugar**

5½ **tablespoons unsalted butter, melted and**
    cooled

1. **CENTER A RACK** in the oven and preheat the oven to 350°F. Butter the insides of six 2½- by 1½-inch-high ring molds, 4-ounce disposable aluminum cups, or 4-ounce muffin tins, dust them with flour, and tap out the excess. Place the molds or cups on a baking sheet (line the sheet with parchment if you're using the ring molds) and keep close at hand.

2. **SIFT THE FLOUR** and baking powder together and reserve.

3. **PUT THE EGG WHITES** and vanilla bean pulp in the bowl of a mixer fitted with the whisk attachment. Beat the whites on low speed until they are broken up and foamy. Increase the speed to medium-high and continue to whip until the whites form soft peaks. Gradually add the sugar and whip until the whites form firm, glossy peaks.

4. **SPOON OUT A LITTLE** of the whipped whites into a small bowl and fold the butter into the whites; reserve. Using a large flexible rubber spatula, fold the flour into the whites in two to three additions. When the flour is incorporated, fold in the egg white and butter mixture. Immediately spoon the batter into the prepared molds.

5. **SLIDE THE BAKING SHEET** into the oven and bake for 8 to 10 minutes, or until a knife plunged into the center of the cakes comes out clean. The cakes should be golden brown and springy to the touch, and they should pull away just a bit from the sides of the molds. Lift off the ring molds, or unmold the cakes, and transfer them to a rack to cool to room temperature.

to serve: For each portion, spoon a circle of marmalade onto the center of a dinner plate. Place a cake on top of the marmalade, then, with a spoon, gently form a shallow hollow in the center of the cake and fill with marmalade.

to drink: A light, sparkling Moscato d'Asti

Ruby Grapefruit with Pomegranate Sabayon

The quality that I love in grapefruit—its bracing tartness—is the same quality that makes grape-fruit difficult to serve as a dessert in anything but a fruit salad. But, because there are so many times when grapefruit's cool appeal is what you want after a meal, I set myself the challenge of creating a grapefruit dessert in which the fruit's refreshing qualities would be evident but not over-powering. Success came when I topped Ruby Reds, a tangy but sweet grapefruit, with sabayon, an ethereally light, moussy mixture of warm beaten egg yolks, sugar, and a spoonful of white wine. The sabayon was the perfect foil for the grapefruit's acidity and it brought its own almost imper-ceptible but much appreciated richness to the table. Of course, it didn't hurt that I macerated the grapefruits in sweet-tart pomegranate juice and added a generous amount of grated ginger to both the fruit and the sabayon—which turned out to be the best way to keep the dessert refreshing, brightly flavored, and still sweet and satisfying.

Pomegranates and Ruby Reds are plentiful in winter, but if, when you want to make this dessert, your market is offering only yellow- or pink-fleshed grapefruits, forge ahead. You'll lose a touch of sweetness, but you'll still have an excellent dessert.

MAKES 4 SERVINGS

the grapefruit:

4 large Ruby Red grapefruit
2 cups pomegranate juice (available at Middle Eastern markets) or about 5 pomegranates, peeled, seeds removed from membranes and reserved

½ cup sugar
2 teaspoons (packed) freshly grated peeled ginger

1. WITH A KNIFE, cut away the skin of the grapefruits, removing every trace of white cottony pith and exposing the moist, glistening fruit. Then cut between the membranes to release the grapefruit seg-ments. Reserve the segments and discard the rest. Remove the seeds from the grapefruit sections.

2. IF YOU ARE NOT USING ready-made pomegranate juice, place the pomegranate seeds in the con-tainer of a blender or food processor and process, scraping down the sides of the container as needed, until the seeds are broken down and have yielded their juice. Strain, discarding whatever solids remain; you should have 2 cups juice. Pour the pomegranate juice into a saucepan. Add the sugar and ginger to the pan and bring to the boil. Add the reserved grapefruit segments, bring the mixture back to a sim-mer, and then pull the pan from the heat. Set aside to cool. (*The grapefruit can be made a day ahead and stored, with its liquid, in a tightly covered container in the refrigerator.*)

the sabayon:

3 large egg yolks

1 tablespoon sugar

1 tablespoon white wine

1 tablespoon grenadine

1 tablespoon water

2 teaspoons (packed) freshly grated peeled ginger

1. PLACE ALL THE INGREDIENTS for the sabayon in a heatproof bowl (if your mixer bowl is heatproof, you can use it) and set the bowl over, not touching, simmering water. Cook, whisking constantly, until the mixture is warm to the touch and thickened. Remove the bowl from the heat and, if necessary, transfer the sabayon to the bowl of a mixer fitted with the whisk attachment. Whip the sabayon on medium-high speed until it is cool to the touch, about 4 to 5 minutes.

2. MEANWHILE, preheat the broiler.

3. DRAIN THE GRAPEFRUIT segments (save the macerating syrup), pat them dry, and divide them among four gratin dishes or ovenproof dinner plates, arranging the segments in a pinwheel pattern. Spoon some of the sabayon into the center of each dish. Run the dishes under the broiler just to evenly brown the sabayon.

to serve: Drizzle a little of the pomegranate syrup around the grapefruit and serve immediately.

to drink: A demi-sec sparkling wine, preferably one from California

Peach-Nougatine Tart

This tart is typically French in conception and universal in its appeal. It is buttery, caramel sweet, peachy to the extreme, and beautifully textured. The base is a disk of puff pastry covered with a single, thin layer of fresh heart-of-summer peach slices. Once baked, the pastry puffs, browns, and crisps and the peaches, brushed with butter and sugar, soften, sweeten, and caramelize. The tart would be fine with nothing more, but what sets it apart is the nougatine topping, a thin sheet of easily made caramel-and-nut candy. The round of almond nougatine (almond is the perfect accompaniment to peach—it intensifies the fruit's flavor) is laid over the tart and run under the broiler briefly so that the nougatine doesn't so much melt into the tart as fuse with it. Make this tart for special occasions—it deserves it—and, with the nougatine made ahead (as it must be) and the puff pastry cut and ready to bake, you'll have no problem baking it during dinner and finishing it à la minute.

MAKES 6 SERVINGS

the crust:

¼ **pound all-butter puff pastry**
   (see Glossary, page 371)

ROLL THE PUFF PASTRY out into a disk 8 inches in diameter and ⅛ inch thick. Slide the disk onto a baking sheet lined with parchment paper, press a piece of plastic wrap over the pastry, and chill until needed. *(The disk can be rolled out up to 3 hours ahead and kept covered in the refrigerator, or wrapped airtight and stored in the freezer for a month.)*

the nougatine:

⅓ **cup sugar**   1½ **teaspoons light corn syrup**
4 **tablespoons unsalted butter**   ¾ **cup sliced blanched almonds, warmed in a**
3 **tablespoons whole milk**   **200°F oven or at room temperature**

1. KEEPING TWO SHEETS of parchment paper and a rolling pin close at hand, place all the ingredients except the almonds in a medium saucepan and bring to the boil over medium heat. Allow the mixture to boil for 3 minutes, just until it's light brown, then remove the pan from the heat and stir in the almonds. Immediately pour the nougatine mixture onto one of the sheets of parchment paper, cover with the second sheet of parchment, and then, working quickly, flatten the nougatine between the parchment sheets by rolling it out with your rolling pin. Slide the parchment-sandwiched nougatine onto a baking sheet and place the baking sheet in the freezer; freeze for at least 30 minutes.

2. CENTER A RACK in the oven and preheat the oven to 425°F.

3. REMOVE THE TOP SHEET of parchment from the nougatine and, using a tart ring as a guide, cut out an 8-inch circle of nougatine. (You can discard the scraps, but you'll be happier if you bake them too and save them for a nibble.) Keep the tart ring around the nougatine and bake it for 5 minutes, or until it is lightly golden. Transfer the baking sheet to a rack, remove the tart ring, and allow the nougatine to cool. *(The nougatine can be made a couple of hours ahead, cooled, and kept in a cool dry place.)*

to assemble and bake:

2 large ripe peaches, peeled, halved, pitted, and cut into ⅛-inch-thick slices

1 teaspoon unsalted butter, melted

2 teaspoons sugar

1. LOWER THE OVEN TEMPERATURE (or preheat it) to 400°F.

2. STARTING AT THE VERY OUTER EDGE of the puff pastry, arrange a pinwheel of peach slices on the crust, overlapping them only slightly. Make a second pinwheel of peaches in the center of the tart so that the puff pastry is completely covered. Brush the peach slices with the melted butter, sprinkle with the sugar, and bake for 30 to 40 minutes, until the pastry is puffed and the peaches are soft and lightly caramelized.

3. TURN THE OVEN to broil and, working gingerly, transfer the somewhat fragile nougatine circle to the top of the tart. Run the tart under the broiler—don't take your eyes off it for an instant—until the nougatine is a dark golden brown, about 1 to 2 minutes.

to serve: Allow the tart to cool for just a few minutes, then serve—it's meant to be served warm.

to drink: A beautiful amber Malvesia della Lipari

Milk Chocolate and Cherry Tart

When I was a kid, I was forbidden to drink alcohol, but I was allowed Mon Chéri, a chocolate-cherry candy that tasted boozy (I later found out it actually had alcohol in it) and made me feel grown-up. This summer tart, which is definitely not kid stuff—the alcohol kick is real—was inspired by those foil-wrapped candies of childhood. It has three elements: a cocoa crust, a layer of port-poached cherries, and a soft, sensuous milk chocolate filling, a cross between a flan and a custard, that covers the cherries.

Because cherries can be very mild and their texture, once baked, can be too soft, I fortified them by poaching them in citrus-infused port. But, even fortified, I wasn't taking any chances that they might be overpowered—that's why I went to the ultimate team player: milk chocolate, not the usual French pastry-chef choice. Paired with the cherries, the milk chocolate offers a fifty-fifty taste experience—each mouthful is half chocolate, half cherry.

A note on the crust: The recipe makes enough dough for two crusts, but if you cut the recipe in half, you won't get the right texture. The extra dough can be frozen for a month and used the next time you make this tart or any tart that needs a chocolate crust—you could even use it to make an ice cream tart.

MAKES 6 SERVINGS

the crust:

8 tablespoons (1 stick) unsalted butter, cut into
    8 pieces, at room temperature
1 cup confectioner's sugar, sifted
1½ cups all-purpose flour

⅓ cup unsweetened cocoa powder,
    preferably Dutch-processed
1 large egg, lightly beaten

1. TOSS THE PIECES of butter into the bowl of a mixer fitted with a paddle attachment and beat on medium speed until the butter is homogenous. Set the speed to low and, one by one, add the sugar, flour, and cocoa, mixing until the dough is crumbly. Pour in the egg and continue to mix on low only until the dough comes together in a ball—take care not to overmix the dough. (Alternatively, you can make the dough in a food processor. Process the ingredients in the same order, scraping down the sides of the work bowl as needed. However, rather than waiting for the dough to come together in a ball in the processor, it's better to stop when the dough is moist and forms curds. Remove the dough from the processor and use your hands to form it into a ball.)

2. DIVIDE THE DOUGH in half, shape each half into a disk, and wrap the disks in plastic wrap. You'll only need one disk to make this tart, so put that disk of dough in the refrigerator to chill for 2 hours and freeze the other disk for another tart. *(Wrapped airtight, the dough can be refrigerated for up to 2 days or frozen for up to a month.)*

3. BUTTER THE INSIDE of an 8- by 1¼-inch fluted round tart pan with a removable bottom, place the pan on a parchment-lined baking sheet, and keep it close at hand. Working on a lightly floured surface, roll the dough into a round with a thickness of ⅛ inch. Gently lift the dough into the pan and fit it over the bottom and up the sides of the pan; run your pin across the top of the tart pan to cut the excess dough level with the rim. (If the dough tears while you're trying to fit it into the pan, just patch it with scraps.) Chill the dough for at least 20 minutes while you preheat the oven.

4. CENTER A RACK in the oven and preheat the oven to 350°F.

5. REMOVE THE TART PAN from the refrigerator, line the tart shell with parchment paper or foil, and fill it with dried beans or rice. Bake for 13 to 15 minutes, or until the crust is firm but not fully baked. Transfer the baking sheet to a rack, remove the paper and beans, and cool the crust to room temperature. *(The crust can be made 8 hours ahead and kept uncovered in its pan at room temperature.)* While the crust is cooling, make the filling.

the filling:

½ **moist, plump vanilla bean**

1½ **cups ruby port**

1 **strip orange zest (pith removed), plus a pinch of grated orange zest**

Juice of 1 orange

½ **pound fresh cherries, halved and pitted**

4½ **ounces milk chocolate, preferably imported, finely chopped**

1 **cup heavy cream**

Scant ¼ cup sugar

2 **large eggs**

Unsweetened whipped cream for serving

1. CUT THE VANILLA BEAN lengthwise in half and, using the back of the knife, scrape the pulp out of the pod. Toss the pulp and pod into a medium saucepan along with the port, the strip of orange zest, and the orange juice and bring to the boil over medium heat. Reduce the heat to low and simmer the mixture for 10 minutes. Add the cherries and bring back to the boil, then immediately pull the pan from the heat. Set aside to cool to room temperature.

2. WHEN THE SYRUP is cool, strain it into a small pan. Pat the cherries dry between paper towels. Boil the syrup until it is reduced to a glaze, then set it aside.

3. CENTER A RACK in the oven and preheat the oven to 300°F.

4. PUT THE CHOCOLATE in a 2-quart measuring cup with a spout or a large bowl and keep it close to the stovetop. Bring the cream and sugar to the boil in a small saucepan, then slowly pour the hot liquid over the chocolate, whisking gently until the mixture is smooth. (Don't whisk vigorously—you don't want to beat air into the mixture.) One by one, whisk in the eggs, mixing until they are incorporated and the mixture is smooth and glossy. Stir in the grated orange zest.

5. ARRANGE THE CHERRY HALVES on the bottom of the crust and pour over the chocolate filling. (It will come nearly to the top.) Slide the baking sheet into the oven and bake the tart for 35 to 40 minutes, or until the center is gently set—if you tap the side of the tart pan lightly, you'll see that the center shimmies only slightly, if at all. Transfer the tart to a rack to cool to room temperature.

to serve: Serve each slice of tart with a drizzle of port glaze—you can put the glaze over the tart or on the plate—and a spoonful of whipped cream.

to drink: A fruity tawny port; it could even be served chilled

Creamy Lemon and Raspberry Tart

This is my favorite lemon tart, bar none. It is tarter than most lemon tarts—because in addition to the zest and juice, it includes lemon pulp. It's also more custardy—because it is based not on a curd or a cream, but on a real custard baked at a low temperature so that it sets to a velvety softness. Because I am inordinately fond of raspberries with lemon, I've packed this tart with the fresh berries, but the tart can be made with blueberries, blackberries, or no berries at all. Lemon alone is also splendid.

MAKES 8 SERVINGS

the crust:

1 partially baked 9½-inch tart shell
   (in a fluted tart pan) made
   from Pâte Sablée (page 353)

IF THE CRUST IS NOT on a parchment-lined baking sheet, transfer it to one and set it aside.

the filling:

2 medium lemons

2 large eggs

2 large egg yolks

½ cup sugar

¾ cup plus 2 tablespoons heavy cream

2 cups raspberries

1. CENTER A RACK in the oven and preheat the oven to 300°F.

2. GRATE THE ZEST of both lemons using the small holes of a box grater; set aside. With a small knife, cut off the top and bottom of each lemon and then carefully cut away the cottony white pith and a tiny bit of flesh from each lemon—the juicy sections of lemon should now be completely exposed. Lay the lemons on their sides and cut each lemon crosswise into ½-inch-thick slices; remove the seeds.

3. PLACE THE LEMON SLICES, eggs, yolks, and sugar in the container of a blender and purée until smooth. Strain the mixture into a bowl and whisk in the reserved zest and the cream. Give the bowl a good rap against the counter to debubble it—if there are bubbles in the cream now, there will be bubbles in your tart later. (It's not tragic, but neither is it attractive.)

4. SCATTER THE BERRIES over the bottom of the crust and pour over the filling. Bake for 35 to 40 minutes, or until the filling is set in the center. Transfer the tart to a rack and cool to room temperature.

to serve: Cut the tart into 8 wedges and serve as is with some lightly sweetened whipped cream, raspberry coulis, or even a spoonful of berry marmalade (page 172).

to drink: A Kir Royale made with a crème de framboise such as Chambord

Chocolate Lollipops with Grand Marnier Sabayon

Nothing could be more whimsical or more delicious than these dark-as-night, deeply rich choco-late lollipops. The pops are inch-long pieces of well-chilled chocolate-truffle ganache that are rolled in crunchy, caramely almond nougatine, pierced with skewers, and served with a sabayon dipping sauce, a featherlight mixture of warm, sweetened egg yolks and orange-scented Grand Marnier.

MAKES ABOUT 60

the nougatine:

¼ cup sugar

1 tablespoon water

½ cup sliced blanched almonds, warmed in a
    200°F oven or at room temperature

1. KEEPING TWO SHEETS of parchment paper and a rolling pin close at hand, stir the sugar and water together in a medium saucepan and bring to the boil over medium heat. Continue to cook, stir-ring until the sugar dissolves, then, once the sugar melts and starts to color, swirling the pan until the sugar is deeply caramelized—its color will be mahogany. Remove the pan from the heat, stir in the almonds, and immediately pour the nougatine onto one of the sheets of parchment paper. Cover with the second sheet of parchment and then, working quickly, flatten the nougatine between the parchment sheets by rolling it out with your rolling pin. Don't worry about making the nougatine any particular size or shape, just make it as thin as you can. Slide the parchment-sandwiched nougatine onto a baking sheet and place the baking sheet in the freezer; freeze for about 30 minutes, or until it's solid.

2. WHEN THE NOUGATINE IS COLD and crackly, peel off the parchment, break it into pieces, and pulverize the pieces in a food processor. *(The nougatine can be made a day ahead and kept in a tightly covered tin away from moisture and heat.)*

the lollipops:

9 ounces bittersweet chocolate, preferably one
    that is at least 70% cocoa solids, finely
    chopped

1 cup heavy cream

½ teaspoon pure vanilla extract

1. PUT THE CHOCOLATE in a heatproof mixing bowl and keep it nearby while you bring the cream and vanilla extract to a boil in a small saucepan. Whisking gently and constantly, slowly pour the cream over the chocolate. Whisk, taking care not to beat in any air, until the mixture, a ganache, is shiny and smooth. Put the bowl in the refrigerator to cool the ganache—stirring every 5 minutes—until it is firm enough to pipe through a pastry bag.

2. LINE A BAKING SHEET with parchment paper. Spoon the ganache into a pastry bag fitted with a $\frac{1}{2}$-inch plain round tip. Pipe the ganache into $\frac{1}{2}$-inch thick logs (the thickness, not the length, is important). Cover the logs lightly with plastic wrap and chill them.

3. WHEN THE LOGS ARE FIRM, cut them, using a knife dipped in hot water and then dried, into 1-inch-long pieces; chill the pieces. Alternatively, you could shape the chilled ganache into small balls using a spoon. *(The logs or the cut pieces can be kept covered in the refrigerator for a day.)* Just before serving, bring the pieces of ganache to room temperature and press some of the nougatine into each piece.

the sabayon:

4 large egg yolks

$\frac{1}{4}$ cup Grand Marnier

2 tablespoons sugar

2 tablespoons water

WHISK ALL THE INGREDIENTS together in a heatproof bowl (if your standing mixer bowl is heatproof, use it) and place the bowl over—not touching—simmering water. Cook, whisking constantly and energetically, until the mixture thickens and is just warm to the touch. Gently scrape the sabayon into the bowl of a mixer fitted with the whisk attachment and beat on high speed until the sauce is cool, about 4 minutes.

to serve: Pierce each piece of ganache with a long hors d'oeuvre skewer or a toothpick. Alternatively, you can serve the lollipops popless and allow guests to dip them into the sabayon with forks. (Fondue forks would work very nicely here—and so would fingers.) Pour the sabayon into a decorative bowl, set the bowl in the center of a serving plate, and surround with the lollipops.

to drink: Marsala, a wine with nougatine's brown sugar and nut flavors

Daniel Boulud *en voyage*

le voyage dishes from lands far and near

The recipes of Le Voyage are inspired by the cultures, ingredients, legends, and chefs of places I've loved visiting and those I long to visit. Some of the recipes, like the one for Gravlax with its mustard-dill sauce, are authentic—it's a version I made when I was a chef in Denmark; others, such as the Cod, Clams, and Chorizo Basquaise, belong to what I think of as the culture of taste—they are inspired by the ingredients of a particular place and have the taste of authenticity, but they are a culinary invention. In this chapter, I invite you to come with me to Italy—the rustic Roasted Chicken with Tuscan Bread Stuffing will transport you there; to Southeast Asia via Crab, Mango, and Cucumber Salad; to Spain via Gazpacho with Anchovy Toast; to the Middle East with Coffee-Cardamom Pots de Crème; and to delicious points in between and beyond.

Soups, Starters, Small Dishes, Lunches, and Anytime Food

Garlic Soup with Bacalao

This soup has the warm, inviting flavors of the Mediterranean—it's a little Spanish, a little Italian, a little Greek. It's hearty and rustic, almost a salt cod chowder (*bacalao* is the Spanish name for salt cod), and it's meant to be kept slightly coarse, the better to appreciate its bold flavors. At Café Boulud, we float a crouton spread with a mix of piquillo peppers, garlic, and parsley in each bowl. I think of the crouton as another part of the dish—it reinforces the flavors that are already in the soup and adds complementary new tastes, another texture, and a dash of color.

MAKES 4 SERVINGS

½ pound salt cod (see Glossary, page 371)

2 tablespoons extra-virgin olive oil

2 stalks celery, peeled, trimmed, and sliced

1 leek, white and light green parts only, split lengthwise, sliced, washed, and dried

1 large onion, peeled, trimmed, and sliced

¼ fennel bulb, trimmed and sliced

8 small cloves garlic, peeled, split, germ removed, and crushed

2 sprigs thyme

1 bay leaf

Herb sachet (1 teaspoon fennel seeds and
   1 teaspoon crushed coriander seeds, tied
   in cheesecloth)

5 cups unsalted Chicken Stock (page 346) or
   store-bought low-sodium chicken broth

¾ pound Yukon Gold potatoes, peeled and cut
   into 1-inch chunks

Pinch of red pepper flakes

1 cup heavy cream

Salt and freshly ground white pepper

1. ONE DAY AHEAD, trim the salt cod by cutting away all the dry parts around the belly and tail. Once trimmed, you should have a perfectly white cod fillet. Cut the fillet into 2- to 3-inch chunks and drop them into cold water. Keep the fish submerged in cold water and refrigerated for 24 hours, changing the water at least three times.

2. THE NEXT DAY, warm the olive oil in a stockpot over medium heat. Add the celery, leek, onion, fennel, garlic, thyme, bay leaf, and herb sachet and cook, stirring, for 15 to 20 minutes, or until the vegetables are tender but not colored. Add the chicken stock and potatoes and bring to the boil. Toss in the soaked cod and the pepper flakes, pour in the cream, adjust the heat so that the soup simmers, and cook at the simmer for another 20 to 30 minutes.

3. PULL OUT AND DISCARD the thyme, bay leaf, and sachet, and, working in batches, purée the soup in a blender. Taste the soup for salt and pepper (it may be salty enough because of the cod, but it will probably need some pepper) and keep it warm while you make the croutons. *(The soup can be made a few hours ahead and then reheated gently at serving time.)*

the croutons:

2 small piquillo peppers (see Glossary, page
   370) or 1 roasted red pepper, cut in tiny dice

2 small cloves garlic, peeled, split, germ
   removed, and very finely chopped

2 sprigs Italian parsley, leaves only, finely
   chopped

3 tablespoons extra-virgin olive oil

Salt and freshly ground white pepper

4 thick slices sourdough baguette (cut on
   the bias)

Fleur de sel or lightly crushed coarse sea salt

1. CENTER A RACK in the oven and preheat the oven to 400°F.

2. MIX THE PEPPERS, garlic, parsley, and oil in a bowl and season with salt and pepper. Spread the mixture over the slices of baguette and put the bread on a parchment-lined baking sheet. Bake just until the bread is crispy, 10 to 12 minutes, then sprinkle with fleur de sel or crushed coarse salt.

to serve: Reheat the soup, if necessary, then ladle the piping-hot soup into warm soup plates. Float a crouton in the center of each plate and serve immediately.

to drink: A toasty, spicy white Rioja

Seafood Paella Soup

When I decided to re-create the Spanish paella as a seafood soup, I looked to the French repertoire for technique. Although rarely made this way nowadays, the classic lobster bisque, a blend of lobsters, tomatoes and onions, Cognac, and tarragon, is thickened with rice. Since rice is the basic ingredient of paella, you can see that the connection between lobster bisque and paella was a natural one.

This soup has everything that makes seafood paella an enduring favorite—the briny freshness of lobsters, shrimp, and mussels, the touch of saffron, the hint of red pepper, the sun-soaked warmth of tomatoes, and the primal earthiness of rice. These robust ingredients are used both in the base of the soup and as the add-ins. First the shellfish shells, vegetables, rice, and herbs are cooked together, then the vegetables and rice are puréed to produce the smooth, lightly thickened base. To finish, nuggets of the lobster, the shrimp, and mussels, as well as rice, red peppers, and peas, are stirred in. Serve a small portion and you'll have a stunning starter; be generous and you'll have a memorable main course.

MAKES 6 STARTER OR 4 MAIN-COURSE SERVINGS

the soup:

Two 1½ pound live lobsters, rinsed under cold water

16 large shrimp, head on if possible

2 tablespoons extra-virgin olive oil

1 medium leek, white part only (reserve the green for the bouquet garni), thinly sliced, washed, and dried

1 medium onion, peeled, trimmed, halved, and thinly sliced

1 stalk celery, peeled, trimmed, and thinly sliced

½ red bell pepper, cored, seeded, deveined, and thinly sliced

4 cloves garlic, peeled, split, and germ removed

3 ounces prosciutto, cut into 3 chunks

Bouquet garni (2 sprigs Italian parsley, 2 sprigs thyme, and 1 bay leaf, wrapped in the reserved leek green and tied)

Salt and freshly ground white pepper

½ pound mussels, scrubbed and debearded

⅓ cup short-grain white rice

2 teaspoons tomato paste

Pinch of saffron threads

3 quarts unsalted Chicken Stock (page 346) or store-bought low-sodium chicken broth

Tabasco sauce

1. **BRING A LARGE POT** of salted water to the boil. Plunge the lobsters into the boiling water and cook for 7 minutes. Remove the lobsters and drain them. When they're cool enough to handle, pull off the heads and clean them by removing the gills and any soft parts; set the heads aside. Crack the claws and remove the claw and knuckle meat, setting the shells aside. Finally, split each tail, remove the meat

(you should be able to pull it out in one piece with a fork), and take out the vein that runs down the back. Cut the meat crosswise into 6 slices, or medallions. Reserve the tail and other shells, tossing away any small pieces of shells from the tails, knuckles, and claws (they'll be too small to find and scoop out of the finished paella); refrigerate them until needed. Refrigerate the lobster meat, covered with a damp towel and plastic wrap.

2. IF THE SHRIMP have heads, pull them off. Shell the shrimp; reserve the heads and shells. Devein the shrimp and keep them covered in the refrigerator until needed.

3. HEAT THE OLIVE OIL in a Dutch oven or large casserole over medium heat, then add the leek, onion, celery, red pepper, garlic, prosciutto, bouquet garni, and salt and pepper to taste. Cook, stirring, until the vegetables are tender but not colored, 10 to 12 minutes. Toss in the mussels, cover the pot, and cook until the mussels open, about 5 minutes. Using a slotted spoon, scoop out the mussels and set them aside. Add the rice, the lobster shells, and the shrimp heads and shells and cook, stirring all the while, until the shells turn red, about 5 minutes. Stir in the tomato paste and saffron, then pour in the stock. Bring to the boil, lower the heat, and simmer for 45 minutes, taking care to skim off the foam that bubbles up to the surface.

4. WHILE THE SOUP is simmering, remove the mussels from their shells. Discard the shells and keep the mussels covered in the refrigerator until needed.

5. SCOOP OUT AND DISCARD the lobster and shrimp shells, the bouquet garni, and the prosciutto from the soup. Working in batches, purée the soup in a blender until smooth, then pass it through a fine-mesh strainer. Taste and add more salt and pepper if you think it needs it, and a few drops of Tabasco. If you're not going to use the soup immediately, cool it, then cover and refrigerate it until needed. *(The soup can be kept covered in the refrigerator for 1 day.)* When you're ready to serve, bring the soup gently back to the boil.

to finish:

¼ **pound shelled fava beans (from about ½ pound in the pod) or fresh green peas (from about ¾ pound in the pod)**

2 **tablespoons extra-virgin olive oil**

½ **small onion, peeled, trimmed, and cut into small dice**

2 **sprigs Italian parsley, leaves finely chopped, stems reserved**

1 **sprig thyme**

2 **small pinches of saffron threads**

½ **cup short-grain white rice**

Salt and freshly ground white pepper

1½ **cups unsalted Chicken Stock (page 346) or store-bought low-sodium chicken broth**

Pinch of cayenne pepper

2 **piquillo peppers (see Glossary, page 370) or 1 roasted red bell pepper, cut into small diamonds**

1. BRING A LARGE POT of salted water to the boil. Plunge the fava beans or peas into the water and boil for about 2 minutes, or until the skins peel off easily. Drain the vegetables and run them under cold water to set their color and cool. Drain again, then pinch the beans or peas between your thumb and index finger to pop off their outer skin. (Because fava bean skins are tough, it's essential to remove them; pea skins are more tender, so removing them is optional.) Set the beans or peas aside.

2. WARM 1 TABLESPOON of the olive oil in a medium sauté pan or skillet over medium heat. Add the onion, parsley stems, thyme, and half the saffron and cook, stirring, until the onions soften but don't color, about 10 minutes. Add the rice, season with salt and pepper, and pour in the chicken stock. Bring to the boil, cover the pan, and adjust the heat so that the stock simmers. Cook for 15 minutes, or until the rice is tender and the liquid has been absorbed. Discard the parsley and thyme.

3. MEANWHILE, when the soup is just about ready, warm the remaining 1 tablespoon olive oil in a large sauté pan or skillet over medium heat. Toss in the shrimp, cayenne, and the second pinch of saffron, season with salt and pepper, and cook, stirring often, until the shrimp are just about cooked through and lightly browned, 1 to 2 minutes. Add the lobster medallions and claws, the mussels, the beans or peas, and the peppers and sauté for 2 minutes more to finish cooking the shrimp and to warm the rest of the ingredients. Pull the pan from the heat.

to serve: Spoon a mound of rice into the center of each warm shallow soup plate. Alternatively, you can place a 2-inch ring mold in the center of each bowl and fill it with rice. Ladle in enough soup to come almost to the top of the rice. Remove the mold, if you've used it, from each plate and arrange the lobster meat—tails, claws, and knuckles—over the rice. Float the shrimp and mussels in the soup, scatter over the fava beans or peas, peppers, and the chopped parsley, and serve immediately.

to drink: A white Irougéguy from the Pays Basque

Alex Lee's Chicken Soup with Mushrooms

This recipe comes from Alex Lee, the executive chef at Daniel and my colleague for ten years. It is a soup his Chinese grandmother made for him and, like chicken soups from every culture, this one soothes, satisfies, and no doubt can cure the common cold—especially when served with grandmotherly love on the side. As is typical in Chinese cooking, the soup is infused with both the fragrance and flavors of cilantro, ginger, garlic, and salty ham. Its primary ingredient, the chicken, plays a double role—it gives the soup its essential character, then it's shredded to provide texture. And the abundant mushrooms act as double agents too—meaty and light, pungent and mild, they're there to add both depth and chew. Ladled straight from the pot, the soup is as comforting as a lullaby; drizzle on a drop or two of the hot zesty scallion oil, and it swings.

If you'd like to make this soup more substantial, you can add some noodles to it. Chinese cellophane noodles would be good (just soften them in warm water before cooking them for a few minutes in the soup), as would a handful of Chinese egg noodles.

MAKES 6 TO 8 SERVINGS

1 ounce dried wood ear mushrooms

1 ¼-inch-thick piece peeled ginger

1 clove garlic, peeled and crushed

2 sprigs cilantro

5 black peppercorns

6 coriander seeds

1 bay leaf

One 3- to 4-pound chicken

¼ pound shiitake mushrooms, stemmed and cleaned

1 package (3½ ounces) enoki mushrooms, trimmed

¼ pound Smithfield ham, cut into short, thin strips (optional)

1 small onion, peeled, trimmed, and cut into short, thin strips

1 stalk celery, peeled, trimmed, and cut into short, thin strips

1 small carrot, peeled and cut into short, thin strips

3½ quarts water

Salt

1. PUT THE WOOD EAR MUSHROOMS in a bowl with enough warm water to cover them generously. Let the mushrooms soak for 20 minutes, then drain and rinse them.

2. WRAP THE GINGER, garlic, cilantro, peppercorns, coriander seeds, and bay leaf in a square of cheesecloth and toss this sachet and all the other ingredients except the water and salt into a deep stockpot. Pour in the water: You want the water to cover the chicken—if it doesn't, chop the chicken in half. Bring the liquid to the boil over high heat, lower the heat so that the liquid simmers, and cook, skimming the foam that rises to the surface, for 1½ hours. Be assiduous about the skimming—it will give you a beautifully clear broth.

3. REMOVE THE CHICKEN from the pot (you can keep the soup at a low simmer or pull the pot from the heat) and, as soon as it's cool enough for you to handle, remove and discard the skin. Using your fingers, pull the meat off the bones in shreds; discard the carcass. Pull out and discard the cheesecloth sachet, and return the chicken meat to the pot. Season the soup with salt and, if necessary, reheat it over low heat; keep it warm over low heat while you make the scallion oil. *(The soup can be made ahead to this point, cooled, and kept tightly covered in the refrigerator for up to 3 days. Bring to the boil before serving.)*

the scallion oil:

1 clove garlic, peeled and crushed
1 scallion, trimmed and chopped
One ¼-inch-thick piece peeled ginger, bruised

1 teaspoon salt
¼ cup vegetable oil

PUT THE GARLIC, scallion, ginger, and salt in a small metal bowl. Pour the oil into a small saucepan and heat it to its smoking point. Standing back, pour the hot oil over the aromatic ingredients in the bowl. Stir well, then allow the oil to stand for 2 minutes. Discard the garlic and ginger before serving.

to serve: Ladle the soup into large hot bowls, making sure that each bowl gets a little of every ingredient. Drizzle a spoonful of scallion oil over each serving and serve immediately.

to drink: Chinese beer

voyage

Clockwise from left:
Seafood Paella Soup (page 188),
White Gazpacho (page 200), and
Alex Lee's Chicken Soup
  with Mushrooms (page 191)

le voyage
Scallop and Oyster Seviche (page 204)

le voyage
Crab, Mango, and Cucumber Salad with Mango Coulis (page 206)

le voyage
Clams Casino (page 216)

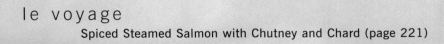

le voyage
Spiced Steamed Salmon with Chutney and Chard (page 221)

le voyage
Moroccan Squab (page 238)
with Chickpea Fries (page 82) and
Broccoli Rabe with Honeyed Grapes (page 289)

le voyage
Spiced Skirt Steak with Braised
Root Vegetables (page 242)

le voyage
Coffee-Cardamom Pots de Crème (page 256)

Duck Dumplings in Broth

This is a sustaining meal-in-a-bowl, fragrant, full-bodied, and Asian in spirit. The dumplings are filled with highly seasoned finely puréed duck meat and poached in a broth invigorated by herbs and spices, mushrooms, tamarind, and lime. And it is the poaching broth that becomes the dumplings' sauce. Like a French *nage,* the liquid in this dish is meant to be minimal. There should be just enough to allow the star ingredient—the dumplings—to float (the verb *nager* means to swim), just enough so that every spoonful can deliver a mini-version of the entire dish: a plump dumpling bobbing in a small pool of delicate, extremely aromatic broth.

MAKES 6 SERVINGS

the duck:

One 4-pound Long Island (Pekin) duck

THE DUCK NEEDS TO BE cut into parts, a job you can do at home or leave to the butcher. To cut up the duck, first remove the legs and skin them—you'll cook the legs in the broth. With the legs out of the way, take both breasts off the bone. Trim away the skin and fat from one breast and leave it on the other. Cut all the breast meat (including the skin and fat) into ½-inch dice. Wrap the diced meat and fat airtight in plastic wrap and keep refrigerated until you're ready to make the dumplings. Keep the carcass, minus skin and excess fat, for the broth.

the broth:

2 quarts unsalted Chicken Stock (page 346) or store-bought low-sodium chicken broth

The reserved duck carcass and 2 legs (from above)

PUT THE STOCK, carcass, and duck legs in a stockpot and bring to the boil. Lower the heat and simmer, skimming off the fat that bubbles to the surface, for 1 hour, or until the duck legs are thoroughly cooked and shreddable. Remove from the heat, lift the legs out of the broth, and, when they're cool enough to handle, use your fingers to shred the meat. Set the meat aside *(it can be cooled, covered, and kept in the refrigerator for up to 1 day),* discard the carcass, and skim off the fat from the broth—this is most easily done when the broth is cold, so, if you have time, chill the broth, then skim off the top layer of fat. *(The broth can be made up to 1 day ahead and kept covered in the refrigerator. When you're ready to finish the dish, bring it back to the boil.)*

the dumplings:

The reserved diced duck breast meat and fat
(from above)

3 scallions, white part only, very thinly sliced

1 clove garlic, peeled, split, germ removed, and
finely chopped

1 teaspoon finely chopped peeled ginger

1 tablespoon soy sauce

3 drops Tabasco sauce

½ teaspoon toasted sesame oil

¼ teaspoon sugar

1 teaspoon thinly sliced mint leaves

1 teaspoon thinly sliced basil leaves

1 teaspoon thinly sliced cilantro leaves

Salt and freshly ground white pepper

1 package wonton wrappers (the wrappers
should be 2½ inches square)

1 egg, beaten with 1 teaspoon cold water, for
egg wash

1 teaspoon vegetable or peanut oil

1. PUT THE BREAST MEAT and fat in the work bowl of a food processor and pulse on and off several times to finely chop the meat, then process for 30 seconds to a minute, just long enough to produce a smooth paste. Scrape the meat out of the work bowl into a large mixing bowl, then fold in the remaining ingredients except the salt and pepper, wonton wrappers, egg wash, and vegetable or peanut oil. Stir well, then season with a pinch each of salt and pepper.

2. TO STUFF AND SHAPE the dumplings, lay a piece of parchment paper out on a work surface and put 3 or 4 wonton wrappers on the paper close to you, placing each wonton so that one point is aimed at your belly—the wontons should look diamond-shaped. (Keep the remaining wontons under a damp cloth so they'll stay moist and pliable.) Brush the edges of each wrapper with a very light coating of egg wash and place a heaping teaspoon of the duck purée in the center of each wrapper. Fold the top half of each wrapper over the filling so you have a triangle, and press down on the edges to seal them. Also press gently around the little blob of filling—this will help you get all the air out of the dumpling so that it won't open during poaching. Turn each dumpling so that the long side of the triangle is closest to you and running from your left to your right. Lift each point of the long side in to the middle—you'll end up with them pointing up. Fold one of the little points over the other and moisten with a little egg wash to seal it. You should have a little bundle that's like a pouch; if you don't—don't worry. As long as you sealed the dumpling when you first folded the wonton wrapper over on itself, you're golden—the first seal is crucial, the rest is just style. Continue making dumplings until you've used all the filling.

3. BRING A MEDIUM POT of salted water to a boil and add the dumplings. Poach for 3 to 4 minutes, then drain and toss the dumplings with the oil. *(The dumplings can be poached, tossed with the oil, and kept covered in the refrigerator for a few hours.)*

to finish:

The reserved duck broth

5 medium shiitake mushrooms, stemmed, cleaned, and thinly sliced

1 package (3½ ounces) enoki mushrooms, trimmed

1 carrot, peeled, trimmed, and cut into matchstick-sized pieces

1 leek, white part only, cut into matchstick-sized pieces and washed

1 stalk lemongrass, stalk and tough outer leaves removed, tender heart of the bulb finely chopped

1 teaspoon finely chopped peeled ginger

1 clove garlic, peeled, split, germ removed, and finely chopped

1 teaspoon tamarind paste (optional)

Salt and freshly ground white pepper

2 plum tomatoes, peeled, seeded, and cut into thin strips

1 tablespoon chopped cilantro leaves

Juice of 1 lime

ABOUT 20 MINUTES before you're ready to serve, bring the broth back to the boil and add all the remaining ingredients except the salt and pepper, tomatoes, cilantro, and lime juice. Reduce the heat to a simmer and cook for 10 to 15 minutes, or until the vegetables are tender and the soup aromatic; season with salt and pepper. Just before you're ready to serve, drop the shredded duck and the dumplings into the broth and warm for a minute or two, then add the tomatoes, cilantro, and lime juice and pull the pot from the heat.

to serve: Ladle the broth and dumplings into warm soup plates and serve while everything is steaming and fragrant.

to drink: An aromatic Riesling from New York State

Oyster Velouté with Lemongrass

This is a sexy French starter with an Asian accent—a velouté, a cold, gently gelled cream soup, with a hint of lemongrass, ginger, and cilantro and a lavish share of oysters and caviar. To get the lemongrass, ginger, and cilantro to whisper rather than shout—left on their own, they'd overpower this dish—they're warmed with the cream, used as an infusion, and discarded once their haunting aromas and the lightest touch of their sharp, bright flavors have been taken in. Tamed, they enliven the soup, set off the essential brininess of the oysters and caviar, and make this a polished beginning for a very special meal.

MAKES 4 SERVINGS

2 cups heavy cream

1 stalk lemongrass, stalk and tough outer leaves removed, tender heart of the bulb coarsely chopped

2 sprigs cilantro

One ½-inch-thick piece peeled ginger, cut in half

1 sheet gelatin (see Glossary, page 367), or ½ teaspoon powdered gelatin softened in 1 tablespoon cold water and then heated until dissolved

3 cups unsalted Chicken Stock (page 346) or store-bought low-sodium chicken broth

2 leeks, white and lightest green parts only, split lengthwise, cut into ¼-inch pieces, and washed

Salt and freshly ground white pepper

24 seasonal North Atlantic oysters, such as Wellfleet, Pemaquid, or bluepoint, well rinsed (you'll need to reserve 1 cup of the oyster liquor; if the fishmonger shucks the oysters for you, make sure to ask for the liquor)

Tabasco sauce

4 ounces osetra caviar (optional)

1. **POUR THE CREAM** into a small saucepan and toss in the lemongrass, cilantro, and ginger. Bring to the boil, then adjust the heat so that the cream is at a steady simmer. Let the cream bubble away until it is thick enough to coat the back of a wooden spoon and reduced to about ⅔ cup. Patience—this might take as long as 30 minutes.

2. **PULL THE PAN** from the heat, cover, and allow the cream to infuse for 1 hour, time enough for it to take in all the flavor of the lemongrass, cilantro, and ginger. Pour the cream through a fine-mesh sieve into a large bowl and keep close at hand; discard the solids.

3. **IF YOU'RE USING** sheet gelatin, soften it in a small bowl of cold water. Meanwhile, bring the chicken stock to a simmer.

4. LIFT THE GELATIN out of the cold water, squeeze it gently between your hands to remove excess moisture, and then whisk it into the warm chicken stock. (If you're using softened and dissolved powdered gelatin, add it now.) When the gelatin has dissolved, whisk the chicken stock into the cream. Let the mixture cool, then cover and refrigerate it, whisking from time to time, until the velouté is well chilled.

5. PUT THE LEEKS in a small sauté pan or skillet with 3 to 4 tablespoons of water. Season with salt and pepper, cover the pan, and cook the leeks until they are tender, 3 to 5 minutes. Drain and cool, then cover and chill.

6. SHUCK THE OYSTERS, putting the oysters in one bowl and their liquor in another. Keep the oysters covered in the refrigerator. Discard the oyster shells and save 1 cup of the liquor.

7. LITTLE BY LITTLE, strain the liquor into the chilled velouté mixture—the amount you add will depend on how briny you want the taste to be and how thick or thin the consistency. Season with pepper and Tabasco and refrigerate until serving time—but for no more than 2 hours.

to serve: Place a spoonful of the leeks in the bottom of each of six small chilled soup bowls and top the leeks with the caviar, if you're using it. Pat the oysters dry between paper towels and put 6 oysters around the leeks in each bowl. Stir the chilled velouté very well and pour it into the bowls. Serve immediately.

to drink: A crisp, fruity New Zealand Sauvignon Blanc

Gazpacho with Anchovy Toast

Gazpacho, one of Spain's most celebrated specialties, is a cold soup that is sometimes aptly described as a liquid salad. Indeed, with its base of puréed tomatoes, peppers, cucumbers, onions, and garlic, it is summer's bounty made drinkable. I've taken a few liberties with this dish, opting to accentuate the freshness of the mix by finishing it with chopped basil and a generous splash of both lemon and lime juice. And, at serving time, I toss in cubes of the same vegetables I blended into the gazpacho. Few soups are as easy to make—this is a push-the-button-on-the-blender soup—and few offer as much satisfaction, satisfaction that is multiplied when you serve the gazpacho with anchovy toast. The toast—a slice of garlic-rubbed baguette sautéed to golden in a little olive oil—is spread with an anchovy-and-chive butter that is lightly salty, extremely savory, and completely captivating.

MAKES 6 SERVINGS

the soup:

1 yellow bell pepper, cored, seeded, deveined, and cut into chunks

1 red bell pepper, cored, seeded, deveined, and cut into chunks

1 green bell pepper, cored, seeded, deveined, and cut into chunks

2 large red tomatoes, quartered

1 yellow tomato (or an additional red tomato), quartered

1 English cucumber, peeled and cut into chunks

½ small red onion, peeled, trimmed, coarsely chopped, rinsed, and dried

3 cloves garlic, peeled, split, and germ removed

Juice of 1 lemon

Juice of 1 lime

½ teaspoon Tabasco sauce

Salt and freshly ground white pepper

¼ cup finely chopped basil leaves

1. **BRING A SMALL POT** of salted water to the boil, add the chunks of yellow, red, and green pepper, and blanch for 2 to 3 minutes, just until tender. Drain the peppers in a sieve and run them under cold water. As soon as they're cool, pat them dry between paper towels.

2. **PUT ALL THE INGREDIENTS** except the salt and pepper and basil into the container of a blender and whir until smoothly puréed. (Work in batches, if necessary.) Taste the gazpacho and add salt and pepper as needed, then strain it. Stir in the basil and chill until needed. *(If possible, give the gazpacho at least 2 and up to 6 hours in the refrigerator—it's really at its best when it's very cold.)*

the vegetable garnish:

½ **yellow bell pepper, cored, seeded, deveined, and cut into ½-inch dice**

½ **red bell pepper, cored, seeded, deveined, and cut into ½-inch dice**

½ **green bell pepper, cored, seeded, deveined, and cut into ½-inch dice**

½ **small red onion, peeled, trimmed, cut into ¼-inch dice, rinsed, and dried**

¼ **cucumber, peeled, seeded, and cut into ½-inch dice**

MIX THE VEGETABLES together and keep them covered and refrigerated until needed. *(The vegetables can be prepared about 2 hours ahead and kept covered in the refrigerator.)*

the toast:

2 **tablespoons unsalted butter, at room temperature**

10 **anchovy fillets, rinsed, patted dry, and finely chopped**

½ **teaspoon finely chopped chives**

½ **teaspoon freshly squeezed lemon juice**

2 **tablespoons extra-virgin olive oil**

6 **slices sourdough baguette**

1 **clove garlic, peeled and split**

1. PUT THE BUTTER in a small bowl and, using a rubber spatula, work it until it is very soft and creamy. Add the anchovies, chives, and lemon juice and blend well.

2. WARM THE OLIVE OIL in a large nonstick sauté pan or skillet over medium heat and toast the bread in the oil until golden on both sides. Remove it from the pan, rub it with the cut garlic, and spread with the anchovy butter.

to serve: Ladle the cold gazpacho into chilled soup bowls or cups. Spoon some of the diced raw vegetables into the center of each bowl and serve accompanied by anchovy toast.

to drink: A well-chilled, pungent Bandol Rosé

White Gazpacho

Like the well-known red gazpacho of Spain, white gazpacho is a chilled uncooked soup. It is entirely different from its crimson cousin, but every bit as tantalizing. The base of this white gazpacho is bread and water, almonds (very traditional), pine nuts (not so traditional), and more than a pound of green grapes. Puréed in a blender, zinged with vinegar, and chilled, the soup needs nothing but a few strands of fresh mint, a couple of sliced grapes, and a handful of nuts as garnish. At Café Boulud, the soup is listed on the menu among the starters, but at home, you may want to serve cups of this refreshing blend in the middle of a summer afternoon—it makes a great pick-me-up.

MAKES 4 SERVINGS

4 slices (about ¼ pound) top-quality white
    bread (a Tuscan country loaf would be
    great), crusts removed
2 cups water
½ cup slivered or sliced blanched almonds,
    very lightly toasted
⅓ cup pine nuts, very lightly toasted
1 small clove garlic, peeled, split, and germ
    removed

1 teaspoon salt, or more to taste
1¼ pounds seedless green grapes, stemmed
6 tablespoons extra-virgin olive oil
2 tablespoons white wine vinegar
½ teaspoon sherry vinegar
Freshly ground white pepper

1. **SOAK THE BREAD** in the water for about 10 minutes.

2. **PUT THE ALMONDS,** pine nuts, garlic, and salt in the container of a blender (first choice) or food processor. Pulse, scraping down the sides of the jar as needed, until the nuts are as finely ground as possible—just take care not to turn them into paste. Add the grapes and whir to purée. Lift the bread from the water (reserve the water) and squeeze the bread between your hands to extract some of the excess liquid. With the motor running, add the bread along with the oil, both vinegars, and one quarter to one half of the water. Check the soup's consistency—it should be as thick as good heavy cream. If the soup's closer to sour cream, add more water.

3. **STRAIN THE GAZPACHO** and taste for seasoning, adding pepper and more salt as needed. *(The gazpacho can be served immediately or poured into a container, covered, and kept in the refrigerator for up to 12 hours.)*

to serve (optional):

1 tablespoon slivered or sliced blanched almonds, very lightly toasted
1 tablespoon pine nuts, very lightly toasted

2 tablespoons finely sliced mint leaves
10 seedless green grapes, cut in half

LADLE THE SOUP into small chilled bowls and, if you wish, top with the toasted nuts, strands of fresh mint, and grape halves, domed side up.

to drink: A puckery Vinho Verde from Portugal

Sardines Escabeche

I turn to escabeche, a Spanish pickled fish dish, when I've got fish that's firm, fatty, and flavorful—which puts sardines at the top of my perfect-for-escabeche list. For this rendition, the sardines are quickly fried in oil, packed into a dish—an earthenware casserole would be attractive and authentic—strewn with herbs, and then submerged in a highly seasoned pickling blend with lots of aromatic spices and vegetables. Chilled for a few hours, the escabeche is delicious served the day it is made, and so many times better the next day—making this a fine party dish. You can be successful using salmon rather than sardines, and you can serve the escabeche with nothing more than a large green salad. In fact, you can dress the salad with some of the liquid from the dish.

MAKES 6 SERVINGS

1¼ cups extra-virgin olive oil
Flour for dredging
Salt and freshly ground white pepper
1¼ pounds sardine fillets, skin on (from about 2½ pounds whole sardines), or 1¼ pounds skinless salmon fillet, cut into ⅓-inch-thick slices
2 sprigs thyme
2 sprigs cilantro
2 sprigs basil
1 tomato, peeled, seeded, and finely diced
6 pearl onions, peeled, trimmed, and thinly sliced crosswise
3 cloves garlic, peeled, split, germ removed, and thinly sliced

2 small carrots, peeled, trimmed, and thinly sliced
2 stalks celery, peeled, trimmed, and thinly sliced
18 fennel seeds, toasted
18 coriander seeds, toasted
2 bay leaves
Pinch of red pepper flakes
1 tablespoon ketchup
1½ teaspoons sugar
½ cup white vinegar
Juice of 2 lemons
Lemon wedges for serving

1. **POUR 2 TABLESPOONS** of the olive oil into a large nonstick sauté pan or skillet and warm it over medium heat. Spread some flour out on a plate, season it with salt and pepper, and dredge only the skin sides of the sardines or one side of the salmon slices in the flour, shaking off the excess. Slip the fish into the pan, flour side down, and fry only on the flour side for 1½ minutes—the fish will be undercooked, but it will finish cooking in the marinade. Lift the fish out of the pan and pat off the excess oil; discard the frying oil, wipe out the pan, and set it aside.

2. ARRANGE THE SARDINE fillets or salmon slices attractively in an overlapping pattern on a rimmed serving platter or in an oval gratin pan that holds them snugly. Strew the thyme, cilantro, basil, and diced tomato over the fish and set the platter aside for the moment.

3. RETURN THE PAN to medium heat and add 2 tablespoons of the olive oil. When the oil is hot, toss in the onions, garlic, carrots, celery, fennel and coriander seeds, and bay leaves and cook, stirring, until the vegetables are almost cooked through, 5 to 7 minutes. Add the remaining 1 cup olive oil and all the other remaining ingredients except the lemon juice and wedges to the pan, bring to the simmer, and cook, stirring occasionally, for 5 minutes. Pull the pan from the heat and stir in the lemon juice.

4. POUR THE HOT SAUCE over the fish. Cover the platter with plastic wrap and allow the mixture to cool to room temperature. Chill the escabeche for at least 6 hours, or overnight, before serving.

to serve: Serve the escabeche with lemon wedges on the side. If you'd like, you can drain off some of the marinating liquid, emulsify it in the blender, and use it as the dressing for an accompanying green salad.

to drink: A big Chardonnay from Australia's Hunter Valley

Scallop and Oyster Seviche

This is a pull-out-the-stops, break-the-bank, celebratory starter that's extraordinarily easy to make. Based on the Spanish seviche, a dish in which fish is cooked by the acidic ingredients in a marinade, my version is composed of thinly sliced rounds of fresh, sweet raw scallops, marinated for only minutes in lime and horseradish, and includes briny oysters, a touch of crunchy celery and radish, and a spoonful of luxe caviar. This can be a sit-down starter served in a bowl or a stand-up hors d'oeuvre, the ingredients presented in one of nature's loveliest serving pieces—an oyster shell.

Because the scallops and oysters are served raw, the success of the dish depends on their perfect freshness and quality. Pristine diver (that is, hand-harvested) sea scallops from Maine are the best for this starter, but other ultra-fresh scallops can be used. If superb scallops, oysters, and caviar are not readily available in your neighborhood, you can order these ingredients by mail from my own supplier (see Source Guide, page 385)—they'll be at your door within twenty-four hours.

MAKES 4 SERVINGS

2 limes

4 very fresh jumbo diver sea scallops (about 1½ to 2 ounces each) or other very fresh large sea scallops

2 teaspoons finely grated horseradish

3 drops Tabasco sauce

Fleur de sel or lightly crushed coarse sea salt

16 bluepoint or other medium briny oysters, shucked and liquor reserved

Leaves from 1 celery stalk from the center of the bunch, finely sliced

1 to 2 small pink radishes, scrubbed, trimmed, and thinly sliced

1 tablespoon finely chopped chives

2 ounces (or more, if you want) sevruga or osetra caviar

Freshly ground white pepper

Slices of buttered pumpernickel, for serving

1. PUT FOUR SMALL BOWLS into the refrigerator to chill. Squeeze the juice from one of the limes, and strain and reserve 1 tablespoon of it. Grate the zest of the second lime and set the zest aside. Then, using a small knife, peel away the lime's pith until the fruit is exposed. Release 8 segments from the lime—they should be free of any membrane—and cut the segments into tiny dice; set these aside too.
2. USING A SHARP THIN KNIFE, cut each scallop crosswise into 5 or 6 slices. Stir the lime juice, zest, horseradish, and Tabasco together in a small bowl. Add the scallops and turn them gently in the lime mixture.

3. AS SOON AS THE SCALLOPS are moistened, divide them among the chilled bowls, arranging the slices in a circle, one slice overlapping another. Sprinkle the scallops with a bit of fleur de sel or crushed coarse salt. Arrange 4 oysters over each portion of scallops and top each serving with an equal amount of celery leaves, radish slices, diced lime, and chives; finish with a small spoonful of caviar.

to serve: Carefully pour a little of the reserved oyster liquor into each bowl and season with pepper. Serve immediately, passing slices of buttered pumpernickel.

to drink: A piercingly acidic white Graves, a classic match with raw seafood

Crab, Mango, and Cucumber Salad

For me, this salad has the same appeal as Vietnamese summer rolls, a favorite of mine—it's got clean flavors, contrasting textures, the unexpected sparkle of mint, and the always welcome crunch of peanuts, a taken-for-granted nut that I like enormously. There aren't many ingredients in this somewhat Indochine salad, but each adds something essential to the whole: The mango is soft, buttery in its own way, and at once cool and rich; the cucumber is crunchy, watery, and refreshing; and the crab is light, sweet, and seawater fresh. The salad is seasoned with cilantro, mint, and lime, dusted with toasted peanuts, and served as is or accompanied by a savory mango coulis. Not unlike the Curried-Pepper Vinaigrette (page 272), this coulis can be both dressing and dip; it can play a walk-on part or shine in the lead.

The full recipe of mango coulis makes about one cup, which is twice as much as you'll need for this crab salad. You can cut the recipe down to size, but I'd suggest you make the full cup, since it will keep for a day and is terrific served as a dipping sauce for boiled shrimp or an assortment of cut-up raw vegetables.

MAKES 4 SERVINGS

the mango coulis (optional):

1 tablespoon extra-virgin olive oil

1 ripe mango, peeled, pitted, and cut into small dice

Salt and freshly ground white pepper

¼ cup water

1 teaspoon freshly squeezed lemon juice

HEAT THE OLIVE OIL in a small pan over medium heat. Add the mango, season with salt and pepper, and cook, stirring, for about 3 minutes, until the fruit is very tender. Add the water, bring to the boil, and then pull the pan from the heat. Stir in the lemon juice, then scrape the mixture into the jar of a mini-blender or, better yet, a container in which you can use an immersion blender. Purée until smooth, let cool, and chill until needed. *(The coulis can be made a day ahead and kept tightly covered in the refrigerator.)*

the salad:

1 pound fresh lump crabmeat, preferably from Maine (see Source Guide, page 385), picked through to remove small pieces of shell or cartilage

1½ tablespoons freshly squeezed lime juice

3 tablespoons extra-virgin olive oil

1 tablespoon finely chopped cilantro leaves, plus 4 whole leaves for garnish

2 teaspoons finely chopped mint leaves, plus 4 whole leaves for garnish

Salt and freshly ground white pepper

Tabasco sauce

1 medium mango, peeled, pitted, and cut into ¼-inch dice

1 cucumber, peeled, seeded, and cut into ¼-inch dice

1 tablespoon unsalted peanuts, toasted and roughly chopped

1. SEASON THE CRABMEAT with 1 tablespoon of the lime juice, half the olive oil, two thirds of the chopped cilantro and mint, salt and pepper to taste, and about 10 drops of Tabasco. Toss the crabmeat lightly with a fork or your fingers. If you're going to present the salad family-style, put the crab in the bottom of a chilled shallow bowl. Or, for individual servings, arrange the crab in four chilled shallow soup plates.

2. SEASON THE MANGO and cucumber with the remaining lime juice, olive oil, and chopped cilantro and mint, salt and pepper to taste, and about 10 drops of Tabasco, and scatter the mixture over the crabmeat. *(If necessary, you can prepare the elements of the salad 1 to 2 hours ahead, keep them covered with plastic wrap in the refrigerator, and assemble them right before serving.)* Sprinkle the salad with the chopped peanuts and top with the whole cilantro and mint leaves.

to serve: If you've made a large bowl of salad, spoon out each portion at the table. Or present the salads in their individual bowls. If you've made it, serve the mango coulis on the side.

to drink: A really cold Alsatian Sylvaner or a Pinot Blanc

Gravlax

This is the gravlax we used to make when, in my early twenties, I was a chef at the Plaza Hotel in Copenhagen, and it's the gravlax I make when I'm nostalgic for my time in Scandinavia. Gravlax is cured salmon, the cure being a mix of salt, sugar, and dill that is rubbed into the fillets and left on the fish for at least two days. The sweet-salty blend not only permeates the fish, it "cooks" it in a way, firming the texture just enough to add a little chew to each satiny slice. I love how the pungent fragrance of the dill is released as it is moistened by the melting salt and sugar. Traditionally served with a mustard-dill sauce, which is the way we serve it at Café Boulud, gravlax, like so many of the greatest dishes, is a model of simplicity—it needs nothing more than slices of dark, nutty pumpernickel bread or rye toast to make it world class.

If you'd like to keep close to Danish custom, you can cut away the salmon skin, slice it into thin strips, and deep-fry the strips until they are brown and crisp. Then, toss the strips over the salmon at serving time.

MAKES 12 SERVINGS

the marinade and salmon:

1½ teaspoons black peppercorns

One 2-pound salmon fillet, skin on

1½ tablespoons coarse sea salt

1 teaspoon sugar

1 bunch dill, feathery tops only

1. PUT THE PEPPERCORNS in a small skillet set over medium heat, shaking the pan frequently, until the peppercorns are lightly toasted and very fragrant. Turn the peppercorns out onto a cutting board and coarsely crush them using the bottom of a heavy pan or the end of a French rolling pin.

2. MAKE A FEW SMALL HOLES in the salmon's skin by poking the skin lightly with the point of a small knife and place the fish skin side down in a nonreactive pan (glass would be perfect here). Mix all the marinade ingredients together with your fingers in a small bowl and then pat the marinade evenly over the fish. Cover the pan tightly with plastic wrap and refrigerate the salmon for 48 to 72 hours.

the sauce:

¼ cup (lightly packed) brown sugar

2 tablespoons white vinegar

½ teaspoon dry mustard

½ teaspoon ground fennel

½ cup Dijon mustard

⅓ cup grapeseed oil

¼ cup finely chopped dill

Salt and freshly ground white pepper

WORKING IN A SMALL microwave-safe bowl, whisk together the sugar, vinegar, dry mustard, and ground fennel. Heat in the microwave oven on high power for 30 seconds, stir, and then heat for 10 seconds more. (Alternatively, you can warm the mixture on the stovetop in a small saucepan over medium heat.) Scrape the mixture into the container of a blender, add the Dijon mustard, and whir to blend thoroughly. With the motor running, add the grapeseed oil in a steady stream and blend to emulsify. Add the chopped dill and pulse to incorporate. Season with salt and pepper. *(The sauce can be made up to 1 day ahead and kept tightly covered in the refrigerator.)*

to serve:
Sliced pumpernickel or toasted rye bread

USING THE BACK of a table knife, gently scrape the marinade off the salmon. Then cut the fish into very thin slices—it's best to cut the fish straight down into slices that are ⅛ inch thick. Fan the slices out on a plate and serve the sauce and bread on the side.

to drink: Caraway Aquavit, with a beer right next to it

Jumbo Shrimp Salad with Fennel and Red Plum Vinaigrette

Here's a shrimp salad that's constructed as though it were French and flavored as though it were Asian. In French fashion, the salad is both cool and warm: The cool parts are the fennel and cilantro, glossed with lemon juice and oil; the warm, and mostly Asian, parts are the lightly sautéed quarters of baby bok choy and the crunchy sesame-coated shrimp. It's the vinaigrette that pulls all the pieces together—it's made from sweet, fat, red plums, cooked to a compote and given added zest with a splash of vinegar and a chunk of fresh ginger.

A word on the shrimp: Large spot prawns are my first choice for this salad, but really, any large shrimp will do—just remember to reduce the cooking time if your shrimp are smaller. No matter the size, there's nothing worse than overdone shrimp—even a plum vinaigrette won't make them better.

MAKES 4 STARTER OR 2 LUNCH SERVINGS

the vinaigrette:

3 ripe red plums (about 10 ounces total), such as Santa Rosa or Dinosaur Eggs, halved and pitted
1 tablespoon water
One ¼-inch-thick piece peeled ginger
3 sprigs cilantro

1 tablespoon grenadine (optional, but good for plums that are not too sweet)
1½ teaspoons red wine vinegar
1 teaspoon sugar
Salt and freshly ground white pepper

SQUEEZE THE FRUIT between your fingers so that the pulp falls in pieces into a small saucepan. Pour in the water, add the ginger, cilantro, the grenadine, if you're using it, vinegar, and sugar, and cook the plums at a simmer until they are very soft and easily mashed with the back of a spoon, 10 to 15 minutes. Pull the pan from the heat, discard the cilantro, and turn the plums into the container of a blender. Purée the plums, then push them through a fine-mesh strainer. Season to taste with salt and pepper and set the vinaigrette aside until needed. *(The vinaigrette can be made up to a day ahead and kept covered in the refrigerator.)*

the salad:

2 tablespoons extra-virgin olive oil
Juice of ½ lime
2 tablespoons cilantro leaves

½ fennel bulb, trimmed and cut into paper-thin slices, preferably on a mandoline
Salt and freshly ground white pepper

USING A FORK, stir together the oil and lime juice in a small bowl until blended. Mix in the cilantro leaves and toss the fennel with this dressing. Season to taste with salt and pepper and set the fennel aside until needed.

the shrimp:

4 baby bok choy

3 tablespoons extra-virgin olive oil

1 tablespoon unsalted butter

Two ¼-inch-thick slices peeled ginger

1 clove garlic, peeled and crushed

1½ pounds spot prawns or jumbo shrimp, peeled and deveined

Salt and freshly ground white pepper

1 tablespoon sesame seeds

1. BRING A SMALL POT of salted water to the boil and toss in the bok choy. Cook just until tender, about 5 minutes, then drain in a strainer and run the boy choy under cold water to stop the cooking and set the color. When it's cool, dry it well. Cut the bok choy into quarters, core, and keep it close at hand.

2. PUT 2 TABLESPOONS of the oil and the butter in a large sauté pan or skillet over medium heat. When hot, toss in the ginger and garlic and cook for a minute or so. Season the shrimp with salt and pepper and toss them with the sesame seeds. Add the sesame-coated shrimp to the pan and cook, turning them once, until they are thoroughly cooked but still moist, about 5 minutes.

3. TRANSFER THE SHRIMP to a warm plate and put the bok choy in the pan. Sauté just until it is warmed through, season with salt and pepper, and pull the pan from the heat.

to serve: Divide the shrimp among plates, top with the fennel salad, and surround with the bok choy. Spoon a few circles of plum vinaigrette around each plate and pour the rest into a sauceboat to pass at the table.

to drink: A rich Santa Barbara Chardonnay with good fruit

Kazu's Pork

Kazuhisa Tamura is a sous-chef at the Imperial Hotel in Tokyo who, for six months, lived in New York and worked at Café Boulud as part of a culinary and cultural exchange program. We often have cooks from other countries in our kitchen, and we always learn a great deal from them, have fun, and, as part of the fun, eat well, as we did when Kazu cooked this traditional *tonkatsu* for us. Tonkatsu is a pork cutlet accompanied by a spicy tomato sauce. The pork for the dish is cut from the tenderloin, deep-fried, sliced into thin cutlets, and, in this version, served with two sauces. The sauce for the pork is as American sounding as my French sauce diable (page 54)—in keeping with the original, it's made with ketchup and Worcestershire sauce and given a tangy edge with the addition of apple and onion. The second sauce, meant to be tossed with lots of crisp shredded cabbage, is a light, cool blend of soy sauce, rice vinegar, and ginger. Assembled, the dish presents a lively mix of textures and plays up the always-appreciated contrast between foods sweet and salty.

MAKES 6 SERVINGS

the cabbage and its sauce:

½ **medium head savoy cabbage, trimmed, cored, and finely shredded**
½ **cup peanut oil**
¼ **cup rice vinegar**

¼ **cup soy sauce**
¼ **onion, peeled, trimmed, and chopped**
1 **teaspoon finely chopped peeled ginger**
Salt and freshly ground white pepper

1. **SOAK THE CABBAGE** in very cold water for 30 minutes, then drain and dry in a salad spinner.
2. **PUT THE OIL,** vinegar, soy sauce, onion, and ginger in the container of a blender and whir until the sauce is smooth. Season the dressing with salt and pepper and then toss it with the cabbage; set the cabbage aside for the moment.

the pork sauce:

2 **teaspoons peanut oil**
½ **onion, peeled, trimmed, and thinly sliced**
½ **apple, peeled, cored, and thinly sliced**

5 **tablespoons Worcestershire sauce**
3 **tablespoons ketchup**
3 **tablespoons sugar**

WARM THE OIL in a medium sauté pan or skillet over medium heat. Add the onion and cook, stirring, until it is softened, about 5 minutes. Add the apple to the pan and cook, stirring, until it is cooked through and lightly browned, about 5 minutes. Transfer the onion and apple to the container of a blender, add the remaining ingredients, and purée until smooth. Set this aside to use as a dipping sauce for the pork.

the pork:

3 cups (approximately) peanut oil, for deep-fat frying

2 pounds pork tenderloin, cut into slices 6-inches-long by ¾-inch-wide

Salt and freshly ground white pepper

Flour for dredging

2 large eggs, lightly beaten

Fresh bread crumbs, preferably panko (see Glossary, page 369), for dredging

1. **POUR THE OIL** into a deep stockpot or casserole, place the pot over medium heat, and heat the oil to 350°F, as measured on a deep-fat thermometer.

2. **WHILE THE OIL** is heating, season the pork with salt and pepper, dredge it in the flour, tapping off the excess, dip it into the eggs, and then dredge it in the bread crumbs, again tapping off the excess. Working in two batches, slip the meat into the hot oil and deep-fry for 8 to 10 minutes, until the crumbs are golden brown and the pork is cooked through. Drain on paper towels to remove any excess oil.

to serve: Cut each piece of pork on the bias into slices about ½ inch thick. For each serving, pile a mound of cabbage just off the center of a large plate and lean the pork slices against it. Spoon some of the pork sauce around the plate and pour the rest into a small bowl to serve on the side.

to drink: Japanese beer

Flash-Cooked Striped Bass Sashimi

The inspiration for this dish came when I was working with Nobu Matsuhiso, the extraordinary Japanese chef, to prepare a gala dinner in Israel. Nobu "cooked" a very thinly sliced fillet of fish by pouring hot oil over it. I loved the mixed sensations of hot and cold, raw and cooked, that the dish offered. In this preparation, I've chosen to cut striped bass into thin fillets (you can also use fluke, salmon, or red snapper) and to flash-cook them in the oven for three minutes. Cooked this way—and for so short a time—the fish comes as close as possible to capturing the vivid freshness of Japanese sashimi without being served raw. Since they are brushed only with a gloss of olive oil and seasoned only with salt and pepper, the fillets are ready to welcome a splash of puckery vinaigrette. Based on lemon juice, horseradish, and cayenne, and dotted with tiny cubes of tomato, cucumber, and celery, the vinaigrette is as sparkling, fresh, and vibrant as the fish. This dish knows no season, but it does know how to whet an appetite for the meal to come, so serve it when you're looking for excitement but want to keep the starter light.

MAKES 4 SERVINGS

the vinaigrette:

1 lemon
¼ cup extra-virgin olive oil
1 teaspoon (packed) grated horseradish
½ small stalk celery, peeled, trimmed, and cut into ⅛-inch dice
½ small cucumber, peeled, seeded, and cut into ⅛-inch dice

1 plum tomato, peeled, seeded, and cut into ⅛-inch dice
1 tablespoon finely chopped chives
1 teaspoon finely chopped cilantro leaves
Pinch of cayenne or a few drops of Tabasco
Salt and freshly ground white pepper

1. **USING A SMALL SHARP KNIFE,** slice away all the peel from the lemon, including the white cottony pith beneath it and the slimmest layer of the fruit, so that the moist, juicy flesh of the lemon is exposed. Slice between the membranes to release half the lemon segments; set the remaining half of the lemon aside. Cut the segments into tiny dice (make sure to remove any seeds) and toss them into a bowl.

2. **WORKING OVER THE BOWL,** squeeze the juice from the remaining lemon half. Gently whisk in the rest of the ingredients, and set the vinaigrette aside while you prepare the fish.

the fish:

Extra-virgin olive oil
¾ pound skinless striped bass, fluke, salmon,
   or red snapper fillet
Salt and freshly ground white pepper

1. CENTER A RACK in the oven and preheat the oven to 325°F. Brush an ovenproof platter with a light coating of olive oil.

2. USING A KNIFE with a very sharp thin blade, cut the fish into very thin slices; each slice should be only about ⅜ inch thick. Season the fish on both sides with salt and pepper and lay the slices on the platter; brush the top of the fish lightly with oil. Bake the fish for 3 to 4 minutes, or until the slices are warm to the touch. Remove the platter from the oven and turn on the broiler. Run the fillets under the hot broiler for just 30 seconds to finish cooking them to rare.

to serve: Spoon the vinaigrette over the fish and serve immediately.

to drink: A Napa Valley Sauvignon Blanc to add some richness to the dish

Clams Casino

I didn't have to voyage far for this dish: A quick trip downtown brought me to New York's Little Italy, where Clams Casino has a permanent spot on just about every trattoria menu. I love this buttery browned dish for its complex saltiness. It's got a brininess from the clams, which I accentuate by adding some prosciutto, the air-dried ham that brings a wonderful light, meaty saltiness to the dish, and the whole thing is balanced by the sweetness of the mushrooms, peppers, and bubbling hot butter. The dish is colorful and inviting and, pulled straight from the oven, would be the perfect starter for a party, since it's impossible not to make friends with people who are licking their fingers—as everyone will be after each clam.

MAKES 4 SERVINGS

4 tablespoons unsalted butter

1 shallot, peeled, trimmed, finely chopped, rinsed, and dried

½ cup dry white wine

16 littleneck clams, scrubbed

1 sprig thyme

2 tablespoons finely chopped prosciutto

4 medium white mushrooms, trimmed, cleaned, and finely chopped

1 scallion, white and light green parts only, finely sliced

½ roasted red bell pepper, finely chopped

1 tablespoon finely chopped Italian parsley leaves

½ teaspoon finely chopped oregano leaves (or a pinch of dried oregano)

1 teaspoon freshly squeezed lemon juice

Freshly ground white pepper

2 tablespoons fresh bread crumbs

1. CENTER A RACK in the oven and preheat the oven to 350°F.

2. MELT 1 TABLESPOON of the butter in a Dutch oven or casserole over medium heat, then add the shallot. Cook and stir until the shallot is translucent, 2 to 3 minutes, then add the wine. Bring the wine to a boil, toss in the clams and thyme, and cover the pan. Cook until the clams pop open, about 7 minutes. Check at the 5-minute mark and each minute thereafter and transfer the clams to a plate as they open. When all the clams have been transferred to the plate, cook the liquid down until it is reduced to 3 tablespoons. Remove the pan from the heat, strain the liquid, and set aside.

3. MELT THE REMAINING 3 tablespoons butter in a small pan over medium heat. Add the prosciutto, mushrooms, scallion, red pepper, parsley, oregano, and lemon juice and season with pepper. Cook, stirring, just to warm the ingredients, then add the reduced clam liquid and cook for 1 minute more over low heat. Pull the pan from the heat and strain the contents; reserve the liquid and solids separately.

4. REMOVE AND DISCARD the top shell of each clam and place the clams on a small baking sheet. Divide the prosciutto and pepper mix evenly among the clams, spooning a little over each one. Sprinkle the clams with the bread crumbs and finish by moistening each clam with a little of the reserved cooking liquid. Slide the baking sheet into the oven and bake the clams for about 7 minutes, until everything is cooked through and bubbling. Turn the oven up to "broil" (or transfer the baking sheet to the broiler) and broil the clams until the tops are lightly golden.

to serve: The clams need to be served immediately, while they're still finger-burning hot. Serve them in small shallow bowls and offer forks, but don't be surprised when your guests treat these as finger food. Whether they are using fingers or forks, they'll want bread to soak up the buttery juices that will be left in the bowls.

to drink: An Alicante, a great match with briny, buttery seafood dishes

Main Courses

Cod, Clams, and Chorizo Basquaise

This dish stakes no claims to authenticity, but it does play up to advantage the typically Basque practice of pairing seafood with spicy meat, in this case chorizo, the Spanish smoked pork sausage. The chorizo is cooked with a mix of peppers and onions known throughout Spain and the Pays Basque as a piperade. Often used as a filling for omelets, a garnish for soups, or a flavor booster for stews, the piperade here forms a savory cushion for the cod and clams and makes a lively mate for the light wine and herb pan sauce. This dish is as tempting as it is simple to make—the fish cooks while the piperade simmers. Remember this dish on weeknights: In addition to its intriguing flavors and eye-catching appeal, it's got time on its side—you can have a remarkably good dinner on the table in forty-five minutes flat.

MAKES 4 SERVINGS

the piperade:

1 tablespoon extra-virgin olive oil

¼ pound chorizo, cut lengthwise in half and
then crosswise into ¼-inch-thick slices

1 medium onion, peeled, trimmed, and cut
lengthwise in half and then crosswise into
¼-inch-thick slices

1 red bell pepper, cored, seeded, deveined, and
cut into ¼-inch-thick strips

1 green bell pepper, cored, seeded, deveined,
and cut into ¼-inch-thick strips

4 plum tomatoes, peeled, cut into 4 wedges
each, and seeded

2 cloves garlic, peeled, split, germ removed,
and finely diced

Pinch of red pepper flakes

Salt and freshly ground white pepper

HEAT THE OIL in a large sauté pan or skillet (choose one that has a cover) over medium heat. Add the chorizo and cook, stirring, for about 4 minutes, or until the sausage is evenly browned. Use a slotted spoon to transfer the chorizo to a plate for the moment. Add the onion and peppers to the pan and cook, stirring frequently and adjusting the heat as necessary, until the onion turns translucent and the vegetables soften but do not color, 10 to 12 minutes. Return the chorizo to the pan along with the tomatoes, garlic, and red pepper flakes. Season the piperade with salt and pepper, lower the heat, cover the pan, and simmer for about 10 minutes more while you cook the fish. *(The piperade can be made up to a day ahead, cooled, and kept covered in the refrigerator. Reheat it gently while you cook the cod and clams.)*

the cod and clams:

3 tablespoons extra-virgin olive oil

Four 6-ounce cod fillets, skin on

Salt and freshly ground white pepper

Flour for dredging

16 Manila or littleneck clams, scrubbed

1 sprig thyme

1 clove garlic, peeled

4 sprigs Italian parsley, leaves only

¼ cup dry white wine

1. HEAT 2 TABLESPOONS of the olive oil in a large sauté pan or skillet (this pan needs to have a cover too) over medium-high heat. Season the cod fillets with salt and pepper and dust the skin side with flour. When the oil is hot, slip the cod, skin side down, into the pan. Cook the fish for 4 minutes before flipping it over. Add the clams, thyme, garlic, parsley, and white wine, arranging the ingredients around the fillets. Cover the pan, lower the heat to medium, and cook for 5 minutes, or until the clams open. (If the clams haven't opened after 5 minutes, remove the fish and continue to cook until they do open.)

2. PULL THE PAN FROM THE HEAT, spoon out and discard the thyme and garlic, and transfer the cod and clams to a plate; keep in a warm place. Strain the pan juices into the container of a blender and whir to blend. Add the remaining 1 tablespoon olive oil and blend again to emulsify the sauce.

to serve:
1 tablespoon extra-virgin olive oil

DIVIDE THE PIPERADE among four warm dinner or shallow soup plates. Top each serving with a fillet of cod and surround with 4 clams. Spoon the sauce over the clams and drizzle some of the olive oil over each fillet. Serve immediately.

to drink: A fragrant Condrieu, a white wine from the Rhône region of France

Spiced Steamed Salmon with Chutney and Chard

This recipe comes with the American Heart Association's stamp of approval. I created it for a gala meal honoring the Association and made sure that less than 30 percent of its not-many calories came from fat and that it had fiber, fruit, antioxidant leafy greens, and, just for good measure, fabulous flavor—not a written requirement on the AHA's list, but certainly one that's high on mine. The recipe has four components, all surprisingly fast and simple to prepare: sautéed Swiss chard, steamed curry-rubbed salmon, a fresh pineapple and dried cherry chutney (a make-ahead condiment that's irresistibly snackable), and a lightly curried broth with head-spinning aroma. And each component can be mixed and matched. When you're looking for a change, try slipping slices of chicken breast into the dish in lieu of salmon or serving the chard, chutney, and broth with rice.

MAKES 4 SERVINGS

the chutney:

1 tablespoon extra-virgin olive oil

½ small onion, peeled, trimmed, and finely diced

½ small apple, peeled, cored, and finely diced

⅛ pineapple, peeled, cored, and finely diced

¼ piquillo pepper (see Glossary, page 370) or roasted red bell pepper, finely diced

1 tablespoon dried cherries, soaked in hot water until plump and soft, drained, and finely diced

2 teaspoons sugar

1 teaspoon Madras curry powder

½ cup rice vinegar

Salt and freshly ground white pepper

WARM THE OIL in a medium sauté pan or skillet over medium heat, then add the onion. Cook, stirring, until the onion is translucent but not colored, about 2 minutes. Toss in the apple, pineapple, pepper, cherries, sugar, and curry powder and cook only until the fruits are tender but not mushy, a matter of a minute or two. Pour in the rice vinegar, bring to the boil, and cook until the liquid is reduced by half. Pull the pan from the heat, season the chutney with salt and pepper, and set it aside until serving time. The chutney can be served warm or at room temperature. *(The chutney can be made up to 2 days ahead and kept well covered in the refrigerator. Bring to room temperature or gently warm before serving.)*

the broth:

2 tablespoons extra-virgin olive oil

1 tablespoon finely diced onion

1 tablespoon finely diced peeled carrot

1 teaspoon Madras curry powder

1 tablespoon grated peeled ginger

1 tablespoon finely chopped lemongrass bulb

½ cup dry white wine

2 cups unsalted Chicken Stock (page 346) or
store-bought low-sodium chicken broth

Salt and freshly ground white pepper

1. WARM 1 TABLESPOON of the oil in a medium sauté pan or skillet over medium heat and, when it's hot, add the onion and carrot. Cook, stirring, until the onion is translucent but not colored, about 2 minutes. Toss in the curry powder, ginger, and lemongrass and cook for 2 minutes more. Deglaze the pan with the white wine, cooking until the wine evaporates. Pour in the chicken stock, bring to the boil, reduce the heat, and allow the broth to simmer for 20 minutes while you prepare the chard.

2. WHEN THE BROTH is ready, pass it through a fine-mesh strainer into a bowl. Discard the solids, season the broth with salt and pepper, and whisk in the remaining 1 tablespoon oil. Set aside in a warm place until serving time. Right before serving, reheat the broth and, if you want, emulsify it with an immersion blender.

the chard:

2 pounds Swiss chard, stems and tough center
ribs removed, washed, and cut into thin
strands

1 tablespoon extra-virgin olive oil

Salt and freshly ground white pepper

1. BRING A POT of salted water to the boil, toss in the chard, and blanch just until it is tender, about 5 minutes; drain well.

1. WARM THE OIL in a large sauté pan or skillet over medium heat and add the chard. Sauté for just 2 to 3 minutes. Season with salt and pepper, then set aside in a warm place until needed.

the salmon:

Four 6-ounce salmon fillets, skin on

1 teaspoon Madras curry powder

Salt and freshly ground white pepper

SEASON THE FILLETS with the curry powder and salt and pepper. Bring a small amount of water to the boil in the bottom of a steamer (a wok with a bamboo steamer, a fish poacher, or a stockpot with a steaming rack is ideal). Place the fillets skin side down on the steamer tray, making sure that the fish does not come into contact with the boiling water, cover, and steam until the fish is opaque around the edges but still moist and rosy inside, about 10 minutes. Remove the tray from the steamer.

to serve: Divide the chard among four warm shallow soup plates. Arrange the salmon over the chard and top each fillet with a spoonful of chutney. Ladle the hot broth around the fish and serve immediately.

to drink: An American Gewürztraminer

Seafood Misto

The ratio of enjoyment to effort for this dish is delightfully high. There's little that's easier than wrapping some seafood in parchment or foil and sliding it into the oven, and little that tastes better. Cooking *en papillote,* in a packet, is a simple way not only to cook food, but to blend flavors, and it works particularly well with this Italian-style misto, or mix, of seafood because it captures the juices that are released from the mussels and clams and uses them to moisten the shrimp and scallops, those delicate creatures that are always in danger of being overcooked or drying out.

If you'd like to make the dish a little more substantial, cook some short penne, toss it with olive oil, season with salt and pepper, and spoon it into the serving bowls before adding the misto.

MAKES 4 SERVINGS

12 bay scallops, left whole, or 4 sea scallops,
   cut crosswise in half
12 littleneck clams, scrubbed
12 mussels, scrubbed and debearded
8 large shrimp, peeled and deveined
4 tablespoons dry white wine
4 tablespoons extra-virgin olive oil
1 tablespoon freshly squeezed lemon juice
2 tablespoons Niçoise olives, pitted and
   quartered
1 tablespoon finely chopped sun-dried tomatoes
   (if the tomatoes are not packed in oil, soak

them in hot water for 15 minutes, drain,
   pat dry, and then chop)
1 tablespoon finely chopped Italian parsley
   leaves
1 tablespoon capers
1 clove garlic, peeled, split, germ removed,
   and finely chopped
Pinch of red pepper flakes
Salt and freshly ground white pepper

1. **CENTER A RACK** in the oven and preheat the oven to 375°F. Cut four rectangles of heavy-duty aluminum foil or parchment paper, each about 16 inches by 12 inches.

2. **LAY OUT THE FOIL** or parchment rectangles in front of you and place 3 bay scallops (or 2 seascallop halves), 3 clams, 3 mussels, and 2 shrimp in the center of each. Divide the remaining ingredients except the salt and pepper evenly among the packets, then season lightly with salt (remember, the seafood is naturally salty) and pepper. Lift up two long sides of each packet, bring them to the middle of the packet, and fold them together to make a narrow band about ½ inch wide, then fold the band over on itself to make a double seal. Now make a similar double fold on each of the two remaining open sides. These seals should be strong enough to hold the packets closed as steam builds up inside. If the

packets don't seem secure (you might have your doubts about the seal you get with parchment), you can give the packets a third fold-over. Just make sure to leave room for expansion.

3. TRANSFER THE PACKETS to a baking sheet and slide the sheet into the oven. Bake for 15 to 20 minutes, at which point the packets should be puffed to the max. (If you're not sure if the seafood is cooked, pull out one packet and take a peek—watch out for the steam; the test is whether or not the mussels and clams have opened. If the seafood isn't cooked, reseal the packet and put it back in the oven.)

to serve: Put each packet—still sealed—in a shallow soup plate and bring the plates to the table. Let each guest puncture his own packet and get the full effect of that first heady whiff of the misto. (If you're serving pasta, have the pasta, moistened with olive oil, in the bottom of the plates, open the packets, and pour over the seafood and its light sauce.)

to drink: A light, crisp, cold Soave

Shrimp over Coconut-Curry Risotto

This intriguing risotto is inspired by the exotic flavors of Southeast Asia. The rice is Arborio, the traditional risotto rice, and it cooks slowly, like a classic risotto, but the flavoring comes from unsweetened coconut milk, which is also the base of the curry sauce. The risotto is topped with deep-fried coconut-coated shrimp and surrounded by the sauce, its aroma, a mix of lemongrass and ginger, Madras curry powder, and Thai chile paste, the first sign you'll have of pleasures to come.

MAKES 4 SERVINGS

the sauce:

2 tablespoons extra-virgin olive oil

1 small onion, peeled, trimmed, and finely diced

3 cloves garlic, peeled, split, germ removed, and finely diced

2 stalks lemongrass, stalk and tough outer leaves removed, tender heart of the bulb thinly sliced

One 1-inch-long piece of peeled ginger, thinly sliced

1 stalk celery, peeled, trimmed, and thinly sliced

½ fennel bulb, outer leaves removed, trimmed, and thinly sliced

Salt and freshly ground white pepper

2 teaspoons Madras curry powder

½ teaspoon Thai red chile paste

½ cup dry white wine

One 14-ounce can unsweetened coconut milk

1 cup unsalted Chicken Stock (page 346), store-bought low-sodium chicken broth, or water

WARM THE OLIVE OIL in a large sauté pan or skillet over medium-low heat and add the onion, garlic, lemongrass, and ginger. Cook, stirring, until the onion is translucent but not colored, 7 to 8 minutes. Toss in the celery and fennel, season with salt and pepper, and cook for 7 to 8 minutes more, or until all the vegetables are tender but still uncolored. Stir in the curry powder and chile paste and cook, continuing to stir, for another 2 minutes. Pour in the white wine and let it cook away, then add the coconut milk and chicken stock or water. Bring the mixture to the boil, lower the heat so that the liquid simmers, and cook until it is reduced by half. Pour the sauce into the container of a blender and purée until smooth, then pass the sauce through a fine-mesh strainer into a small saucepan, pressing against the solids. Taste and add more salt and pepper if needed. Cover the sauce with a piece of plastic wrap pressed directly against its surface and keep it in a warm place until just before serving, then reheat gently. *(The sauce can be made up to a day ahead, cooled, and kept tightly covered in the refrigerator. Reheat gently before serving.)*

the risotto:

5 cups (approximately) unsalted Chicken Stock (page 346) or store-bought low-sodium chicken broth

3 tablespoons unsalted butter

½ medium onion, peeled, trimmed, and finely chopped

1 clove garlic, peeled, split, germ removed, and
   finely chopped
2 cups Arborio rice

Salt and freshly ground white pepper
½ cup dry white wine
One 14-ounce can unsweetened coconut milk

1. POUR THE STOCK into a saucepan and bring to the boil. Keep the stock at a slow, steady simmer.

2. WORKING OVER MEDIUM HEAT, melt the butter in a large sauté pan or skillet with high sides. Add the onion and cook, stirring, until it softens, about 5 minutes. Add the garlic and cook, stirring, for 5 minutes more. Add the rice, season with salt and pepper, and cook for 2 minutes, until it is hot and coated with butter. Pour in the wine, scraping the bottom of the pan. Cook and stir until the wine almost completely evaporates, then add ½ cup of the coconut milk and cook, again stirring, until it too almost evaporates. Add 1 cup of the stock and cook, stirring often, until the rice absorbs all but 3 tablespoons of the liquid. Add another cup of stock and cook and stir as before. Continue cooking, stirring and adding stock 1 cup at a time, until you've added 4 cups. Meanwhile, start the shrimp.

3. ADD THE REMAINING coconut milk to the risotto, stir until it is absorbed, and then taste the rice—it may need another ½ to 1 cup of stock and a few more minutes to cook. When the rice is cooked, adjust the seasoning, adding more salt and pepper if needed, and immediately remove the pan from the heat.

the shrimp:

2 to 3 cups peanut oil, for deep-frying
12 large shrimp, peeled, deveined, tails on
Salt and freshly ground white pepper
Flour for dredging
1 large egg, lightly beaten

¼ cup unsweetened dried shaved coconut
   (available in health food markets)
2 sprigs basil, leaves only, finely sliced, for
   garnish

1. POUR THE OIL into a deep pot and heat it to 350°F, as measured on a deep-fat thermometer.

2. SEASON THE SHRIMP with salt and pepper, dredge them in flour, and tap off the excess. Run the shrimp through the beaten egg and then coat them with the shaved coconut. Fry the shrimp for 2 minutes, or until the coconut is golden brown and the shrimp tails are red. Drain the shrimp on paper towels.

to serve: Divide the risotto among four warm shallow soup plates. Top with the shrimp and spoon the curry sauce around the rice. Sprinkle each plate with strands of basil and serve immediately.

to drink: An aromatic Vouvray Sec

Bay Scallop and Tomato Gratin

Bay scallops, small, succulent, and almost sweet enough to snack on like candy, are such a treat that I'm always creating dishes to showcase them when they're in season. Sometimes I'll use scallops raw in a seviche (page 204), sometimes I'll make them part of a seafood mélange (page 224), and sometimes I'll make them the star of a simple gratin, such as this one, whose flavorings are *molto Italiano*. There's enough garlic in this dish to give it a strong, but not overpowering, personality, and enough herbs—parsley, thyme, and basil—to set the scallops, tomatoes, and bread crumbs in balance.

The most important thing to remember with scallops is to get the freshest ones you can and then not to cook them any longer than absolutely necessary—you don't want to risk toughening them. Here, the scallops are cooked to perfection. First, they're given a quick toss on the stovetop, so that they take on some color, then they're spooned into individual gratin dishes (you could do this in one pan—a pie dish, even), covered with a garlic and herb crust, and run under the broiler for a crispy, golden finish. This is short-order cooking at its best.

MAKES 6 SERVINGS

¾ cup fresh bread crumbs

6 sprigs Italian parsley, leaves only, finely chopped

3 sprigs thyme, leaves only, finely chopped

3 sprigs basil, leaves only, finely chopped

6 cloves garlic, peeled, split, germ removed, and finely chopped

Salt and freshly ground white pepper

9 tablespoons extra-virgin olive oil

2¼ pounds bay scallops

3 large ripe tomatoes, peeled, seeded, and cut into ½-inch dice

1. TOSS TOGETHER THE BREAD CRUMBS, half the parsley, the thyme, basil, and three quarters of the garlic, season with salt and pepper, and set aside.

2. PREHEAT THE BROILER. Butter six shallow gratin dishes. (The dishes should be only about 1 inch deep and about 6 inches in diameter.)

3. HEAT 3 TABLESPOONS of the olive oil in a large sauté pan or skillet over high heat until it is very hot. Pat the scallops dry, then season them with salt and pepper and slip them into the pan. (Do this in batches if necessary.) Cook, turning the scallops as needed, until they're golden on both sides, 2 minutes. Toss in the diced tomatoes along with the remaining parsley and garlic and cook, stirring, for 1 minute more, to cook off some of the tomato juice.

4. DIVIDE THE SCALLOP mixture evenly among the gratin dishes and sprinkle an equal amount of the seasoned bread crumbs over each dish. Drizzle 1 tablespoon of olive oil over each gratin and slide the dishes under the broiler for 2 minutes—watch them closely—or until the tops are golden brown. Immediately pull the dishes from under the broiler.

to serve: The herb-crusted scallops should be served in their gratin dishes, so place the hot dishes on heatproof dinner plates and rush the gratins to the table. (If you've prepared this in a single dish, divide the scallops among heated dinner plates and serve immediately.)

to drink: A Pinot Grigio, in keeping with the dish's Italian style

Tonnato Vitello

This is my rendition of the Italian classic, vitello tonnato. Usually it is a cold dish composed of thin slices of veal *(vitello)*, and every inch of the meat is covered with a tangy mayonnaise that always includes a little canned tuna *(tonnato)*. But I've turned the dish around, replacing the veal with thin slices of glisteningly fresh tuna, seasoned sparingly with hazelnut oil. The tuna is accompanied by quickly sautéed sweetbreads, whose straight-from-the-skillet heat, rich flavor, and luxurious texture are a sensational match for the cool tuna. Both the tuna and the sweetbreads benefit from a drizzle of the sauce, an almost traditional version of the classic, a mayonnaise with chopped capers, parsley and chives, anchovies, and, of course, canned tuna. Although the sweetbreads must be sautéed at serving time, the mayonnaise and tuna can be prepared ahead, making this a dish to consider when you want something elegant—but not expected—for a dinner party.

A planning note: Both tuna and sweetbreads need to be prepared when they are at their peak of freshness, so plan to make this dish the same day you purchase these ingredients. Also, you might want to call your fishmonger to make certain he has a 6-ounce center-cut piece of sushi-quality tuna that's about 3½ by 3½ inches in cross-section. He may have to order it for you.

MAKES 2 MAIN-COURSE OR 4 STARTER SERVINGS

the sauce:

1 large egg yolk
1 teaspoon Dijon mustard
Freshly ground white pepper
¼ cup extra-virgin olive oil
3 anchovy fillets, rinsed, dried, and finely
 chopped

1 tablespoon capers, rinsed, dried, and finely
 chopped
1½ teaspoons finely chopped canned white tuna
1 tablespoon finely chopped Italian parsley
 leaves
1 teaspoon finely chopped chives

START THE SAUCE by whisking the yolk, mustard, and pepper to taste together in a small bowl. Whisking all the while, drizzle in the olive oil and continue to whisk until you've got a silky mayonnaise. Fold in the remaining ingredients, cover the bowl, and chill until needed. *(The sauce can be made several hours ahead and kept covered in the refrigerator. It should be served cold.)*

the tuna:

One 6-ounce piece sushi-quality center-cut
 tuna loin, about 3½ by 3½ inches in cross-
 section and the same thickness along its
 entire length

Hazelnut or extra-virgin olive oil
Salt and freshly ground white pepper

1. **CHILL THE TUNA** until it's very cold (when it's easiest to slice), then cut it into 12 to 16 thin slices.

2. **DRIZZLE A TINY BIT** of hazelnut or olive oil over the bottom of each chilled dinner plate and sprinkle the oil with a little salt and pepper. If this is a main course for two people, place half the slices of tuna in the center of each plate, overlapping the slices neatly. If you're serving this as a starter, divide the tuna among four plates. Pour the sauce into a squeeze bottle and draw a square of sauce around the tuna—or simply spoon the sauce around the tuna. Cover the plates and chill them until needed. *(The dish can be made up to this point 2 hours ahead and kept covered and refrigerated.)*

the sweetbreads:

5 ounces (1 lobe) sweetbreads	**Flour for dredging**
Salt and freshly ground white pepper	**1 teaspoon extra-virgin olive oil**

1. **ASK YOUR BUTCHER** to clean the sweetbreads and to cut them into 8 pieces. Season the pieces with salt and pepper and dredge them in flour, shaking off the excess.

2. **WARM THE OIL** in a medium sauté pan or skillet and, when it's hot, add the pieces of sweetbread. Cook, stirring occasionally, just until they are lightly browned and slightly firm, 2 to 4 minutes. Remove from the heat and serve immediately.

to finish:

8 hazelnuts, toasted, skinned (see Glossary, page 369), and cut in half	**Celery leaves (choose pale yellow leaves from the heart) for garnish**
Extra-virgin olive oil	**Hazelnut or extra-virgin olive oil**
Fleur de sel or lightly crushed coarse sea salt	**Salt and freshly ground white pepper**

WHILE THE SWEETBREADS are cooking, garnish the tuna: Place hazelnuts in the corners of the sauce squares. Brush the tuna very lightly with olive oil—just to give it a sheen—and sprinkle it with fleur de sel or crushed coarse sea salt. Toss the celery leaves with a drop of hazelnut or olive oil, season with salt and pepper, and place a small bouquet of leaves on the tuna.

to serve: Divide the sweetbread among the plates, placing the pieces on top of the tuna. Serve immediately, so that everyone can enjoy the play of hot against cold.

to drink: An unoaked Premier Cru or Grand Cru Chablis

Grilled Mackerel on Pickled Eggplant

When you savor this combination, first you'll taste the rich, oily mackerel, briefly marinated in a gingery soy-sesame vinaigrette and quickly sautéed, then the strips of stir-fried colorful peppers, and finally the eggplant, sharply pickled and uncharacteristically, but very appealingly, plump and spongy. Before I pickle the eggplant in a mixture of ginger, wine, and vinegar, I poach it—an odd way of cooking eggplant, but one that I've been using for years. Poaching eggplant increases its capacity to absorb flavorful liquids and transforms its texture, making it softer, silkier, and even sensuous—not a word I'd normally use to describe eggplant. This is a dish with a strong personality, and I like to serve it with greens that can hold their own, so I choose tender mustard greens or bunches of peppery cress—greens with attitude.

If you'd like to vary this recipe, try using striped bass or bluefish in place of the mackerel.

MAKES 4 SERVINGS

the eggplant:

¾ **pound eggplant, peeled, trimmed, and cut into sticks, each 1½ inches long and ⅓ inch on a side**

¼ **cup dry white wine**

2 **tablespoons white wine vinegar**

Four ¼-**inch-thick slices peeled ginger**

Pinch of salt

1. **BRING A MEDIUM POT** of salted water to the boil over high heat and drop in the eggplant. Bring the water back to the boil—a matter of about 30 seconds—and immediately drain the eggplant. (This is not meant to cook the eggplant, just to take the edge off its natural bitterness.)

2. **WORKING IN A SMALL SAUTÉ PAN** or skillet over medium heat, stir together 1 cup water, the wine, vinegar, ginger, and salt and bring to the boil. Lower the heat and simmer for 5 to 7 minutes, to allow the flavors to meld.

3. **DROP THE EGGPLANT** into the pan and let it simmer in the mixture for 5 minutes; you want to pickle the eggplant, but you don't want it to be mushy, so keep a close eye on it, and drain it as soon as it's tender and tasty. Set the eggplant aside to cool to room temperature.

the mackerel:

6 **tablespoons extra-virgin olive oil**

1 **teaspoon finely chopped peeled ginger**

½ **teaspoon finely chopped garlic**

2 **tablespoons freshly squeezed lime juice**

2 **tablespoons soy sauce**

1 **teaspoon toasted sesame oil**

1½ **tablespoons sesame seeds, toasted**

1 pound Spanish mackerel, striped bass, or
bluefish fillets, skin on

1 yellow bell pepper, cored, cut into quarters,
seeded, and deveined

1 red bell pepper, cored, cut into quarters,
seeded, and deveined

8 scallions, white and light green parts only,
cut on the bias into 2-inch lengths

3 tablespoons cilantro leaves

Salt and freshly ground white pepper

¼ pound young mustard greens or peppery
cress, trimmed, washed, and dried

1. WARM 1 TABLESPOON of the olive oil in a small sauté pan or skillet over low heat and toss in the ginger and garlic. Cook for 30 seconds, then pull the pan from the heat. Whisk in the lime juice, another 3 tablespoons of the olive oil, the soy sauce, sesame oil, and sesame seeds; set this vinaigrette aside.

2. CUT EACH FILLET lengthwise down the center to remove the blood line and pinbones, then cut each fillet on the diagonal into 1-inch-thick slices. Toss the fish with 2 tablespoons of the vinaigrette and set it aside to marinate while you prepare the vegetables.

3. BRING A SMALL POT of salted water to the boil, then add the yellow and red peppers. Cook for about 10 minutes, or until they're tender, then remove them with a slotted spoon, drain, and pat dry. Keep the water at the boil and add the scallions; cook for 5 minutes, or until tender. Drain and dry the scallions too.

4. THE PEPPERS NEED TO BE PEELED—their skin should come off easily now that they're cooked—and cut into small pieces. You can cut the peppers any way you want, but they're attractive cut into triangles. Toss the peppers, blanched scallions, the reserved eggplant, and the cilantro leaves with 3 tablespoons of the vinaigrette; set aside.

5. WARM THE REMAINING 2 tablespoons olive oil in a sauté pan or skillet over medium heat. Season the fish with salt and pepper and slip the fish into the pan. Sear for 1 to 2 minutes on a side, or until the fish is medium-rare (the fillets will be like warm sushi). Carefully transfer the fish to a warm plate.

6. WITH THE PAN ON LOW HEAT, add the remaining vinaigrette and stir with a wooden spoon to pick up any bits that may be at the bottom of the pan. Add the vegetables and give them a quick toss, just to warm them, then remove the pan from the heat.

to serve: Divide the fish among warm dinner plates and spoon over a little of the pan juices. Top with equal amounts of the pickled eggplant and peppers and finish with the mustard greens or cress.

to drink: A very cold floral Daiginjo sake

Lacquered Chicken with Noodle Salad

Here's a chicken for a casual Sunday afternoon meal, an elbows-on-the-table supper that every-one—kids included—will enjoy. The charm of this recipe is its marinade, a quick-change artist. Built on an Asian-flavored blend of soy sauce and sesame oil, honey and orange, ginger, garlic, and scallions, it is used to marinate the cut-up chicken, baste it while it's in the oven, and then lacquer it under the broiler. Finally, it becomes the sauce for both the chicken and the noodle salad, a colorful toss of spaghetti and ribbons of carrots, cucumber, celery, and leek.

MAKES 4 SERVINGS

One 3- to 4-pound chicken, cut into 8 pieces
½ cup soy sauce
2 tablespoons honey
Grated zest of ½ navel orange and juice from
   the whole orange
1 tablespoon finely chopped peeled ginger
6 scallions, white and light green parts only, 5
   coarsely chopped, the remaining scallion cut
   into slender matchsticks
2 cloves garlic, peeled, split, germ removed,
   and crushed
1 tablespoon toasted sesame oil

½ pound thin spaghetti
1 tablespoon extra-virgin olive oil
1 carrot, peeled, trimmed, and cut into slender
   matchsticks
1 leek, white part only, cut into slender matchsticks and washed
1 stalk celery, peeled, trimmed, and cut into
   slender matchsticks
½ cucumber, peeled, seeded, and cut into
   slender matchsticks
Salt and freshly ground white pepper

1. **RINSE THE CHICKEN** pieces and pat them dry. Place them in a bowl or in a large heavy-duty plastic bag with a zipper-lock top; set aside. Put the soy sauce, honey, orange zest and juice, ginger, the chopped scallions, and the garlic in the work bowl of a food processor and whir until puréed. Add the sesame oil and pulse just to blend. Pour the marinade over the chicken, making sure that all the pieces are well covered. Let the chicken marinate in the refrigerator for at least 1 hour and up to 3 hours.

2. **WHILE THE CHICKEN** is marinating (or, if it's more convenient for you, wait until the chicken is in the oven), cook the noodles in a large quantity of boiling water. (You don't have to salt the water for this recipe.) Drain them well, put them in a bowl, and toss them with the olive oil. Set aside to cool.

3. **BRING A SMALL POT** of salted water to the boil. One by one, blanch the carrot, leek, celery, and the scallion matchsticks in the boiling water, cooking only until the vegetables are crisp-tender, 2 to 3 minutes; as each vegetable is cooked, scoop it out of the water with a slotted spoon and run it under cold water to set the color and cool. Drain the vegetables and pat them dry. Toss the cooled vegetables

and the cucumber with the noodles. *(The salad can be made up to 4 hours ahead and kept covered in the refrigerator.)*

4. CENTER A RACK in the oven and preheat the oven to 350°F.

5. PLACE THE CHICKEN in a single layer, skin side up, in a small roasting pan or a baking dish. Pour three quarters of the marinade over the chicken—reserve the remaining marinade for the noodles—and slide the pan into the oven. Roast the chicken, basting frequently, for 45 minutes, or until the chicken is cooked through. Check by piercing a leg—the juices should run clear. (If some pieces are cooked before others, remove the cooked pieces and keep them warm.)

6. WHEN THE CHICKEN is cooked, turn on the broiler and put the chicken under it for about 5 minutes, continuing to baste frequently, or until the chicken is beautifully lacquered.

7. MEANWHILE, bring the reserved marinade to a boil and boil for 1 minute. Pour this over the noodles, toss well, and taste for salt and pepper. The noodle salad can be served at any temperature—from slightly warm, as it would be if you made it when the chicken was roasting, to chilled, as it would be if you made it ahead.

to serve: Spoon the pan juices over the lacquered chicken and serve the chicken on hot dinner plates with the noodle salad on the side.

to drink: An off-dry Tokay Pinot Gris

Roasted Chicken with Tuscan Bread Stuffing

I wouldn't be surprised if this became your "house chicken," the recipe you turn to whenever you want a perfect chicken for a family dinner or a meal with good friends. This simple recipe produces a chicken with vigorous country flavors. It's the stuffing that sets it above others. Made of chicken livers and prosciutto, rosemary, garlic, onions, and sage, it is bound together by cubes of toasted Tuscan bread and tucked not inside the chicken, but under its skin. As the chicken roasts, the juices from the prosciutto and the livers, and the flavors from the onions, garlic, and herbs, perfume the meat. The chicken goes into the oven lumpy and bumpy, the stuffing making hillocks under the bird's skin, and comes out deeply golden, its skin cracklingly crisp; it is wildly fragrant and thoroughly inviting.

MAKES 4 SERVINGS

the stuffing:

2 slices Tuscan-type country bread, crusts removed

1 tablespoon extra-virgin olive oil

3 chicken livers (about ¼ pound total)

Salt and freshly ground white pepper

3 tablespoons unsalted butter

½ onion, peeled, trimmed, and cut into ¼-inch dice

3 cloves garlic, peeled, split, germ removed, and finely chopped

2 ounces prosciutto, cut into ¼-inch dice

5 sage leaves, finely chopped

2 tablespoons finely chopped Italian parsley leaves

1 sprig rosemary, leaves only, finely chopped

1. **CENTER A RACK** in the oven and preheat the oven to 350°F.

2. **PUT THE BREAD** in the oven—right on the rack is OK—and bake just until it's slightly dried, 5 to 8 minutes. When the bread's cool enough to handle, cut it into ¼-inch cubes.

3. **WARM THE OLIVE OIL** in a large sauté pan or skillet over medium heat. Add the chicken livers, season with salt and pepper, and cook, stirring, for 4 minutes, or until the livers are browned on the outside but still rosy within. Remove the pan from the heat, put the livers on a cutting board, and cut them into ¼-inch dice.

4. **WIPE OUT THE PAN** and return it to medium heat. Melt 1 tablespoon of the butter in the pan, add the onion and garlic, and season with salt and pepper. Cook and stir just until the onions are translucent but not colored, about 5 minutes. Add the prosciutto and sauté for 2 minutes, then return the chicken livers to the pan. Cook for another 2 minutes and stir in the bread cubes. When the bread is blended, fold in the herbs and season with salt and pepper. Add the remaining 2 tablespoons butter and stir it into the mixture. When the butter has melted, remove the pan from the heat and turn the stuffing into a bowl; cool.

the chicken:

One 3½-pound chicken, rinsed and dried; neck reserved

2 tablespoons (approximately) extra-virgin olive oil

2 tablespoons unsalted butter, melted

Salt and freshly ground white pepper

¼ cup unsalted Chicken Stock (page 346) or store-bought low-sodium chicken broth

1. CENTER A RACK in the oven and preheat the oven to 350°F.

2. IN ORDER TO GET the stuffing under the chicken's skin, you've got to gingerly separate the skin from the body, a job best done with your fingers. Clear the way by tucking the bird's wings back and under themselves. Then, with your fingers, rub a little olive oil under the skin and over the flesh: Pull the skin from the belly area back, run your fingers under the breast skin as far as you can, and then run them around the leg meat. Do the same thing from the neck end. Now, start putting stuffing under the skin: Press the stuffing over and around the legs and against the breast—the breast area will take the most stuffing. Get as much stuffing as you can under the skin and then, if there's any stuffing left over, toss it into the cavity. Pull the neck skin as taut as you can and tuck it under the chicken; pull the belly skin taut and tuck it between the chicken's legs. Cross the chicken's legs and tie them with kitchen twine. The chicken will look lumpy, bumpy, and plump—and that's perfect.

3. YOU'RE GOING TO USE the chicken's neck as a roasting rack, so cut the neck into 3 pieces and put them in the center of a small roasting pan. Brush the chicken all over with some of the melted butter and season the skin generously with salt and pepper. Put the chicken on top of the neck pieces—the "rack"—and slide the roasting pan into the oven. Roast the chicken for 15 minutes, basting twice with the remaining melted butter. Continue to roast the chicken for another 1 hour and 15 minutes, basting every 20 minutes or so with olive oil or with the juices that accumulate in the bottom of the pan. Remove the chicken from the oven and allow it to rest for 10 minutes.

4. SPOON OFF HALF THE FAT from the pan, leaving the juices. Put the pan over medium heat and add the chicken stock. Stir and scrape up whatever bits and scraps may have stuck to the bottom of the pan and simmer the sauce for 2 to 3 minutes. Season with salt and pepper and pull the pan from the heat.

to serve: Carve and serve the chicken, straining some of the pan sauce over each portion.

to drink: A full-bodied, rustic Langhe from Italy

Moroccan Squab

The pleasures of this dish start as soon as you begin blending the spices to be brushed over the roasting squabs. Stir together the cumin and coriander, cinnamon, and hot cayenne, then add garlic and cilantro and bits of sweet-salty lemon zest confit, and you'll revel in the way the exotic aromas of Morocco fill the kitchen. Squab seem like special-occasion fare, when, in fact, they should be considered fast food: A few minutes in the oven, and they're done—to rare, the way I always serve them. With this recipe, I like to stay with the flavors of Morocco, and I often serve the squab with Vegetable Couscous (page 297), but they're also extremely good with Broccoli Rabe with Honeyed Grapes (page 289), another dish that plays with the seductive scents of North Africa.

MAKES 2 SERVINGS

1 tablespoon honey

1 tablespoon finely chopped lemon zest confit
   (page 146)

Juice of 1 lemon

1 clove garlic, peeled, split, germ removed, and
   finely chopped

6 sprigs cilantro, leaves and tender stems only,
   finely chopped

1 teaspoon ground cumin

1 teaspoon ground coriander

1 teaspoon salt

¼ teaspoon ground cinnamon

⅛ teaspoon cayenne pepper

Freshly ground white pepper

1 tablespoon extra-virgin olive oil

1 tablespoon unsalted butter

Two 1-pound squab

1. **CENTER A RACK** in the oven and preheat the oven to 450°F.

2. **MIX EVERYTHING** except the oil, butter, and squab together in a bowl. Put the oil and butter in a small roasting pan and slide it into the oven just to heat the oil and melt the butter. Pull the pan out and turn the squab in the hot fat just to coat the skin, then set the squab breast side up in the pan and roast for 10 minutes, basting them with the fat in the pan twice during this period. At the 10-minute mark, brush the squab with about three quarters of the spice mixture and return them to the oven to roast for another 5 minutes. At this point, the squab will be rare, which is the best way to serve them. (The meat will actually be red—and that's the way it's supposed to be.) If you press the squab, it should feel like a medium-rare steak (or the fleshy part of your thumb). Pull the pan from the oven, turn on the broiler, and let the squab rest in a warm place for 5 minutes.

3. **RIGHT BEFORE SERVING**, run the squab under the broiler for a minute or two just to rewarm and crisp the skin.

4. MEANWHILE, pour the remaining spice mix into a small saucepan and bring it just to the boil, then remove the pan from the heat.

to serve: The squab can be served whole or cut up. To cut up a squab, steady it on a cutting board by holding it on its side with a carving fork, taking care not to pierce the breast. Using a pair of poultry shears, cut the squab in half, cutting out the backbone first and then splitting the breast down the bone. Place an entire split squab or a whole squab on each warm dinner plate. Spoon over a little of the hot spice sauce and serve immediately, with whatever you've chosen as an accompaniment.

to drink: A Russian River Pinot Noir, for its spice, fruit, and soft tannins

Oxtail Rioja

Slow cooking gathers and deepens the flavors in this Spanish-style stew. Oxtail, one of my favorite cuts for braising, is mixed with Serrano ham and the trinity of the Spanish kitchen, onions, peppers, and tomatoes, before being slipped into a casserole with Spain's best red wine, the complex rioja. After hours in the oven, moistening the meat and vegetables, the wine imbues the entire stew with its fruit and spice. I can't think of a better dish for a chilly evening—it makes you feel as snug and pampered as you do when you're curled up in front of the hearth.

MAKES 4 SERVINGS

4 pounds oxtails, cut into 2-inch-thick pieces
1 tablespoon sweet paprika
Salt and freshly ground black pepper
Flour for dredging
¼ cup extra-virgin olive oil
¼ pound Serrano ham, cut into ½-inch dice
1 head garlic, cut crosswise in half
1 large onion, peeled, trimmed, and cut into
   ½-inch dice
1 large carrot, peeled, trimmed, and cut into
   ½-inch dice
1 pound green frying peppers, cored, seeded,
   deveined, and diced
1 tablespoon tomato paste

1 pound tomatoes, cored, cut lengthwise in
   half, and seeded, each tomato half cut into
   4 wedges
Herb sachet (1 bay leaf, 2 sprigs Italian parsley, and 1 sprig thyme, tied in cheesecloth)
4 cups rioja wine
1 quart unsalted Chicken Stock (page 346) or
   store-bought low-sodium chicken broth
½ cup sliced blanched almonds, toasted

1. **SEASON THE OXTAILS** on all sides with the paprika and salt and pepper, then dredge them in flour, shaking off the excess. Place a large sauté pan or wide casserole over medium heat and pour in the olive oil. When the oil is hot, add the oxtails (you might have to do this in batches) and cook, turning to brown all sides, about 10 minutes. Transfer the oxtails to a plate and pour off all but 2 tablespoons of the fat from the pan.

2. **STILL WORKING OVER MEDIUM HEAT**, add the ham, garlic, onion, carrot, and green peppers to the pan. Cook, stirring frequently, until the vegetables are soft but not colored, about 15 minutes. Stir in the tomato paste and tomatoes. Return the oxtails to the pan along with the herb sachet and red wine. Bring the wine to the boil, skimming the foam that rises to the surface, and cook until the wine is reduced by half. Add the chicken stock and bring to the boil, then adjust the heat so that the liquid

simmers. Cover the pan and cook at a steady simmer for 2½ hours. During this time, it's important to be diligent about skimming off whatever foam and solids bubble up to the top. (When you've got the cover off to skim, check that the liquid isn't boiling, and adjust the heat as needed.)

3. REMOVE THE COVER and continue to simmer for 30 minutes more, or until the sauce is reduced and slightly thickened. The sauce won't be very thick, but it should coat the oxtails. Remove and discard the garlic and sachet before serving.

to serve: If you've cooked the oxtails in an attractive pan or casserole, you can serve them in the pot. If you'd prefer, transfer the oxtails, vegetables, and sauce to a serving platter. In either case, sprinkle the oxtails with the almonds right before serving.

to drink: A Rioja, of course

Spiced Skirt Steak with Braised Root Vegetables

This is steak au poivre with a soft Asian touch, a lot of heat and almost as many kinds of pepper as you can find at the spice counter. I toast some of the spices, then mix together white, black, green, and Szechwan peppercorns, cayenne, allspice, and fresh ginger, pulverize them, and press them deeply into skirt steaks. Cooked quickly over high heat, the steaks are fiercely spicy, all the better to enjoy with chunks of butter-glazed root vegetables.

MAKES 4 SERVINGS

the spices and steak:

1 teaspoon white peppercorns

½ teaspoon black peppercorns

½ teaspoon Szechwan peppercorns

½ teaspoon allspice berries

½ teaspoon green peppercorns

½ teaspoon red pepper flakes

¼ teaspoon finely chopped peeled ginger

Four 6-ounce skirt steaks

1. PUT THE WHITE, black, and Szechwan peppercorns in a small sauté pan or skillet along with the allspice. Place the pan over medium heat and warm the spices, shaking the pan to keep them from heating too much on one side, until they are very lightly toasted but highly aromatic. Remove the pan from the heat, turn the spices out onto a cutting board, and add the green peppercorns, red pepper flakes, and ginger. Crush the spices by bashing them with the bottom of a heavy pan or the end of a French rolling pin, or by working them with a mortar and pestle.

2. PUT THE STEAKS in a container that can hold them comfortably and, using your fingers and the heel of your hand, press the spices evenly over both sides of the steaks. Cover the steaks with plastic wrap and marinate at room temperature for 30 minutes. (*The steaks can be kept covered in the refrigerator for up to 2 hours. Bring to room temperature before cooking.*)

the vegetables:

1 tablespoon extra-virgin olive oil

1 medium carrot, peeled, trimmed, and cut into ¼-inch-thick rounds

1 small celery root, peeled, trimmed, and cut into 8 wedges

1 large turnip, peeled, trimmed, and cut into 8 wedges

Salt and freshly ground white pepper

1 medium celery stalk, peeled, trimmed, and cut into ½-inch-thick slices

1 medium fennel bulb, trimmed and cut into 8 wedges

2 sprigs thyme

2 cups unsalted Chicken Stock (page 346) or store-bought low-sodium chicken broth

2 tablespoons unsalted butter

WARM THE OIL in a Dutch oven or large casserole over medium heat. Toss in the carrot, celery root, and turnip, season with salt and pepper, and cook, stirring frequently, for 5 minutes—keep the heat down and the ingredients moving so that the vegetables don't color. Add the celery, fennel, and thyme and cook, stirring, for 5 minutes more. Finally, pour in the chicken stock, add the butter, and bring the stock to the boil. Lower the heat and simmer the vegetables for 25 to 30 minutes, or until almost all of the liquid has evaporated and the vegetables are very tender and glazed with the butter and stock. Add more salt and pepper if needed, remove from the heat, and pull the thyme out of the pot. Keep warm while you cook the steaks. *(The vegetables can be made up to a day in advance, cooled completely, and kept covered in the refrigerator. At serving time, gently reheat the vegetables with a bit more butter or stock.)*

to finish:

1 tablespoon extra-virgin olive oil	**½ cup dry white wine**
Salt	**2 tablespoons unsalted butter**

1. WARM THE OLIVE OIL in a large sauté pan or skillet over high heat until the oil is smoking hot. Season the steaks on both sides with salt and slip them into the pan. Brown the steaks for about 2 minutes on each side for medium-rare, a little longer for better-done meat. Transfer the steaks to a heated platter and keep warm for a moment.

2. SPOON OFF THE FAT in the pan and add the wine. Boil the wine until it reduces by half, then add whatever juices may have accumulated on the platter with the steaks. Pull the pan from the heat and swirl in the butter.

to serve: The steaks can be sliced or not—it's your call. Divide the vegetables among four warm dinner plates. Place the steak or slices of steak (sliced across the grain on a sharp diagonal) alongside the vegetables and spoon some sauce over each portion of steak. Serve immediately.

to drink: An Australian Shiraz with generous fruit and spice

Veal Chops Stuffed with Fontina and Porcini

This looks like a steak-house special and tastes like an Italian culinary treasure. I've taken thick veal chops, butterflied them so that each has a roomy pocket, and filled the pockets generously with ingredients more precious than many currencies: thinly sliced prosciutto, Italian Fontina, and meaty porcini. Hearty but refined, bold but polished, the dish is glorious. I like it served with Braised Carrots (page 73).

MAKES 4 SERVINGS

10 ounces fresh porcini, trimmed and cleaned

Four 10-ounce veal rib chops (bone-in)

4 slices prosciutto, each cut in half

3½ ounces Italian Fontina, cut into 8 thin slices

Salt and freshly ground white pepper

3 tablespoons extra-virgin olive oil

1 clove garlic, peeled and crushed

1 sprig thyme

1 shallot, peeled, trimmed, finely chopped, rinsed, and dried

½ cup dry white wine

1. **CENTER A RACK** in the oven and preheat the oven to 400°F.

2. **SLICE HALF THE PORCINI** into ¼-inch-thick slices and quarter the remaining porcini. Keep the slices and quarters separate but nearby.

3. **THE VEAL CHOPS** need to be butterflied, a job you can do easily at home or one you can have the butcher do. Working with a long sharp knife, cut the meaty round part of each chop in half horizontally just to the bone, deep enough so that you can open the chop up and stuff it. Done right, when you open the chop the bone will run down the center and the meat will form two circles on either side of the bone. (It will be like a lowercase "db" monogram.) Open one chop. Working on one side of the chop, place one eighth of the sliced mushrooms, a piece of prosciutto, and a slice of Fontina, then repeat so that you've got two complete layers of stuffing; close the chop. Do this for the remaining 3 chops, season them with salt and pepper, and then tie them with kitchen twine to keep the stuffing in place and the chops in shape.

4. **WARM 1 TABLESPOON** of the olive oil with the garlic and thyme in a medium sauté pan or skillet over medium heat. Toss in the quartered mushrooms, season with salt and pepper, and cook, stirring, for 3 to 5 minutes, or until the mushrooms have released their moisture and it has cooked down. Pull the pan from the heat and set aside. Gently reheat the mushrooms right before serving.

5. **WARM THE REMAINING** 2 tablespoons olive oil in a large ovenproof sauté pan or skillet (or work in two pans, each with 1 tablespoon oil) over medium-high heat. When the oil is hot, slip the chops into the pan and cook to color, about 3 minutes on each side and 1 to 2 minutes around the edges (7 to 8 minutes total). Slide the pan into the oven to finish the cooking, figuring on 4 minutes a side. Remove

the pan from the oven, transfer the chops to a warm plate, and keep them warm while you make the sauce. (This resting period is important for the chops—it will give their delicious juices a chance to settle back into the meat.)

6. SKIM THE FAT off the pan juices, put the pan over low heat, and add the shallot. Cook the shallot for 1 to 2 minutes, then add the wine and cook until the wine reduces by half. Pour in whatever juices may have accumulated on the plate with the chops. Taste the sauce and season with salt and pepper if needed, then strain it.

to serve: Place one chop on each of four heated dinner plates, spoon over a little of the pan juices, and divide the mushrooms among the plates.

to drink: A rich, barrel-aged Napa Valley Chardonnay, an older one if you can find it

Veal Gremolata with Kale Polenta

Gremolata is a piquant mix of chopped garlic, freshly grated lemon zest, and parsley that's used in Italy to add vitality to roasts and casseroles. Sometimes the gremolata is treated as a condiment, set on the table and sprinkled onto dishes in quantities that depend on each diner's taste; that's the way it's used in the classic Italian osso buco. And sometimes the gremolata is made part of the dish, as it is in this preparation, in which it is blended with bread crumbs, patted onto sautéed veal medallions, dotted with butter, and run under the broiler to brown. Either way, the gremolata adds a distinctive flavor to a dish—tangy but well balanced, ideal with the mild veal medallions and a good companion to the diced tomatoes and black olives that brighten the pan sauce.

To keep the Italianate nature of this dish, I serve it with polenta—but it's polenta with a twist. When the polenta is almost cooked through, I add finely sliced kale. I love the play of the smooth, only slightly corn-flavored polenta against the hearty, only slightly bitter-flavored kale. For this dish, I don't keep the polenta completely creamy. Once it's cooked, I chill the polenta, then cut it into serving-sized portions and brown it, giving it a golden crust that provides just the right proportion of crunchiness to creaminess.

If you want, you can prepare the polenta the day before; that way, you'll only need to give it a last-minute sauté.

MAKES 4 SERVINGS

the polenta:

½ **pound kale, stems and tough center ribs removed**
2½ **cups whole milk**
Salt and freshly ground white pepper

½ **cup instant polenta**
Semolina flour or finely ground cornmeal for dredging
2 **tablespoons extra-virgin olive oil**

1. **BRING A LARGE POT** of salted water to the boil. Plunge the kale into the pot and boil for 8 to 10 minutes, until it is tender. Drain the kale, run it under cold water, and then, when it is cool, squeeze the leaves between your hands to get rid of excess moisture. Pat the leaves dry between paper towels. Cut the kale into ½-inch-thick strips and reserve.
2. **LINE A 9-INCH SQUARE PAN** with parchment paper. Cut another sheet of parchment as large as the pan, and keep everything close at hand. (Or, line the pan with plastic wrap and then use plastic wrap to cover the finished polenta.)
3. **POUR THE MILK** into a medium saucepan, season with salt and pepper, and bring to the boil over medium heat. Lower the heat so that the milk simmers steadily and, whisking constantly, add the polenta

in a slow stream. When all the polenta is in the pan, cook over low heat, whisking without stop, for 3 to 4 minutes. Stir in the kale and cook and stir for 1 minute more. Scrape the polenta into the prepared pan, spreading it evenly so that it is about ¼ inch thick. Working quickly, run a spatula over the polenta to smooth and even the top surface, rap the pan against the counter to knock out any air bubbles, and then cover the polenta with the second sheet of parchment (or plastic wrap), pressing lightly against the parchment to create an airtight seal—this will keep a skin from forming on the polenta. Chill the polenta in the refrigerator for 2 to 3 hours, or, better still, overnight.

4. JUST BEFORE SERVING TIME—or a few hours ahead—use a cookie cutter to cut the polenta into twelve 2-inch circles or, using a sharp knife dipped in hot water, cut it into comparably sized squares or triangles. (If you've cut out the polenta ahead of time, wrap the pieces in plastic wrap and keep them refrigerated until needed.)

5. AT SERVING TIME, when the veal gremolata is almost finished, dip the smooth side of each piece of polenta into the semolina or cornmeal and tap off the excess. Warm the olive oil in a large nonstick sauté pan or skillet over high heat and, when it is hot, add the polenta cakes, semolina side down. Brown the cakes for 2 to 3 minutes, or until they're crispy and golden, then flip them over and brown the other side. Drain the cakes on paper towels before serving. (If you're still a few minutes away from serving time, put the polenta cakes on a baking sheet and tuck them into a 200°F oven until you need them—they'll be fine for about 10 minutes.)

the veal gremolata:

5 tablespoons finely chopped Italian parsley
  leaves
1½ tablespoons grated lemon zest
2 tablespoons fresh bread crumbs
1 tablespoon finely chopped garlic
Salt and freshly ground white pepper
2 tablespoons extra-virgin olive oil
12 veal tournedos (medallions) cut from the
  tenderloin, each 2 ounces and 1 inch thick
2 tablespoons unsalted butter, cut into tiny bits

1 medium shallot, peeled, trimmed, finely
  chopped, rinsed, and dried
½ cup dry white wine
1 cup unsalted Chicken Stock (page 346) or
  store-bought low-sodium chicken broth
2 plum tomatoes, peeled, seeded, and cut into
  ¼-inch dice
2 tablespoons Niçoise olives, pitted and cut
  into ¼-inch dice

1. TO MAKE THE GREMOLATA, mix 4 tablespoons of the parsley, the lemon zest, bread crumbs, and garlic together in a small bowl. Season with salt and pepper and set aside.

2. SET THE BROILER RACK about 5 inches below the heating element and preheat the broiler.

3. WARM THE OLIVE OIL in a large sauté pan or skillet over high heat. Season the veal with salt and pepper and slip the medallions into the pan. Brown the meat for 2 minutes, then flip the medallions over and cook for another 2 minutes—the veal will be medium-rare; cook the medallions for a minute or two longer on each side if you like your veal better done.

4. PULL THE PAN from the heat and transfer the veal to a baking sheet—but don't wipe out the pan. Sprinkle the medallions with the gremolata and dot the tops with the butter. Set the veal aside briefly while you prepare the sauce. (If you haven't started to brown the polenta cakes, this is a good time to get them going.)

5. SET THE PAN you used to brown the veal over medium heat and toss in the shallot. Cook, stirring and scraping up whatever bits may have stuck to the bottom of the pan, until the shallot softens, about 1 to 2 minutes. Pour in the white wine and let it cook until it evaporates, then add the stock and allow it to reduce by half. Add the remaining 1 tablespoon parsley to the pan and stir in the tomatoes and olives. As soon as all the ingredients are warm, remove the pan from the heat, season the sauce with salt and pepper if needed, and set the pan aside while you finish the veal medallions.

6. SLIDE THE VEAL under the broiler and cook—keeping a close eye on the medallions—just until the gremolata topping is golden, a matter of a minute or two.

to serve: Place 3 polenta cakes on each of four warm dinner plates. For each serving, arrange 3 veal medallions on the polenta and spoon over some sauce.

to drink: A new-style Tuscan Chardonnay with some oak

Desserts

Pistachio Coconut Pain Perdu
with Kumquat Marmalade

What Americans call French toast, the French call *pain perdu,* or lost bread, because the dish is prepared with bread so stale it normally would be lost to the table. And while both Americans and French have the same idea of what pain perdu is, they differ on when to serve it—Americans eat French toast for breakfast, the French eat it for dessert. This version, for dessert, is not really French or American, but inspired by the flavors of Asia. The bread is soaked in a vanilla-scented batter based on coconut milk, and then crusted with shredded coconut and chopped pistachio nuts. Served with a golden kumquat marmalade, or the best-quality store-bought orange marmalade you can find (this is not a French toast for maple syrup), it is both warm and comforting and fresh and bright tasting.

the marmalade:

½ **pound kumquats, cut into** ¼**-inch-thick**
  slices and seeded
¼ **moist, plump vanilla bean**

2½ **teaspoons sugar**
3 **cups water**

1. **PUT THE KUMQUATS** in a medium saucepan with water to cover by 1 inch and bring to the boil. As soon as the water comes to the boil, drain the kumquats and cool them under cold running water; repeat this process two more times to rid the skins of some of their bitterness. After the last blanching, drain the kumquats well and return them to the pan.

2. **CUT THE VANILLA BEAN** lengthwise in half and, using the back of the knife, scrape the pulp out of the pod. Add the pulp, pod, and sugar to the kumquats, stir in the water, and bring to the boil. Lower the heat so that the water just simmers and cook the mixture, stirring frequently, for 1½ to 2 hours, until the kumquats are very tender. If, while the marmalade is cooking, it gets too thick and looks as though it's in danger of sticking to the bottom of the pan, add ¼ cup of water.

3. **USING A HAND-HELD** immersion blender, process the marmalade until it is puréed but not completely smooth. Alternatively, you can purée the marmalade by pulsing it in a food processor.

4. **LINE A PLATE** with a sheet of plastic wrap and spread the marmalade over the plastic in a thin layer. Top with another piece of plastic wrap, pressing the wrap against the kumquat marmalade to create an airtight seal. Chill in the refrigerator, then, when the marmalade is cool, remove the vanilla bean. *(Packed airtight, the marmalade will keep for at least 1 week in the refrigerator.)*

the pain perdu:

Four ¾**-inch-thick slices stale brioche or other**
  egg bread, such as challah
2 **large eggs**
2 **tablespoons sugar**
Pulp from ¼ **moist, plump vanilla bean**
  (scraped as above; reserve the pod for
  another use, if desired)

Pinch of salt
¾ **cup unsweetened coconut milk**
1 **tablespoon dark rum**
½ **cup chopped skinned unsalted pistachio nuts**
2 **tablespoons unsweetened dried shredded**
  coconut (available at health food markets)
2 **tablespoons unsalted butter**

1. **PLACE THE SLICES** of bread in a deep flat dish or a baking pan. (If you don't have a dish large enough to hold the four slices in one layer, soak the bread in two dishes.) Whisk together the eggs,

sugar, vanilla bean pulp, and salt in a bowl, add the coconut milk and rum, and whisk to combine. Pour this mixture over the bread. Soak the bread, turning it over as needed so that it absorbs the liquid evenly, about 10 minutes.

2. TOSS THE PISTACHIO NUTS and coconut together on a plate and keep the plate close to the stove. Melt the butter in a large sauté pan or skillet, preferably one that is nonstick, over high heat. When the butter is foamy, one by one, dip the slices of bread into the pistachio-coconut mixture—you only need to coat one side of each slice of bread—then slip the bread, nut side down, into the pan. Cook until the bread is golden brown on the first side, then flip the bread over and cook until the other side is equally golden, a total of about 4 to 6 minutes.

to serve: Get the pain perdu from pan to plate as quickly as you can, and serve with a spoonful of the marmalade.

to drink: A glass of dark rum to go with the dessert's tropical flavors

Arroz con Leche with Sangria Figs and Cherries

Inspired by the flavors of Spain, this rice pudding—*arroz con leche*—is both nursery-dessert soothing and boldly flavored. The soothing part is the pudding itself, Arborio rice lightly flavored with cinnamon, vanilla, and lemon. The punch comes from the poached fruit and syrup that serve as a topping. I've based the syrup on Spain's most popular summertime thirst quencher, sangria, the sweetened red wine made lusty with the addition of oranges and lemons, cloves, cinnamon, and vanilla. And I use the syrup to cook Black Mission figs and red cherries. It's a marriage of opposites—the pudding is cool and mellow, the topping is warm and wild—but it's a happy marriage.

This is a great party dessert because both the fruits and the pudding must be made a day ahead. Right before you're ready to serve, you have only to boil the sangria down to a glaze and warm the fruits in it.

MAKES 4 SERVINGS

the fruit:

½ plump, moist vanilla bean

2 cups red wine, preferably a full-bodied wine, perhaps a Grenache

⅔ cup sugar

Three ¼-inch-thick orange slices

Three ¼-inch-thick lemon slices

1 cinnamon stick

3 whole cloves

8 medium Black Mission figs

12 fresh sweet cherries, pitted

1. CUT THE VANILLA BEAN lengthwise in half and, using the back of the knife, scrape the pulp out of the pod. Put the pulp and pod into a medium saucepan along with all the other ingredients except the figs and cherries; bring to the boil. Pull the pan from the heat, cover, and allow to infuse for 10 minutes.

2. UNCOVER THE PAN, return it to medium heat, and bring to the boil again. Drop in the figs, lower the heat, and poach the figs at a simmer for 3 minutes. Add the cherries and poach for just 2 minutes more. Remove the pan from the heat and cool to room temperature, then store, tightly covered, in the refrigerator overnight.

the arroz con leche:

¾ cup Arborio rice

Pinch of salt

3 cups whole milk

1 cinnamon stick

½ moist, plump vanilla bean, split and scraped as above

1 strip lemon zest (pith removed)

3 tablespoons sugar

1. **LINE A BAKING PAN** or a shallow bowl with a sheet of plastic wrap.

2. **IN A MEDIUM SAUCEPAN,** bring the rice, salt, and 1½ cups water to the boil. Lower the heat and simmer until the rice absorbs almost all of the water. Meanwhile, stir the milk, cinnamon, vanilla bean pod and pulp, and lemon zest together in a small saucepan and warm over medium heat.

3. **ADD ½ CUP OF THE WARM MILK** to the rice and cook, stirring constantly with a wooden spoon, until the rice has just about absorbed the milk. Add another ½ cup milk and cook, stirring, until it is almost all absorbed. (Work just as if you were making a risotto.) When all the milk has been added, continue to cook—stirring without stopping—until the rice is creamy, not soupy. Stir in the sugar and pull the pan from the heat.

4. **IMMEDIATELY SPREAD THE RICE** pudding over the plastic-lined pan or bowl in a thin layer. Top with another piece of plastic wrap, pressing the wrap against the pudding to create an airtight seal. Chill in the refrigerator, then, when the pudding is cool, remove the cinnamon stick, vanilla bean, and lemon zest. *(The pudding can be made up to 8 hours ahead and kept covered in the refrigerator.)*

to finish:

1. **SPOON THE FIGS** and cherries out of the sangria syrup and keep them aside. Strain the syrup into a saucepan, bring to the boil, and boil until the sangria is reduced to ½ cup glaze.

2. **LOWER THE HEAT** under the glaze and add the figs and cherries to the pan. Basting constantly, cook until the fruit is warm and covered with a thick, shiny coating of glaze. Remove the pan from the heat and set the fruit and glaze aside to cool slightly, about 5 minutes, basting the fruit frequently with the glaze during this time.

to serve: Spoon an equal amount of chilled rice pudding into each of four small bowls. Cut the figs lengthwise in half. Make a small hollow in the center of each pudding and, for each serving, spoon in 4 warm fig halves and 3 cherries. Drizzle with some of the warm sangria glaze and serve.

to drink: Setubal, like Madeira, a Spanish fortified wine

Mango, Kiwi, and Coconut Custard Tart

I've always had a fondness for custard in general and custard tarts in particular, since they lend themselves so readily to variation, allowing me to reinvent them, drawing on the flavors that interest me at the moment or the exotic foods I sometimes find in the market. In this version, I've gone tropical, creating a tart that showcases contrasting flavors—it plays the warmth of coconut and cream against the citrusy freshness of mango and kiwi. And it does so in a very unusual way. While mango and kiwi are most often used as a decorative topping in desserts, I make them an integral—baked-in—part of this dessert. Thoroughly blended with the coconut custard and softened by the oven's heat, they show a different, gentler side of their personalities.

MAKES 8 SERVINGS

the crust:

**1 partially baked 8- by ¾-inch tart shell
   (in a tart ring) made from Pâte Sablée
   (page 353)**

KEEP THE CRUST, with the tart ring still in place, on the parchment-lined baking sheet. *(You can make the crust up to 8 hours ahead and keep it in its ring at room temperature.)*

the filling:

**1 cup unsweetened dried shredded coconut
   (available at health food markets)**
⅓ cup sugar
1 large egg
1 large egg yolk
1½ tablespoons all-purpose flour

½ cup whole milk
½ cup heavy cream
**½ small mango, peeled, pitted, and cut into ¾-
   inch cubes**
**2 small kiwis, peeled and cut into ¾-inch
   cubes**

1. PUT ALL THE INGREDIENTS except the mango and kiwis in the jar of a blender (or the container of a food processor) and purée until smooth. Pour the mixture into a jar or bowl, cover with plastic wrap, and refrigerate for 1 hour. *(The filling can be made up to this point 1 day ahead and kept covered in the refrigerator.)*

2. CENTER A RACK in the oven and preheat the oven to 300°F.

3. SCATTER THE MANGO and kiwi cubes evenly over the bottom of the crust. Gently stir the filling with a whisk (stir, don't beat—you don't want air in the mixture), then pour it over the fruit. Carefully slide the baking sheet into the oven and bake for 20 to 25 minutes, or until the filling is set; the edges of the tart will be lightly browned and a knife inserted in the center of the custard will come out clean. Pull the baking sheet from the oven and cool the tart to room temperature on a rack.

to serve: Once the tart is cooled, cut it into 8 wedges for serving.

to drink: A well-balanced Canadian Riesling ice wine

Coffee-Cardamom Pots de Crème

The idea for these small custards came to me while thinking about the way coffee is drunk in Middle Eastern countries: through a cardamom pod held in one's teeth. Cardamom's flavor is slightly sharp, like citrus, but also warm and round, like vanilla. And, like citrus and vanilla, it is a good mixer. In this recipe, crushed cardamom pods are cooked with chopped coffee beans and sugar until the sugar caramelizes—this is the best way to extract the most flavor from both the pods and beans. The sugar is then cooked with milk and cream, and finally mixed with egg yolks. Prepared this way, the cardamom and coffee are perfectly blended into the custard and their flavors lose none of their intensity. The finished pots de crème taste as though thick, rich cream had been added to a cup of Middle Eastern coffee.

MAKES 6 SERVINGS

3 ounces (1 cup) coffee beans, preferably an
    espresso roast
2 tablespoons cardamom pods
¾ cup sugar

2 cups (approximately) heavy cream
1 cup whole milk
7 large egg yolks

1. **PUT THE COFFEE BEANS** and cardamom pods in the work bowl of a food processor and pulse on and off several times to roughly chop—not grind—them. Turn the chopped beans and pods into a medium saucepan and add ½ cup of the sugar. Put the pan over medium heat and cook, stirring constantly with a wooden spoon, until the sugar starts to melt. Once the sugar has melted, continue to cook, still stirring without stop, until the sugar caramelizes—you want the color of the caramel to be deep amber, almost mahogany. Now, standing away from the stove so you don't get splattered, slowly pour in 1 cup of the cream and the milk. Don't panic—the caramel will immediately seize and harden, but it will all smooth out as the liquids warm and the sugar melts again. Bring the mixture to a boil and, when the sugar has melted and everything is smooth again, pull the pan from the heat. Cover the pan (we do this with plastic wrap at the Café to get a good seal) and allow the mixture to infuse for 20 minutes.

2. **CENTER A RACK** in the oven and preheat the oven to 300°F.

3. **WORKING IN A BOWL** that's large enough to hold all the ingredients, whisk the yolks and the remaining ¼ cup sugar together until the mixture is pale and thick. Strain the coffee-cardamom liquid into a measuring cup (discard the beans and pods) and add enough heavy cream to bring the liquid up to 2 cups. Very gradually and very gently—you don't want to create air bubbles—whisk the liquid into the egg mixture; skim off the top foam, if there is any.

4. ARRANGE SIX 4-OUNCE ESPRESSO or custard cups in a small roasting pan, leaving an even amount of space between them, and fill each cup nearly to the top with the custard mixture. Carefully slide the pan into the oven; then, using a pitcher, fill the roasting pan with enough hot water to come halfway up the sides of the espresso cups. Cover the pan with plastic wrap (don't worry—it can stand the heat) and poke two holes in two opposite corners. Bake the custards for about 40 minutes, or until the edges darken ever so slightly and the custards are set but still jiggle a little in the center when you shake them gently.

5. REMOVE THE PAN from the oven and let the custards sit in the water bath for 10 minutes. Peel off the plastic wrap, lift the cups out of the water, and cool the custards in the refrigerator. *(The pots de crème can be prepared a day ahead and stored in the refrigerator; when they are cool, cover them with plastic wrap.)*

to serve: The pots de crème are at their best at room temperature, so remove them from the refrigerator and keep them on the counter for about 20 minutes before serving.

to drink: A deluxe cream sherry, perhaps a Pedro Ximénez

Sacher Torte

Although Austria's pastry heritage is long and rich, its most widely known sweet, the Sacher Torte, is a relative newcomer. It was created by Prince Metternich's pastry chef in 1814 or 1815 to celebrate the Congress of Vienna, and there isn't a restaurant or pastry shop in Vienna that doesn't offer its own version of this classic dense, deep, dark chocolate cake. At Café Boulud, we too make our own, one that can hold its own in the deep and dark departments against any Sacher Torte here or abroad. The Café Boulud torte, like all the others, begins with nuts and bittersweet chocolate and it's finished with a shiny chocolate glaze. But instead of the more traditional apricot coating, it has raspberry jam—simply because I prefer it that way.

MAKES 8 SERVINGS

6 tablespoons almond flour (see Glossary, page 362) or finely ground blanched almonds

¼ cup all-purpose flour

¼ cup unsweetened cocoa powder, preferably Dutch-processed

4 ounces extra-bittersweet chocolate, preferably one that is at least 70% cocoa solids, finely chopped

8 tablespoons (1 stick) unsalted butter, at room temperature

¾ cup confectioner's sugar, sifted, plus extra for dusting

5 large eggs, 4 separated and 1 left whole, at room temperature

½ teaspoon freshly squeezed lemon juice

¼ cup raspberry jam (with seeds)

1. **CENTER A RACK** in the oven and preheat the oven to 425°F. Butter the inside of an 8- by 2-inch round cake pan, dust the inside with flour, tap out the excess, and set aside.

2. **SIFT TOGETHER** the almond flour or ground almonds, the all-purpose flour, and cocoa powder and set this mixture aside.

3. **MELT THE CHOCOLATE** in a heatproof bowl set over (not touching) simmering water or in a microwave set on low to medium power; set aside.

4. **WORKING IN A MIXER** fitted with the paddle attachment, beat the butter and confectioner's sugar together until the mixture is pale and creamy. One by one, add the whole egg and the yolks and continue to beat until the mixture is thick. Transfer the mixture to a large bowl, and wash and dry the mixer bowl.

5. **FIT THE MIXER** with the whisk attachment and the clean, dry bowl. Working on medium-low speed, beat the egg whites with the lemon juice just until they are foamy. Increase the speed to medium-high and continue to beat until the whites hold soft peaks.

6. **USING A LARGE FLEXIBLE RUBBER SPATULA** and a light hand, fold the melted chocolate into the egg yolk mixture, followed by the almond flour–cocoa mixture. Next, fold in the beaten egg whites

in 3 additions, and scrape the batter into the prepared pan; it will fill it only to the halfway mark. Slide the pan into the oven and bake for 20 to 22 minutes, or until a knife inserted in the center of the cake comes out clean. Unmold the cake onto a cooling rack, invert it, and cool to room temperature right side up on a rack. *(The cake can be wrapped airtight and frozen for up to a month.)*

7. IF THE TOP of the cake is domed or a little uneven, use a long serrated knife to slice away a sliver of the top to level it. Then cut the cake horizontally in half. Place the bottom half of the cake, cut side up, on a cardboard cake round or the removable metal bottom of a tart pan, preferably one that is slightly smaller than the cake. Spread the top of this half evenly with the raspberry jam, top with the other half of the cake, and put the cake aside while you make the ganache.

to finish:

5 ounces extra-bittersweet chocolate, preferably one that is at least 70% cocoa solids, finely chopped

2 cups heavy cream
½ cup raspberries
Confectioner's sugar for dusting

1. PUT THE CHOCOLATE in a bowl. Pour 1 cup of the heavy cream into a small saucepan and bring it to the boil. At the boil, pull the pan from the heat and slowly pour the hot cream over the chopped chocolate, whisking the mixture gently until you have a smooth, glossy ganache. Using an offset metal icing spatula, spread a thin layer of the ganache over the sides and top of the cake—this is just a coat to keep the crumbs from spoiling the final coat, so don't overdo it; it should be a very thin gloss. (If the ganache doesn't stick to the cake, cool the ganache for about 3 minutes.) Slide the cake into the freezer for 5 minutes to set the crumb coat; keep the ganache in a warm place.

2. CHOOSE A BOWL that is smaller in diameter than the cake and invert it on a piece of parchment or waxed paper—you're going to glaze the cake and you want the excess glaze to drip off the cake. Pull the cake out of the freezer and place it on the bowl. Pour the remaining warm ganache over the cake and smooth it across the top and sides with the offset metal icing spatula. The glaze will set in about 20 minutes, at which point the cake can be served or set aside at room temperature for 1 to 2 hours.

3. JUST BEFORE SERVING, dust the raspberries with confectioner's sugar and place them around the top edge of the cake. Whip the remaining 1 cup heavy cream until it holds soft peaks.

to serve: Put the cake on an attractive plate and cut it at the table, serving a dollop of the cream with each slice of Sacher Torte.

to drink: An espresso and/or a wild raspberry eau-de-vie

Ricotta Tart with Blueberries and Honey

The combination of honey and ricotta is typically Italian and very popular around Eastertime, when cheesecakes reign in Italy. At Café Boulud, the goodness of this cheesecake tart knows no specific holidays. The filling is as moist and creamy, silky even, as you'd expect it to be if it were made from cream cheese, a quality that comes from blending the ricotta until it is curdless. Mixed with eggs, flavored with lemon zest and vanilla, and lightened by whipped egg whites, the filling holds a small surprise—a bottom layer of fresh blueberries. The blueberries provide a touch of tartness, a nice contrast to the filling's milkiness, but they're not the only possibility for this layer. For variety, consider raspberries, blackberries, or even rum-soaked golden raisins. Any of these would go well with the filling and the tart's glistening topping—a thin layer of honey and pine nuts.

MAKES 8 SERVINGS

the crust:

**1 partially baked 8- by ¾-inch tart shell (in a
   tart ring) made from Pâte Sablée (page 353)**

KEEP THE CRUST, with the tart ring still in place, on the parchment-lined baking sheet. *(You can make the crust up to 8 hours ahead and keep it in its ring at room temperature.)*

the filling:

½ cup whole-milk ricotta cheese	**Pinch of salt**
2 tablespoons whole milk	**¼ teaspoon freshly squeezed lemon juice**
¼ moist, plump vanilla bean	**1 cup blueberries**
2 large eggs, 1 separated, 1 left whole	**½ cup pine nuts**
1 tablespoon sugar	**1 tablespoon honey**
Grated zest of ½ lemon	

1. CENTER A RACK in the oven and preheat the oven to 425°F.

2. PUT THE RICOTTA and 1 tablespoon of the milk in the container of a blender or food processor (or use a hand-held immersion blender) and blend until the ricotta is perfectly smooth. Scrape the ricotta into a bowl that's large enough to hold all the ingredients.

3. CUT THE VANILLA BEAN lengthwise in half and, with the back of the knife, scrape the pulp out of the pod; discard the pod (or reserve it for another use). Whisk the whole egg and the yolk into the ricotta, followed by the sugar, the remaining 1 tablespoon milk, the zest, the vanilla bean pulp, and salt.

4. WHIP THE EGG WHITE and lemon juice in a mixer fitted with the whisk attachment (or with a hand-held beater) on medium-low speed just until the white is broken up and foamy. Increase the speed to medium-high and continue to whip until the white holds medium peaks. Using a large flexible rubber spatula, delicately fold the white into the ricotta mixture.

5. SCATTER THE BLUEBERRIES over the bottom of the tart crust, then scrape the ricotta mixture over the berries, using the spatula to smooth the top. Slide the baking sheet into the oven and bake for 15 minutes, or until the top of the tart is golden and puffed; a knife inserted in the center of the tart should come out clean. Transfer the tart to a rack to cool to room temperature, during which time the top will sink—don't worry, it's normal.

6. WHILE THE TART IS COOLING, put the pine nuts and honey in a sauté pan and cook, stirring often, until the nuts are golden brown. Pour the mixture over the cooled tart, then use a metal offset spatula to smooth it evenly across the surface.

to serve: The tart is ready to be served when the pine-nut-and-honey topping has cooled. Cut the tart into 8 wedges.

to drink: A honey-flavored Juraçon Moelleux

Daniel Boulud at the farm

le potager   vegetarian dishes that celebrate the bounty of the garden

Le potager, the kitchen garden or vegetable plot, has been a source of profoundly happy memories in my life. My parents and theirs before them were farmers, and from the time I was old enough to dig potatoes or shuck peas, I worked in the garden with my family. Having grown up with a farmer's reverence for the earth's bounty, I have spent my years in the kitchen creating dishes that allow the infinite flavors, fragrances, and textures of vegetables to shine. Here is a selection of my favorite recipes from the potager, all completely vegetarian. Some of the recipes, like Heirloom Tomato and Goat Cheese Salad or A Dozen Spring Vegetables poached with ginger and basil, are light and simple; others, like the Root Vegetable Cassoulet, Cranberry Bean and Kale Stew, or sumptuous Wild Mushroom Civet cooked in red wine, are robustly flavored, complexly textured, and filling; but every recipe shows off to stunning advantage the natural goodness of the treasures we take from the garden.

Soups, Starters, Small Dishes, Lunches, and Anytime Food

Soupe au Pistou

Soupe au Pistou, a Provençal favorite, is a vegetable soup (it's minestrone's cousin) made potent with a dollop of pistou, France's answer to Italy's pesto. There are no rules for the soup itself—anything that's in season can be used, and the more variety, the better. In this rendition, I keep to the spirit of Provence by using chickpeas and potatoes, zucchini, plum tomatoes, and some haricots verts, swizzle-stick-thin green beans. Then I hop over the border and spoon in pesto rather than pistou for the last touch. The only difference between pesto and pistou is pine nuts—pesto's got them, pistou doesn't—but I like the body and richness that a few ground nuts bring to this soup. Whether made with pesto or pistou, the soup is bound to be one you'll turn to often, because it's made quickly and easily, it's full of flavor, and it's transporting: Swirl the pesto around in the bowl, catch a whiff of the warm basil and garlic, leeks, and potatoes, and then pinch yourself to prove you're not in Provence—or Liguria.

MAKES 4 SERVINGS

2 tablespoons extra-virgin olive oil

1 stalk celery, peeled, trimmed, and cut into ½-inch dice

1 small onion, peeled, trimmed, and cut into ½-inch dice

1 medium leek, white part only, cut into ½-inch dice, washed, and dried

4 cloves garlic, peeled, split, germ removed, and finely chopped

Salt and freshly ground white pepper

Spice sachet (½ teaspoon black peppercorns, ¼ teaspoon fennel seeds, ¼ teaspoon coriander seeds, and 1 bay leaf, tied in cheesecloth)

Bouquet garni (2 sprigs Italian parsley, 2 sprigs thyme, 1 sprig basil, wrapped in a leek green and tied)

6 cups unsalted Vegetable Stock (page 346), store-bought low-sodium vegetable broth, or water

1 large Yukon Gold potato, peeled and cut into ½-inch dice

1 medium carrot, peeled, trimmed, and cut into ½-inch dice

¼ pound haricots verts, trimmed and cut into ½-inch lengths

½ cup cooked chickpeas (see Glossary, page 366), or canned chickpeas, rinsed and drained

1 small zucchini, scrubbed, trimmed, and cut into ½-inch dice

2 plum tomatoes, peeled, seeded, and cut into ½-inch dice

½ cup pesto (page 274)

4 leaves basil, cut into thin strands

1. WARM THE OLIVE OIL in a Dutch oven or large casserole over medium heat. Stir in the celery, onion, leek, and garlic, season with salt and pepper, and cook, stirring, until the vegetables are translucent, about 10 to 12 minutes. Toss in the sachet and bouquet garni and pour in the stock or water. Bring to the boil, lower the heat so that the liquid simmers, and cook for 10 minutes, skimming off whatever foam rises to the surface.

2. ADD THE POTATO and carrot and simmer for 10 minutes more. Add the haricots verts and simmer for 5 minutes, then add the chickpeas and zucchini. Let the soup simmer for another 5 minutes or so, at which point the beans should be tender, then stir in the tomatoes and pull the pot from the heat. Scoop out and discard both the sachet and bouquet garni.

to serve: Ladle the soup into warm shallow soup plates and top each portion with a generous tablespoonful of pesto. Scatter over the basil leaves and serve.

to drink: A Provençal rosé

Wild Mushroom and Barley Soup

As comforting as a down blanket, this soup is a soothing bone-warmer for a blustery day. It gets its deep flavor from toasted barley and root vegetables, a bundle of herbs, and several kinds of mushrooms, both dried and fresh. The dried mushrooms are intensely and characteristically musky, while the fresh, depending on their variety, can be woodsy, hearty, or even light. In order to get the best flavor and texture, you really should put at least three different kinds of mushrooms into the soup. My favorite combination, a mix of exotic mushrooms, uses half chanterelles, the other half an equal blend of porcini and black trumpets. But if only cultivated mushrooms are available, you'll get an excellent soup from a blend that's half cremini and the rest a mix of shiitakes and oyster mushrooms.

This soup is complete as is, but I often bolster each portion with a small goat cheese flan and a parsley-garlic crouton—just float the flan in the soup and serve the crouton on the side.

MAKES 8 TO 10 SERVINGS

2 ounces dried mushrooms, preferably an assortment (such as morels, porcini, shiitakes, and chanterelles)

3 tablespoons unsalted butter or extra-virgin olive oil

1 cup pearl barley

1 stalk celery, peeled, trimmed, and cut into ¼-inch dice

1 medium leek, white part only, split lengthwise, cut into ¼-inch-thick slices, washed, and dried

1 medium onion, peeled, trimmed, and cut into ¼-inch dice

1 medium carrot, peeled, trimmed, and cut into ¼-inch dice

1 medium turnip, peeled, trimmed, and cut into ¼-inch dice

2 cloves garlic, peeled, split, germ removed, and finely chopped

Salt

6 leaves sage, finely chopped (reserve the stems for the herb sachet)

¾ pound mushrooms, preferably an assortment, trimmed, cleaned, and cut in half (or quartered if large)

3½ quarts unsalted Vegetable Stock (page 348) or store-bought low-sodium vegetable broth

Herb sachet (6 sage stems—reserved from above—4 sprigs Italian parsley, 2 sprigs thyme, 1 bay leaf, ¼ teaspoon fennel seeds, ¼ teaspoon coriander seeds, and ¼ teaspoon black peppercorns, tied in cheesecloth)

Freshly ground white pepper

Goat Cheese Flans with Garlic-Herb Croutons (page 290; see headnote) (optional)

1. PUT THE DRIED MUSHROOMS in a bowl and pour 2 cups of warm water over them. Let the mushrooms soak for at least 30 minutes, longer if it's more convenient for you. Remove the mushrooms from the water and squeeze them in your hands to get rid of the excess moisture; discard the soaking liquid.

2. WARM 1 TABLESPOON of the butter or oil in a small sauté pan or skillet over medium heat and, when it's hot, add the barley. Cook the barley, stirring regularly, for about 5 minutes, or until the grains are lightly toasted. Pull the pan from the heat and set the barley aside for the moment.

3. WARM THE REMAINING 2 tablespoons butter or oil in a stockpot or large casserole over medium heat. Add the celery, leek, onion, carrot, turnip, and garlic, season with salt, and cook, stirring, until the vegetables soften but do not color, about 10 minutes. Add the sage and all the mushrooms (fresh and reconstituted), season with salt again, and continue to cook just until the mushrooms release their moisture, a matter of minutes. Stir in 3 quarts of the stock and toss in the herb sachet and barley. Bring the soup to a boil, lower the heat so that it simmers gently, and cook until the barley is tender and the broth is thoroughly infused with the rich flavors of the mushrooms, about 1 hour and 10 minutes.

4. THIS IS REALLY A SOUP, not a thin stew, so, if you think your soup isn't soupy enough, bring the remaining 2 cups stock to the boil and add it to the pot. (If you're planning to refrigerate the soup and serve it later, don't add the extra broth now. Since the barley will absorb liquid as it rests, it's wiser to add the remaining broth when you're reheating the soup.) Taste and add more salt and some pepper if needed. (*The soup can be cooled, poured into a covered container, and kept in the refrigerator for about 4 days, or packed airtight and frozen for a month.*) Bring to the boil before serving.

to serve: Ladle the soup into warm bowls and, if you're serving them, float a flan in each bowl and offer a crouton on the side.

to drink: A light, earthy Oregon Pinot Noir

Soupe Glacée of Cavaillon Melon

The melon of choice for this refreshing, heady concoction—a soupe glacée, a chilled soup—is the highly perfumed cavaillon, a small orange-fleshed melon that's grown in France, Spain, and the Caribbean. Expensive even in France, it can be very expensive and a bit difficult to find here, but in its place you can use cantaloupe. The important thing is to buy a melon with a fragrance strong enough to set your head spinning when you sniff it at the market. Aroma is one of the primary pleasures of this soup, in which one portion of the melon is cooked down to concentrate its flavor and another is added to the soup raw, its fruitiness fresh and untouched. I think you'll find the base of the soup—cream infused with lemongrass, purple basil, and a touch of kaffir lime leaf—an unexpected but inspired match for the melon.

MAKES 4 SERVINGS

the melon:

4 ripe cavaillon melons or 2 large very ripe
  cantaloupes, peeled, halved, and seeded

1. **CUT ENOUGH OF** one of the melons into ¼-inch dice to make ½ cup and set this aside, covered, in the refrigerator. Cut the rest of the melon into small chunks and toss the chunks into a food processor; whir to purée.

2. **POUR OUT ¼ CUP** of the purée and keep it covered in the refrigerator. Pour the rest of the purée into a small saucepan and cook it over medium heat until it reduces just a bit, about 10 minutes. Pour the hot purée into a bowl and set the bowl into another larger bowl filled with ice cubes and water. Keep the purée over ice until needed, or, once it's cooled down, cover it and put it in the refrigerator. (*The purée can be kept, covered, in the refrigerator for up to 4 hours.*)

the soup base:

1 stalk lemongrass
1 whole star anise
1 cinnamon stick
10 fennel seeds
½ teaspoon coriander seeds
8 black peppercorns
1½ cups heavy cream

1 small kaffir lime leaf (optional)
Grated zest and juice of 1 lime
Three ¼-inch-thick slices peeled ginger
1 sprig basil, opal basil if available
Salt and freshly ground white pepper
3 drops Tabasco sauce

1. **YOU'RE GOING TO BE USING** some of the lemongrass for the soup base and some for the garnish, so it's most convenient to prepare it for both now. Discard the outer part of the stalk, trim the lemongrass so that it's about 5 inches long, and cut the white bulb away from the green stalk. Peel away the tough outer leaf from the bulb and finely chop enough of the tender heart of the lemongrass (the inside of the white bulb) to make 1 tablespoon—you'll use this for the garnish; cover and refrigerate. Use the heel of a chef's knife to bruise the green part of the lemongrass, which will flavor the soup base.

2. **PUT THE STAR ANISE,** cinnamon stick, fennel seeds, coriander seeds, and peppercorns in a medium saucepan over medium heat and warm, shaking the pan, until the spices are toasted and very aromatic, about 4 minutes. Add the cream, the kaffir lime leaf, if you're using it, half the lime zest (reserve the rest for the garnish), the ginger, basil, and the bruised lemongrass stalk. Bring to the boil, lower the heat, and simmer for 5 minutes. Season with salt and pepper and simmer for 5 minutes more. Strain the soup base into a bowl and set the bowl into an ice-water bath to cool.

3. **WHEN THE BASE IS WELL CHILLED,** stir in both the reserved ¼ cup uncooked melon purée and the cooled cooked purée, the Tabasco, and half of the lime juice (save the rest to finish the soup). Taste for seasoning and add more salt and pepper, if you want it. Strain the soup again and keep it refrigerated until needed.

the garnish:

The reserved melon dice, lemongrass, and lime juice and zest (from above)
1 sprig basil, opal if available, leaves only, finely chopped, plus 2 sprigs, leaves only (left whole)

1 small kaffir lime leaf, finely chopped (optional)
Salt and freshly ground white pepper
Tabasco sauce
1 sprig cilantro, leaves only

PUT THE DICED MELON in a bowl and season it with the reserved chopped lemongrass, lime juice, and zest, the chopped basil, and the kaffir lime leaf, if you're using it. Add salt and pepper, if needed, and just a drop or two of Tabasco.

to serve: For each serving, spoon one quarter of the diced melon into the center of a chilled small soup bowl and top with a few whole basil and cilantro leaves. Pour the well-chilled soup around the garnish and serve immediately, while everything is really cold.

to drink: An Oregon Pinot Blanc with bright melon flavors

Chilled Borscht with Scallion Sour Cream

Borscht, a time-honored specialty of Russian kitchens, is usually served hot and can be made with or without meat, but it must always have beets—they're what keep borscht from being just another vegetable soup. This version, my favorite, served icy cold, is so full of beets that its color rivals that of garnets. While I like beets and use them often, they're best when they've got a good partner or two to support them. Here, I made the borscht with a traditional soup base of sautéed leeks, onions, and celery (they soften the earthy edge common to beets), tossed in some diced leeks for texture and sweetness, and added a scallion cream that, once stirred into the borscht, smooths the flavors and draws them all together. If you want to take this soup luxe (and, in the process, make it not completely vegetarian), put a small spoonful of caviar on top of the scallion cream—the extra touch of saltiness is sensational.

MAKES 6 TO 8 SERVINGS

the borscht:

3 tablespoons extra-virgin olive oil

3 medium leeks, white and light green parts
   only, thinly sliced and washed

2 medium onions, peeled, trimmed, and thinly
   sliced

2 small stalks celery, peeled, trimmed, and
   thinly sliced

2¼ pounds beets, peeled and cut into
   ½-inch dice

Salt and freshly ground white pepper

Herb sachet (3 sprigs Italian parsley,
   2 sprigs thyme, 2 cloves garlic, peeled and
   crushed, 1 bay leaf, and 10 black peppercorns, tied in cheesecloth)

2 quarts unsalted Vegetable Stock
   (page 348) or store-bought low-sodium
   vegetable broth

Splash of sherry vinegar

1. **WARM THE OLIVE OIL** in a stockpot or large casserole over medium heat and, when it's hot, add the leeks, onions, and celery. Cook, stirring, until the vegetables soften but don't color, about 10 minutes. Toss in the beets, season with salt and pepper, and continue to cook and stir for another 10 minutes or so. Add the herb sachet and stock to the pot and bring to the boil, then lower the heat and simmer the borscht until the beets are tender, about 35 minutes.

2. **REMOVE AND DISCARD** the sachet, then, working in batches, ladle the soup into the container of a blender and whir until the borscht is smooth. Season with salt and pepper as needed and a touch of sherry vinegar, then strain the borscht into a container and refrigerate to chill. *(The borscht can be made up to 1 day ahead and kept tightly covered in the refrigerator.)*

the leeks and beets:

2 tablespoons extra-virgin olive oil

1 small leek, white part only, split lengthwise, cut into ¼-inch dice, washed, and dried

Salt and freshly ground white pepper

1 small beet, peeled, trimmed, and cut into ¼-inch dice

WARM 1 TABLESPOON of the oil in a small sauté pan or skillet over medium heat. Add the leek, season with salt and pepper, and cook, stirring, until the leek is tender but not colored, about 5 minutes. Transfer the leek to a plate to cool, and wipe out the pan. Warm the remaining 1 tablespoon oil in the pan, add the beet, season with salt and pepper, and cook, stirring, until it too is tender, about 10 minutes. Transfer the beet to another plate to cool.

the scallion cream:

2 teaspoons extra-virgin olive oil

1 bunch scallions, white part only, finely sliced

Salt and freshly ground white pepper

1 cup cold sour cream

1. WARM THE OLIVE OIL in a small sauté pan or skillet over low heat, then add the scallions. Cook slowly, stirring them frequently, until they are tender. Season with salt and pepper and set the scallions aside to cool.

2. FOLD THE COOLED SCALLIONS into the cold sour cream. Season with additional pepper.

to serve: Ladle the cold borscht into small chilled soup bowls, scatter over some of the cooled leek and beet, and top each with a dollop of scallion cream.

to drink: A Russian vodka, preferably one that's peppered

Curried-Pepper Vinaigrette with Asparagus

A cross between a dip and a dressing, this quickly made sunflower-yellow vinaigrette is ideal with steamed or poached vegetables. I serve it with asparagus as a predinner nibble or as a buffet dish, but it's also very good with artichokes and, if you're not preparing an all-*potager* meal, mussels, shrimp, or the Asparagus and Lobster Salad (page 118). The vinaigrette is neither hot nor spicy, neither aggressively curried nor overly saffroned. Its up-front flavor is that of mild, sweet yellow bell peppers, which is why it's such a good companion to so many other vegetables.

MAKES 4 SERVINGS

the curried-pepper vinaigrette:

2 tablespoons extra-virgin olive oil

2 yellow peppers, cored, seeded, deveined, and
   cut into ¼-inch dice

1 teaspoon Madras curry powder

½ teaspoon saffron threads

Pinch of cayenne pepper

Salt and freshly ground white pepper

2 tablespoons water

1½ teaspoons white vinegar

WARM THE OLIVE OIL in a small sauté pan or skillet over medium heat. Add the diced peppers, curry powder, saffron, and cayenne and season with salt and pepper. Cook, stirring frequently, for 10 minutes, or until the peppers are very soft but not in the least colored. Add the water and warm it for a minute or two, then remove the pan from the heat. Using an immersion or regular blender, purée the mixture, then push it through a fine-mesh strainer. Stir in the vinegar, and taste for salt and pepper. *(The vinaigrette can be made up to a day ahead and kept covered in the refrigerator.)*

the asparagus:

24 stalks pencil-thin asparagus, peeled and
   trimmed

PUT A POT OF SALTED WATER up to boil. Starting at the tips, cut the asparagus into 2- to 3-inch lengths; discard any short pieces that remain. When the water is boiling, plunge the asparagus into the pot and cook at the boil until tender but still very green, 3 to 4 minutes. Gently lift the asparagus out of the pot and run it under cold water to stop the cooking and cool it. When it's cool, pat dry between kitchen towels. *(The asparagus can be cooked a few hours ahead and kept covered in the refrigerator.)*

to serve: Spoon the vinaigrette into a bowl, surround with the asparagus, and let everyone dip.

to drink: Limoncello-ade, a mix of lemonade, water, and Limoncello

Salsa Cruda with Horseradish and Avocado Mousse

Salsa cruda is a liquidy summer salad, almost a gazpacho. Its flavors, based on sun-ripened tomatoes and sharpened by horseradish, chile, and lime, sing out with freshness. Since this has to be served very cold, keep your mixing bowl over ice and plan to serve the salsa cruda as soon as you've made its luscious mousse. I'm calling the avocado topping a mousse for lack of another name. Whirred in a food processor, it has the creamy texture of a mousse, but it's made with only avocado, lime juice, and a pinch of salt. Here, everything depends on the avocado—choose the ripest one you can find.

MAKES 4 SERVINGS

the salsa:

2 large very ripe tomatoes, cored and cut into ¼-inch cubes

3 scallions, white part only, thinly sliced

2 red radishes, trimmed, washed, dried, and cut into ¼-inch dice

1 small cucumber or a 6-inch length of an English cucumber, peeled, seeded, and cut into ¼-inch dice

1 serrano chile, halved, seeds removed, and finely chopped

2 tablespoons extra-virgin olive oil

1 tablespoon (packed) freshly grated horseradish

1 tablespoon freshly squeezed lime juice

10 leaves cilantro, finely chopped

6 leaves mint, finely chopped

4 large leaves basil, finely chopped

¾ teaspoon salt, or to taste

Freshly ground white pepper

PLACE A BOWL in another larger bowl filled with ice cubes and water. Gently stir all the ingredients together in the smaller bowl and keep the salsa on ice while you prepare the mousse.

the mousse:

1 large very ripe (but not overripe) avocado, halved, pitted, and peeled

1 tablespoon freshly squeezed lime juice

½ teaspoon salt

1 tablespoon finely chopped chives, for garnish

1 red radish, trimmed, washed, dried, and cut

PLACE THE AVOCADO, lime juice, and salt in the work bowl of a food processor and whir, scraping down the sides of the bowl as needed, until the mousse is perfectly smooth and very creamy.

to serve: Spoon the salsa cruda into chilled small bowls, top each with a spoonful of mousse, sprinkle the mousse with minced chives, and surround with slices of radish.

to drink: A salt-rimmed margarita

Heirloom Tomato and Goat Cheese Salad

As much as I love this salad, I only make it when I've got perfect, absolutely ripe, filled-with-juice tomatoes, which means this is a heart-of-summer salad. At Café Boulud, we make this salad when the farmers at the Union Square Greenmarket are offering their best heirloom tomatoes or when Alex Lee, the executive chef at Daniel, brings in a basket of tomatoes from his garden. As good as everything is that goes into this salad—the pesto, mixed with the seasoned juice from the tomatoes, and the fresh, soft goat cheese and herbs—the salad will be only just good enough if your tomatoes aren't exceptional.

MAKES 6 SERVINGS

the salad:

4 large ripe, juicy heirloom tomatoes, peeled
   and cored
18 small tomatoes, such as cherry, grape, or
   pear tomatoes, cut in half
1 shallot, peeled, trimmed, finely chopped,
   rinsed, and dried
1 tablespoon finely chopped Italian parsley
   leaves

1 tablespoon finely chopped oregano leaves
2 teaspoons salt
Pinch of freshly ground white pepper
Pinch of red pepper flakes
2 tablespoons balsamic vinegar
1 tablespoon sherry vinegar

CUT THE HEIRLOOM tomatoes lengthwise in half. Working over a strainer set over a large bowl, seed the tomatoes, discarding the seeds and saving the juice in the bowl. Cut each tomato into 8 wedges and put the tomatoes, along with all the other ingredients, into the bowl with the juice. Mix everything together gently and allow to sit at room temperature for 30 minutes. (If you need to leave the tomatoes for up to an hour or even an hour and a half, that's OK.)

the pesto:

2 bunches basil (about 8 ounces), leaves only,
   washed
½ clove garlic, peeled and germ removed

1 teaspoon pine nuts, very lightly toasted
1 teaspoon finely grated Parmesan cheese
½ cup extra-virgin olive oil

1. PUT A POT OF SALTED WATER up to boil. Plunge the basil into the boiling water and blanch for 2 minutes. Drain the leaves and run them under cold water to stop the cooking and cool them. Drain, then squeeze the leaves free of excess moisture between your palms.

2. PUT ALL THE INGREDIENTS in the container of a food processor and whir until smooth. Transfer to a bowl, cover, pressing a piece of plastic wrap against the surface, and set aside until needed. *(The pesto can be made up to a day ahead and kept tightly covered in the refrigerator. Stir the pesto and bring it to room temperature before using.)*

to finish:
Salt and freshly ground white pepper
6 ounces (1 cup) soft goat cheese

DRAIN THE TOMATOES, reserving the tomato juice, and arrange them on a large serving platter or in a shallow bowl. Pour up to ¾ cup of the reserved juice into the pesto and mix well: You might want a little less tomato juice, but you probably won't want more. What you're looking for is a fairly thin, very tasty pesto—taste as you mix. Season with salt and pepper, if needed.

to serve: Top the tomatoes with dollops of cheese and drizzle the entire salad with the pesto. Pass the extra pesto in a sauceboat at the table.

to drink: A chilled Pouilly-Fumé from the Loire Valley

Vegetables en Rémoulade

Think of rémoulade sauce as the French equivalent of tartar sauce. Like its American cousin, it's got a mayonnaise base to which pickles and other salty, vinegary ingredients are added. But unlike tartar sauce, which is served almost exclusively with fried fish, rémoulade sauce finds itself served alongside vegetables, raw or cooked, crunchy or soft (for a very simple salad, pair it with nothing more than hearts of romaine), fruit and vegetable salads (try it with a combination of pears and celery), cold meats, chilled seafood, and, of course, fried fish.

For this dish, the rémoulade is served as a dipping sauce, and the dippers are a combination of crisp, raw vegetables and some that are lightly blanched and therefore slightly softened. With the colorful vegetables arranged on a large platter and the pickle-polka-dotted sauce in the center, the salad is not only delicious but great looking too.

MAKES 6 SERVINGS

the rémoulade:

2 large egg yolks

1 tablespoon freshly squeezed lemon juice

2 teaspoons Dijon mustard

1 teaspoon sherry vinegar

1/4 teaspoon salt, or more to taste

Pinch of freshly ground white pepper, or more to taste

1 cup vegetable oil

1 large hard-boiled egg, finely chopped

1 1/2 tablespoons chopped cornichons (bottled French gherkins)

1 1/2 tablespoons chopped capers

1 tablespoon chopped Italian parsley leaves, plus extra for garnish

1 1/2 teaspoons chopped tarragon leaves, plus extra for garnish

1 small clove garlic, peeled, split, germ removed, and finely chopped

MAKE THE MAYONNAISE base by whisking together the yolks, lemon juice, mustard, vinegar, salt, and pepper in a medium bowl. Whisking constantly, drizzle in the vegetable oil—start by adding the oil in droplets and then, when the mixture starts to look thick and creamy, pour the oil into the bowl in a slow, steady stream. Fold in the remaining ingredients, taste the rémoulade sauce, and add more salt and pepper if needed. Set the sauce aside briefly, or refrigerate it until needed. *(The sauce can be made up to 1 day in advance and kept well covered in the refrigerator.)*

the vegetables:

6 ounces haricots verts, trimmed

12 stalks asparagus, peeled and trimmed

1 small fennel bulb, trimmed and cut into 6 wedges

1 tomato, peeled, cut into 6 wedges, and seeded

1 small head romaine, cored and cut into 6 wedges

1 small cucumber, peeled, seeded, and cut lengthwise into 6 pieces

3 stalks celery, peeled, trimmed, and cut crosswise in half

6 red radishes, trimmed, washed, dried, and cut crosswise in half

PUT A LARGE POT of salted water up to boil. When the water is at a rolling boil, add the haricots verts and cook just until they are tender, 4 to 5 minutes. Scoop the beans out of the pot with a slotted spoon and run them under cold water to set their color and cool them; drain. Next, blanch the asparagus for 4 to 5 minutes, run it under cold water, and drain. Finally, blanch the fennel until tender, 5 to 8 minutes, drain, cool under cold water, and drain again. Dry the vegetables well between layers of paper towels.

to serve: Spoon the rémoulade sauce into a bowl, sprinkle with the extra parsley and tarragon, and place the bowl in the center of a serving platter. Arrange all the vegetables (blanched and raw) around the rémoulade and serve, inviting everyone to pick and dip.

to drink: A refreshing cold pale beer

Tapenade Salad

Tapenade, a highly seasoned purée of black olives, is as much a kitchen staple in the South of France as ketchup or mayonnaise is here in America. Coal-black, garlicky, salty, pleasantly oily, and olivey, to be sure, tapenade can be spread on bread to add zip to a sandwich, swirled into soups, offered as a dip, or used as a salad dressing, as it is in this lively mix of shaved fennel, roasted peppers, tomatoes (a natural partner for tapenade), and peppery arugula. I like this as a first-course salad topped with shards of Parmesan and served with a garlic-and-herb crouton on the side. Consider starting everyone off with just a touch of tapenade—it's powerful stuff—and bringing the rest to the table so that those with a taste for the pungent can serve themselves more.

If you want the tapenade but don't want to commit to the whole salad, do what I often do: Spread the tapenade evenly over the inside of a roasted sweet pepper, top with a few fresh basil leaves, and serve with a knife and fork, or set the pepper on a toasted round of crusty bread, to be eaten like an open-faced sandwich.

MAKES 4 SERVINGS

the tapenade:

1 cup Niçoise or Kalamata olives, rinsed, dried, and pitted

½ cup extra-virgin olive oil

20 leaves basil

1 tablespoon capers, preferably salt-packed, rinsed and dried

1 tablespoon pine nuts, lightly toasted

½ clove garlic, peeled and germ removed

½ teaspoon grated lemon zest

Salt and freshly ground white pepper

PUT ALL THE INGREDIENTS except the salt and pepper in the work bowl of a food processor and whir, scraping down the sides of the bowl as needed, until the olives are puréed and the ingredients blended. Taste for seasoning—you'll want to add some pepper, but the olives and capers may provide all the salt you'll need. (*The tapenade can be made up to 1 week in advance and kept tightly covered in the refrigerator.*)

the salad:

1 small fennel bulb, trimmed

8 red radishes, trimmed, washed, dried, and thinly sliced

1 roasted red bell pepper, cut into 8 pieces

1 roasted yellow bell pepper, cut into 8 pieces

1 pint cherry tomatoes, halved

1 small cucumber, peeled, seeded, and cut into 2-inch lengths

1 scallion, white part only, thinly sliced on the bias

1 bunch arugula, tough stems removed,
    washed, and dried
½ stalk celery, peeled, trimmed, and thinly
    sliced on the bias

Finely grated zest of ½ lemon and the juice of
    the whole lemon
Fleur de sel or lightly crushed coarse sea salt
    and freshly ground white pepper

CUT THE FENNEL into quarters and, using a mandoline or box grater, shave it into thin slices. Toss the fennel into a mixing bowl along with all the other vegetables. Season the salad with the lemon zest and juice, salt, and pepper.

to serve:
Shaved Parmesan cheese
2 tablespoons pine nuts, toasted
Garlic-Herb Croutons (page 290) (optional)

ARRANGE THE SALAD on four chilled plates and top with the Parmesan and a smattering of toasted nuts. Dot the plates with some of the tapenade and spoon the rest into a bowl; let everyone serve themselves more if they want. Serve with the croutons, if you've made them.

to drink: A chilled spicy, summery, red Barbera d'Alba

Stuffed Grape Leaves with Herbed Yogurt Dipping Sauce

This is finger food, perfect for a party, a buffet, or an outdoor lunch, or as an accompaniment to apéritifs. The grape leaves are stuffed with lemony white rice and currants and served with a yogurt sauce seasoned with vegetables, spices, and herbs. Actually, it's a sauce when the grape leaves are served on a plate, as they will be if you make this dish a sit-down starter, and a dip when the packets are pick-up food. Either way, you'll find other occasions to serve the yogurt sauce, since it goes nicely with greens of many varieties. Just a note about the rice: Resist the temptation to cook it all the way through at the start; it's meant to be parboiled because it will finish cooking—perfectly—when the packets are braised.

MAKES 4 LUNCH OR 6 STARTER SERVINGS

the sauce:

1 cup plain yogurt

2 small red radishes, trimmed, washed, dried, and finely grated (on the small or medium holes of a box grater)

⅓ small cucumber, peeled, seeded, and finely grated (on the small or medium holes of a box grater)

2 tablespoons finely chopped cilantro leaves

1 tablespoon freshly squeezed lemon juice

1 small clove garlic, peeled, split, germ removed, and finely chopped

Pinch of ground coriander

Pinch of ground cumin

Pinch of cayenne pepper

Salt and freshly ground white pepper

1. **LINE A FINE-MESH STRAINER** with a double thickness of damp cheesecloth and set the strainer over a bowl. Spoon the yogurt into the strainer. Chill the setup for at least 1 hour and for up to 6 hours, time enough for the yogurt to drain off some of its moisture.

2. **TURN THE YOGURT** into a bowl, and squeeze the grated radishes and cucumber between your hands to remove the excess moisture. Stir them into the yogurt along with the remaining ingredients. Taste for salt and pepper. The sauce can be served immediately or refrigerated until needed. *(The sauce can be made up to 3 hours ahead and kept covered in the refrigerator.)*

the grape leaves:

½ jar (or ½ pound) grape leaves

SEPARATE THE GRAPE LEAVES and put them in a heatproof bowl. Pour enough boiling water over the leaves to cover them and let the leaves soak for at least an hour, then rinse the leaves twice under cold running water and pat them dry between layers of paper towels.

the filling:

1 cup imported basmati rice

Salt

5 tablespoons extra-virgin olive oil

½ medium onion, peeled, trimmed, and finely
   diced

Freshly ground white pepper

½ cup finely chopped herbs, preferably a mix of
   Italian parsley, cilantro, mint, and dill

¼ cup pine nuts, lightly toasted

¼ cup (packed) currants or golden raisins

Finely grated zest of 1 lemon

Freshly squeezed juice of ½ lemon

1. PUT THE RICE in a medium saucepan with 3 cups water and 1 teaspoon salt and bring to the boil. Lower the heat and allow the rice to cook at a simmer for 10 minutes. (It won't be fully cooked at this point—that's fine.) Drain the rice, run it under cold water, drain it again, and then chill it while you prepare the rest of the filling.

2. WARM 1 TABLESPOON of the olive oil in a medium sauté pan or skillet and add the onion. Season with salt and pepper and cook, stirring, just until the onion is tender but not colored, about 5 minutes. Turn the onion into a bowl and stir in the remaining ingredients. Add the cooled rice and season the filling with salt and pepper.

3. SO THAT THE GRAPE LEAVES will fold into tidy packets, cut off the stems and enough of the bottom of each leaf to make a straight edge. Flatten one leaf on a cutting board, keeping the straight side (the stem end) closest to you. Place a mounded tablespoonful of filling close to, but not on, the straight edge and fold the sides of the leaf over the filling—don't stretch the leaf, just turn the sides in. Now, working from the bottom, roll the leaf up to make a secure packet. It's best if you have only a single layer of leaf on top of the filling, so when you've rolled the packet over and made that top layer, cut off and discard the rest of the leaf. Place the leaf seam side down in a sauté pan or skillet large enough to hold all the stuffed leaves. Continue filling and folding leaves until you've used all the filling. Check the pan: The packets should be snug but not overcrowded; you need to give the leaves a bit of room since the rice is going to finish cooking, and expand a little, in the next step.

to cook:

1½ **cups water**   1 **sprig thyme**

2 **tablespoons extra-virgin olive oil**   1 **bay leaf**

½ **teaspoon salt**

MIX ALL THE INGREDIENTS together and pour them over the grape leaves. Cut a round of parchment paper to fit inside the pan (see Glossary, page 369), then cut a small air vent in the center of the paper. Press the parchment against the grape leaves and set the pan over medium heat. When the liquid comes to the boil, lower the heat so that it simmers gently and braise the packets, checking on their progress occasionally, for 30 to 35 minutes, at which point the rice should be fully cooked and the liquid absorbed. Remove the packets from the pan and arrange them on a serving platter. *(The stuffed grape leaves can be served now, while they're warm, or when they reach room temperature. They can be made up to 12 hours ahead and kept covered and chilled; bring the packets to room temperature before serving.)*

to serve: If you are serving this as a sit-down first course, spoon some of the yogurt sauce onto the center of each plate and top with about 6 stuffed grape leaves. Or, if you want to use the grape leaves on a buffet or as a nibble with apéritifs, just arrange the packets in a pyramid in the center of a platter and offer the yogurt sauce in a bowl on the side.

to drink: A light, dry Malvesia

Asparagus Tart

This is a tart I make often in spring. It's based on an asparagus purée that's enlivened with ramps, those wild onions that look like very skinny baby leeks or floppy scallions but taste bigger and sharper. (When the market is no longer offering ramps, I switch to garlic to get a similar edge.) The purée is blended with eggs and cream, poured into a crust that's been layered with sautéed mushrooms, Texas bulb onions, and sliced blanched asparagus, and baked slowly, the better to get a lovely, smooth custard texture. My favorite accompaniment for this tart is a small salad of asparagus spears, greens, and mushrooms, drizzled with nut oil and sherry vinegar. The salad complements the tart's lightness and adds a touch of chill. Think of it as the yang to the tart's yin.

MAKES 8 SERVINGS

the crust:

1 unbaked 9½-inch tart shell (in a fluted tart pan) made from Pâte Brisée (page 352), chilled

1 large egg white, lightly beaten

1. CENTER A RACK in the oven and preheat the oven to 350°F.

2. FIT A PARCHMENT PAPER round into the bottom and up the sides of the crust and fill with dried beans or rice. Back the crust for 18 to 20 minutes, remove the paper and beans, and bake for 3 to 5 minutes more, until golden. Brush the inside of the hot crust with the lightly beaten egg white and bake for just 1 minute longer. Transfer the crust to a rack to cool to room temperature.

the filling:

23 stalks jumbo asparagus, peeled

6 ramps, trimmed, washed, and leaves and bulbs separated, or 4 cloves garlic, peeled, split, and germ removed

1 tablespoon unsalted butter

2 Texas or Vidalia spring bulb onions, bulbs and some green only, split lengthwise and cut into thin slices

½ teaspoon finely chopped rosemary leaves

2 large very firm porcini or white mushrooms, trimmed, cleaned, and cut into thin slices

Salt and freshly ground white pepper

1 cup heavy cream

2 large eggs

1 large egg yolk

Pinch of cayenne pepper

1 tablespoon very finely grated Parmesan

1. PUT A LARGE POT of well-salted water up to boil. The asparagus is going to be cut in two different ways—you'll use 5 tips and all of the stalks for the tart and the remaining tips for the salad. The easiest way to do the cutting is to start from the tip of each asparagus and cut off a 4-inch-long piece. Then cut the next 3 inches of the stalk into ¼-inch-thick slices and discard what remains of the stalk.

Plunge the spears into the boiling water and cook for 5 minutes, then lift them from the pot and run them under cold water to stop the cooking and set their color. Drain and set aside. Add the ramp bulbs (or garlic) to the pot and boil for 5 minutes, then add the asparagus slices and ramp leaves. Boil for another 2 minutes, then drain the vegetables, run them under cold water until they are cool, and drain them again. Squeeze the moisture from the ramp leaves and pat the asparagus spears and slices, as well as the ramp bulbs, dry with several changes of paper towels.

3. MELT THE BUTTER in a medium sauté pan or skillet over medium heat. Add the onions and rosemary and cook, stirring, until the onions are soft but not colored, about 5 minutes. Add the mushroom slices, season with salt and pepper, and continue to cook and stir for 5 minutes more. Turn the ingredients out of the pan onto a plate and allow them to cool.

4. CENTER A RACK in the oven and preheat the oven to 275°F. Place the crust on a parchment-lined baking sheet and keep it close at hand.

5. PUT HALF THE ASPARAGUS slices and the ramp leaves and bulbs (or the garlic) into the work bowl of a food processor and pulse on and off to chop them. Add the cream, eggs and yolk, cayenne, and salt and pepper to taste and process until the mixture is smooth. Using a spatula, spread the sautéed onions and mushrooms over the bottom of the crust and scatter over the remaining asparagus slices. Pour the custard into the crust; it will come almost to the rim. Arrange 5 of the asparagus spears in a pinwheel in the center of the tart. Sprinkle the Parmesan evenly over the top of the tart and bake until the custard is set in the center, 40 to 45 minutes. Cool the tart on a rack while you make the salad.

the salad:

The reserved asparagus spears (from above)
2 large very firm porcini or white mushrooms,
   trimmed, cleaned, and cut into very thin slices
¼ pound purslane or tender baby spinach,
   stems removed, washed, and dried

Hazelnut or walnut oil
Sherry vinegar
Salt and freshly ground white pepper

TOSS THE ASPARAGUS SPEARS, mushrooms, and purslane or spinach together in a large bowl. Drizzle over some nut oil and a little vinegar, season with salt and pepper, and toss again to dress the salad evenly.

to serve: Cut the slightly cooled tart into 8 wedges and place a wedge and some salad on each dinner plate.

to drink: A well-balanced, not very sweet Alsatian Vendage Tardive Riesling

Cremini and Fontina Tart

I had quiche on my mind when I created this tart for the debut menu at Café Boulud. I wanted something with the custardy texture of quiche, but I wanted it to have more complexity. To start, I was after a certain roastedness, an underlying warmth, that I was able to build into the recipe by caramelizing the onions to make a confit, or compote, that I layered into the tart. Then, still thinking quiche, I replaced the traditional ham with thick slices of firm cremini and had rich, buttery Italian Fontina cheese stand in for the more expected Gruyère, a wonderful cheese, but one that would have been too sharp and nutty for this tart. After tinkering and tasting, I finally got what I wanted: a sophisticated dress-up tart with cozy, country-café appeal.

MAKES 8 SERVINGS

the crust:

1 unbaked 9½-inch tart shell (in a fluted tart pan)
   made from Pâte Brisée (page 352), chilled
1 large egg white, lightly beaten

1. CENTER A RACK in the oven and preheat the oven to 350°F.

2. FIT A PARCHMENT PAPER round into the bottom and up the sides of the crust and fill with dried beans or rice. Bake the crust for 18 to 20 minutes, remove the paper and beans, and bake for 3 to 5 minutes more, until golden. Brush the inside of the tart with the lightly beaten egg white and bake for just 1 minute longer. Transfer the crust to a rack to cool to room temperature.

the filling:

5 tablespoons extra-virgin olive oil
2 cloves garlic, peeled
¾ pound cremini mushrooms, trimmed,
   cleaned, and cut into ¼-inch-thick slices
1 sprig thyme
Salt and freshly ground white pepper
1 large onion, peeled, trimmed, halved, and
   finely sliced
½ teaspoon sugar

2 tablespoons sherry vinegar
1 large shallot, peeled, trimmed, finely
   chopped, rinsed, and dried
2 large eggs
⅔ cup heavy cream
¼ pound Italian Fontina cheese, cut into
   ¼-inch dice
½ cup finely grated Parmesan cheese

1. CENTER A RACK in the oven and preheat the oven to 375°F. Place the tart pan on a parchment-lined baking sheet and keep it close at hand.

2. WARM 2 TABLESPOONS of the olive oil in a sauté pan or skillet over medium heat. Crush 1 of the cloves of garlic and add it to the pan along with the cremini and thyme. Season with salt and pepper and cook, stirring often, until the mushrooms are tender and just lightly browned, about 5 minutes. Remove and discard the garlic and thyme and transfer the cremini to a bowl to cool.

3. WARM 2 MORE TABLESPOONS of the oil in the same pan over medium-high heat. Toss the onion with the sugar and salt and pepper to taste in a small bowl. Add the onion to the pan and cook, stirring frequently, for 8 to 10 minutes, until evenly caramelized. Stir in the sherry vinegar and cook, continuing to stir, until the vinegar boils away completely. Pull the pan from the heat.

4. SPLIT THE REMAINING CLOVE of garlic, remove and discard the germ, and finely chop the garlic. Warm the remaining 1 tablespoon olive oil in a small sauté pan or skillet over medium heat. When it's hot, add the garlic and shallot, season with salt and pepper, and cook, stirring, until the garlic and shallot are soft but not colored, about 3 minutes. Remove from the heat and let cool.

5. TOSS THE GARLIC-SHALLOT mixture with one quarter of the cremini (keep the remaining cremini aside). Season with salt and pepper, scrape the mixture into the jar of a blender, and add the eggs and cream; purée until smooth. (Take care not to overprocess this mixture—you don't want to thicken the cream.)

6. POUR HALF OF THE CREAM mixture into the crust, then, leaving any juices that may have accumulated in the bowl, arrange the remaining cremini in an even layer over the cream. Follow with a layer of the caramelized onions, again leaving any liquid in the bowl, and then a layer of the Fontina cheese. Pour in enough of the remaining cream mixture to come to the rim of the crust; there may be some cream left over. Sprinkle the tart with the Parmesan cheese and very carefully slide the baking sheet into the oven. Bake for 20 to 25 minutes, or until the top is nicely browned and the custard is set.

to serve: The tart should be served while it is still very hot. Give it a 5-minute rest after it comes from the oven, then slice and serve.

to drink: A toasty, nutty, rich white wine, such as a Chassagne-Montrachet

Cheese-Topped Stuffed Artichoke Hearts

Whenever you see garlic, tomatoes, basil, and black olives, some of the ingredients I use to stuff these artichokes, you're bound to think Niçoise. Indeed, I was thinking of the warm, piquant flavors of Nice when I created this dish. Although there are many vegetables that go well with the classic Niçoise combination—eggplant and fennel come to mind immediately—artichokes, with their edge of sweetness, make an especially fine match. This recipe makes enough stuffing to fill the six artichoke hearts and then some—spread the leftover stuffing along the bottom of the baking dish. This bit of extra filling keeps the artichokes from drying in the oven and also makes a nice cushion for the artichoke hearts at serving time.

MAKES 6 SERVINGS

3 lemons, halved

6 globe artichokes

1½ tablespoons extra-virgin olive oil, plus more for drizzling

1 small onion, peeled, trimmed, and cut into ¼-inch dice

1 clove garlic, peeled, split, germ removed, and finely chopped

½ pound white mushrooms, trimmed, cleaned, and cut into ¼-inch dice

Pinch of thyme leaves

Salt and freshly ground white pepper

8 pieces Tomato Confit (page 350) or drained oil-packed sun-dried tomatoes, cut into ¼-inch dice

¼ cup Niçoise olives, pitted and roughly chopped

2 tablespoons finely chopped Italian parsley leaves

2 tablespoons finely sliced basil leaves

2 ounces (approximately) fresh mozzarella, thinly sliced

1. **SQUEEZE THE JUICE** of 1 lemon into a medium bowl and pour in a couple of cups of water; keep the bowl close at hand. One at a time, stem and trim the artichokes down to their hearts (see Glossary, page 362) and, using a small knife or spoon, hollow out the center of each heart—this will be the bowl for the filling. As soon as you've trimmed a heart, drop it into the acidulated water to keep it from turning brown while you work on the other artichokes.

2. **PUT A LARGE POT** of salted water up to boil and add the juice of the remaining 2 lemons. Drain the artichoke hearts and drop them into the pot. Lower the heat to a simmer and cook the artichokes until they are tender when pierced with the tip of a knife, about 12 minutes. Drain and set aside to cool.

3. **WARM THE OLIVE OIL** in a medium sauté pan or skillet over medium heat. Add the onion and garlic and cook, stirring, until they soften but do not take on any color, 5 to 6 minutes. Add the mushrooms and thyme, season with salt and pepper, and continue to cook and stir for 3 minutes more.

Remove the pan from the heat and stir in the tomatoes, olives, parsley, and basil. Taste and season the stuffing again with salt and pepper if needed. *(The stuffing can be made up to a day ahead, cooled, and kept tightly covered in the refrigerator.)*

4. CENTER A RACK in the oven and preheat the oven to 425°F.

5. LIGHTLY BUTTER THE INSIDE of a baking pan just large enough to hold the artichoke hearts comfortably, and spread a thin layer of the stuffing over the bottom of the pan. Season the artichoke hearts with salt and pepper and divide the remaining stuffing evenly among them, spooning the stuffing into the hollows you created and mounding it slightly. Set the artichokes over the layer of stuffing in the pan. *(The artichokes can be prepared up to 1 to 2 hours ahead and kept covered with plastic wrap in the refrigerator.)*

6. COVER EACH ARTICHOKE with mozzarella, and drizzle a bit of oil over the cheese. Slide the pan into the oven to bake for 15 to 20 minutes, or until everything is piping hot. (If you've taken the artichokes from the refrigerator, they'll need another 10 or 15 minutes to heat through.)

to serve: For each serving, spoon a little of the stuffing that was in the pan into the center of a warm plate and top with a cheese-covered artichoke heart. Serve immediately.

to drink: A chilled Muscadet with racy acidity

le potager
Salsa Cruda with Horseradish and Avocado Mousse (page 273)

le potager
Soupe Glacée of Cavaillon Melon (page 268)

le potager
Vegetable Couscous (page 297)

le potager
Root Vegetable Cassoulet (page 300)

le potager

Andrew Carmellini's Bow Tie Pasta with Tomato, Arugula, and Mozzarella (page 306)

le potager
Lemon-Lime Risotto with Asparagus (page 308)

le potager
Zucchini-Ricotta Layers with Zucchini Pesto (page 310)

Stuffed Romaine in Red Wine (page 326)

le potager

Potato Gratin Forestier (page 318)

le potager
Vanilla Blueberries, aka Bill's Blues (page 340)

Broccoli Rabe with Honeyed Grapes

I have a taste for bitter greens and appreciate the bite of broccoli rabe, but I like the greens even more when they've got a little something sweet to bite against. Here, I add a few slivers of sweet pepper or tomato and some sliced grapes tossed in a bit of honey—it's an unusual, but unusually good, combination. Serve this either as a light starter or an original side dish.

MAKES 4 SERVINGS

1 pound broccoli rabe, tough ends trimmed and coarse leaves removed

2 tablespoons extra-virgin olive oil

Pinch of red pepper flakes

4 pieces piquillo peppers (see Glossary, page 370) or Tomato Confit (page 350), cut into thin slivers, or 1 plum tomato, peeled, seeded, and cut into thin slivers

Salt and freshly ground white pepper

2 teaspoons honey

$\frac{1}{4}$ teaspoon ground cumin

$\frac{1}{2}$ cup seedless green grapes, thinly sliced

$\frac{1}{4}$ cup slivered blanched almonds, toasted

1. **BRING A LARGE POT** of salted water to the boil. Plunge the broccoli rabe into the boiling water to cook for 5 minutes, or until it is tender but still very green. Drain in a colander and run the broccoli rabe under cold water to stop the cooking and set the color. Drain again, then squeeze the broccoli rabe between your hands to extract as much of the excess moisture as you can.

2. **WARM THE OLIVE OIL** in a large sauté pan or skillet over medium heat, then add the red pepper flakes. Toss the broccoli rabe and the pepper or tomato strips into the pan and cook, stirring almost constantly, just until the ingredients are heated through. Season with salt and pepper and transfer the vegetables to a heated platter.

3. **WIPE OUT THE PAN** and add the honey. When the honey bubbles, add the cumin and then the grapes, stirring until the grapes are lightly glazed with the honey.

to serve: Spoon the honeyed grapes over the broccoli rabe, sprinkle with the toasted almonds, and serve immediately.

to drink: A Russian River Pinot Noir

Goat Cheese Flans with Garlic-Herb Croutons

The word *flan* can refer to tarts or cup custards, sweet or savory. My goat cheese flan is a simple, savory, crustless cup custard with a mild flavor and silky texture. Made in small custard cups (or even smaller espresso cups, if you want) the flan is an appealing spoon-food starter if you serve it alongside a simply dressed salad and add a garlic and herb crouton to the plate. Sometimes we serve the flan-salad-crouton trio intact at Café Boulud, and sometimes we skip the salad and pair the croutons and flans (made in very small cups) with robust Wild Mushroom and Barley Soup (page 266)—we just float a flan in the center of each bowl of soup and serve a crouton on the side.

MAKES 6 SERVINGS

the flans:

6 ounces (1 cup) soft fresh goat cheese, at
    room temperature
6 large eggs, at room temperature
1 cup heavy cream or half-and-half, at room
    temperature

Large pinch of freshly grated nutmeg
Salt and freshly ground white pepper

1. **CENTER A RACK** in the oven and preheat the oven to 300°F. Butter or spray (with a nonstick cooking spray) the insides of six 4-ounce custard cups or aluminum foil cups and place the cups in a small baking pan.

2. **WHISK THE GOAT CHEESE** and eggs together in a large bowl until you've worked out all the lumps. When the mixture is smooth, whisk in the heavy cream or half-and-half and nutmeg and season with salt and pepper. Whisk just to combine—whipped cream isn't what you're after.

3. **DIVIDE THE FLAN MIXTURE** evenly among the custard cups and slide the pan into the oven. Pour in enough hot water to come halfway up the sides of the custard cups. Cover the pan tightly with a double layer of plastic wrap—don't worry: it's not going to melt in the oven—and poke two holes in two opposite corners of the pan. Close the oven door and bake the flans for 50 minutes, or until they are just set—if you tap the custard cups gently, the flan shouldn't jiggle.

4. **REMOVE THE PAN** from the oven and leave the cups in their water bath with the plastic cover intact for 10 minutes. Remove the plastic wrap, lift the cups out of the water, and transfer to a rack to cool for no more than 10 minutes. *(If you're not serving the flans now, you can cool and then cover them with plastic and keep them refrigerated for a day. Just before serving, warm them by putting them in a skillet with an inch or so of simmering—not boiling—water, or warm them in the microwave oven on low power.)*

the croutons:

4 tablespoons extra-virgin olive oil

12 thin slices sourdough baguette

2 cloves garlic, peeled and split

2 teaspoons finely chopped Italian parsley
leaves

1 teaspoon finely chopped chives

4 leaves (not sprigs) rosemary, finely chopped

2 sprigs thyme, leaves only, finely chopped

Salt and freshly ground white pepper

WARM 2 TABLESPOONS of the oil in a large sauté pan or skillet over medium heat. Arrange the slices of baguette in a single layer in the pan and toast them evenly on one side. Flip the bread over, add the remaining 2 tablespoons oil, and toast the other side. Remove the bread from the pan, rub each piece with the cut side of a clove of garlic, sprinkle with some of the chopped herbs, and season with salt and pepper.

to finish:

Mixed salad greens

Extra-virgin olive oil

Sherry vinegar

Salt and freshly ground white pepper

Grated aged goat cheese (optional)

TOSS THE SALAD GREENS with oil and vinegar, season with salt and pepper, and sprinkle with a little grated cheese, if you're using it.

to serve: Run a blunt knife around the edge of each warm flan and invert the flans onto dinner plates. Arrange a mound of salad to one side and lean 2 croutons against the salad. If you're using the aged goat cheese, you can grate some over the flans too before bringing the plates to the table.

to drink: A chilled Sancerre Blanc

Butternut Squash Chutney

Butternut squash is pumpkin's closest kin and, like pumpkin, it's beautifully orange, easily cooked down to softness, and content to fill that special spot between sweet and savory, as it does in this chutney. The chutney is seasoned with ingredients associated with curry—coriander seeds, cumin, tamarind, cinnamon, and Madras curry powder—and balanced with sweet-tangy fruits—raisins, mango, and dried apricots or pears. You can serve it warm or at room temperature, the day it is made or a day or two later, and, on any day and at any temperature, it's particularly good with sautéed spinach, pan-roasted vegetables, or any vegetables left over from couscous (page 297).

For a quickly made accompaniment, peel and trim some turnips and cut them into chunky slices, each about ½ inch thick. Sauté the turnips in butter, just to give them a bit of color, add some water to the pan, cover, and braise until they're tender. If the turnips haven't absorbed all the liquid, simmer it away and then pour in a little honey. Turn the turnips around in the honey until they're glazed, season with salt and pepper, and bring them to the table with the chutney.

MAKES 4 TO 6 SERVINGS

1 cup golden raisins

8 dried pear halves or apricots, cut into
  ¼-inch dice

½ cup white vinegar

1 teaspoon Madras curry powder

2 whole star anise, finely crushed

½ teaspoon coriander seeds, finely crushed

½ teaspoon ground cumin

½ teaspoon tamarind paste (optional)

Pinch of cayenne pepper

Pinch of ground cinnamon

1 tablespoon extra-virgin olive oil

1½ medium onions, peeled, trimmed, and cut
  into ½-inch dice

1½ pounds butternut squash, peeled, seeded,
  and cut into ½-inch cubes

Salt and freshly ground white pepper

1 large mango, peeled, pitted, and cut into
  ½-inch dice

1 teaspoon sugar

1 cup water

1. **IF THE RAISINS,** pears, or apricots are not plump and moist, toss them into a small pot of boiling water and let them sit for a minute, then drain and dry them.

2. **WORKING IN A MEDIUM BOWL,** stir together the vinegar, raisins, and pears or apricots and allow the fruit to steep while you prepare the rest of the ingredients. (*If it's more convenient, the fruits can steep for an hour or so at room temperature or overnight in the refrigerator.*)

3. **STIR TOGETHER THE CURRY** powder, star anise, coriander, cumin, tamarind, cayenne, and cinnamon; reserve.

4. WARM THE OLIVE OIL in a large sauté pan or casserole over medium heat. Add the onions and cook, stirring, for about 5 minutes, or until they are soft but not colored. Add the squash to the pan, season with salt and pepper, and sauté for 10 to 15 minutes, or until the squash is tender. Toss in the reserved spice mix, the dried fruits and their steeping liquid, and the mango, stirring well to make certain the ingredients are well blended. Sprinkle the sugar over the mixture, add the water, and give the pan another good stir.

5. CUT A PARCHMENT PAPER circle to fit inside the pan (see Glossary, page 369), cut out a small air vent in the center, and press the parchment against the ingredients. Cook the chutney over very low heat for 40 to 50 minutes. Remove the paper, taste the chutney, and adjust the seasoning, adding more salt and pepper if needed. Allow the chutney to cool until it is warm, or cool it further, until it reaches room temperature.

to serve: The chutney can be served the day it is made, but it gains in flavor if it's allowed to rest overnight in the refrigerator. If you chill the chutney, gently warm it or bring it to room temperature before serving.

to drink: A Belgian wit beer

Grains, Beans, Pasta, and Risotto

Summer Bean Casserole

There is a happy moment in summer when the greenmarket's farmers are offering bushels of just-picked beans, and that's the time we make this casserole at Café Boulud. It's an uncomplicated mix of beans, aromatic vegetables, and chopped herbs, braised stovetop until there's just a gloss of liquid in the pan and then served in shallow soup plates. Although it's fine served as is, I like to put a mound of arugula and herbs in the bottom of each plate. Adding an uncooked ingredient to the dish brings a hint of summer's freshness back to the savory cooked beans.

A word on the Romano beans that are part of the dish. Romanos are my favorite beans, but only when they're properly cooked—which means when they're tender. This isn't a bean that takes to being served crisp or crunchy—when they're not cooked enough, Romanos are all starch and no sweetness. As they cook past the point of crunch, they absorb water and give up starch, which is just what has to happen for them to be at their best.

½ cup dried cannellini beans, picked over and rinsed

Salt and freshly ground white pepper

¼ pound Romano beans, trimmed and cut on the bias into 1-inch lengths

¼ pound green beans, trimmed and cut on the bias into 1-inch lengths

¼ pound yellow wax beans, trimmed and cut on the bias into 1-inch lengths

1 tablespoon unsalted butter

1 teaspoon extra-virgin olive oil

1 clove garlic, peeled, split, germ removed, and finely chopped

1 small carrot, peeled, trimmed, and cut into ¼-inch dice

1 small stalk celery, peeled, trimmed, and cut into ¼-inch dice

½ medium onion, peeled, trimmed, and cut into ¼-inch dice

Salt and freshly ground white pepper

2 tomatoes, peeled, seeded, and cut into ¼-inch dice

1 tablespoon finely chopped Italian parsley leaves

1 tablespoon finely chopped tarragon leaves

1½ teaspoons tomato paste

2 cups unsalted Vegetable Stock (page 348) or store-bought low-sodium vegetable broth

1. THE NIGHT BEFORE you make the casserole, put the dried beans in a pot with enough cold water to cover them by at least an inch. Let the beans soak overnight in the refrigerator, then rinse and drain them. (Or, if you're in a rush—or you haven't planned far enough in advance—bring the water with the beans to a boil, boil for 2 minutes, pull the pot from the heat, and soak the beans for an hour. Rinse the beans under cold water and drain.)

2. BRING A LARGE POT of well-salted water to the boil. Blanch the Romano, green, and wax beans in the boiling water for 2 minutes, then drain them and run them under cold water to stop the cooking and set their color. When the beans are cool, drain them well.

3. WORKING OVER MEDIUM HEAT, warm the butter and oil in a large sauté pan or skillet. When the butter is melted and hot, add the garlic along with the carrot, celery, and onion, season with salt and pepper, and cook, stirring, until the vegetables soften but do not take on color, about 10 minutes. Add the cannellini beans and cook, stirring, for 3 minutes, then add the tomatoes, the blanched beans, the chopped parsley and tarragon, and more salt and pepper. When the ingredients are warmed, about 3 minutes, add the tomato paste, stirring to incorporate it evenly, and then the vegetable stock. Bring the stock to the boil.

4. CUT A CIRCLE of parchment paper to fit inside the pan (see Glossary, page 369) and press the paper gently against the ingredients. Adjust the heat so that the liquid simmers steadily and cook for 40 to 45 minutes, or until the vegetables are tender and the cooking juices just glaze the beans. If you've got too much liquid, uncover the casserole and cook it a few minutes more to reduce the juices to a glaze. Taste and add more salt and pepper if needed.

to serve:

1 pound arugula, tough stems removed,
    washed, dried, and cut into ¼-inch-wide
    strands
Fresh herb leaves, including mint, tarragon, and
    basil, to mix with the arugula

Extra-virgin olive oil
Salt and freshly ground white pepper

TOSS THE ARUGULA with the herbs, drizzle with a little olive oil, and season with salt and pepper. Divide the arugula among four warm shallow soup plates and ladle over the casserole.

to drink: A light red wine, such as a Chinon from the Loire Valley

Vegetable Couscous

Couscous—the word refers to both the dish and its main ingredient—is a specialty of northern Africa that has nestled itself comfortably into French cuisine. Often thought of as a grain—indeed, it's treated like a grain—couscous is really a semolina pasta that, when raw, resembles coarse yellow cornmeal. Once cooked, the granules soften to a sort of cereal or porridge, but one with a little grit, a bit of coarseness that adds interest to any dish. Traditional couscous is cooked in a couscousière, a special steamer, and must be raked a few times during the process. Not so instant couscous, which is what's used here—all you've got to do is pour hot broth over the couscous, wait five minutes for it to soak it up, fluff the grains with a fork, and head for the table.

Couscous alone is interesting; couscous with its traditional accompaniments is exceptional. For this couscous, a spiced, aromatic broth is used to cook large wedges of vegetables, each vegetable adding more flavor to the broth. The broth is ladled over the couscous to cook it, and then you stir in dried fruits and nuts, a sweet touch that plays against the spice. Finally, there's the never-to-be-omitted harissa, the cayenne and red pepper condiment that can change couscous from a comfort dish to a fiery challenge—the amount you use is up to you, since it's served on the side.

Make this dish when you want a casual but festive meal. You need no additional accompaniments, just a convivial group that will be happy to play with the food, ladling on more broth, adding more harissa, and choosing among the various vegetables, of which the fennel is always my favorite.

MAKES 4 SERVINGS

the harissa:

3 tablespoons extra-virgin olive oil

½ onion, peeled, trimmed, and finely chopped

1 clove garlic, peeled, split, germ removed, and finely chopped

1 teaspoon fennel seeds

½ teaspoon cumin seeds

½ teaspoon cayenne pepper, or to taste

¼ teaspoon red pepper flakes, or to taste

Salt

4 pieces Tomato Confit (page 350), coarsely chopped, or 1 tablespoon tomato paste

½ tomato, peeled, seeded, and cut into chunks

1 roasted red pepper, coarsely chopped

WARM 1 TABLESPOON of the olive oil in a medium sauté pan or skillet over medium heat, and add the onion and garlic, spices, and salt to taste. Cook, stirring, until the onion softens and turns lightly golden, about 8 minutes. Add the tomato confit or paste, the fresh tomato, and the roasted pepper and continue to cook and stir for 3 minutes more. Turn the ingredients into the container of a blender or food processor, add the remaining 2 tablespoons olive oil, and pulse on and off just until the mixture is finely chopped—it shouldn't be a purée. Set aside to cool. *(The harissa can be made up to 5 days ahead and kept in a tightly sealed jar in the refrigerator.)*

the broth:

10 cardamom pods

2 allspice berries

1 cinnamon stick

1 bay leaf

1 whole clove

½ teaspoon cumin seeds

½ teaspoon fennel seeds

½ teaspoon black peppercorns, crushed

Small pinch of red pepper flakes

¼ ounce dried mushrooms

2 sprigs mint

2 sprigs Italian parsley

7 cups water

1 tablespoon salt

4 cipollini or 8 pearl onions, peeled and
  trimmed (cut the cipollini in half)

2 carrots, peeled, trimmed, and cut into
  1-inch chunks

½ fennel bulb, trimmed and cut into 4 wedges

1 turnip, peeled, trimmed, and cut into 4
  wedges

½ small head savoy cabbage, trimmed, cored,
  and cut into 4 wedges

1 medium zucchini, scrubbed, trimmed, and
  cut into 1-inch dice

1 scallion, white and light green part only, cut
  into 1-inch lengths

1. TIE THE CARDAMOM, allspice, cinnamon, bay leaf, clove, cumin and fennel seeds, crushed peppercorns, red pepper flakes, and mushrooms together in a double thickness of cheesecloth. Tie the mint and parsley sprigs together with kitchen twine.

2. POUR THE WATER into a tall stockpot or large casserole and add the salt and the spice sachet. Bring to the boil, then lower the heat to a steady simmer. Add the onions, carrots, and fennel to the pot and simmer for 10 minutes. Toss in the turnip and simmer for 5 minutes, then add the cabbage and cook at a simmer for another 5 minutes. Add the zucchini and scallion and continue to cook the vegetables and broth for 10 minutes more. Turn off the heat and add the mint and parsley bundle. Leave everything to infuse another 5 minutes.

3. SPOON THE VEGETABLES into a large serving bowl or platter and keep warm. Strain the broth into a saucepan, discarding the spice sachet and herb bundle.

the couscous:

1½ cups quick-cooking couscous

1 tablespoon extra-virgin olive oil

¼ cup plump golden raisins

¼ cup plump dried cranberries

4 soft, plump dried apricots, cut into
   ¼-inch dice

2 soft, plump dried pear halves, cut into
   ¼-inch dice

2 tablespoons pine nuts, lightly toasted

2 tablespoons skinned pistachio nuts, lightly
   toasted

1½ cups vegetable broth (from above)

1. STIR THE COUSCOUS, olive oil, raisins, cranberries, apricots, pears, and nuts together in a serving bowl.

2. BRING THE BROTH to a boil and pour it over the couscous. Immediately tightly cover the bowl with plastic wrap and let the couscous rest for 5 minutes, time enough for it to absorb the broth and soften. Remove the plastic wrap and fluff the couscous with a fork.

to serve: You can serve the couscous and vegetables in separate bowls, or you can arrange the vegetables around the couscous. Either way, put the harissa in a small bowl and pour the remaining hot broth into a pitcher or a sauceboat. Set the table with individual shallow soup plates and allow guests to serve themselves, encouraging them to pour over as much of the hot broth as they wish and to spice up their portions with harissa.

to drink: An Israeli Gewürztraminer with good fruit

Root Vegetable Cassoulet

When I put this on my opening menu at Café Boulud, I smiled and thought, "I wouldn't dare serve this in Toulouse." Cassoulet is the dish that defines the cuisine of Toulouse, a city in southwestern France. There, the base of the casserole or stew—cassoulet is not so easily pigeonholed—is beans, as it is in my version. But in Toulouse, they strive to make their cassoulet rich by combining duck confit with goose and pork, sausages, and lamb. My cassoulet, inspired by France but made for America, is richly flavored but not at all rich. The beans are as creamy as those of the original, but the deep, cooked-into-the-beans flavor comes from generously cut vegetables, fresh herbs, and ample amounts of garlic. And the crust, the final touch on any cassoulet, is garlicky and golden—just as it should be.

MAKES 6 SERVINGS

2 cups dried cannellini beans, picked over and
    rinsed
3 tablespoons extra-virgin olive oil
½ onion, peeled, trimmed, and cut into ¼-inch
    dice
3 large cloves garlic, peeled, split, germ
    removed, and finely chopped
Salt and freshly ground white pepper
1 tablespoon tomato paste
2 tomatoes, 1 peeled, seeded, and cut into ¼-
    inch dice, the other just cut in half
7 cups unsalted Vegetable Stock (page 348) or
    store-bought low-sodium vegetable broth

6 stalks celery, peeled, trimmed, and cut into
    3-inch lengths
3 medium carrots, peeled, trimmed, and cut
    into 3-inch lengths
2 large turnips, peeled, trimmed, and quartered
1 medium fennel bulb, trimmed and quartered
Bouquet garni (3 sprigs Italian parsley,
    2 sprigs sage, and 2 sprigs thyme, tied
    together with kitchen twine)

1. THE NIGHT BEFORE you want to make the cassoulet, put the dried beans in a pot with enough cold water to cover them by at least an inch. Let the beans soak overnight in the refrigerator, then rinse and drain them. (Or, if you're in a rush—or you haven't planned far enough in advance—bring the water with the beans to a boil, boil for 2 minutes, pull the pot from the heat, and soak the beans for an hour. Rinse the beans under cold water and drain.)

2. WARM 1 TABLESPOON of the olive oil in a small sauté pan or skillet over medium heat. When it's hot, add the onion and garlic and season with salt and pepper. Cook, stirring, until the onion and garlic are tender but not colored, about 10 minutes. Stir in the tomato paste and, when it's incorporated evenly, add the diced tomato; pull the pan from the heat and set aside.

3. PUT THE BEANS in a Dutch oven or large casserole. Pour in the stock and bring to the boil. Add the celery, carrots, turnips, fennel, the split tomato, and the bouquet garni. Cut a parchment paper circle to fit inside the pot (see Glossary, page 369) and press the paper gently against the ingredients. Lower the heat so that the liquid bubbles at a steady simmer, and cook, stirring now and then, until the beans are tender, about 1 hour. Season the casserole with salt and pepper shortly before the beans are cooked through. When the beans are done, pull the pot from the heat and remove and discard the bouquet garni and whatever is left of the tomato. Drain the liquid from the pot into a pitcher and keep close at hand. Working gently, transfer the vegetables to a bowl.

4. SPOON THE BEANS into a baking dish—a pottery casserole would be perfect—and stir in the onion-tomato paste mixture along with the remaining 2 tablespoons olive oil. Add enough of the reserved cooking liquid to just cover the beans. Top with the vegetables and moisten with more of the cooking liquid. Reserve the remaining liquid if you are going to reheat the cassoulet. *(The cassoulet can be made up to this point a day in advance, cooled, and stored tightly covered in the refrigerator. Bring it to room temperature, then reheat it for about 1 hour in a 350°F oven, adding some of the reserved cooking liquid if the casserole seems dry. Fifteen minutes before the cassoulet's ready, put on the crust and turn up the oven temperature, as directed below.)*

the crust:

1 cup fresh bread crumbs	¼ cup finely chopped Italian parsley leaves
2 large cloves garlic, peeled, split, germ removed, and very finely chopped	3 tablespoons unsalted butter, melted

1. CENTER A RACK in the oven and preheat the oven to 400°F.

2. TOSS TOGETHER THE BREAD CRUMBS, garlic, and parsley and stir in the melted butter. Spread the mixture evenly over the cassoulet and slide the casserole into the oven. Bake for 12 to 15 minutes, or until the crumbs are golden brown and crusty.

to serve: Bring the casserole to the table and serve immediately, spooning crust, vegetables, and beans into warm soup plates.

to drink: A brawny white wine, such as a Châteauneuf-du-Pape

Cranberry Bean and Kale Stew

I think you'll want to quickly fold this dish into your repertoire of favorites for weekdays: It's homey, easy to prepare, open to variation, and fully satisfying. My first choice for the dish is a combination of hearty kale and mild fresh cranberry beans, but you can substitute Swiss chard, turnip greens, or beet tops for the kale and use canned cannellini beans if the season for cranberry beans is past. Whichever you use, be sure to set out a bowl of fleur de sel or crushed coarse sea salt and a peppermill so that everyone can season the dish to their own liking. Most important, pour some of your favorite olive oil over the stew just before you bring it to the table. That last little drizzle of oil glistens and has a come-hither appeal.

MAKES 4 SERVINGS

2 tablespoons extra-virgin olive oil

1 medium red onion, peeled, trimmed, and cut into ½-inch dice

3 cloves garlic, peeled and crushed

1 medium carrot, peeled, trimmed, and cut into ½-inch dice

1 stalk celery, trimmed, and cut into ½-inch dice

Pinch of red pepper flakes

Salt and freshly ground white pepper

2 medium tomatoes, peeled, seeded, and roughly chopped

¾ pound kale, stems and tough center veins removed, washed, dried, and cut into ½-inch-wide strips

2 cups unsalted Vegetable Stock (page 348) or store-bought low-sodium vegetable broth

1½ pounds cranberry beans, shucked (to make 2¼ cups), or two 15-ounce cans cannellini beans, rinsed and drained

Best-quality extra-virgin olive oil for serving

Fleur de sel or lightly crushed coarse sea salt

1. **CENTER A RACK** in the oven and preheat the oven to 350°F.

2. **WARM THE OLIVE OIL** in a large ovenproof sauté pan or skillet over medium heat. Add the onion, garlic, carrot, celery, red pepper flakes, and salt and pepper to taste and cook, stirring, until the onions and celery are soft but not colored, about 10 minutes. Stir the tomatoes and kale into the pan and cook for 2 to 3 minutes, just to wilt the kale. Add the stock and cranberry beans, season with salt and pepper, and bring to the boil. (If you're using canned beans, don't add them yet.)

3. **COVER THE PAN** and then slide it into the oven. Let the stew simmer for 20 minutes, then remove the cover, stir, and simmer for 30 minutes more. (If using canned beans, add them about 15 minutes before the stew is done.) The stew is done when the beans are tender and most of the liquid

has evaporated. If the stew seems too soupy, put the pan over medium heat and cook the liquid down until just a few spoonfuls remain. Adjust the seasoning, adding more salt and pepper as needed.

to serve: Ladle the stew and a little of its sauce into heated shallow soup plates. Drizzle some very good olive oil around the stew and have fleur de sel and a peppermill on the table.

to drink: An earthy Hautes-Côtes de Beaune red, maybe one that's 4 to 5 years old

Angel Hair Pasta and Vegetable Ribbons

With its sesame-and-soy-accented broth, soft angel hair pasta, and abundance of thin colorful vegetable ribbons, this good-looking dish is ideal for casual suppers. The ribbons, a fanciful addition, require nothing but a little wrist action and a good vegetable peeler: After you've peeled the vegetables, just keep peeling and soon you'll have a mound of ribbons, which become part of the broth, flavoring it as they cook. When the broth is finished, it's ladled over the pasta and finished with lots of crisp fried shallots, toasted sesame seeds, and a few cilantro leaves. While you can cook the pasta and fry the shallots ahead of time, the most efficient way to make this dish is to do a few things at once: Get the vegetables and broth going and while they simmer, boil the pasta and set to work on the shallots. Play it right, and you'll have dinner on the table in thirty minutes.

For something extra, finish this with hot scallion oil (page 192).

MAKES 4 SERVINGS

the shallots:

2 medium shallots, peeled, trimmed, and very thinly sliced crosswise on a mandoline, with the fine-slicing blade of a food processor, or with a sharp knife

2 cups flavorless oil, preferably grapeseed oil

Salt

SOAK THE SHALLOTS in cold water for about 5 minutes, then drain and pat them completely dry between paper towels. Put the shallots and oil in a small saucepan over medium heat and warm for 5 to 10 minutes, during which time the oil will bubble and the shallots will brown. Scoop the shallots out of the oil with a slotted spoon and transfer them to a plate lined with a triple thickness of paper towels. Separate the shallots, salt them, and keep them aside until needed.

the broth and vegetables:

4 stalks celery, peeled and trimmed

1 medium carrot, peeled and trimmed

1 medium leek, white part only, quartered lengthwise and washed

One 1-inch length of lemongrass stalk, bruised

3 sprigs cilantro, leaves and stems separated

4 cups water

2 tablespoons soy sauce

1 teaspoon salt

16 shiitake mushrooms, stemmed, cleaned, and quartered

2 packages (7 ounces total) enoki mushrooms, trimmed

1 bunch scallions, trimmed, washed, and cut
 on the bias into 1-inch lengths
1 tablespoon finely slivered peeled ginger
1 teaspoon toasted sesame oil
Pinch of red pepper flakes

½ pound angel hair pasta
1 lime, halved
Scallion oil (page 192) (optional)
2 tablespoons sesame seeds, toasted

1. **PUT A LARGE POT** of salted water up to boil for the pasta.

2. **USING A VEGETABLE PEELER,** cut long ribbons from the celery and carrot by running the peeler down the length of the vegetables. Don't worry if they're not all the same size—just try to keep the ribbons long and thin. When you're working on the carrot, draw the peeler down one side until you get to the core, then rotate the carrot and work the other sides; discard the core. Drop the carrot and celery ribbons along with the leek into cold water to cover; set aside while you prepare the broth.

3. **TIE THE LEMONGRASS** and cilantro stems together with kitchen twine. Pour the water into a large saucepan and add the lemongrass and cilantro stems, the soy sauce, salt, mushrooms, scallions, and ginger and bring to the boil, then lower the heat and simmer for 15 minutes. Drain the carrots, celery, and leek and add them to the pot along with the sesame oil and red pepper flakes; simmer for 5 to 7 minutes more.

4. **MEANWHILE,** as soon as you've tossed the vegetables into the pot, put the pasta up to boil—it should cook until al dente, about 5 minutes.

to serve: Drain the pasta and divide it evenly among four warm shallow soup plates. Squeeze the juice of the lime into the broth and spoon a generous amount of broth and vegetables over each serving of pasta. If you're using scallion oil, drizzle it in now. Top each serving with some crispy shallots, a few cilantro leaves, and a sprinkling of the toasted sesame seeds.

to drink: An amber beer

Andrew Carmellini's Bow Tie Pasta with Tomato, Arugula, and Mozzarella

This recipe comes from Andrew Carmellini, the executive chef at Café Boulud. It's a pasta dish with summer's best tomatoes and pasta's best additions: garlic, basil, mozzarella, and grated Parmesan. Its sauce of slowly cooked tomatoes is intensely flavored with olive oil infused with garlic, red pepper flakes, and fresh basil. Toss the small bow tie pasta with the sauce, top with cubes of mozzarella, peppery arugula, and cherry tomatoes, and you'll have a new idea about what pasta and tomato sauce can be.

A word on the pasta: The sauce for this dish is so good that it will go with just about any pasta, but the best choice would be a small pasta, like the bow ties, that has ruffles, ridges, curves, and crevices to catch and hold the sauce. When you're looking for a variation, try penne, ridged or not, rigatoni, orecchiette, frilly radiatori, or even fanciful wagon wheels.

MAKES 4 MAIN-COURSE OR 6 STARTER SERVINGS

6 ripe beefsteak tomatoes, peeled, seeded, and coarsely chopped

½ cup plus 2 tablespoons extra-virgin olive oil

1 bunch basil, leaves only, washed and dried

2 cloves garlic, peeled and crushed

Pinch of red pepper flakes

Salt and freshly ground white pepper

1 pound small bow tie pasta

2 tablespoons finely grated Parmesan cheese

1. **PUT THE CHOPPED TOMATOES** in a medium saucepan over medium-low heat and cook, stirring occasionally, until they are reduced by half, about 35 minutes. Turn the tomatoes into a large bowl and set aside.

2. **MEANWHILE, PUT THE ½ CUP OLIVE OIL,** the basil, garlic and red pepper flakes in a medium saucepan and cook over medium heat until the oil reaches 190°F, as measured on an instant-read thermometer, or until the basil leaves start to pop. Remove the pan from the heat and allow the oil to infuse for 15 minutes.

3. **CAREFULLY POUR THE OIL** through a fine-mesh strainer into the cooked tomatoes. Discard the solids in the strainer and toss the oil and cooked tomatoes together. Season the sauce with salt and pepper. *(The sauce can be made 1 day ahead, cooled, and then covered, and refrigerated. Reheat gently before serving.)*

4. **BRING A LARGE POT** of salted water to the boil, add the pasta, and cook until done. Drain the pasta and turn it into a large warm bowl. Toss the bow ties with the remaining 2 tablespoons olive oil, then stir in the tomato sauce and grated Parmesan.

to serve:

1 bunch arugula, preferably baby arugula,
   trimmed, washed, and dried

¼ pound mozzarella, cut into ⅛-inch cubes

1 pint baby cherry tomatoes, peeled

3 tablespoons finely grated Parmesan cheese,
   or more to taste

TOP THE PASTA with the remaining ingredients and serve immediately.

to drink: Vino Nobile di Montepulciano—it's a highbrow Chianti

Lemon-Lime Risotto with Asparagus

The combination of creamy rice and distinctively flavored asparagus is a natural. But introduce lemon and lime to the mix, and what was predictable becomes original. The lemon and lime cut the risotto's richness, elevate the asparagus's flavor, and, most surprisingly, make this a warm-weather dish. If you have some on hand, you can add a sprig of rosemary to the pan; it's another good partner for asparagus, lemon, and lime.

MAKES 4 MAIN-COURSE OR 6 STARTER SERVINGS

the asparagus:

16 stalks asparagus, peeled and trimmed

PUT A POT OF SALTED WATER up to boil. Plunge the asparagus into the boiling water and cook at a steady simmer until it can be pierced easily with the tip of a knife, 6 to 7 minutes. Gently lift the asparagus out of the pot and run it under cold water to stop the cooking and set the color. When it is cool, pat dry between kitchen towels. Cut off the top 2 inches of each asparagus spear and cut the tips lengthwise in half. Cut the next 2 to 3 inches of each spear into ¼-inch-thick rounds; discard whatever remains. *(You can do this a day ahead and keep the asparagus covered in the refrigerator.)*

the risotto:

7 cups (approximately) unsalted Vegetable Stock (page 348) or store-bought low-sodium vegetable broth

2 lemons

2 limes

4½ tablespoons unsalted butter, at room temperature

½ small onion, peeled, trimmed, and finely diced

2 cups Arborio rice

½ cup finely grated Parmesan cheese

1 tablespoon crème fraîche

1. **POUR THE STOCK** into a large saucepan and bring to the boil. Keep the stock at a slow, steady simmer. Grate the zest of half a lemon and half a lime; toss together and set aside. Working over a measuring cup, squeeze enough juice from the lemons and limes to produce ⅓ cup lemon-lime juice; set aside.
2. **WORKING OVER MEDIUM HEAT,** melt 3 tablespoons of the butter in a Dutch oven or a large sauté pan or skillet with high sides. Add the onion and zests and cook, stirring with a wooden spoon, just until the onion is translucent, about 5 minutes. Add the rice and cook, still stirring, for about 5 minutes more. Pour in the juice, stir and scrape the bottom of the pot, and cook, stirring once or twice, until the juice has almost completely evaporated, then add 1 cup of the hot stock. Cook, stirring often, until the rice

absorbs most of the liquid. While there's no hard-and-fast rule with risotto, and every rice reacts differently, usually you can count on adding more liquid when there's just about 3 tablespoons of liquid left in the pan. Add another cup of the hot stock and cook and stir as before. Continue cooking, stirring regularly and adding the stock 1 cup at a time, until you've added 6 cups of stock. At this point, taste the rice. Usually, the rice will need another ½ to 1 cup stock and a few more minutes to cook.

3. STIR IN 1 TABLESPOON of the butter and the Parmesan. Add the crème fraîche and asparagus rounds to the pot, stir to warm the asparagus, and remove the pot from the heat.

4. MEANWHILE, working quickly, melt the remaining ½ tablespoon butter in a small sauté pan or skillet, toss in the asparagus tips, and heat, stirring, just until they are warmed through.

to serve: Spoon the risotto into heated soup plates, top with the warmed asparagus tips, and serve immediately.

to drink: A Mosel Riesling, a really acidic wine to work with—not against—the lemon-lime juice

Roasted, Stuffed, and Braised Vegetables

Zucchini-Ricotta Layers with Zucchini Pesto

The inspiration for this dish was lasagna, but I've replaced what would have been lasagna's broad noodles with rounds of baked-until-just-barely-tender zucchini. The filling is ricotta, as it would be in lasagna, but it's neither layered with a red sauce nor baked. Although there is a touch of red in this dish—it comes from petals of tomato confit or sun-dried tomatoes—the only thing saucy is the brilliantly emerald pesto, a blend of basil and the greenest part of the zucchini. I find the best way to show this recipe off to advantage is to plate the dishes in the kitchen, constructing alternating layers of zucchini, ricotta, and tomato, and to accompany each portion with a Parmesan tuile.

MAKES 4 SERVINGS

the zucchini pesto:

1 small zucchini, scrubbed

Salt and freshly ground white pepper

1 bunch basil, leaves only, washed and dried
(about ¼ cup packed)

1 small clove garlic, peeled, split, and germ
removed

1 tablespoon finely grated Parmesan cheese

1 tablespoon pine nuts

½ cup extra-virgin olive oil, or more as needed

1. PUT A POT OF SALTED WATER up to boil. Cut off the ends of the zucchini and stand the zucchini on end. Slice the zucchini on one side from top to bottom, cutting off only the flesh and leaving the seeds. Rest the zucchini on the long side you just cut, and cut the other three sides in the same way—only the core of seeds should be left. Discard the core of seeds and cut the zucchini into ½-inch chunks.

2. PLUNGE THE ZUCCHINI into the boiling water and blanch for 2 minutes, then scoop out the pieces with a slotted spoon and run them under cold water to set their color and cool them. Blanch the basil leaves in the boiling water for 2 minutes, drain, and run them under cold water. Dry the zucchini between kitchen towels; dry the basil by squeezing the leaves between your palms.

3. PUT ALL THE INGREDIENTS in the container of a blender or food processor and whir until smooth. The pesto should be brilliantly green, smooth, and as thick as yogurt. If it's too thick, add a drizzle more olive oil. Transfer to a bowl, cover, pressing a piece of plastic wrap against the surface, and set aside briefly, or chill until needed. (*The pesto can be made a day ahead and kept tightly covered in the refrigerator. Bring it to room temperature before using.*)

the tuiles (optional):

½ cup finely grated Parmesan cheese

1. CENTER A RACK in the oven and preheat the oven to 300°F.

2. WORKING ON A NONSTICK BAKING SHEET, make 8 circles of cheese, each 2½ to 3 inches in diameter, sprinkling the cheese in an even layer that is just thick enough that you can't see the pan through the cheese. Bake for 2 minutes, or until the cheese melts, then, ever so carefully, lift the tuiles off the baking sheet—a flexible plastic dough scraper is great for this job. If you want flat tuiles, put them on a cool baking sheet; for curved tuiles, lay the tuiles over a rolling pin and press them gently against the pin's curve. *(The tuiles can be made up to 4 hours ahead of time and kept in a dry place until needed.)*

the zucchini and ricotta:

3 tablespoons (approximately) extra-virgin olive oil

2 medium zucchini, scrubbed and trimmed

Salt and freshly ground white pepper

4 cloves garlic, peeled and crushed

1 sprig thyme, leaves only

¾ cup whole-milk ricotta cheese

2 tablespoons finely grated Parmesan cheese

1 tablespoon chopped Italian parsley leaves

1 large egg yolk (optional)

12 pieces Tomato Confit (page 350) or drained oil-packed sun-dried tomatoes

¼ cup Niçoise olives, pitted and halved

1. **CENTER A RACK** in the oven and preheat the oven to 375°F. Line a baking sheet with foil and brush the foil lightly with 1 tablespoon of the oil.

2. **CUT THE ZUCCHINI** on the bias into slices about 3 inches long and ¼ inch thick and brush the slices on both sides with about 1 tablespoon of the olive oil. Arrange the slices in a single layer on the baking sheet, season with salt and pepper, and scatter over the garlic and thyme. Slide the baking sheet into the oven and bake for 10 to 12 minutes, or until the zucchini is just tender.

3. **WHILE THE ZUCCHINI IS BAKING,** make the ricotta mix. Whisk together the ricotta, Parmesan, parsley, the egg yolk, if you're using it, the remaining 1 tablespoon olive oil, and salt and pepper to taste until well blended. *(The ricotta mixture can be made the day before and kept well covered in the refrigerator. Bring to room temperature before using.)*

to serve: Construct each serving on a dinner plate. Spoon some pesto into the center of each plate, top with 3 slices of zucchini, then a spoonful of ricotta, 2 pieces of tomato arranged in a single layer, a few more slices of zucchini, another spoonful of ricotta, and another piece of tomato. Circle the plates with the olive halves and some more pesto. Serve with Parmesan tuiles, if you've made them.

to drink: An Italian Pinot Nero

Panzanella-Stuffed Eggplant

I admire eggplant for the smoothness it acquires when baked. However, it can add silkiness or sameness to a dish, according to what else is added to the mix. With eggplant, everything depends on its costars. In this recipe, which I think of as "Tuscany meets Provence," I've taken my inspiration from panzanella, the well-seasoned Italian bread salad. The bread in the stuffing adds body to the eggplant, the toasted nuts add depth, and the herbs give the flavors a lift. Left like this, with a crust of herbs and Parmesan cheese, the eggplant would be fine, but incomplete. That's why I add a Provençal-style tomato, onion, and artichoke ragout under the eggplant—it serves as a base for the dish in every sense of the word.

MAKES 4 SERVINGS

the eggplant:

3 tablespoons extra-virgin olive oil

4 small eggplants (each about 6 ounces)

3 cloves garlic, peeled and crushed

2 sprigs thyme, leaves only, finely chopped

½ sprig rosemary, leaves only, finely chopped

Salt and freshly ground black pepper

1. **CENTER A RACK** in the oven and preheat the oven to 325°F. Line a baking pan with aluminum foil and brush it with 1 tablespoon of the oil.

2. **CUT EACH EGGPLANT** lengthwise in half, then, using a small sharp knife, score the flesh in a criss-cross pattern, making the little squares in the crosshatch about 1 inch on a side. Brush the flesh with the remaining 2 tablespoons olive oil, sprinkle with the garlic, herbs, and salt and pepper, and place flesh side up on the foil-lined pan. Bake the eggplants for about 30 minutes, then flip them over and bake for 15 minutes more, or until they give when squeezed but aren't verging on collapse.

3. **WHEN THE EGGPLANTS** are cool enough to handle, choose the 4 softest halves and scoop out the flesh from the insides, working around the seeds; discard the seeds and the shells. Scoop out and reserve the flesh from the remaining shells, but this time leave a thin wall of flesh to hold the stuffing; set these shells aside. *(The eggplants can be prepared to this point a day ahead and kept tightly covered in the refrigerator.)*

the ragout:

Juice of 1 lemon

8 baby artichokes, trimmed, or 2 globe artichoke hearts (see Glossary, page 362)

2 tablespoons extra-virgin olive oil

1 medium onion, peeled, trimmed, cut in half,
and thinly sliced

Salt and freshly ground white pepper

1 small clove garlic, peeled, split, germ
removed, and finely chopped

2 sprigs thyme

½ sprig rosemary

¼ cup white wine

3 medium tomatoes, peeled, seeded, and cut
into ½-inch dice

1. **FILL A MEDIUM BOWL** with cold water and add half the lemon juice. Using a mandoline (or the thin slicing blade of a food processor), slice the artichokes or artichoke hearts ⅛ inch thick and toss the slices into the acidulated water; reserve.

2. **POUR THE OLIVE OIL** into a large sauté pan or skillet and place the pan over medium heat. Drain the artichokes, pat them dry, and, when the oil is hot, toss them into the pan along with the onion. Season with salt and pepper and cook, stirring regularly, for about 5 minutes, just until the vegetables soften, without coloring. Add the garlic, thyme, and rosemary and continue to cook and stir for 10 minutes more. Pour in the wine, bring to a boil, and allow it to simmer until it has almost evaporated. Stir in the tomatoes and cook for 2 minutes more, just to combine the flavors. Remove the pan from the heat, discard the rosemary and thyme, and stir in the remaining lemon juice. Season the ragout with salt and pepper and set aside until needed.

the stuffing:

1½ slices (or enough to make 3 ounces) stale
Tuscan bread, crust left on, cut into ¼-inch
cubes

Salt and freshly ground white pepper

The reserved eggplant flesh (from above)

1 tomato, peeled, seeded, and coarsely
chopped

¼ cup sliced blanched almonds, toasted

10 large leaves mint, finely chopped

8 large leaves basil, finely chopped

1 clove garlic, peeled, split, germ removed, and
finely chopped

3 tablespoons extra-virgin olive oil

Pinch of cayenne pepper

1. **PREHEAT THE OVEN** to 350°F.

2. **SEASON THE BREAD CUBES** with salt and pepper and lay them in a single layer on a baking sheet. Toast the bread in the oven for 5 to 10 minutes, or until the cubes are dry. Toss the cubes into a large mixing bowl.

3. **COARSELY CHOP THE EGGPLANT** and add it to the bowl along with the tomato, almonds, mint, basil, garlic, and olive oil. Season the stuffing well with salt and pepper and the cayenne. Divide the stuffing among the 4 eggplant shells, mounding it with a spoon.

to finish:

⅓ cup finely grated Parmesan cheese

2 tablespoons (approximately) extra-virgin olive oil

2 leaves basil, finely chopped

2 leaves mint, finely chopped

1. **CENTER A RACK** in the oven and preheat the oven to 425°F. Butter the bottom of a gratin or baking pan just large enough to hold the eggplant comfortably.

2. **TURN THE RAGOUT** into the pan and spread it evenly along the bottom of the pan. Arrange the stuffed eggplants over the ragout, sprinkle the stuffing with the Parmesan, and drizzle over some of the olive oil. Slide the pan into the oven and bake for 25 to 30 minutes, drizzling the topping frequently with olive oil so that it forms a crispy crust. When the crust is browned, the eggplant is done.

to serve: Spoon some of the ragout into the center of each warm plate, top with a stuffed eggplant, and sprinkle with the basil and mint leaves. Serve while everything is still very hot.

to drink: A Provençal wine such as Bandol Blanc

Oven-Roasted Vegetable Casserole

For anyone who appreciates fine ingredients, takes pleasure in cooking, and enjoys the way cooking and eating engage our senses, this very simple dish will have extraordinary appeal. I find it a pleasure to tend the vegetables as they roast, turning them over gently in the warm olive oil and watching them soften, give up their sweet juices, and turn golden. It is a delight to toss the fresh basil leaves into the casserole and breathe in their heady aroma. And it is a treat to savor these vegetables, caramel brown, naturally sweet, and oven-tender. This is a family-and-friends dish, made more inviting when you set out a bottle of olive oil, a bowl of salt, and a few wedges of lemon and encourage everyone around the table to finish the dish to their own taste.

MAKES 4 SERVINGS

⅓ cup extra-virgin olive oil, plus more for serving
8 small turnips, peeled and trimmed
8 small to medium fingerling potatoes, washed
8 small carrots, peeled and trimmed
8 cipollini onions, peeled and trimmed
8 medium white mushrooms, stemmed and cleaned
8 medium pink radishes, washed, dried, and trimmed
2 to 3 stalks celery, peeled and cut into eight 3-inch pieces
2 large cloves garlic, peeled
Bouquet garni (1 bay leaf, 1 sprig thyme, and the reserved basil stems—from below—tied together with kitchen twine)

1 teaspoon crushed coriander seeds, tied in cheesecloth
Salt and freshly ground white pepper
½ cup Niçoise olives
½ bunch basil, washed, dried, and stems and leaves separated (stems used for the bouquet garni)
1 lemon, cut into 4 wedges
Fleur de sel or lightly crushed coarse sea salt
Grated Pecorino Romano or Parmesan cheese (optional)

1. PREHEAT THE OVEN to 350°F.
2. WARM 3 TABLESPOONS of the olive oil in a shallow casserole or ovenproof sauté pan over medium heat. Add the turnips, potatoes, and carrots and cook, turning frequently, for 8 to 10 minutes, or until the vegetables take on a little color. Add the remaining oil, the onions, mushrooms, radishes, celery, garlic, bouquet garni, and coriander sachet. Season well with salt and pepper and cook, stirring, for another 8 to 10 minutes, until the newly added vegetables are also lightly and evenly browned.

3. TRANSFER THE PAN to the oven and roast for about 30 minutes, stirring two or three times during this period, until the vegetables test tender when pierced with a knife. Remove the pan from the oven, discard the garlic, bouquet garni, and coriander sachet, and stir in the olives and half the basil leaves.

to serve: Scatter the remaining basil leaves over the vegetables—don't stir them in—and bring the casserole to the table. Serve the oven-roasted vegetables and their cooking juices directly from the pan. Offer the lemon, fleur de sel or coarse salt, pepper, and olive oil at the table and, if desired, top each serving with some grated cheese.

to drink: A light, crisp, unoaked Chardonnay

Potato Gratin Forestier

As a son of the Dauphiné, the French region famous for its potato gratins, it would be unthinkable for me not to have at least one of these soul-soothing casseroles in my repertoire. Actually, I have several potato gratins in my files, but the potato-mushroom gratin—*forestier* always means there are mushrooms in the dish—is a favorite and one I've made for many years. Early in my career, I was the chef at the Baron of Beef, the famed restaurant of the Hotel Plaza in Copenhagen. The restaurant was named for its specialty, a combination of two top rounds of beef carved tableside, and I always served the dish with a potato gratin, most often one like this in which the potatoes are layered with wild mushrooms, drenched with heavy cream, and baked until they are soft, custardy, and saturated with the cream. Topped with a dusting of Parmesan that browns as the potatoes bake, this gratin would sit easily next to chicken or beef, or take center plate with a well-dressed salad on the side.

MAKES 4 MAIN-COURSE OR 6 TO 8 SIDE-DISH SERVINGS

1 pound assorted wild mushrooms, trimmed, cleaned, and separated by variety

2 tablespoons (approximately) unsalted butter

Salt and freshly ground white pepper

2 cloves garlic, peeled, split, germ removed, and finely chopped

¼ teaspoon finely chopped thyme leaves

3 cups heavy cream

Freshly grated nutmeg

4 pounds Idaho potatoes

¼ cup finely grated Parmesan cheese

1. **WORKING IN A MEDIUM SAUTÉ PAN** or skillet over medium heat, sauté each variety of mushroom in just enough butter to keep the mushrooms from sticking. Season the mushrooms with salt and pepper and cook, stirring, just until they are tender but not colored, a few minutes for each batch. When one type of mushroom is cooked, drain, turn it into a bowl, and repeat with the next type. You need to sauté the mushrooms separately because each type has a different cooking time but, once cooked, all the mushrooms should be mixed together in the bowl, along with the garlic and thyme. Set aside at room temperature until needed. *(The mushrooms can be sautéed up to 2 hours ahead and kept covered with plastic wrap at room temperature.)*

2. **CENTER A RACK** in the oven and preheat the oven to 350°F. Butter the bottom and sides of an ovenproof 10-inch sauté pan or skillet.

3. **POUR THE CREAM** into a large bowl and whisk in salt and pepper and freshly grated nutmeg to taste. (Add more salt than you might normally, because the potatoes will need it.) One at a time, peel the potatoes and slice them into ⅛-inch-thick rounds. The best way to get rounds this thin is to use a

mandoline. Lacking that, use the thinnest slicing blade on the food processor or a sharp knife. Toss the potatoes into the cream as you slice them.

4. USING YOUR HANDS, pull enough potato slices out of the cream to make a single layer on the bottom of the buttered pan, arranging them in even, slightly overlapping concentric circles. Make a second layer of potato slices and then pour some cream over the layers. Press down on the potatoes to compact the layers—when you do this, some of the cream should rise up between the slices. Spread the mushrooms (minus whatever liquid may have accumulated in the bowl) over the potatoes and pour in more cream, again using your hands to press down on the ingredients and bring the cream to the top. Arrange the remaining potatoes in attractive layers over the mushrooms, pouring in cream and pressing down as you finish each layer. You may not need all of the cream—you'll know you've added enough when, without pressing down, you see cream at the edges of the pan. Dust the gratin evenly with the Parmesan cheese and place the pan on a foil-lined baking sheet that can act as a drip-catcher. (If you'd like your gratin to look like the one in the photograph [see the insert following page 288], don't extend the last layers of potatoes all the way to the edges of the pan. Leave a border of mushrooms visible and give the mushrooms only the lightest dusting of Parmesan.)

5. BAKE THE GRATIN for 45 minutes, then check that it's not getting too brown. If necessary, lower the oven temperature to 300°F to keep the gratin from coloring too much. Bake for 15 minutes more, or until you can easily pass a slender sharp knife through all the layers.

6. REMOVE THE GRATIN from the oven and let it stand in a warm place for about 20 minutes, time enough for the potatoes to soak up more cream. If it's more convenient, you can keep the gratin warm in a 200°F oven.

to serve: Bring the gratin to the table and cut it into wedges.

to drink: A light, earthy Givry from the Côte Chalonnaise

Eggplant Like a Pizza

This looks like a pizza, despite its lack of a dough. It boasts a stunning medley of vegetables any pizza would be proud to claim, and enough textural interest to fool you into thinking there's more here than meets the eye. This is a recipe to vary to your heart's content. The only thing that's immutable is the double layer of batter-dipped and panfried eggplant—it's the crust. After that, the sautéed vegetables that you layer over the crust are a cook's choice. I think the cloves of roasted garlic are a great all-round flavor booster, so I'd suggest you keep them, but the rest is up to your imagination. Only one caveat: Make sure you cook the vegetables all the way through before you assemble the pizza, since the baking time for the assembled pizza is only just long enough to heat—not cook—the ingredients.

MAKES 6 TO 8 SERVINGS

1 to 2 medium eggplants
Salt
3 to 4 tablespoons extra-virgin olive oil
1 green bell pepper, cored, seeded, deveined,
    and cut into thin strips
Freshly ground white pepper
1 small red onion, peeled, trimmed, halved,
    and thinly sliced
½ zucchini, scrubbed, trimmed, and cut into
    ¼-inch-thick rounds
½ yellow squash, scrubbed, trimmed, and cut
    into ¼-inch-thick rounds
2 cups (approximately) flavorless oil, such as
    grapeseed or vegetable, for deep-frying

Flour for dredging
5 leaves basil, torn into pieces
1 roasted red bell pepper, cut into thin strips
1 roasted yellow bell pepper, cut into thin strips
1 tablespoon finely chopped Italian parsley
    leaves
12 pieces Tomato Confit (page 350) or drained
    oil-packed sun-dried tomatoes, quartered
1 head Roasted Garlic (page 349), garlic
    pushed out of the peel
12 Niçoise olives, pitted
1 tablespoon finely grated Pecorino Romano or
    Parmesan cheese
2 ounces feta cheese, crumbled

1. PEEL ONE OF THE EGGPLANTS and cut it into ⅛-inch-thick rounds. (The easiest way to get rounds this thin is to use a mandoline or a meat slicer—lacking either, do the best you can do with a knife.) You'll need about 20 slices for the pizza, so count what you've got to determine whether or not you need to use the second eggplant. Sprinkle the slices on both sides with salt and place them between a triple layer of paper towels; set aside for 45 minutes. (The salting will rid the eggplant of some of its natural bitterness and make it less likely to absorb large quantities of oil when it is fried.)

2. WHILE THE EGGPLANT IS RESTING, sauté the vegetables: Warm 1 tablespoon of the olive oil in a small sauté pan or skillet over medium heat. When it's hot, add the green pepper strips, season with

salt and pepper, and cook, stirring, just until the pepper is tender but not colored, 5 to 8 minutes. Spoon the pepper onto a small plate and set aside. Put the pan back over the heat and, if necessary, add a little more olive oil. Warm the oil, then add the red onion slices to the pan. Season with salt and pepper and cook the onion until it too is tender but not colored. Set the onion aside on another small plate and repeat with the zucchini and then the yellow squash, adding only as much oil as you need to keep the vegetables from sticking. *(The vegetables can be sautéed a few hours ahead and kept covered at room temperature or in the refrigerator.)*

3. FOR THE "CRUST," pat the salted eggplant dry between paper towels. Place a rack over a baking pan and put it close to the stovetop. Pour the 2 cups oil into a deep saucepan and put the pan over medium-high heat. Dredge the eggplant slices a few at time in the flour, tapping off the excess flour. When the oil is hot (about 350°F, as measured on a deep-fat thermometer), fry the eggplant in batches—don't crowd the pan—just until the pieces are golden at the edges and lightly crispy. Lift the slices out of the oil with a slotted spatula and onto the rack to drain.

4. CENTER A RACK in the oven and preheat the oven to 400°F. Line a baking sheet with foil. Brush the inside of a 10-inch cake ring or the ring (not the base) of a springform pan with oil, place the ring on the baking sheet, and brush the area inside the ring very lightly with oil.

5. START CONSTRUCTING the pizza by arranging a layer of fried eggplant slices, each slice slightly overlapping the previous slice, within the cake ring. Top with another layer of eggplant—this makes the crust—season with salt and pepper, and scatter over the basil leaves. Lay the red and yellow pepper strips over the basil and sprinkle these with the parsley. Next, arrange a layer of yellow squash and zucchini rounds and lay the green pepper strips over the squash. Top this with the pieces of tomato and roasted garlic cloves. Finish with the sautéed onions and the black olives. Dust the pizza with the grated cheese and scatter the feta evenly over the pie. Drizzle with olive oil and slide the pan into the oven.

6. BAKE FOR 15 TO 20 MINUTES, or until the pizza is very hot and the cheese is melted. Remove the pan from the oven, take off the cake ring, and, using two broad spatulas, lift the pizza onto a cutting board or serving plate.

to serve: Not surprisingly, the easiest way to cut the pizza is with a pizza wheel. Divide the pizza into 6 or 8 slices and serve on warm plates.

to drink: A fruity wine such as a Cassis Blanc from Provence

Wild Mushroom Civet

The classic civet, a red wine stew, is based on wild hare and cooked only during hunting season. Because it's a recipe too good to put away when the season closes, cooks have adapted the structure of the dish over the years to fit other foods, most especially lobster (lobster cooked in red wine is a marvel) and duck (see page 56 for my rendition of a duck civet). For me, it was an easy jump to a wild mushroom civet, a dish for the foraging season. Mushrooms and red wine make a good marriage: The mushrooms bring texture, depth, sweetness, and an earthy aroma to the mixture, while the red wine gives fruit, spice, and a touch of acidity. Try to use an assortment of mushrooms, if you can—complexity is always welcomed in a braised dish—and serve the civet with garlic-herb croutons and, if you're feeling ambitious, any of the offerings that traditionally keep a wild hare civet company: roasted apples, pears, or chestnuts; dried prunes; cracked walnuts; and/or soft, silky mashed potatoes.

MAKES 4 SERVINGS

¼ pound dried porcini mushrooms

4 cups red wine

5 tablespoons unsalted butter

1 tablespoon extra-virgin olive oil

1 clove garlic, peeled, split, germ removed, and finely chopped

1 onion, peeled, trimmed, and cut into ¼-inch dice

1 carrot, peeled, trimmed, and cut into ¼-inch dice

1 stalk celery, peeled, trimmed, and cut into ¼-inch dice

Salt and freshly ground white pepper

½ pound wild mushrooms, preferably an assortment, trimmed, cleaned, and cut in half (or quartered if large)

¼ cup Niçoise or Kalamata olives, pitted

1 tablespoon finely chopped Italian parsley leaves

5 sprigs thyme

2 leaves sage, finely chopped

1 bay leaf

1 tablespoon all-purpose flour

1½ cups water

4 Garlic-Herb Croutons (page 290)

1. **PUT THE DRIED MUSHROOMS** in a medium bowl and pour 3 cups of warm water over them. Let the mushrooms soak for at least 30 minutes, longer if it's more convenient for you, then lift them from the water and squeeze them between your palms to rid them of excess moisture; reserve the mushrooms and discard the soaking liquid.

2. **POUR THE WINE** into a medium saucepan, bring to the boil over medium heat, and boil until the wine is reduced by half.

3. MEANWHILE, working over medium heat, warm 1 tablespoon of the butter and the oil in a large sauté pan or skillet with high sides. When the butter is melted and hot, add the garlic along with the diced onion, carrot, and celery. Season with salt and pepper and cook, stirring, until the vegetables soften but do not take on color, 8 to 10 minutes. Add the mushrooms, both fresh and reconstituted, and 2 table-spoons of the butter and cook and stir for another 5 to 7 minutes, or until the mushrooms are tender. Stir in the olives, parsley, thyme, sage, and bay leaf, then add the flour. Cook and stir for 2 minutes more, then add the reduced red wine and bring it to the boil.

4. CUT A PARCHMENT PAPER CIRCLE to fit inside the pan (see Glossary, page 369) and press the parchment lightly against the ingredients. Set the heat to very low—the liquid should simmer gen-tly—and braise for 15 minutes. Add the water and cook for 25 to 30 minutes more, until all the veg-etables are meltingly tender and the sauce is full flavored. Remove the parchment and, if there's too much liquid in the pan—it should be saucy, not soupy—cook the civet uncovered for a few minutes more. Discard the bay leaf, taste the civet, and add more salt and pepper if needed.

5. REMOVE THE PAN from the heat and swirl in the remaining 2 tablespoons butter. *(The civet can be cooled—don't add the butter in this case—and stored tightly covered in the refrigerator for a day or two. To reheat, cover the pan with a parchment paper lid and warm over low heat; then swirl in the butter.)*

to serve: For each serving, put a garlic-herb crouton in the bottom of a warm shallow soup plate and top with the civet.

to drink: A Nuits-Saint-Georges, a wine with big flavors and some tannins

A Dozen Baby Spring Vegetables with Vanilla, Ginger, and Basil

This dish, a stovetop mix of vegetables, was on Café Boulud's opening menu. We started with autumn vegetables, then changed the selection as the seasons changed. Whatever vegetables you use, it's important to have a variety, and it's important that you leave a little of each vegetable's firmness to preserve its individuality. You can make this with just about any combination of vegetables you find in the market. That said, don't give up the vanilla, ginger, and basil. The vanilla, famously fragrant, adds a caramely underflavor that's not easy to place but is irreplaceable—it brings a sensuality to the dish that I'd hate to lose. The ginger is just the opposite—it's a bright flavor lifter, the counterpoint to the vanilla. As for the basil, few herbs bring so much to so many vegetables. A good mixer, basil is the needed last touch—scattered over the hot vegetables, it's like a touch of perfume on a pulse point.

MAKES 4 SERVINGS

1 bunch basil, leaves only, washed and
    dried
One 3-inch-long piece peeled ginger
1 moist, plump vanilla bean
4 small new potatoes, each about 1 to
    1½ inches across, scrubbed
2 baby fennel bulbs, trimmed, halved length-
    wise, and washed
4 baby leeks, white part only, well washed
4 baby turnips, peeled and greens trimmed to
    ½ inch
4 spring onions, white part with ½ inch of
    green only
4 small icicle radishes, roots trimmed, greens
    trimmed to ½ inch, and washed

8 baby carrots, peeled and greens trimmed
    short
4 green baby pattypan squash, washed (or 2
    baby zucchini, cut into 1-inch lengths)
4 yellow baby pattypan squash, washed (or 2
    baby yellow squash, cut into
    1-inch lengths)
8 yellow wax beans, trimmed
8 haricots verts, trimmed
8 snow peas
1 plum tomato, peeled, seeded, and cut into
    ¼-inch dice
1 lemon
2 tablespoons extra-virgin olive oil
Salt and freshly ground white pepper

1. TAKE A HANDFUL of the smaller, tender basil leaves, wrap them in a damp towel, and tuck them into the refrigerator until needed. Grate enough of the ginger to make ½ teaspoon and set that aside covered, then cut the remaining ginger into 4 pieces. Cut the vanilla bean lengthwise in half and, using the back of the knife, scrape the pulp out of the pod. Cover the pulp and set it aside for the moment. Tie the pieces of ginger, the remaining basil, and the vanilla bean pod in cheesecloth and keep this sachet close at hand.

2. BRING A GALLON of salted water to the boil in a large pot. Toss the sachet into the water along with half of the vanilla pulp and boil for 10 minutes. Keeping the water at a boil, add the potatoes and boil for 4 minutes. Toss in the fennel and boil for 3 minutes more, then add the leeks and turnips and boil for 1 more minute. Now add the onions and radishes and boil for 2 minutes more before tossing in the baby carrots. After 4 minutes, add the squash, wax beans, haricots verts, and snow peas. Boil for 3 minutes—at this point, all the vegetables should be tender. Drain immediately, pull out and discard the sachet, and cool the vegetables down in the refrigerator. When they are cool, peel the potatoes and slice them into ¼-inch-thick rounds. *(The vegetables can be made up to this point and kept covered with plastic wrap in the refrigerator for up to 6 hours.)*

3. PUT THE DICED TOMATO in a small bowl and keep it nearby. Finely grate the zest of half the lemon and toss the zest into the bowl with the tomatoes. Using a small sharp knife, cut away the zest and white cottony pith from the entire lemon, cutting deep enough to expose the moist flesh. Slicing between the membranes, release half the segments. Pick out and discard the seeds from the lemon segments and then slice them into small dice. Add the dice to the tomatoes, then squeeze the juice from what remains of the lemon over the tomatoes. Toss the tomato, zest, dice, and juice together and set aside.

4. HEAT THE OLIVE OIL, the reserved grated ginger, and the remaining vanilla pulp in a large sauté pan or skillet over high heat. Add the vegetables, season with salt and pepper, and cook, stirring constantly, until they are hot, about 3 minutes. Toss in the tomato and lemon mixture and stir to combine, then pull the pan from the heat.

to serve: Divide the vegetables among four warm shallow soup plates and top with the reserved basil leaves. Serve immediately, while everything is hot and the fragrance of the just-strewn basil is at its peak.

to drink: A lightly oaked Pinot Grigio from Italy

Stuffed Romaine in Red Wine

If all you've ever thought romaine lettuce was good for was Caesar salad, you're in for a treat. Stuffed with root vegetables, seasoned with sage, and sauced with a reduction of red wine and port, the leafy lettuce becomes a deeply flavorful bitter green, a mysteriously complex wrapper, and the principal player in a thoroughly satisfying cold-weather dish. For double satisfaction, serve the romaine with creamy polenta (page 246) or bread—you'll want a sopper-upper for every drop of the sauce.

You can simplify this dish by making an unstuffed version. Blanch and drain the leaves of romaine just as you would if you were stuffing them, then roll them into balls. Line the pan with the vegetables that would have been the stuffing—they'll braise with the sauce—settle the lettuce balls on the bed of vegetables, and carry on.

MAKES 4 SERVINGS

the stuffing:

18 white mushrooms, stemmed and cleaned

6 medium turnips, peeled, trimmed, and roughly chopped

2 large carrots, peeled, trimmed, and roughly chopped

2 large parsnips, peeled, trimmed, and roughly chopped

2 small celery roots, peeled and roughly chopped

3 tablespoons unsalted butter

2 large onions, peeled, trimmed, and finely chopped

Salt and freshly ground white pepper

4 leaves sage, finely chopped (reserve the stems for the sauce)

1. **PLACE THE MUSHROOMS,** turnips, carrots, parsnips, and celery root in the work bowl of a food processor (depending on the size of your work bowl, you may have to this in batches) and pulse on and off until the vegetables are chopped into pieces about ½ inch in size—don't overdo it.

2. **MELT THE BUTTER** in a large sauté pan or skillet over medium heat. Add two thirds of the onions and cook, stirring, until they are soft but not colored, about 5 minutes. Add two thirds of the chopped vegetables to the pan (the remaining vegetables and chopped onions will be used in the sauce), season with salt and pepper, and continue to cook and stir until they are tender but not colored, another 10 minutes or so. Remove the pan from the heat, stir in the chopped sage leaves, and taste for salt and pepper. Set the stuffing aside to cool.

the sauce:

2 tablespoons extra-virgin olive oil

The reserved chopped onion, chopped vegetables, and sage stems (from above)

Salt and freshly ground white pepper

5 cups red wine

1 cup ruby port

1. WARM THE OLIVE OIL in a medium saucepan over medium heat. When the oil is hot, stir in the reserved chopped onion and cook, stirring, until it is soft but not colored, about 5 minutes. Add the reserved vegetables and sage stems, season with salt and pepper, and continue to cook until the vegetables soften just a little, another 5 minutes. Pour in the wine and port and bring to a boil, then lower the heat to medium and allow the liquid to simmer until it is reduced to 1 cup. Be patient—this might take about 45 minutes. (You can work on the romaine while the sauce is reducing.)

2. WHEN ONLY 1 CUP of liquid remains, strain the sauce through a chinois or a fine-mesh strainer set over a saucepan, pressing hard against the solids to extract as much of the liquid as possible. Discards the solids and set the sauce aside until needed.

the romaine:

8 small heads romaine lettuce

Salt and freshly ground white pepper

1 tablespoon unsalted butter

1. PUT A LARGE POT of salted water up to boil. Center a rack in the oven and preheat the oven to 375°F. Generously butter a flameproof oval gratin pan or small roasting pan.

2. REMOVE ANY TOUGH OUTER LEAVES from the romaine. Drop half the heads into the pot of boiling water and boil for about 3 minutes, or until the ribs of the romaine are pliable. (If the romaine pops above the water as it cooks, press it down with a skimmer or colander to keep it submerged.) Scoop out the romaine and run it under cold water to stop the cooking. Repeat with the remaining romaine.

3. SQUEEZE THE ROMAINE between your hands to get rid of some of the excess water. Cut off and discard the bottom 2 inches of each head and pat the lettuce dry between layers of towels. One at a time, unroll each head of lettuce and spread out the leaves just enough to have them make a rough square. Remove and discard the small core leaves and season the romaine with salt and pepper.

4. FOR EACH ROMAINE, scoop up a rounded soupspoonful of stuffing, put your cupped hand against the stuffing and press against it lightly and then place the compacted ball of stuffing close to what was the core end of the romaine. Bring the lettuce up around the stuffing to make a ball. (If, once you've made the ball, there are leaves or ribs that won't fold into the ball, cut them off and discard them.) Wrap the packet in a kitchen towel, twist the ends of the towel, and squeeze the packet to remove excess moisture and give it a rounder, more uniform shape. Unwrap the packet and place seam side down in the buttered gratin dish. Spoon the sauce over the romaine. Cut a piece of parchment paper to fit inside the dish (see Glossary, page 369), and press it lightly against the packets.

5. SLIDE THE PAN into the oven and braise the lettuce, basting occasionally, for 45 minutes. Remove the pan from the oven and transfer the lettuce to a warm platter. Keep the romaine warm while you finish the sauce.

6. COOK THE SAUCE at a boil on top of the stove until it is reduced to about 6 tablespoons. Pull the pan from the heat and swirl in the butter.

to serve: Place 2 stuffed romaine lettuces on each of four warm dinner plates, spoon over the hot sauce, and serve immediately.

to drink: A good Gigondas from a ripe vintage

Desserts

Potato and Almond Cake

Potato may not jump to mind as the ingredient of choice for a fabulous dessert, but it's the secret of this cake's soft, smooth, sensuous, almost custardy consistency. The cake batter is made from the baker's basic mix of butter, sugar, eggs, and cream, and the flavor is mild, slightly vanilla-ish, sweet, and—just in case you were wondering—not a bit like a baked potato. (The only way you'd place the potato is if you said "potato" three times before taking your first bite.) Pound cake lovers will be content to eat this cake plain, but at the restaurant we pair it with a light vanilla bean syrup with slivers of sweet dates and a remarkable whipped cream flavored with roasted coffee beans, a touch of chicory, and melted milk chocolate. I'll be surprised if you don't find yourself making this cream often and serving it with cookies. Try it with the small, buttery Trao-Mad cookies (page 98), or think of it the next time you've got a vanilla or chocolate cake that needs a boost.

the syrup:

1 moist, plump vanilla bean

1½ cups water

¼ cup sugar

8 pitted dates, each cut into 8 slivers

CUT THE VANILLA BEAN lengthwise in half and, using the back of the knife, scrape the pulp out of the pod. Bring the water, sugar, and vanilla bean pod and pulp to a boil in a small saucepan. As soon as the syrup comes to the boil, pull the pan from the heat, stir in the dates, and set aside to cool. *(The dates and syrup can be made a day in advance and, once cooled, kept covered in the refrigerator.)*

the cream:

1 to 1½ cups heavy cream

1 tablespoon chicory (see Source Guide, page 385)

⅓ cup coffee beans, roughly crushed

5½ ounces milk chocolate, preferably imported, finely chopped

1. PUT 1 CUP of the cream, the chicory, and coffee beans in a medium saucepan and bring to the boil. Pull the pan from the heat, cover, and set the cream aside to infuse for 15 minutes. Meanwhile, place the chocolate in a metal bowl and set out a glass measuring cup.

2. STRAIN THE INFUSED CREAM into the measuring cup and, if it doesn't come up to the 1-cup mark, add enough additional heavy cream to make an even cup. Wash and dry the saucepan, pour in the cream, and bring back to the boil. Add the cream to the chocolate in two additions, each time very gently whisking the cream into the chocolate. You don't want to beat air into the mixture, nor do you want to overwork it, so just go slowly and easily. When the cream is homogenous, press a piece of plastic wrap against its surface to create an airtight seal and chill it in the refrigerator. *(If you have the time, this is best left to chill overnight in the refrigerator.)* Before serving, whisk the cream until it is firm enough for you to form a rounded spoonful.

the cake:

1 pound Idaho potatoes

2 tablespoons all-purpose flour

½ teaspoon baking powder

½ cup sugar, plus extra for topping

2 large eggs, separated

Pulp from ½ moist, plump vanilla bean (scraped as above; pod reserved for another use, if desired)

3½ tablespoons unsalted butter, melted

2 tablespoons heavy cream

1 large egg yolk

¼ cup sliced blanched almonds

1. **PEEL THE POTATOES,** cut them into quarters, and toss them into a pot of cold salted water. Bring to the boil and cook until the potatoes can be pierced easily with a knife. Drain the potatoes, then put them back into the pot and, shaking the pot constantly over medium heat, heat the potatoes just enough to cook off the excess moisture. Purée the hot potatoes through a food mill or potato ricer and cool them to room temperature. Reserve 1 (packed) cup of potato purée.

2. **CENTER A RACK** in the oven and preheat the oven to 400°F. Butter an 8- by 2-inch round cake pan, dust it with flour, tap out the excess, and place the pan on a baking sheet.

3. **WHISK TOGETHER** the flour, baking powder, and 2 tablespoons of the sugar and set aside.

4. **WORKING IN A MIXER** fitted with the whisk attachment, beat the egg whites with the vanilla bean pulp on medium-low speed until they are foamy and start to come together, about 2 minutes. Increase the speed to medium-high and, when the whites form very soft peaks, start adding the remaining 6 tablespoons sugar in a slow, steady stream. Continue to beat until the whites are firm but still glossy. Set aside for the moment.

5. **IN A LARGE BOWL,** whisk together the cooled mashed potatoes, the butter, cream, and egg yolks until smooth. Switch to a rubber spatula and gently but thoroughly stir the flour mixture into the potatoes. Finally, delicately fold in the beaten egg whites. (You might find it easiest to stir about a quarter of the beaten whites into the mixture, just to lighten it, then to fold in the rest.)

6. **FILL THE PAN** with the batter, gently smoothing the top. Sprinkle the top with the almond slices and about 1 tablespoon sugar. Slide the baking sheet into the oven and bake for 20 to 25 minutes, rotating the sheet front to back at the 10-minute mark. When baked, the cake should be golden brown, just pulling away from the sides of the pan, and springy to the touch.

7. **RUN A SMALL BLUNT KNIFE** between the cake and the sides of the pan and unmold the cake onto a cooling cake; invert the cake to cool to room temperature right side up on the rack.

to serve: Cut the cake into 8 slices and place one piece of cake in the center of each of eight dinner plates. Arrange some date slivers in a few crisscrosses on one side of each plate and garnish each with a scoop of chicory cream. Drizzle the vanilla syrup around the cake and serve.

to drink: A 10-year-old tawny port

Candied Yellow Tomatoes

What botanists have long known, dessert lovers are only just beginning to accept: The tomato is a fruit—one with sweet possibilities. Here, the firm, succulent flesh of nonacidic yellow tomatoes is macerated overnight in a syrup of lemongrass and vanilla to make a fruit salad of unusual finesse. It can be served with a premium-quality vanilla ice cream, but if you have an ice cream maker, I urge you to churn a batch of subtly flavored thyme ice cream—in concert with the candied tomatoes, it is extraordinary.

MAKES 8 SERVINGS

8 medium yellow tomatoes
3 cups water
1 cup sugar
1½ stalks lemongrass (the half from a stalk split lengthwise), bulb and 4 to 5 inches of the stalk only, bruised

½ moist, plump vanilla bean, split lengthwise
Thyme Ice Cream or Vanilla Ice Cream (page 341), for serving

1. BRING A LARGE POT of water to the boil. Cut a small X in the base of each tomato, then toss the tomatoes into the boiling water (in batches, if necessary) and blanch for just 1 minute. Drain the tomatoes and run them under cold water to cool. Using a small knife, peel the tomatoes and cut each into 6 wedges. With each wedge set on its rounded side, cut between the firm flesh and the pulp and seeds, following the curve of the flesh; discard the pulp and seeds and place the pieces of peeled tomato in a bowl.

2. BRING THE 3 CUPS WATER, the sugar, lemongrass, and split vanilla bean to a boil in a medium saucepan. Pull the pan from the heat, cover tightly with plastic wrap, and let steep for 10 minutes.

3. POUR THE SYRUP over the tomatoes. Cool to room temperature, then cover the bowl with plastic wrap and refrigerate overnight. Discard the lemongrass and vanilla bean pod before serving.

to serve: For each portion, arrange 6 tomato wedges in a small chilled bowl or compote dish. Spoon over some of the syrup and top with a scoop of thyme or vanilla ice cream.

to drink: a New York State late-harvest Riesling

Orange Salad

In this salad, orange finds its soul mates: fresh rosemary and vanilla. Except for a couple of spoonfuls of sugar to round out the flavors and turn the orange juice into a light syrup, that's it—nothing more, and nothing more needed. The salad is cool, fresh, surprising, and ideal for any meal—including brunch. At Café Boulud, we often serve the salad alongside a small bowl of Apple-Quince Marmalade (page 336) and a few crunchy cookies, but it's satisfying on its own, particularly after a hearty meal, and lovely spooned over a slice of lightly toasted pound cake or with the Far Breton (page 86). (For a change of pace, have the oranges from this salad stand in for the berries in the center of the Light Vanilla Cakes, page 172.)

MAKES 4 SERVINGS

8 navel oranges

2 sprigs rosemary

½ plump, moist vanilla bean

2 tablespoons sugar

1. **WITH A KNIFE,** cut away the skin of the oranges, removing every trace of white cottony pith and exposing the moist, glistening fruit. Working over a bowl, cut between the membranes, releasing the orange segments and allowing them and their juices to drop into the bowl. If you'd like, you can cut the orange segments into smaller pieces. As you finish each orange, squeeze the remaining juice from the membranes into the bowl before discarding the membranes. Add the rosemary.

2. **CUT THE VANILLA BEAN** lengthwise in half and, using the back of the knife, scrape the pulp out of the pod. Add the vanilla bean pod and pulp along with the sugar to the bowl and stir gently. Cover the bowl with plastic wrap and chill for 12 hours before serving.

to serve: Discard the rosemary and vanilla bean and spoon the oranges and some of their syrup into small bowls.

to drink: A mimosa

Apple, Almond, and Pine Nut Tart

In France, an almond cream tart is almost always topped with thinly sliced poached pear halves—not this one. This recipe works a fresh twist on the classic and gives the almond cream something spicier to play against: a slim layer of vanilla-and-cinnamon-scented applesauce. First the applesauce is spooned into the crust, then it's topped with the almond cream. Both layers are soft, smooth, and comforting. The textural contrast comes from the almondy crust—aptly named Sublime—and the pine nuts, scattered across the top of the tart like so many golden stepping stones.

MAKES 6 TO 8 SERVINGS

The crust:

1 partially baked 8- by-³⁄₄ -inch tart shell (in a
   tart ring) made from Pâte Sublime
   (page 355)

KEEP THE CRUST, with the tart ring still in place, on its parchment-lined baking sheet. *(You can make the crust up to 8 hours ahead and keep it in its ring at room temperature.)*

the filling:

½ moist, plump vanilla bean
1 large (about 12 ounces) Gala apple, peeled,
   cored, and cut into 1-inch chunks
1 tablespoon sugar
½ cinnamon stick
3 tablespoons water

1 recipe Almond Cream (page 359), at room
   temperature
⅓ cup pine nuts
Confectioner's sugar for dusting

1. CUT THE VANILLA BEAN lengthwise in half and, using the back of the knife, scrape the pulp out of the pod. Put the vanilla bean pod and pulp, apple, sugar, cinnamon, and water into a saucepan, stir well to combine, and set over medium heat. Cook, stirring now and then, until the apple starts to release some of its juice, about 5 minutes. At this point, lower the heat, cover, and cook gently, stirring from time to time, until the apple is soft enough to be mashed into a sauce with a fork, about 30 minutes. Mash the apple, take the pan off the heat, remove the vanilla bean and cinnamon stick, and set the applesauce aside to cool.

2. CENTER A RACK in the oven and preheat the oven to 400°F.

3. TURN THE APPLESAUCE into the tart shell and smooth its surface with a spatula. Fill the tart shell with the almond cream, again smoothing the top, and sprinkle over the pine nuts. Bake the tart for 20 minutes, or until the almond cream is golden and slightly puffed and the nuts are golden brown. Transfer to a rack and cool to room temperature.

to serve: The tart is best served at room temperature the day it is made. Sprinkle it with a little confectioner's sugar right before bringing it to the table.

to drink: A sparkling dessert wine made from apples, such as a Pommeau de Bretagne

Apple-Quince Marmalade

Not really a spread-on-toast marmalade and not really a compote or an applesauce, this hauntingly spiced mix is an easy spoon food to serve on its own, with Orange Salad (page 333), or, like the orange salad, with a few cookies for crunch. I like apple and quince together and use the combination for dishes both savory (see the Honey-Glazed Chicken with Quinces and Apples, page 150) and sweet. The fruits have a natural affection for one another but, because the quince never softens enough to be as saucy as the apples, there's always a little textural give-and-take going on when they're together. What catapults this simple mix to sophistication is the blend of spices—exotic star anise, warm vanilla, and heady clove and cinnamon.

MAKES 4 SERVINGS

½ moist, plump vanilla bean
⅓ cup plus 1 tablespoon sugar
3 whole star anise
1 cinnamon stick
1 whole clove

1 quince, peeled, halved, cored, and cut into
   ½-inch-thick slices
4 Granny Smith apples, peeled, cored, and cut
   into ½-inch cubes
1 cup water

1. CUT THE VANILLA BEAN lengthwise in half and, using the back of the knife, scrape the pulp out of the pod. Put the vanilla bean pod and pulp and 2 cups of water into a medium saucepan. Add the ⅓ cup sugar, the star anise, cinnamon, and clove and bring to a boil; drop in the slices of quince. Poach at a simmer until the slices are tender, about 30 minutes.

2. WHEN THE QUINCE IS TENDER enough to be pierced easily with the tip of a knife, drain, discarding the poaching syrup and spices. Cool, then cut the quince into small dice.

3. MEANWHILE, make the apple compote: Toss the apples into another medium saucepan along with the water and the remaining 1 tablespoon sugar. Cover and cook over low heat, stirring occasionally, until the apples are so soft that they fall apart when stirred, about 30 minutes.

4. STIR THE QUINCE into the apple compote and pull the pan from the heat; cool to room temperature. The marmalade can be served at room temperature or chilled. *(The marmalade can be made up to 2 days ahead and kept tightly covered in the refrigerator.)*

to serve: Spoon the marmalade into small bowls or cups and serve alone or with cookies, if you have them.

to drink: A traditional Tokaji Aszú

Crisp Raspberry Tuiles with Lemon Cream

A triple treat for anyone who loves raspberries, this dessert is really a small tower of raspberry tuiles (the cookies named for French roof tiles), crisp and slightly caramely, honeycombed, and wholly raspberry flavored. (These are so remarkable we serve them on their own on our petits fours plate at the Café.) The tuiles are layered with lemon pastry cream that's been lightened with whipped cream and enlivened with fresh raspberries. Then the tower is set on a plate that's drizzled with brilliantly red raspberry sauce. The dessert looks highly polished and very professional, but it's easily accomplished at home because the elements are made ahead and assembled at serving time.

For a simpler presentation, spoon the lemon cream and whole berries into small cups, top with a tuile or two, and finish with a swirl of sauce—different look, same exceptional flavors.

MAKES 6 SERVINGS

the tuiles:

¼ **pound (about 1 cup) fresh raspberries**

2 **tablespoons unsalted butter, at room temperature**

¾ **cup confectioner's sugar, sifted**

2 **tablespoons all-purpose flour**

1. **PURÉE THE RASPBERRIES** in a blender or food processor (or use an immersion blender) until smooth. Spoon the purée into a fine-mesh strainer set over a bowl and press to get as much pulp as possible through the strainer. Discard the seeds in the strainer and reserve 3 tablespoons of the purée from the bowl.

2. **WORKING IN A SMALL BOWL** with a rubber spatula, blend the butter and confectioner's sugar together. Add the raspberry purée and mix to incorporate. Add the flour and mix until smooth. Cover the tuile batter with a piece of plastic wrap, pressing the plastic against the batter to get an airtight seal, and refrigerate for at least 1 hour, or, preferably, overnight.

3. **CENTER A RACK** in the oven and preheat the oven to 300°F. Set out two nonstick baking sheets. Make a template so that you'll be able to shape tuiles of a consistent size: Make it from a large plastic top, such as the type that comes with yogurt or ice cream, by cutting out an interior circle that's 2½ inches in diameter; leave the rim intact.

4. **FOR EACH TUILE**, drop about ¾ teaspoon of batter onto the baking sheet, leaving about 4 inches between each drop of batter. (You should be able to get 12 tuiles on a sheet.) Position the template flat against the baking sheet with a drop of batter in the center of the circle and, using a small metal offset spatula, spread the batter evenly across the template; lift off the template and repeat with the remaining tuiles, scraping whatever batter sticks to the template back into the bowl. Even if you've shaped

tuiles on both baking sheets, it's best to bake these one sheet at a time, so just set the second sheet aside for the moment.

5. BAKE THE TUILES for 8 to 10 minutes, or until they are lacy and very lightly browned. (If the tuiles don't brown, they'll be chewy, not crisp.) You'll need to remove each tuile from the sheet as soon as it's ready even though all the tuiles might not be ready at the same time—so don't leave the kitchen. Let the baked tuiles rest a minute, then remove them from the baking sheet by sliding a flexible plastic dough scraper or a broad thin spatula under each cookie and then immediately turning the tuile onto a flat surface—metal or marble is ideal. Return the baking sheet to the oven to bake any remaining tuiles. Bake the second sheet of tuiles and, as soon as the first baking sheet is cool, form and bake more tuiles. (You need 18 tuiles to construct 6 desserts, but it's best to make more in case some break or burn—besides, it's nice to have extras to nibble with coffee.) When the tuiles are cool, they can be stored in an airtight container. *(If you live in a humid climate, it's best to make the tuiles right before serving.)*

the sauce:

½ **pound (about 2 cups) raspberries**
1 tablespoon sugar

PURÉE THE RASPBERRIES and sugar together in a blender or food processor (or use an immersion blender) and press the purée through a fine-mesh strainer into a bowl. Keep the sauce tightly covered in the refrigerator until needed. *(The sauce can be made up to a day in advance and kept in an airtight container in the refrigerator.)*

the cream:

½ **recipe Lemon Pastry Cream (page 358)**
½ **cup heavy cream, whipped to soft peaks**

SCRAPE THE PASTRY CREAM into a medium bowl and whisk it lightly, just to loosen it. Gently fold the whipped cream into the pastry cream.

to finish:

½ **pound (about 2 cups) raspberries**
Confectioner's sugar for dusting

PLACE 1 TUILE in the center of each of six dinner plates. Spoon a generous dollop of lemon cream in the center of each tuile, then, using half the berries, make a ring of raspberries around each portion of cream. Top with another tuile and repeat with another layer of cream and berries. Finish each with another tuile.

to serve: Dust the desserts lightly with confectioner's sugar and drizzle each plate with raspberry sauce. Serve immediately.

to drink: A festive Champagne cocktail with raspberry liqueur and/or fresh raspberries

Vanilla Blueberries, aka Bill's Blues

The "Bill" in this dessert's name refers to President Bill Clinton, the guest of honor for whom we made this couldn't-be-simpler sweet. The Café Boulud team and I were chosen to prepare a special summer dinner for the President when he was making a whirlwind tour of Long Island, and on the spur of the moment—inspired by a bushel of small, fragrant wild blueberries—we put this together. The berries are very lightly sweetened, flavored with a bit of vanilla bean and a scraping of lemon zest, warmed, spooned into bowls, and topped with vanilla ice cream, which melts and makes its own luscious sauce. Although we hesitated for a moment, concerned that this sweet was too rustic for a presidential meal, we forged ahead and, at the end of the dinner, knew we'd made the right choice—not one bowl came back with a spoonful left over.

MAKES 4 SERVINGS

½ **moist, plump vanilla bean**
¾ **pound blueberries, wild or cultivated**
¼ **cup water**
1 **tablespoon sugar**

Grated zest of ¼ small lemon
Vanilla ice cream, homemade (page 341) or
    store-bought

CUT THE VANILLA BEAN lengthwise in half and, using the back of the knife, scrape the pulp out of the pod (reserve the pod for another use, if desired). Put the blueberries, water, sugar, vanilla pulp, and lemon zest in a sauté pan or skillet over medium heat and cook, stirring often but gently, until the berries start to release their juices. Pull the pan from the heat.

to serve: Divide the warm berries among four small bowls. Top with ice cream and serve immediately.

to drink: A white-chocolate liqueur

Vanilla Ice Cream, and Herb Variations

With homemade vanilla ice cream in your freezer, you'll never be at a loss for a great dessert. This is a classic French-style ice cream based on a cooked custard, or crème anglaise, a base that I think produces the smoothest, most elegant ice cream. Since all of its flavor comes from the pod and pulp of one vanilla bean, it's important to choose a bean that is moist, plump, and very aromatic. Vanilla beans come, most commonly, from Tahiti, Madagascar, and Mexico, and each country produces a bean with a different flavor and aroma. My favorite is the Tahitian bean (see Source Guide, page 385), but I urge you to taste different beans and find your own favorite.

MAKES ABOUT 1½ PINTS

1 plump, moist vanilla bean	½ cup sugar
2 cups whole milk	4 large egg yolks

1. CUT THE VANILLA BEAN lengthwise in half and, using the back of the knife, scrape the pulp out of the pod. Put the vanilla bean pulp and pod, the milk, and ¼ cup of the sugar into a saucepan; bring to the boil. Pull the pan from the heat, cover with plastic wrap, and set aside to infuse for 10 minutes. Fill a large bowl with ice cubes and water and set aside a heatproof bowl that will fit into this water bath.

2. WHISK THE YOLKS and the remaining ¼ cup sugar together in a medium bowl until the mixture thickens slightly and turns pale. Strain the vanilla-infused milk into a medium saucepan and bring it back to the boil. While whisking the egg mixture without stop, gradually pour half the hot milk over the egg yolks. Whisk so that all the ingredients are well combined, then pour this mixture back into the saucepan. Cook over medium heat, stirring constantly—this time with a wooden spoon—until the mixture thickens just enough to coat the back of the spoon. If you run your finger down the length of the spoon's bowl, the custard shouldn't run into the track you've created. Strain the custard into the heatproof bowl and put the bowl in the ice-water bath; cool completely. You can use the custard now, or you can cover it with plastic wrap and store it in the refrigerator overnight.

3. FREEZE THE CUSTARD in an ice cream maker following the manufacturer's instructions. When churned, scrape the ice cream into a container, cover well, and put it in the freezer for an hour or two to ripen before serving.

verbena ice cream: Omit the vanilla bean and infuse the milk with ⅛ ounce dried verbena leaves. You can use the verbena leaves that you would use to make verbena tea or a verbena tisane.

thyme ice cream: Omit the vanilla bean and infuse the milk with 2½ teaspoons chopped fresh thyme leaves.

Lemon-Thyme Sorbet

You may not be able to place the thyme in this mostly lemon-flavored sorbet—the thyme is not very strong—but you will notice an unusual and exceptionally appealing depth of flavor.

MAKES ABOUT 1½ PINTS

1 cup sugar
1 tablespoon chopped thyme leaves
2 cups water
1 cup freshly squeezed lemon juice

1. **PUT THE SUGAR,** thyme, and water in a saucepan and bring to the boil. Pull the pan from the heat, cover with plastic wrap, and set aside to infuse for 15 minutes.

2. **STIR THE LEMON JUICE** into the syrup, strain, and cool to room temperature. You can use the syrup now, or you can cover it with plastic wrap and store it in the refrigerator overnight.

3. **FREEZE THE THYME MIXTURE** in an ice cream maker following the manufacturer's instructions. When churned, scrape the sorbet into a container, cover well, and put it in the freezer for an hour or two to ripen before serving.

Pineapple-Basil Sorbet

Basil, an herb with surprising affection for fruit, works as an intensifier in this sorbet, adding a touch of licorice flavor to the pineapple so that the fruit's honey sweetness and light tang truly stand out.

MAKES ABOUT 1½ PINTS

1 pineapple (about 2½ pounds)
1 cup sugar
2 tablespoons chopped basil leaves
⅔ cup water

1. CUT OFF THE TOP and bottom of the pineapple and stand the pineapple upright on a cutting board. Following the form of the fruit, and cutting from top to bottom, slice away the tough skin and eyes. Quarter the pineapple lengthwise, slice off the tough center core, and cut the pineapple into chunks. Toss the chunks into the jar of a blender and purée until smooth. Press the purée through a fine-mesh strainer. Measure out 2 cups of purée and reserve.

2. PUT THE SUGAR AND BASIL in a saucepan with the water and bring to the boil. Pull the pan from the heat, cover with plastic wrap, and set aside to infuse 15 minutes.

3. STRAIN THE SYRUP into a bowl, then stir in the reserved pineapple purée and cool to room temperature. You can use the mixture now, or you can cover it with plastic wrap and store it in the refrigerator overnight.

4. FREEZE THE PINEAPPLE mixture in an ice cream maker following the manufacturer's instructions. When churned, scrape the sorbet into a container, cover well, and put it in the freezer for an hour or two to ripen before serving.

base recipes

Chicken Stock

I can't urge you strongly enough to set aside some time to make a batch of chicken stock. Homemade stock, with its rich flavor, honey color, and slight gel, is rarely the star player in a preparation, but its supporting role can elevate just about anything.

MAKES ABOUT 1 GALLON

4 pounds chicken necks, backs, and wings or chicken parts, skinned, fat trimmed, and rinsed

2½ gallons cold water

2 medium onions, peeled, trimmed, and cut into quarters

2 small carrots, peeled, trimmed, and cut into 2-inch-long pieces

1 stalk celery, trimmed, and cut into 2-inch-long pieces

1 medium leek, trimmed, split lengthwise, and washed

½ head garlic, split crosswise in half

1 bay leaf

5 sprigs Italian parsley, washed

1 teaspoon white peppercorns

1. **PUT THE CHICKEN** and 7 quarts of the cold water in a tall stockpot and bring to a rolling boil. Add the remaining 3 quarts water (it should be very cold) and skim off the fat that rises to the top. Adjust the heat so that the water simmers and simmer—skimming regularly—for 10 minutes.

2. **ADD THE REMAINING INGREDIENTS** to the pot and simmer for 3 hours, continuing to skim so that the stock will be clear. Drain the stock in a colander. Allow the solids to drain for a few minutes before discarding them, then strain the stock through a chinois or fine-mesh strainer. Cool and then refrigerate. *(The stock can be kept tightly covered in the refrigerator for 4 days or frozen for up to a month.)*

Beef Stock

This stock gets its depth of flavor from the beef shank that is cooked in it. Once the shank has done its work flavoring the stock, it should be given a second life—shredded or cubed, the meat is good in salads, tossed with pasta, or added to soups.

MAKES ABOUT 2½ QUARTS

1 large onion, peeled, trimmed, and halved crosswise

2 whole cloves

2 tablespoons vegetable oil

1 beef shank (about 6 pounds)—ask the butcher to cut it crosswise into 2-inch-thick slices, bone included, and to trim excess fat

Salt and freshly ground white pepper

6 quarts water

6 large mushrooms, trimmed, cleaned, and halved

4 stalks celery, trimmed, and cut into 2-inch-long pieces

3 carrots, peeled, trimmed, and cut into 1-inch-long pieces

6 cloves garlic, peeled and crushed

5 sprigs Italian parsley

2 sprigs thyme

2 bay leaves

1 teaspoon coriander seeds, toasted

1. YOU NEED TO BLACKEN the cut sides of the onion: This is best done by placing it on a very hot flat surface, such as a griddle, and letting it cook until it is truly burnt. If you don't have a griddle, place the heaviest pan you've got over medium heat and then put the onion cut side down in the pan. Cook until it is as dark as you can get it. Remove the blackened onion halves from the pan and stick a clove in each half; set aside.

2. HEAT THE OIL in a large sauté pan or skillet—nonstick is best—over high heat. Season the meat with salt and pepper and brown the pieces a few at a time (it's important not to crowd the pan), making sure you get them really brown on all sides. As the pieces of meat are browned, transfer them to a large stockpot.

3. WHEN ALL THE MEAT is browned and in the stockpot, pour in the water, add the remaining ingredients, and bring to the boil. Lower the heat to a simmer and cook for 2 hours, diligently skimming off the foam and fat that bubbles up to the surface. Don't skimp on the skimming—it's very important to remove all the impurities and as much of the fat as you can.

4. STRAIN THE STOCK through a colander and then pass it through a chinois or fine-mesh sieve. Cool to room temperature, then cover and refrigerate. *(The stock can be kept, packed airtight, in the refrigerator for up to 4 days or in the freezer for up to 1 month.)* When the stock is chilled, the fat will rise to the top. Before reheating the stock, spoon off and discard the fat.

Vegetable Stock

Clear and pure and full of the deep flavors of root vegetables and herbs and the sharp tastes of garlic and onion, this vegetable stock is bound to become a staple in your freezer. It can be used as the base for all vegetarian soups and stews and it's what you'll turn to when you want to make a *potager* risotto or other grain dishes. Like all stocks, this one should be made without salt so that, when you need to cook it down and concentrate its flavors in any recipe, it doesn't end up unbearably salty.

MAKES ABOUT 1 GALLON

5 onions, peeled, trimmed, and quartered

5 carrots, peeled, trimmed, and cut into
   1-inch-long pieces

4 stalks celery, trimmed and cut into
   1-inch-long pieces

2 small to medium leeks, split lengthwise, cut
   into 1-inch-long pieces, and washed

½ fennel bulb, trimmed, and cut in half

2 small heads garlic, cut crosswise in half

2 small bay leaves

1 bunch Italian parsley, washed

1½ teaspoons white peppercorns

1½ teaspoons coriander seeds

1½ teaspoons juniper berries

2½ gallons water

1. PUT ALL OF THE INGREDIENTS in a tall stockpot—a lobster pot works well here. Bring to the boil, lower the heat to a simmer, and cook, skimming the foam that rises to the surface, for 3 hours.

2. STRAIN THE STOCK through a colander and then through a chinois or fine-mesh sieve; discard the solids. Cool to room temperature, then cover and refrigerate. *(The stock can be kept tightly covered in the refrigerator for 4 days or frozen for up to a month.)*

Roasted Garlic

It's remarkable how heat transforms garlic. Potent and pungent when raw, slightly more mellow when sautéed, it is mild, caramelish, and almost sweet when roasted. Roasted garlic, used as a component of some recipes, can also be used on its own—it's wonderful spread on thick slices of toasted country bread.

MAKES 1 HEAD

1 head garlic, cut crosswise in half but not
    peeled
1 tablespoon extra-virgin olive oil

Salt and freshly ground white pepper
2 sprigs thyme

1. CENTER A RACK in the oven and preheat the oven to 375ºF. Line a baking sheet with parchment paper and keep it close at hand.

2. DRIZZLE THE CUT SIDE of each garlic half with the olive oil, season with salt and pepper, and top each with a sprig of thyme. Turn the halves over onto the parchment-lined baking sheet so that their flat, seasoned side is against the parchment (tuck the thyme under the garlic if it slipped off when you flipped the garlic) and bake the garlic for 1 hour, or until the cloves are so tender they can be popped out of their peels with just the slightest pressure. The garlic can be used immediately or cooled to room temperature. Pop the garlic out of its peel before serving, or bring the cut halves to the table and let guests pop their own cloves. *(The garlic can be made a day ahead and kept in its peel, wrapped well, in the refrigerator.)*

Tomato Confit

Tomato halves, brushed with olive oil, sprinkled with a pinch of sugar and a shower of sliced garlic, seasoned with fresh herbs, and slow-roasted in the oven, turn tender and soft, sweet and exceptionally companionable. The petals, the term I use for the confited tomato halves, can be used in salads, stirred into a sauté at the last minute, chopped and added to stuffings, fillings, and sauces, or called into service whenever you want the deeply concentrated flavor of tomato. In fact, I use tomato confit in recipes in which I might, if I didn't have these on hand, use tomato paste.

MAKES 40 TOMATO HALVES

3 tablespoons (approximately) extra-virgin olive oil, plus extra if storing

Salt and freshly ground white pepper

3 cloves garlic, peeled, split, germ removed, and finely sliced

10 leaves basil, torn

4 sprigs thyme, leaves only

2 bay leaves, broken

20 ripe plum tomatoes, peeled

¼ to ½ teaspoon sugar

1. **CENTER A RACK** in the oven and preheat the oven to 200°F.

2. **LINE A BAKING SHEET** (a jelly-roll pan is good here) with foil and pour about 2 tablespoons olive oil evenly over the pan. Sprinkle the oil with salt and pepper. Strew a little of the garlic, basil, thyme, and bay leaves over the oil.

3. **CUT EACH TOMATO** lengthwise in half and carefully, with your fingers or a tiny spoon, remove the seeds. Lay the tomato halves cut side down in the pan, wiggling the tomatoes around if necessary so that each tomato has a gloss of oil on its cut side. Using a pastry brush, give the tops of the tomatoes a light coat of olive oil. Season the tops of the tomatoes with salt and pepper and a little sugar, and scatter over the rest of the garlic, basil, thyme, and bay.

4. **SLIDE THE PAN** into the oven and bake the tomatoes for 2½ hours, or until they are very tender but still able to hold their shape; turn the tomatoes over at half-time and open the oven for just a second every 30 minutes or so to get rid of the moisture that will build up in the oven. Cool the tomatoes to room temperature on their pan.

5. **WHEN THE TOMATOES** are cool, transfer them to a jar, stacking them neatly. Pour whatever oil remains in the pan over the tomatoes and then, if you plan to keep the tomatoes longer than a day or two, pour in enough olive oil to cover them. Refrigerate. (*Covered in oil, with the jar tightly closed, the tomatoes can be kept in the refrigerator for up 2 weeks—the oil will pick up the concentrated flavor of the tomatoes and you can use it to make a dressing for vegetables or salads.*)

Mustard Vinaigrette

This is a basic vinaigrette, a salad dressing that's good with just about any kind of lettuce, but particularly good with bitter greens.

MAKES ABOUT ¼ CUP

½ clove garlic, peeled and germ removed
Salt
1 tablespoon Dijon mustard
1 tablespoon red wine vinegar

Freshly ground white pepper
3 tablespoons peanut oil
A drop of walnut oil (optional)

PUT THE GARLIC and about ⅛ teaspoon salt in a small bowl. Working with the back of a table fork, crush the garlic with the salt. Continuing to use the fork, or working with a small whisk, mix in the mustard and wine vinegar. Season with salt and pepper and then, little by little, add the peanut oil, mixing until the vinaigrette is homogeneous. If you're using it, stir in the touch of walnut oil. *(The vinaigrette can be made up to 2 days ahead and kept tightly covered in the refrigerator. Whisk to bring it together before serving.)*

Pâte Brisée

This the tart dough from which all other tart doughs in the French repertoire come. It is the basic nonsweet dough used for quiches and savory tarts. Quickly made in the food processor, once chilled (as all pastry doughs must be), it is remarkably easy to roll out—making it an ideal dough for pastry neophytes.

MAKES A 9½-INCH TART

1 cup plus 3 tablespoons all-purpose flour
6 tablespoons unsalted butter, chilled

⅛ teaspoon salt
1 large egg, lightly beaten

1. PUT THE FLOUR, butter, and salt in the work bowl of a food processor fitted with the metal blade and pulse until the ingredients are crumbly. Add the beaten egg and continue to pulse until the mixture forms moist curds—don't overprocess it. You don't want to work the dough long enough for it to form a ball.

2. TURN THE DOUGH out onto a work surface and, if necessary, knead it once or twice to pull it together. Flatten it into a disk and wrap the disk in plastic wrap. Chill the dough for at least 1 hour. *(Wrapped airtight, the dough can be kept refrigerated for 2 days or frozen for up to a month.)*

3. TO ROLL OUT THE DOUGH, place a buttered tart pan with a removable bottom or a tart ring on a parchment-lined baking sheet. Dust a work surface (marble is perfect for rolling out dough) lightly with flour, dust the top of the disk of dough, and roll the dough into a round that is about ⅛ inch thick (or the thickness specified in the recipe you're following). As you roll, lift the dough off the work surface from time to time to make certain it's rolling evenly and not sticking and, if necessary, dust with flour again. Roll the dough up and around your rolling pin and then unroll the dough over the tart pan or ring. (Alternatively, you can fold the dough in half or quarters, lift it up and into the pan, and then unfold it.) Fit the dough into the bottom and up the sides of the pan, taking care not to stretch the dough as you work—what you stretch now will shrink later. Run the rolling pin over the top of the pan to remove the excess dough and, if the recipe calls for it, use the tines of a fork to prick the dough all over. If the dough cracks while you're working, use the scraps to fill the cracks, lightly moistening the edges of the filler-dough to glue it to the dough in the pan. Refrigerate the tart shell for at least 30 minutes before baking.

4. TO BAKE THE TART SHELL, preheat the oven to 350°F.

5. FIT A PARCHMENT PAPER round into the bottom and up the sides of the crust and fill with dried beans or rice. To partially bake the crust, bake the crust for 18 to 20 minutes, remove the paper and beans, and bake for 3 to 5 minutes more, or until it is only lightly colored. If the crust needs to be fully baked, remove the parchment and beans and bake for another 5 to 7 minutes, until golden. Remove the crust to a rack to cool to room temperature. *(The crust can be kept at room temperature for 8 hours.)*

Pâte Sablée

This is the basic sweet pastry dough of the French kitchen, as important in the Gallic tradition as pie dough is in the American, as irresistibly good as it is indispensable. *Sablée* means sandy, and it's a good description of this sweet, crumbly cookie-like dough that is at once tender and crisp.

This recipe makes enough dough for two tart shells. You may not need all this dough at once, but you'll find it easier to work with the ingredients—and you'll get a better-textured dough—if you make the full recipe. It won't go to waste, since extra dough can be wrapped and frozen for a month. Either defrost the dough, still in its wrapper, overnight in the refrigerator or leave it at room temperature for 45 minutes to an hour before rolling.

MAKES TWO 9 ½-INCH TART SHELLS

9 tablespoons unsalted butter, at room
    temperature
1 cup plus 2 tablespoons confectioner's sugar
1¾ cups all-purpose flour

¼ teaspoon salt
1 large egg, lightly beaten

1. **PUT THE BUTTER,** confectioner's sugar, flour, and salt in the bowl of a mixer fitted with the paddle attachment. Mix on medium-low speed just until the mixture is crumbly. Add the egg and continue to mix only until the mixture comes together to form a moist, soft dough—then stop. You don't want to overwork the dough. Alternatively, if you want to make the dough in a food processor fitted with the metal blade, start by processing the butter and confectioner's sugar until smooth. Add the flour and salt and process until the mixture is again smooth. Add the egg and process only until the dough forms moist curds and clumps.

2. **TURN THE DOUGH** out onto a work surface and, if necessary, knead it once or twice to pull it together. Divide the dough evenly in half, flatten each half into a disk, and wrap the disks individually in plastic wrap. Chill the dough for at least 1 hour. *(Wrapped airtight, the dough can be kept refrigerated for 2 days or frozen for up to a month.)*

3. **TO ROLL OUT THE DOUGH,** place a buttered tart pan with a removable bottom or a tart ring on a parchment-lined baking sheet. Dust a work surface (marble is perfect for rolling out dough) lightly with flour, dust the top of the disk of dough, and roll the dough into a round that is about ⅛ inch thick (or the thickness specified in the recipe you're following). As you roll, lift the dough off the work surface from time to time to make certain it's rolling evenly and not sticking and, if necessary, dust again with flour. Roll the dough up and around your rolling pin and then unroll the dough over the tart pan or ring. (Alternatively, you can fold the dough in half or quarters, lift it up and into the pan, and then unfold it.) Fit the dough into the bottom and up the sides of the pan, taking care not to stretch the dough as you

work—what you stretch now will shrink later. Run the rolling pin over the top of the pan to remove the excess dough and, if the recipe calls for it, use the tines of a fork to prick the dough all over. If the dough cracks while you're working, use the scraps to fill the cracks, lightly moistening the edges of the filler-dough to glue it to the dough in the pan. Refrigerate the tart shell for at least 30 minutes before baking.

4. TO BAKE THE TART SHELL, preheat the oven to 350°F.

5. FIT A PARCHMENT PAPER round into the bottom and up the sides of the crust and fill with dried beans or rice. To partially bake the crust, bake the crust for 18 to 20 minutes, remove the paper and beans, and bake for 3 to 5 minutes more, or until it is only lightly colored. If the crust needs to be fully baked, remove the parchment and beans and bake for another 5 to 7 minutes, until golden. Remove the crust to a rack to cool to room temperature. *(Crusts can be kept at room temperature for 8 hours.)*

Pâte Sublime

This version of pâte sablée is called sublime because it is—and it's the addition of almond flour that makes it so. As sweet, tender, and crumbly as your favorite butter cookie, this is, in fact, a cookie dough pressed into the service of a tart crust. If you have scraps or leftovers, think of rolling them out, cutting them into rounds, brushing them with a little beaten egg, sprinkling them with sugar, and baking them in a 375°F oven until they're firm but not colored, about 8 to 10 minutes.

This recipe makes enough dough for three tart shells. You may not need all this dough at once, but you'll find it easier to work with the ingredients—and you'll get a better-textured dough—if you make the full recipe. It won't go to waste, since extra dough can be wrapped and frozen for a month. Either defrost the dough, still in its wrapper, overnight in the refrigerator or leave it at room temperature for 45 minutes to an hour before rolling.

MAKES THREE 9½-INCH TART SHELLS

½ pound (2 sticks) unsalted butter, at room
temperature
¾ cup plus 2 tablespoons confectioner's sugar
¾ cup plus 1 tablespoon almond flour
(see Glossary, page 362) or finely ground
blanched almonds

1¾ cups all-purpose flour
1 large egg white

1. PUT THE BUTTER, confectioner's sugar, and almond flour in the bowl of a mixer fitted with the paddle attachment. Mix on medium-low speed just until the ingredients are combined, about 20 seconds. Add the flour and mix for 20 seconds, just until the dough is crumbly. Add the egg and continue to mix only until the mixture comes together to form a moist, soft dough—then stop. You don't want to overwork the dough. Alternatively, if you want to make the dough in a food processor fitted with the metal blade, start by processing the butter and confectioner's sugar until smooth. Add the almond flour and flour and process until the mixture is again smooth. Add the egg and process only until the dough forms moist curds and clumps.

2. TURN THE DOUGH OUT onto a work surface and, if necessary, knead it once or twice to pull it together. Divide the dough evenly into thirds, flatten each piece of dough into a disk, and wrap the disks individually in plastic wrap. Chill the dough for at least 1 hour. *(Wrapped airtight, the dough can be kept refrigerated for 2 days or frozen for up to a month.)*

3. TO ROLL OUT THE DOUGH, place a buttered tart pan with a removable bottom or a tart ring on a parchment-lined baking sheet. Dust a work surface (marble is perfect for rolling out dough) lightly with flour, dust the top of the disk of dough, and roll the dough into a round that is about ⅛ inch thick (or the thickness specified in the recipe you're following). As you roll, lift the dough off the work surface from time to time to make certain it's rolling evenly and not sticking and, if necessary, dust again with flour. Roll the dough up and around your rolling pin and then unroll the dough over the tart pan or ring. (Alternatively, you can fold the dough in half or quarters, lift it up and into the pan, and then unfold it.) Fit the dough into the bottom and up the sides of the pan, taking care not to stretch the dough as you work—what you stretch now will shrink later. Run the rolling pin over the top of the pan to remove the excess dough and, if the recipe calls for it, use the tines of a fork to prick the dough all over. If the dough cracks while you're working, use the scraps to fill the cracks, lightly moistening the edges of the filler-dough to glue it to the dough in the pan. Refrigerate the tart shell for at least 30 minutes before baking.

4. TO BAKE THE TART SHELL, preheat the oven to 350°F.

5. FIT A PARCHMENT PAPER round into the bottom and up the sides of the crust and fill with dried beans or rice. To partially bake the crust, bake the crust for 18 to 20 minutes, remove the paper and beans and bake for 3 to 5 minutes more, or until it is only lightly colored. If the crust needs to be fully baked, remove the parchment and beans and bake for another 5 to 7 minutes, until golden. Remove the crust to a rack to cool to room temperature. *(Crusts can be kept at room temperature for 8 hours.)*

Vanilla Pastry Cream

A lissome pastry cream is a classic filling for a fruit tart, a plain cake, or a cream puff. Essentially a crème anglaise made thicker and more stable by the addition of flour and cornstarch (you need both to make a great cream; make a pastry cream with only flour or only cornstarch, and you'll be disappointed with the results), it's easy to make—quick too—but it requires attention and a little elbow grease. Keep an eye on the pot and don't stop stirring for a nanosecond, and you'll be rewarded with a sensuously smooth, rich, properly vanilla-scented cream, a pâtissier's gem.

MAKES ABOUT 2 CUPS

1 moist, plump vanilla bean
2 cups whole milk
½ cup sugar

4 large egg yolks
3 tablespoons all-purpose flour
3 tablespoons cornstarch

1. LINE A DEEP RIMMED PLATE with plastic wrap, leaving ample overhang. Cut the vanilla bean lengthwise in half and, using the back of the knife, scrape the pulp out of the pod.

2. POUR THE MILK into a medium saucepan. Stir in ¼ cup of the sugar, add the vanilla bean, pod and pulp, and bring to the boil. While the milk is coming to the boil, vigorously whisk the yolks and the remaining ¼ cup sugar together in a bowl until the mixture turns pale, then whisk in the flour and cornstarch—you should have a thick mixture.

3. WHISKING WITHOUT STOP, very gradually add half the hot milk to the egg mixture. Now that the eggs are tempered—that is, acclimated to the heat—pour them into the saucepan and, still whisking energetically and constantly, cook over medium heat until the pastry cream thickens and starts to boil. Allow the pastry cream to boil for 30 seconds—don't give up on the vigorous whisking—then scrape it onto the plastic-lined plate. Smooth the top of the cream with a rubber spatula and cover the cream with the overhanging plastic wrap (or another sheet of wrap). Press the plastic against the surface of the pastry cream—you don't want the cream to come in contact with air and develop a skin—and transfer the plate to the refrigerator until the cream is chilled. Remove the vanilla bean when the cream is cold. *(The pastry cream can be made up to 2 days in advance and kept covered airtight in the refrigerator.)*

Lemon Pastry Cream

Because this cream is half milk and half lemon juice, it tastes lighter and cooler than the classic recipe from which it is derived—just the ticket for desserts like the Crisp Raspberry Tuiles with Lemon Cream (page 337).

MAKES ABOUT 1 CUP

½ cup whole milk

½ cup freshly squeezed lemon juice

¼ cup sugar

3 large egg yolks

1 tablespoon all-purpose flour

1 tablespoon cornstarch

1. LINE A DEEP RIMMED PLATE with plastic wrap, leaving ample overhang.

2. POUR THE MILK and lemon juice into a medium saucepan (don't worry if it looks curdled), stir in 2 tablespoons of the sugar, and bring to the boil. While the milk is coming to the boil, vigorously whisk the yolks and the remaining 2 tablespoons sugar together in a bowl until the mixture turns pale, then whisk in the flour and cornstarch—you should have a thick mixture.

3. WHISKING WITHOUT STOP, very gradually add half the hot lemon milk to the egg mixture. Now that the eggs are tempered—that is, acclimated to the heat—pour them into the saucepan and, still whisking energetically and constantly, cook over medium heat until the pastry cream thickens and starts to boil. Allow the pastry cream to boil for 30 seconds—don't give up on the vigorous whisking—then scrape it onto the plastic-lined plate. Smooth the top of the cream with a rubber spatula and cover the cream with the overhanging plastic wrap (or another sheet of wrap). Press the plastic against the surface of the pastry cream—you don't want the cream to come in contact with air and develop a skin—and transfer the plate to the refrigerator until the cream is chilled. *(The pastry cream can be made up to 2 days in advance and kept covered airtight in the refrigerator.)*

Almond Cream

A basic blend of ground almonds, sugar, butter, and eggs, French almond cream, similar to Italian frangipane, is traditionally used as the base for fruit tarts, but at Café Boulud we often use almond cream in tandem with other fillings (try the Apple, Almond, and Pine Nut Tart, page 334), spreading just enough of the almond cream across a pastry to provide another, albeit very subtle, layer of flavor.

MAKES ABOUT 1 CUP

4 tablespoons unsalted butter, at room
   temperature
½ cup confectioner's sugar
½ cup almond flour (see Glossary, page 362)
   or ground blanched almonds

1 large egg
1 tablespoon all-purpose flour

PUT THE BUTTER, confectioner's sugar, and almond flour in the bowl of a mixer fitted with the paddle attachment and beat on medium-low speed until the ingredients are well blended. Add the egg and flour and beat on medium speed until homogeneous. If you're not using the almond cream immediately, scrape it into a small container and cover with plastic wrap, pressing the plastic against the surface of the cream. *(The cream can be made up to 2 days ahead and kept covered airtight in the refrigerator.)*

glossary

of terms, ingredients, and techniques

ALMOND FLOUR: Used often in pastries, almond flour is not milled flour as we know it, but blanched almonds ground as fine as flour. The most finely ground almond flour is commercially made (see Source Guide, page 385), but you can produce a satisfactory substitute at home in a food processor—if you pay attention. The problem with grinding any kind of nut in a processor is that you risk overprocessing it and turning it into nut butter. To help prevent this, process the blanched almonds with a little confectioner's sugar, about 2 teaspoons for every cup of almonds. (This shouldn't be enough sugar to throw off a recipe, but if you're concerned, you can decrease the amount of sugar called for in the recipe.) Process the almonds and sugar, pulsing on and off, for about 30 to 45 seconds, at which point the mixture will be finely ground (pulse some more if you think the grind isn't fine enough), but not fluffy and light—that's the oil in the almonds at work. Strain the flour. Almond flour can be packed airtight and kept in the freezer for a month.

ARTICHOKES: I use three kinds of artichokes in my kitchen, globe, baby, and Jerusalem, which isn't really an artichoke at all, despite its name. Globe artichokes are the ones most commonly seen in the market. They're large and green, with lethally pointy leaves, which will soften when cooked. Always look for artichokes whose leaves are compact and cling to the artichoke's body, a sign that the vegetable isn't ancient. For the recipes in this book, you'll use the artichoke hearts, which you get to by cutting off all the leaves. The easiest way to do this is to cut the stem of the artichoke flush with its bottom and then, holding the artichoke in one hand (you might want to keep a dish towel in the artichoke-holding hand to avoid getting poked by the leaves) and a sturdy knife in the other, turn the artichoke against the blade of the knife to remove the leaves. There will remain a cluster of softer but prickly pinkish inner leaves—gather the leaves together and pull them out by hand. Then, using a small knife and following the bowl shape of the artichoke heart, trim away the fuzzy choke on top of the heart. Trim off any green remaining on the sides or bottom of the heart. When the choke is removed, you will have exposed the slightly concave heart. Because artichokes discolor almost as soon as they're exposed to air, make sure to either rub them with a cut lemon or dunk them into a bowl of cold water to which you've added some lemon juice.

Baby artichokes don't need to be babied as much as their bigger brethren, the globes. Since the chokes in baby artichokes are not a problem, all you've got to do to get baby artichokes ready for cooking is to trim their stems, then, starting at the bottom, cut away or peel off the outer leaves until the bottom half is yellow and the top half is green; cut off the top half. Like all artichokes, these turn brown quickly, so always rub them with a cut lemon or submerge them in cold water to which you've added some lemon juice.

Jerusalem artichokes don't look at all like globe artichokes. Oval or lumpy and bumpy, Jerusalems look like water chestnuts or ginger. In fact, eaten raw, they even taste like water chestnuts—they're crisp, crunchy, and refreshing. Their flavor turns more artichoke-like once they are cooked. I use

Jerusalem artichokes in soups and do nothing more than scrub them before adding them to the pot—their thin skins add character to a soup.

ASPARAGUS: Asparagus must always be peeled before it is used. It's the precious tip of the stalk that is the treasure of the asparagus so, when you are peeling the stalk, make sure to guard the tip. Using a swivel-blade peeler, the most efficient tool for this job, and protecting the tip, remove the peel from the stalk, leaving the tip intact and unpeeled. Once the asparagus is peeled, cut away the tough woody lower section of the stalk.

BACON: I don't think it's possible to be French and not love bacon. I love it for the light smokiness it imparts to a dish and for the way its fat carries flavors throughout a dish. For the most part, I use slab bacon—we cut it as we need it in the kitchen. Having a hunk of bacon, rather than precut slices, gives you the freedom to cut the bacon in different ways for different purposes. For instance, there will be times when you'll want the flavor of bacon and you won't want the bacon in the final dish—that's when you'll be glad to be able to drop a chunk of bacon into a pot and retrieve it to discard it later. Or, perhaps you'll want lardons for a fricassee or a salad. Lardons are short, stubby, ¼-inch-thick pieces of bacon and they're easily cut from a slab of bacon. Of course, when you want crispy bacon to break up into bits, or bacon to wrap around something, like stuffed trout (page 139), presliced bacon is ideal. It's also fine when slab bacon is not available.

In addition to bacon, you'll find recipes that use Italian pancetta and prosciutto.

BALSAMIC VINEGAR: Aged balsamic vinegar that is artisanally made in Modena, Italy, and labeled *tradizionale,* your guarantee of authenticity, is an Italian treasure, and it's priced like a treasure—a small (under 4 ounces) bottle can start at about $75 and go up into the hundreds. Authentic balsamic vinegars are aged in a series of wooden casks, each succeeding cask a smaller size and made from a different wood, and not bottled and sold until they are at least 12 years old, or 25 years old or older still. Used less like ordinary vinegar and more like a liqueur, traditional balsamic is measured out in drops and spoonfuls rather than cups. When you want to finish a special salad or a dish with a drizzle of balsamic, this is the vinegar you want. But when you're marinating something or adding a good deal of balsamic to a sauce, you're meant to reach for something less pricey—this is when an industrially made balsamic is fine. If you think your balsamic lacks character, you can improve it by concentrating it. If you cook the vinegar down, you'll lower its acidity and increase its depth of flavor.

BEETS: Beets are messy, and that's that. But they're too good to let the mess get in the way of enjoying them. At the Café, we wear tight-fitting latex gloves when we handle beets—they keep our fingers from being stained red. If you can't find these gloves, use regular kitchen rubber gloves—and cover your cutting board with a layer or two of parchment paper—it's not the perfect solution, but it helps. It also helps if you don't mix beets into a dish until the last minute—waiting gives you a fighting chance of not turning the entire mix red.

BLANCHING: The process of blanching is simple—an ingredient is cooked in salted boiling water and then run under cold water or plunged into an ice-water bath to stop the cooking and, often, to set its color. Some foods are blanched to firm them or, in the case of bacon, to remove some of their salt. Others, like vegetables and fruits, are blanched so that you can peel them—think of tomatoes, peaches, or fava beans—or to soften them for dishes in which they either will be cooked again very briefly or not at all. For example, when you make the zucchini-basil pesto for the Zucchini-Ricotta Layers (page 310), you blanch both the zucchini skins and the basil and never cook them again. The blanching removes their raw taste, softens them sufficiently, and sets their color so that they won't darken in the blender. Whenever you're blanching, make certain you're prepared to rinse the food or dunk it into cold water immediately. This cooling process is called shocking—think of blanching and shocking as culinary Siamese twins.

BOUQUET GARNI: This is the name given to a bundle of herbs used to season slow-cooking dishes such as soups, stews, and braises. While there's no set rule as to what's in a bouquet garni, it usually includes parsley, thyme, and a bay leaf, and is often tied up in a washed leek green. When you want to use dried herbs or spices, they should be wrapped in a cheesecloth packet—and are then, usually, called a sachet. To make a sachet, place the ingredients in a double thickness of cheesecloth, fold the cheesecloth over to enclose them, and then secure the packet with kitchen twine.

BUTTER: All the recipes are made with unsalted butter.

CAVIAR: Few foods are as sumptuous—or as expensive—as caviar, so it's important to buy caviar from a trusted dealer (see Source Guide, page 385). Whether you're buying beluga caviar, the most expensive caviar, with the largest eggs and subtlest flavor; osetra, the caviar many connoisseurs prefer for its complex, somewhat nutty flavor; or sevruga, the smallest eggs, with the strongest flavor, you should always look for the same signs of quality: a well-sealed tin, eggs that are compact and whole, and an aroma that is as fresh as the sea. Color is not an indication of caviar's quality—the eggs can range from a pearly ivory color to a light silvery gray to jet-black. Always keep tinned caviar in the refrigerator and, once you open it, keep the caviar cold. Finally, if you've opened a tin of caviar, it's best to finish it quickly—this is not a delicacy that improves with age. In fact, this is a prime reason for buying your caviar from a dealer who does a brisk business and whose stock turns over regularly.

CHESTNUTS: It takes a little work to get to the creamy, distinctively flavored meat of a chestnut, but it's always worth the effort. To peel chestnuts, put a pot of water up to boil. With a sturdy chef's knife, cut off the pointy tips of the chestnuts, then cut a small X in the flat side of each shell. Toss the chestnuts into the boiling water and cook for about 5 minutes, then lift the chestnuts out of the water with a slotted spoon. (Leave the water on the heat just in case you need to put a few chestnuts back.) Unfortunately, chestnuts peel most easily when they're hot, so, being careful, remove the shell as well as the thin brown skin that's under it. If the shells and skin are too hard to peel, boil the chestnuts for another minute and try again.

In place of chestnuts in their shells, you can buy peeled chestnuts. Look for jars or vacuum-sealed packages that contain dry-packed (but not dried) chestnuts. For recipes that call for peeled fresh chestnuts, avoid tinned chestnuts packed in water.

CHICKEN: Look for chickens that are labeled free-range, or, better still, free-range and organic. Although chicken can be kept for a day or two in the coldest part of your refrigerator, or well wrapped and frozen for a month, I think you should buy the chicken the day you need it and keep it refrigerated until you're ready to use it. When you're ready to prepare it, rinse it inside and out under cold running water and then pat the bird dry with paper towels. If the recipe says that the chicken should be cut into eight parts, here's what you or the butcher should do: First, cut off the legs—this will make it easier for you to handle the rest of the chicken—then cut each leg in two, separating the thigh from the drumstick. Next, using your knife or a pair of poultry shears, detach the backbone all the way to the neck; chop both the backbone and neck into 2 to 3 pieces—keep these aside either for the recipe or for making stock. Finally, split the pair of breasts down the center and then split each breast crosswise in half. Whether or not you want the wings on the breast meat is up to you. If you decide to detach the wings, you can either cook them along with the other eight pieces of chicken, or keep them with the neck and backbone and use them for stock. Of course, this cutting plan works equally well for duck and other poultry.

When it comes to roasting a chicken, we rarely put a metal rack in our roasting pans at the Café. Instead, we make a "rack" from chicken parts. Using poultry shears, clip the chicken wings at the second joint and put the clippings, along with the neck, cut into 2 or 3 pieces, in the center of the roasting pan. Voilà—a rack. Just center the chicken on the bones and carry on.

CHOCOLATE: We use imported bittersweet, milk, and white chocolates in our pastry kitchen. While food is extremely personal, chocolate seems to be even more personal—everyone's got his favorite. For each chocolate recipe, I've included both the type of chocolate I use—for instance, bittersweet—and the percentage of cocoa solids in the chocolate. Cocoa solids listings are always given on imported chocolates and now on a handful of American-made chocolates. The percentage can be used as a rough indication of the strength or depth of chocolate flavor, but none of this as important as the taste and—most important—whether or not it pleases you. I suggest that you use the cocoa solids percentages as a guide and urge you to taste as many chocolates as you can until you find the ones you like the most—these are the chocolates you should use. That said, I would urge you to use imported chocolate when a recipe calls for milk or white chocolate, since imported milk and white chocolates usually have a higher percentage of cocoa solids than domestic brands (many domestic brands of white chocolate have no cocoa solids at all) and deeper, truer flavors.

COCOA POWDER: When you see "cocoa powder" in a recipe, it's unsweetened cocoa powder. At the Café, we use imported cocoa powder that has been Dutched, meaning it has been treated with alkali so that its color is darker and its flavor milder than non–Dutch-processed cocoa.

CORNICHONS: A favorite French pickle, cornichons are gherkins. Cornichons are never sweet and always very vinegary. They are the traditional accompaniment to pâtés and an ingredient in sauces like rémoulade and charcutière.

COUSCOUS: Couscous looks like a grain and even tastes like one, but it is really a semolina pasta. Popular in North Africa and the Middle East, couscous is both the name of the pasta and the traditional stew that uses it as its base. For my recipes, I use instant couscous, available in most supermarkets.

CRÈME FRAÎCHE: Crème fraîche is often referred to as France's sour cream, and while it does have a certain tangy edge, as does sour cream, it's got so much more. Crème fraîche is milder than sour cream, more tolerant to heat—it won't separate when it's cooked—and it can be whipped like heavy cream. Specialty stores sometimes sell imported crème fraîche, and domestic crème fraîche is available under the Vermont Cheese Company label. In a pinch, you can make your own crème fraîche. For every cup of crème fraîche, combine 1 tablespoon buttermilk and 1 cup heavy cream, or ½ cup sour cream and ½ cup heavy cream, in a clean jar with a tight-fitting lid. Shake the jar for a minute, then leave it at room temperature until the cream thickens slightly. The amount of time it takes for the cream to thicken will depend on the room's temperature—count on at least 12 hours and as long as 24. Once it's thickened, chill the crème fraîche in the refrigerator for at least a day before using. Crème fraîche can be kept, tightly sealed, in the refrigerator for up to 2 weeks—just keep in mind that it will get tangier and tangier as it sits.

DRIED BEANS: The good news about dried beans is that they're inexpensive, nutritious, and good-tasting; the bad news is that you have to plan ahead if you want to use them, since beans need to be soaked. The best way to soak beans is to keep them submerged in a generous amount of water overnight in the refrigerator. But if you've left things to the last minute, you can hasten the process by bringing the water and beans to a boil, boiling for 2 minutes. and then letting the beans soak in the hot water for an hour before draining and rinsing them. Either way, keep in mind that beans should not be cooked in salted water—the salt will toughen them. Add salt to the pot only during the last few minutes of cooking.

EGGS: Recipes were tested with Grade A large eggs.

FOIE GRAS: When I refer to foie gras in a recipe, I mean fresh—not tinned—foie gras. Fresh foie gras is the liver of specially raised ducks and, more rarely nowadays, geese. It is silky, sexy, very expensive, and always a treat. Foie gras is easiest to cut and clean when it is cold and your knife is hot. To clean a whole foie gras, separate its two lobes and remove any globules of fat at the connecting point and any veins, using your fingers or the point of a small sharp knife. (See the Source Guide, page 385, for a mail-order resource for fine foie gras.)

FLEUR DE SEL: Literally "flower of salt," fleur de sel is the top layer of sea salt that is raked from the waters around Guérande in France. Fleur de sel is expensive and rare—it is not always available—and never used carelessly. It is not the salt you reach for when you want to salt a pot of boiling water for pasta, nor is it even the salt you'd use to season something before sautéing it. It is meant to be used after the dish is cooked or on uncooked food, such as salads, croutons, or crudités. It is really a finishing salt, more a condiment than a seasoning. If you're looking for the crunch of fleur de sel but do not have fleur de sel at hand, you can get a similar texture by crushing coarse sea salt.

FROMAGE BLANC: This is a fresh cheese that is very popular and widely available in France. Fromage blanc has a mild flavor with a tinge of tang and it can be used with equal success in both sweet and savoy dishes. I use fromage blanc as the basis of my Cervelle de Canut (page 26). Some specialty cheese shops produce their own fromage blanc, but it is available commercially, marketed under the Vermont Cheese Company label.

GARLIC: I'm never happy when a dish is overly garlicky. I love the flavor of garlic, but I always want it to work with the other flavors in a dish. To help ensure that garlic doesn't run roughshod over a recipe, I often remove the germ from a clove of garlic. Split a clove of garlic lengthwise and you'll see the germ running down the center of the clove. Often, when garlic is too strong or not easily digestible, the germ is the culprit. Remove it, and you'll be using the best of the clove.

GELATIN: As chefs in the majority of restaurants both here and abroad do, we use sheet rather than powdered gelatin in our kitchen. A piece of sheet gelatin looks like a rectangle of glassine or plastic—it's shiny, transparent, and brittle. Sheet gelatin is tasteless and never lumps, and mixtures made with it tend to melt quickly and pleasantly on the tongue. To prepare sheet gelatin to go into a recipe—it's usually used in a dessert or a velouté, a lightly thickened cream soup—the gelatin is first soaked in cold water until it is pliable, then gently squeezed to extract excess water and stirred into a hot liquid. Sheet gelatin dissolves almost instantly in hot liquid. At the Café, we use sheet gelatin that weighs 2 grams/sheet. If you want to try substituting powdered gelatin for sheet, the rule of thumb is that 1 package of powdered gelatin equals 3 gelatin sheets. Follow the package directions for preparing the powdered gelatin for use.

HERBS: With very rare exception, I use fresh herbs, not dried, in the kitchen.

HERB SACHET: When you want to flavor a dish with herbs but don't want to incorporate the herbs themselves, that's the time to turn to a sachet, a little packet of herbs, often including seeds and peppercorns as well, wrapped in a double thickness of cheesecloth and secured with kitchen twine. A sachet is always discarded before serving.

LEEKS: It won't take you long to notice that I use leeks often in my cooking—I love the soft sweetness they bring to a dish. You may also notice that, unlike other vegetables that are washed before they are cut, I specify that you cut the leeks first, then wash them. Leeks are dirty—their layers often harbor clumps of real from-the-garden dirt, even a speck of which can spoil a dish. Because leeks' layers are compact, it's easier and more effective to cut the leeks the way the recipe says you should, and then to rinse them really well. If you are going to sauté the cut leeks, then you'll need to dry them between layers of paper or kitchen towels; if they're going into a broth, just shake them free of excess water.

LEMONGRASS: The flavor of lemongrass, a stalwart of the Asian kitchen, is hard to describe, impossible to miss. It straddles citrusy and gingery and has a remarkable perfume. We use both its stalk and bulb in our kitchen. When you buy fresh lemongrass, it will have a long stalk. When I'm using the stalk, I usually don't use all of it, but I often bruise it, giving it a bash or two with the heel of a chef's knife to soften it a bit. Most often, I'll use the stalk to flavor a broth and discard it before serving. If I'm going to use lemongrass as an ingredient that will remain in a dish, I use the bulb, and then only the heart, or tender center, of the bulb. To get to the heart, peel away the tough outer leaves.

LENTILS: The lentils we serve at Café Boulud are the green lentilles de Puy, sometimes called French lentils, and they're very different in size and color from the light green lentils you find in the supermarket. Lentilles de Puy are smaller than light green lentils and much darker—they range in color from gray to almost black, but they're usually referred to as dark green lentils. The lentils should be cooked just until they are tender but still hold their shape. Lentilles de Puy are available in most specialty food shops and in many supermarkets.

MILK: The milk used in these recipes is whole milk.

NUTS: If you were in the kitchen at Café Boulud, you'd notice that every time a cook grabs some nuts to use in a dish, he or she smells and tastes them first—and you should too. Because nuts are so rich in oil, they are highly perishable. Buy your nuts from a reliable supplier who does a lively business and has a high turnover, keep them tightly sealed, preferably in the freezer, and taste as you go.

We often toast nuts before we add them to a dish. To toast nuts, spread them out in a single layer on a baking sheet and roast them in a 350°F oven, shaking the sheet a couple of times, until they are golden. Cool the nuts before chopping or adding them to a mixture. If you're using hazelnuts, you'll need to skin them before you use them. The easiest way to do this is to toast the hazelnuts until their thin, papery (but stubbornly attached) skins start to peel away. Turn the nuts out onto a clean kitchen towel, wrap the towel around the nuts, and rub the nuts against one another until the skins come off. Don't be discouraged when a few pieces of skin resist your efforts—it's impossible to skin hazelnuts perfectly.

OLIVE OIL: Our standard oil in the kitchen is extra-virgin olive oil. For sautéing and roasting, we use an olive oil with a very mild flavor; for making salad dressings and uncooked sauces, we often choose oils with more personality. The best way to choose an olive oil is to taste it—oils run the flavor gamut and what pleases you may not please someone else. While it's not a hard-and-fast rule, in general, you can expect olive oils from Liguria and Provence to be mild, while those from Tuscany and Corsica may be more pungent, and oils from California can be either. But that just touches the tip of the topic. The best-known olive oils come from Italy and France, but California is producing some superb oils, and just about every country around the Mediterranean Sea makes olive oil, many of them, particularly those from Spain and Greece, exceptionally good. Again, I urge you to taste, taste, taste.

PANCETTA: Pancetta is a type of cured bacon that is not smoked. Look for slab pancetta at your butcher shop or specialty Italian market.

PANKO: Panko, Japanese bread crumbs, are the bread crumbs we use when we want a really crispy coating, particularly when we're deep-frying something. Panko have a little sugar and some fat so they brown better than bread crumbs made from just bread and they have a better texture. We don't use them for everything, but when I do call for them, it's because I want to give a dish something more in the crispy department.

PARCHMENT: Parchment is the waxed paper of the professional kitchen. A strong paper with a light silicone coating, it's used for everything from lining baking sheets and making lids for pots to cooking foods en papillote. You can buy a roll of parchment paper, sometimes called cooking paper, in the supermarket, but it will be less expensive if you buy the paper from a kitchen supply shop, where it comes in large sheets. You may have to buy a box of 50 sheets, but you'll find you'll use them. (For example, if you line a baking sheet with parchment before you put down cookie dough, the sheet automatically becomes nonstick, the cookies bake more evenly, and you don't have to wash the sheet—and often you can reuse the parchment.)

I use parchment paper as a lid for foods that I'm simmering or braising because the parchment can be pressed gently against the ingredients, reducing the air space that would exist between the ingredients and a conventional lid and thereby avoiding having the steam condense on the underside of the lid and drip down on the food as water. To make a lid, cut out a round of parchment that's 2 to 3 inches larger than the pot. Snip the extra inches of parchment at 2-inch intervals to make an all-around fringe. Place the parchment over the ingredients, pressing gently and allowing the fringe to press against the sides of the pan. If you want to make an air vent in the center of the parchment lid, just cut a small circle out of the center.

PARMESAN: To get the full flavor that I want, I use only Parmigiano-Reggiano, Parmesan cheese imported from the Emilia-Romagna region of Italy, the only region that produces authentic Parmesan.

PEPPER: The peppermills in the Café Boulud kitchen are filled with white peppercorns. I prefer the mildness of white pepper to the heat of black and like that the color of ground white pepper is inconspicuous in a finished dish.

PEPPERS: Peppers need to be cored, seeded, and deveined before they are used, unless you are going to roast them. The fastest way to roast peppers is to roast them whole over an open flame—something that's easily done if you have a gas range. Impale a pepper on a long-tined fork, turn the heat to high, and char the pepper evenly on every side. When the pepper's skin is black and blistered, either drop the pepper into a plastic bag and seal the bag or drop it into a bowl and cover the bowl with plastic. When the pepper is cool enough to handle, place it on a cutting board and use the back of a knife or your fingers to scrape off the skin, then slice open the pepper lengthwise, trim away its green cap, remove the seeds, and cut away the veins. If you don't have a gas burner, you can char the pepper under the broiler. Put the pepper on a foil-lined pan, put it under the broiler, and turn it to char it evenly. Seal the charred pepper and then peel, seed, and devein it as above. Roasted peppers can be submerged in olive oil and kept in a tightly sealed jar for at least 3 days in the refrigerator.

PIQUILLO PEPPERS: These roasted peppers, from Navarre in the northeastern part of Spain, are at the heart of many specialties of Spain and the Pays Basque. Not found on supermarket shelves—yet—they are worth the trouble to track down or order by mail (see Source Guide, page 385) because they are both sweet and hot (but not explosively so), firm, and fantastic for stuffing. Shaped like stubby, broad-necked hot frying peppers, piquillos are roasted, skinned, and then canned or jarred—you never find them here fresh. They are more expensive than other kinds of roasted peppers, but they are so much more flavorful that they'll spoil you for anything else. However, in recipes that call for piquillo peppers, you can substitute roasted red bell peppers if necessary.

PROSCIUTTO: The prosciutto we use at the Café is imported from Italy; it is usually a prosciutto di Parma. Prosciutto is an air-dried cured ham that does not need to be cooked before it is eaten. I cut it into cubes for stuffing and love to oven-dry paper-thin slices of it as a garnish (see page 131). Oven-dried, the prosciutto may remind you of the best jerky you've ever eaten.

PUFF PASTRY: Perhaps the most elegant—and certainly the most magical—dough in the pastry chef's repertoire, puff pastry is made by encasing butter, lots of it, in a dough, then rolling the dough out until it is three times longer than it is wide, folding it in thirds, like a business letter, and repeating this process, called a turn, five more times. Done properly, the rolling and folding results in a dough that, when baked, puffs extravagantly, producing almost a thousand layers of pastry, the reason you sometimes hear it referred to as *mille-feuilles,* literally, a thousand leaves, in French. To be accurate, puff pastry results in 944 layers of pastry separated by 943 layers of butter—and butter is the only thing that should be used in puff pastry. Puff pastry is a project to make at home, so it's fortunate that there are excellent all-butter puff pastries available commercially (see Source Guide, page 385)—you can enjoy the wonder of it without the work.

SALT: We use sea salt in the kitchen—coarse sea salt at times, and fine sea salt most often. If I think you should use coarse salt or fleur de sel (see above), I've specified it in the recipe; the default salt is fine sea salt.

SALT COD: Cod is an ancient fish, and when you look at salt cod you can imagine our ancestors using a fish not different from what we use today. Then, as now, salt was used to cure and preserve the fish. And now, as then, you can't use the fish until you've soaked it for a day, changing the soaking water every 6 to 8 hours. Soak and poach the cod, and you'll be rewarded with a tender, flaky, full-flavored fish that will make a wonderful brandade (page 30) or a Spanish-accented soup (page 186). If you don't have a reliable merchant from whom to buy salt cod, you can order it from my supplier (see Source Guide, page 385).

SPICES: You'll notice that we use dried spices (and herbs) in three different ways: whole, crushed, and ground. No matter the state in which we use spices, we often toast them. Toasting enhances the flavor and fragrance of spices and is easily accomplished. Put the spices in a small heavy sauté pan or skillet—cast iron is perfect for this—and put the pan over medium heat. Heat the spices, swirling the pan occasionally to keep them moving, until they are warm and their fragrance apparent, about 3 to 5 minutes. If you want to bruise (that is, crack) or crush the spices, the easiest thing to do is to wrap them in a tea towel (or not—you can work directly on the counter) and bash them with the bottom of a heavy pan or the end of a French rolling pin. Finally, if you want to grind the spices, the best thing to use is a spice or coffee grinder, although you can use a mortar and pestle.

TOMATOES: We rarely use tomatoes with their peels and most often we remove their seeds as well. To peel tomatoes, bring a saucepan of water to the boil and put a bowl filled with ice cubes and water close to the stove. Make a tiny, very shallow X in the bottom of each tomato. Working with just a few tomatoes at a time, drop the tomatoes into the boiling water and count 15 seconds, then lift the tomatoes out of the pan and drop them into the ice-water bath. When the tomatoes are cool enough to handle, their peels should just slip off. If they don't, put them back into the boiling water for a few seconds and try again. Cut out the core of the tomato and, if the tomato needs to be seeded, cut it crosswise in half (or lengthwise, or in wedges, depending on the recipe) and use your fingers or a small spoon to scoop out all the seeds and the jelly-like pulp that surrounds them. Discard the seeds and pulp and save the flesh.

TRUFFLES: These are the most mysterious of generally mysterious fungi. They grow underground around oak trees, they can't be cultivated, and no one can know where they'll turn up within regions that are fortunate enough to have truffles at all, Provence and the Southwest of France, as well as parts of Spain and Italy. Sniffed out by specially trained dogs, truffles are understandably expensive, but to a truffle lover, a good truffle always merits its price. The prize of a truffle is its perfume—it's intoxicating. A good truffle is firm, round (in its own bumpy way), and wildly aromatic. Never wash a truffle—just brush it lightly with a moist brush. See the Source Guide, page 385, for information on where to buy premium-quality truffles.

VANILLA BEANS: You'll rarely use a vanilla bean whole—if you did, you'd miss out on much of its flavor: the fragrant pulp within the pod. When choosing a vanilla bean, look for one that is moist, plump, pliable, and perfumed. Beans come most popularly from Madagascar, Mexico, and Tahiti and each country produces a bean with its own distinctive perfume and flavor. If you can, try different beans and choose the one that pleases you the most. (See the Source Guide, page 385, for a place that offers a variety of vanilla beans.) To keep the beans moist and fragrant, wrap them very well in several layers of plastic wrap and keep them refrigerated. To get the most out of a bean, use a sharp paring knife to slice the bean lengthwise in half, then use the back of the knife to scrape the soft, sticky pulp away from the pod. Some recipes will call for the pulp only and others will instruct you to use the pod as part of an infusion and then, when it has flavored the mixture, to discard it. If you'd like, you can save the pod, rinse it well, dry it in a low oven or on a rack at room temperature, and use it to flavor sugar. Keep tossing your used pods into the sugar bin, and soon you'll have a batch of beautifully perfumed vanilla sugar. Alternatively, you can pulverize the bean with sugar in a food processor.

If a recipe calls for vanilla extract, please use pure vanilla extract—use imitation vanilla extract, and you'll spoil the recipe.

YEAST: Recipes using yeast were tested with soft fresh, or compressed, yeast.

batterie de cuisine

a short guide to kitchen tools

Pots and Pans

Buy good pots and pans and you'll be able to pass them along to the next generation of cooks in your family. In general, you should look for pots and pans that are well crafted, well balanced, quick to heat and just as quick to cool down. They should have sturdy, heatproof handles that are securely attached to the pot's or pan's body, and, since the pots and pans should work superbly on the stovetop and then be able to go into the oven and work well there too, the handles should be ovenproof.

Pots and pans worth their steep price tags—and good pots and pans are expensive—can be made of several different materials, among them: Lined copper, which is very expensive and hard to clean, but very sensitive to heat and absolutely gorgeous—think about copper for a pan that you'll cook in and then bring to the table; anodized (or coated) aluminum, which takes advantage of aluminum's light weight and excellent conductivity, and, through the coating, makes aluminum nonreactive (left on its own, aluminum changes color when it comes in contact with acidic food and can, in turn, give an off-taste or color to these foods); and clad (or sandwiched) stainless steel, which uses strong, nonreactive, nonstaining (but poorly conductive) stainless steel on the outside and inside of the pot or pan, and gives it an inner layer of highly conductive copper or aluminum. Each of these materials is used to make pots and pans of varied sizes and shapes, and most can be made with nonstick finishes. The choice is personal.

As for me, for years, I've been a devoted fan of All-Clad Metalcrafters pots and pans—stainless steel cooking equipment sandwiched with aluminum or, in some cases, copper. They are the pots and pans we use at Café Boulud every day for every kind of cooking.

DUTCH OVEN OR LARGE CASSEROLE: This is the pot your grandmother probably referred to as her "large pot." And it is large—larger than a saucepan but not as tall or capacious as a stockpot. Heavy bottomed, with two short, sturdy handles and a cover, Dutch ovens are sold according to their capacity, which is most commonly 3 quarts, 5 quarts, or 6 quarts, and can be anywhere from 8- to 12-inches high. The 5- and 6-quart sizes are the handiest, while the 3-quart size is the least useful for most cooks. The pot is ideal for a big batch of soup, for casseroles, civets and stews, braises and ragouts, preparations that call for browning ingredients before adding the liquid.

ROASTING PAN: A roasting pan has to be able to work well on top of the stove (where you'll sear the ingredients at the start and make the sauce at the finish) and in the oven (where the food is actually roasted), so choose one that has a bottom as heavy and as sensitive to heat changes as a sauté pan's. Equally, if not more, important is the structure of the pan's handles. A roasting pan is heavy even when empty; put a roast or a turkey in the pan and you're going to want handles that you can grip easily and trust completely. Look for a roasting pan with heavy-duty handles securely attached to the pan, and make sure the handles have plenty of grab-room—you're going to have to get your hands and an oven mitt into them and you're going to have to feel confident of your grip. (This is a piece of equipment you should heft in the store before you haul it home.) While it's a nice luxury to have two roasting pans, one about 16 inches long and the other about 14 inches, it's only a necessity to have one—choose the larger size.

SAUCEPANS: Every kitchen needs a heavy-bottomed, long-handled, lidded 2- to 3-quart saucepan— better yet, two. This is the "medium" saucepan in which to boil water to blanch a small amount of cubed vegetables, make pastry cream, mix up sauces, make hot cereal, and boil rice. A good 2- to 3-quart saucepan is so useful you may never remove it from your stovetop. Although you won't use it nearly as often, it's nice to have a small saucepan to keep your medium pan company. I'd suggest a 1- to 1½-quart saucepan for small jobs such as melting butter or making lemon zest confit. Larger saucepans, those that are more than 3 quarts, can be convenient, but they are not necessary.

SAUTÉ PANS OR SKILLETS: What distinguishes a sauté pan from a skillet is the height of the pan— a sauté pan's sides are usually almost 3 inches high, a skillet's only about 2 inches. Both have long handles, but the sauté pan usually has an additional shorter handle, like the ones you find on a Dutch oven, to give you another grab point. For most recipes, you can use a sauté pan interchangeably with a skillet, but if you're outfitting your kitchen, I'd suggest you buy at least two sauté pans—a small pan, about 8 inches in diameter, and a large one that's between 12 and 13 inches in diameter. If you've got the budget and space for another, choose a 10-inch pan. At least one of your larger pans should be non-stick and they should all have lids.

STOCKPOT: A large-volume stockpot (8-quart is a good size, 12-quart even better) is just what you need for making stock in quantity or for cooking lobsters, blanching large chunks of vegetables, or boiling pasta. Look for a stockpot that is as wide as it is tall so that you can stir things easily. The best stockpots have heavy bottoms, so that you can effectively brown ingredients in them, lids, and hefty handles that stand far enough away from the pot so that you can work with them over heat without risking burnt knuckles.

Baking Pans

BAKING SHEETS: Sometimes called jelly-roll pans, these are the low-rimmed baking pans you'll use to make cookies and tuiles, and, of course, jelly rolls. They're the pans you'll pull out when you're making tarts in bottomless tart rings, or even when you want to bake tarts or cakes in pans with standard bottoms—they provide support and a level bottom, and they make getting delicate baked goods in and out of the oven less of an adventure. Baking sheets come in two sizes, 10 ½ by 15 ½ by 1 inch and 12 ½ by 17 ½ by 1 inch. Buy the largest pan that will fit into your oven, allowing at least 1 inch of air space (preferably 2) all around. In fact, buy two—or, if you've got storage space, four. Since nothing should ever go into the oven on a hot baking sheet, having backups means that when you're making cookies, you can have one set of sheets in the oven and the next set ready to go. When you're shopping for baking sheets, buy the heaviest sheets you can find so they won't buckle under high heat, and buy at least one (if not all) with a nonstick finish.

CAKE PANS: Our cake pans at the Café are heavyweight round pans with sides that are 2 inches high. While we have an assortment, you can start your collection with a pan that's 8 inches across. That's the size you'll need for the Far Breton, the Sacher Torte, and the Potato and Almond Cake. To make the Endive, Prosciutto, and Pecan Clafoutis, you'll need a 6-inch round pan, but that's a recipe that can be made successfully in a disposable foil cake pan from the supermarket.

CRÊPE PAN: If you like crêpes and plan to make them often, then it's good to have an 8-inch nonstick crêpe pan in your batterie de cuisine, however, you can make both the Souffléed Lemon Crêpes and the Socca—as well as just about every other crêpe recipe you'll come across—in an 8-inch omelette pan.

CUSTARD CUPS, SOUFFLÉ CUPS, OR RAMEKINS: Eight 4-ounce custard cups, soufflé cups, or ramekins are a kitchen nicety, not a necessity, since you can make most custards, flans, or pots de crème in disposable foil cups from the supermarket or, depending on their size, espresso or coffee cups.

RING MOLDS OR ROUND CUTTERS: At the Café, we'll often present a dish with a compact round of ingredients in the center of the plate. We build these rounds within the containing wall of a ring mold, a round metal circle. Ring molds for presentation are obviously not a home kitchen must-have. However, if you'd like to present your dishes as we do at the Café, you can buy a pair of ring molds (2 ½-inch rings are the most versatile) or you can buy a box of round cutters and use some of the larger cutters for molds. Round cutters are expensive but versatile—they're meant to be used as cookie and biscuit cutters and there's always a use for those. Of course, you can always experiment with cans— remove both ends of the can, scrub the tin really well, stack the ingredients in the ring, and then lift it off the plate.

TART PANS AND TART RINGS: Depending on what we're serving at Café Boulud, we'll use tart rings, ¾-inch-high metal rings with no bottoms, or fluted metal tart pans with removable bottoms. You'll be able to make all of the recipes in this book if you have a 9 ½-inch round fluted tart pan with removable bottom and two tart rings, one 8 inches across and the other 9 inches across. When you use a tart ring, place the ring on a parchment-lined baking sheet and fit the tart dough into the ring by pressing it evenly over the parchment and up the sides of the ring.

Small Hand Tools and Equipment

BASTING BRUSHES: Essentially small paintbrushes, basting brushes are what you'll pull out when you need to brush butter onto fish fillets or into the nooks and crannies of a baking pan, or when you need to glaze a cake or tart with warm preserves. Buy an assortment of brushes in widths ranging from narrow to broad. Although they're available in kitchen supply and specialty shops, they're often cheaper at the hardware store.

CHINOIS: A chinois, or China cap, is a conical strainer that guarantees fine and formidably lump-free sauces, soups, and purées, but you shouldn't think of it as a replacement for a fine-mesh strainer or two—often the bowl shape of a traditional strainer will be more convenient for the job at hand.

COLANDER: Nothing more than a large, coarse metal strainer on feet, a colander is indispensable in the kitchen when you've got chunky or bulky ingredients to drain. It's what you'll use when you're draining pasta, lobster, or other large foods, and it's what you'll dunk into a pot of boiling salted water when you're blanching a bunch of vegetables and want to be able to pull one type of vegetable out before the others. Although it is a close member of the strainer family, it should never be used in lieu of a fine-mesh strainer or chinois—its holes are too big.

CUTTING BOARDS: With cutting boards, cleanliness is next to godliness. (It's for this reason that wooden cutting boards are forbidden in commercial kitchens—as beautiful and traditional as they are, they can't be properly cleaned.) When buying cutting boards, make sure to buy boards that are not only dishwasher-safe, but small enough to fit into your dishwasher. That said, buy the biggest one that will fit into your dishwasher, because you want to give yourself plenty of room to slice, dice, and chop.

FORK, LONG-TINED: For prodding and gripping meats and poultry, keep a sturdy long-handled, two-tined, long-tined fork at the ready. Whether the tines are curved or straight is a matter of preference, not performance.

KNIVES: Knives are so important—and so personal—that every cook in the Café kitchen has his or her own set. I can't encourage you strongly enough to buy the best knives you can afford: Well-made, well-balanced knives will serve you for half a century or more. (And there aren't all that many things that can make—and keep—that promise.) Look for knives that are forged, not stamped, with tangs or shanks that extend into the handle of the knife. Some knives that are made this way are the German knives by Henckels or Wüsthof, and the French knives by Sabatier. Recently, I've seen well-made American knives from LamsonSharp. If you can, buy your knives from a store that will allow you to test-drive them—a knife that feels comfortable in one person's hand may feel awkward in another's. (The size and strength of your hand as well as your agility and skill with a knife will have a lot to do in determining what works best for you.) The basic knives you should own include at least one chef's knife, perhaps a 9- or 10-inch knife, but preferably two or three—8-inch, 10-inch, and 12-inch—to handle every chopping and dicing chore and many slicing jobs too; a pair of paring knives, perhaps a 4-inch and a 6-inch; a long, thin-bladed slicing knife; and a serrated slicing knife. No matter which knife you choose, remember that it will only be as good as the sharpness of its edge—keep a sharpening steel close at hand.

MANDOLINE: Nothing can cut vegetables to see-through-thinness as well as a mandoline. And while it's not an absolute necessity in the home kitchen, it's awfully nice to have on hand when you want to make fast work of slicing or have a yen for paper-thin chips. A mandoline used to be one of the most expensive pieces of non-electric equipment in a kitchen, but now most cooks use Japanese mandolines that cost under $30 and work really well. No matter the mandoline you choose, use it with care—and always use the safety holder that comes with it. Mandolines can cut fingers and fennel with equal efficiency.

MIXING BOWLS: Small and large, shallow and deep, a supply of mixing bowls is an absolute must in the kitchen. The most versatile bowls are those made of metal because, in addition to being unbreakable, they can be placed over heat or, more usually, over a pan of simmering water to serve as the top of double boiler. Similarly, they can withstand cold and quick temperature changes. For easy storage, buy a set—or two—of nesting mixing bowls.

PASTRY BAG AND TIP: When a recipe calls for piping, you're meant to use a pastry bag, one made of nylon or plasticized canvas (or a disposable bag made of clear flexible plastic) fitted with a piping tip; the recipe will specify the size of the tip and whether it should be plain or star-shaped. Properly used, a pastry bag gives you complete control over how much batter, dough, or cream you use and where you place it. Pastry bags allow you to make perfect meringue disks, to fill zucchini flowers with just the right amount of crab cake mixture, or to form lovely whipped cream rosettes on top of a cake. (However, in almost every case—the rosettes are the exception—you can get by without a pastry bag. If you need to fill something, you can use a spoon; and if you need to shape something, like the meringue disks, you can turn a plastic bag into a pastry bag—fill the bag with the batter, draw up the opening of the bag, and give it a twist, or zipperlock it, snip a tiny bit off a bottom corner of the bag, and pipe away.) When you've piped your fill, make sure to clean both the pastry bag and the tip scrupulously. To clean the bag, use soapy water and a soft-scrub pad and make sure to clean both the inside and outside; air-dry the bag by draping it over a long-necked bottle. To clean the tip, use a baby bottle brush or a toothbrush, both will help remove ingredients like stuck-on chocolate or dried-on meringue.

PASTRY OR DOUGH SCRAPER: There are two kinds of scrapers: one, a fairly flexible rectangle of metal attached to a wooden or hard plastic grip; the other an almost teardrop-shaped piece of flexible plastic or rectangle of flexible plastic with one curved side. The metal scraper is particularly good if you're working with heavy yeast doughs—you can use the scraper to lift the dough as you're kneading, and it makes an excellent counter cleaner when kneading is finished. The plastic scraper is a good bowl cleaner—you can use the scraper to get the last of a batter out of a mixing bowl. It's also just the right tool for gently lifting delicate cookies, such as tuiles, off their baking sheets.

ROLLING PIN: It's not just because I'm French that I recommend a French rolling pin—it's because these are the pins that give you the greatest control and flexibility. Because a French pin doesn't have handles—it's about 18 inches long and a uniform 2 inches in diameter—your hands are close to the dough and you get a good feel for how the dough is rolling, its thickness and elasticity. It's important to keep your pin clean and nick-free so that it will slide smoothly over dough. Clean the pin with a damp cloth or, if necessary, scrape it down lightly with the back of a knife or pastry scraper.

SHARPENING STEEL AND ELECTRIC KNIFE SHARPENER: To keep the best edges on your knives, you should have both a sharpening steel and an electric knife sharpener. You'll use the steel often, maybe even daily, and the electric sharpener less frequently, but together they'll keep your knives in top form.

SPATULAS, METAL: It's best to equip your kitchen with several metal spatulas of different proportions. You'll need one or two large spatulas of the pancake-turner variety, with a long handle and a flipper that's offset, meaning it's angled just below the handle. Look for those that have a few cutouts in their flippers—these will allow you to lift and drain simultaneously. A slotted flexible spatula with a shorter handle and somewhat angled flipper, called a Peltex, is indispensable for turning delicate foods such as fish fillets, thin slices of vegetables, potato cakes, and the like. It's likely you'll have to go to a specialty kitchenware shop or a restaurant supply store to buy this spatula, but your effort will be rewarded every time you flip a fillet. Finally, you'll need thin offset spatulas—sometimes called icing spatulas—for spreading creams and jams, fillings, and frostings over cakes and tarts. You might want a short offset icing spatula for small finishing jobs, but you'll certainly want one that's at least 10 inches long for smoothing the tops of 8- and 9-inch cakes.

SPATULAS, RUBBER: Sturdy, flexible restaurant-grade rubber spatulas will come in handy whether you're making dinner or dessert. Buy a couple of small and a couple of large spatulas and keep them close at hand for stirring, folding, and getting the last of anything out of a bowl or jar. Scrub the spatulas well after each use, or put them in the dishwasher. Look for the new heat-resistant spatulas (they're made of silicone)—they won't fray around the edges when you use them to stir something over heat.

SPATULAS, WOODEN: A wooden spatula, preferably a largish paddle-shaped spatula, is not a must in the kitchen, but it's my tool of choice for stirring a risotto, a pastry cream, or a crème anglaise.

SPOONS, METAL: You should have a large metal spoon for stirring and tasting, a slotted spoon for lifting ingredients out of liquids that should remain over heat, and a ladle. Make sure to buy spoons with long handles. Many long-handled spoons come with hooked ends so they can be hung on a rack or with holes in the handles so they can be hung on hooks—a nice convenience. (All-Clad makes an excellent set of hangable long-handled metal spoons, spatulas, and skimmers.)

SPOONS, WOODEN: Long-handled wooden spoons, like wooden spatulas, are good for stirring risottos and creams; they're also fine when you're making caramel or doing anything that requires scraping up cooked and caramelized bits that may be stuck to a sauté or roasting pan.

STRAINERS: For making lumpless creams, smooth puréed soups, and silky custards, make certain you have both small and large fine-meshed strainers. Good strainers are expensive, but they're worth the price because they'll hold up under the pressure of spoons pushing purées through them. The finest and strongest strainers are double mesh. You can get good results from a single mesh strainer, but it will be fragile. Because often the foods you'll be passing through a strainer are acidic—think tomatoes and lemons—it's best to buy stainless steel strainers; with stainless steel, you don't have to worry that acidic foods will discolor them or that they, in turn, will give an off taste to the foods.

THERMOMETERS: You should have at least three different thermometers in your kitchen: a deep-fat frying thermometer, an instant-read thermometer, and an oven thermometer.

Although a deep-fat thermometer won't always be an absolute necessity—there will be times when you'll know the oil is the right temperature just because when you drop a piece of whatever you're frying into it, the oil bubbles around the morsel immediately—you'll need the thermometer when you're making Pommes Frites (page 85) and have to fry the potatoes twice, each time at a different temperature. Of course, as with so many other tools, once you have one, you'll have many occasions to use it. Look for a thermometer with a large read-out—you don't want to have to squint over a pot of 350° F oil.

An instant-read thermometer is a tool a chef is never without. Chefs want an instant-read at the ready to take the temperature of roasts of all kinds (in the kitchen, we never use the type of meat thermometer that stays in the meat during cooking), as well as custards, creams, chocolates, and yeast breads. Good quality instant-read thermometers come with analog or digital read-outs—take your pick.

Even if you think your oven is perfect—it's a good idea to make certain by buying a mercury thermometer and keeping it in the oven at all times.

TONGS: While they are not essential, you might find a pair of long spring-loaded tongs a handy tool for turning roasts in the oven or meat or chicken during sautéing (fish is usually too delicate to use tongs with). Tongs allow you to get a good grip on awkwardly shaped foods (and chicken on the bone can be just that) without piercing them. Choose tongs that have scalloped or rounded pincers—sharp serrated pincers defeat the nonpiercing aspect of this inexpensive tool.

VEGETABLE PEELERS: I've listed this tool in the plural because I think that every cook should have two different kinds of vegetable peelers: one with a swivel blade and one with a stationary blade. The swivel-bladed peeler is good for peeling delicate fruits and vegetables—it's the one I use for peeling asparagus. The stationary-bladed peeler is just what you need when you want to remove thicker slices of peel or when you're working with tougher peels, such as those on squash or celery root. Since the blades on most vegetable peelers are the same, you should choose a peeler that feels good in your hand and, in the case of the swivel peeler, one that swivels freely. Keep in mind that the blade on a peeler cannot be sharpened—when it dulls, it must be replaced.

WHISKS: Whisks come in various lengths and widths. In general, narrow whisks are used for sauces and wide whisks, called balloon whisks, are used when you need to beat air into a mixture—they're the ones for whipping cream and egg whites. To start, equip your kitchen with one sauce whisk and one not-too-wide balloon whisk. Whether narrow or wide, a whisk should have sturdy, flexible stainless steel wires that are securely fitted into the handle. At the point where the wires meet the handle, there should be a cap or other closing (you shouldn't be able to see into the handle), so that you can clean the whisk thoroughly. Today, whisk handles are most often made of metal or plastic; choose the material that feels best in your hand.

ZESTER/GRATER: A zester removes thin, even, pith-free strands of zest from citrus fruits. The zester's handle (of plastic or wood) is mounted with a small metal piece that has five holes at its end. Run the holes, with their sharpened interiors, against the zest and presto!—you've got lovely strands. If a recipe calls for strands of zest, you're finished; if you need chopped zest, just gather the strands together on a cutting board and chop away—the zester gives you a head start on fine chopping. While you can grate zest on a box grater, a rasp-type grater (the one I like is made by Microplane) produces a shower of finely grated zest quickly and effortlessly. The rasp grater looks more like a woodworker's tool than a kitchen gadget.

Electric Tools

BLENDER: The blender is my tool of choice when I want to purée soups. The shape of its container and the variable speeds of its blade make it ideal for this job. However, no matter how efficient your blender, for a really velvety smooth soup, you'll have to strain the soup after it's been blended.

BLENDER, IMMERSION: Not as powerful as the stand blender, but so convenient, the immersion (or hand) blender is a like a magic wand—it's got a long straight stick for a handle and at its end, a blender blade. Plug-in or battery-operated, the immersion blender can purée soups or sauces, blend dressings or froth soups, drinks or vinaigrettes directly in their pot, mixing bowl, glass, or serving bowl. With an immersion blender, there's always one less thing to wash.

ELECTRIC KNIFE: I know that electric knives have gone out of favor in most home kitchens, but I keep an electric knife at the ready at each station in the kitchen. Nothing beats an electric knife for cutting delicate foods, such as the Sea Bass en Croûte, Spiced Pork Belly, Mustard-Crusted Calf's Liver, or terrines.

FOOD PROCESSOR: The food processor is a revolutionary tool that changed the way we do things in the kitchen, particularly the home kitchen. The processor chops and grinds, mixes and blends, and makes spectacular tart dough in a flash. Although a processor is an expensive piece of equipment, it's an important tool for serious cooks. If you're buying one for the first time, buy the sturdiest processor you can afford.

MIXER, STAND: While we have mixers of many sizes in the kitchen, the ones that get the greatest work-outs are our 5-quart KitchenAid mixers. The pastry department uses the mixers most often, to make doughs and cake batters, creams, fillings, meringues, and more, but the cooks are always flipping them on to whip cream, mash vegetables, or, with the special attachment, grind meats. A good mixer is very expensive but extremely long lasting. Treat it right and you'll only have to buy one in your life. When you're buying a mixer, look for one that has at least three attachments: a whisk, a paddle, and a dough hook. And, if you can, buy an extra bowl for the mixer—a blessing when a batter needs beaten egg whites.

Source Guide

All-Clad Metalcrafters
424 Morganza Road
Canonsburg, PA 15317
Telephone: 800-ALL-CLAD
Fax: 724-746-5035
www.allclad.com
Top-quality cookware

Browne Trading Co.
260 Commercial Street
Portland, ME 04101
Telephone: 800-944-7848
Fax: 207-766-2404
www.browne-trading.com
Daniel Boulud's Private Stock Caviar and Smoked Salmon, crabmeat, oysters, salt cod, diver and other sea scallops, and other pristine fish and seafood

D'Artagnan Inc.
280 Wilson Avenue
Newark, NJ 07105
Telephone: 800-DARTAGN or 973-344-0565
Fax: 973-465-1870
www.dartagnan.com
Duck breast prosciutto, duck confit, foie gras, partridge, pheasant, squab, venison, and other game

Gourmand Inc.
2869 Towerview Road
Herndon, VA 20171
Telephone: 703-708-0000
Fax: 703-708-9393
Almond flour, chicory, chocolate, fleur de sel, sheet gelatin, piquillo peppers, puff pastry, truffles, vanilla beans, and other best-quality foodstuffs

J.B. Prince
36 East 31st Street, 11th Floor
New York, NY 10016
Telephone: 212-683-3553
Fax: 212-683-4488
www.jbprince.com
Knives, mixers, blenders, small electrical tools, baking pans and equipment, and assorted cookware

Marché aux Délices
PO Box 1164
New York, NY 10028
Telephone: 888-547-5471
Fax: 212-860-4927
www.auxdelices.com
Exotic mushrooms

Many thanks to the following companies for providing props for photography: All-Clad Metalcrafters, Williams-Sonoma, Bernardaud, L'Olivier, Staub, Bourgeat, Spiegelau, Orfe, Rivolta

Acknowledgments

Many hands make light work. In the case of this book, there were many hands and not only did they make the work light, they made it better and more exciting.

The recipes were first tested during the summer that Café Boulud was being built. As the restaurant was being renovated, we were in the kitchen dodging workmen and cooking the foods that would debut in the Café and find their way to these pages. For their talent, as well as for their boundless energy and enthusiasm, we thank the cooks who worked along with us: Alex Lee, now executive chef at Daniel, and the Daniel sous chefs, Cyrille Allannic and Bertrand Bouquin; Andrew Carmellini, now executive chef at Café Boulud, and the sous chefs of Café Boulud, Brad Thompson and Jean-Francois Bruel; Pierre Calmels; Olivier Guyon; Nicki Reiss; Jeremy Lieb; Jeff Butler; Kazu Tamura; Christine Patton; Café Boulud's executive pastry chef, Remy Funfrock, and his assistant during this time, Fabrice Collingnon; and Andrew Bolsterli, whom we lost tragically and remember warmly. And cheers to Stephen Beckta, Café Boulud's sommelier, and Jean-Luc Le Du, the sommelier at Daniel, for the excellent "to drink" suggestions that follow each recipe.

Having passed the first round of testing, the recipes were then retested by Rica Buxbaum. In addition to being an ace tester, Rica, who knew even when we didn't where all the pieces of this project were at all times, kept us on track, proved an invaluable organizer, and was the best first reader a writer could have.

In the Café Boulud family, we are grateful to Hilary Tolman, Daniel's assistant, for taking the demands of this project in stride and with humor, and to Brett Traussi, operations manager, who kept everything up and running while the construction crew made progress in the dining room and threatened our progress in the kitchen. And we are greatly appreciative of all that Georgette Farkas, director of marketing, did to get the word out on our book.

Having done our part at the Café, we were exceptionally fortunate to have "book people" who knew their parts so well. Merci mille fois to our agent Robert E. Tabian, first for finding such a good home for our baby, and then for continuing to be such an attentive, nurturing godfather.

We were warmly welcomed into the Scribner family. While there are more Scribner angels than we can thank here, we want to single out for thanks and admiration Carolyn Reidy, president of Simon & Schuster; Susan Moldow, Scribner's publisher; Roz Lippel, associate publisher; John Fontana, art director; M. C. Hald, copyediting supervisor; the all-fixing Judith Sutton, our copyeditor; Matthew Thornton, our editor's assistant; and Beth Wareham, director of publicity, who was exceedingly generous with her prodigious talents. Authors couldn't ask for more.

Certainly, we couldn't have asked for more attention from our editor, Maria Guarnaschelli. Maria provided guidance at every stage of this project, helping us to shape the book at the start and to fashion its look at the end. We owe her a special debt of thanks for putting together a remarkable design team for the book. Andrea Gentl and Marty Heyers's photographs brilliantly capture the spirit of each dish, as does the prop styling by Helen Crowther and Julia Baier, and Britta Steinbrecht's design for the pages make working from *The Café Boulud Cookbook* a pleasure.

It was a joy to work with so many gifted people.

Daniel Boulud and Dorie Greenspan

Index